The Collected Courses of the Academy of European Law
Series Editors: Professor Gráinne de Búrca, *European University Institute, Florence*;
Professor Bruno de Witte, *European University Institute, Florence*; and
Professor Francesco Francioni, *European University Institute, Florence*
Assistant Editor: Barbara Ciomei, *European University Institute, Florence*

VOLUME XV/2
The Institutional Framework of European Private Law

The Collected Courses of the Academy of European Law
Edited by Professor Gráinne de Búrca,
Professor Bruno de Witte, and Professor Francesco Francioni

This series brings together the Collected Courses of the
Academy of European Law in Florence. The Academy's mission is to
produce scholarly analyses which are at the cutting edge of the two
fields in which it works: European Union law and human rights law.
A 'general course' is given each year in each field, by a
distinguished scholar and/or practitioner, who either examines the
field as a whole through a particular thematic, conceptual or
philosophical lens, or who looks at a particular theme in the context
of the overall body of law in the field. The Academy also publishes
each year a volume of collected essays with a specific theme in each
of the two fields.

The Institutional Framework of European Private Law

Edited by

FABRIZIO CAFAGGI

Academy of European Law
European University Institute

OXFORD
UNIVERSITY PRESS

OXFORD
UNIVERSITY PRESS

Great Clarendon Street, Oxford OX2 6DP

Oxford University Press is a department of the University of Oxford.
It furthers the University's objective of excellence in research, scholarship,
and education by publishing worldwide in

Oxford New York

Auckland Cape Town Dar es Salaam Hong Kong Karachi
Kuala Lumpur Madrid Melbourne Mexico City Nairobi
New Delhi Shanghai Taipei Toronto

With offices in

Argentina Austria Brazil Chile Czech Republic France Greece
Guatemala Hungary Italy Japan Poland Portugal Singapore
South Korea Switzerland Thailand Turkey Ukraine Vietnam

Oxford is a registered trade mark of Oxford University Press
in the UK and in certain other countries

Published in the United States
by Oxford University Press Inc., New York

© the several contributors, 2006

The moral rights of the authors have been asserted
Database right Oxford University Press (maker)

Crown copyright material is reproduced under Class Licence
Number C01P0000148 with the permission of OPSI
and the Queen's Printer for Scotland

First published 2006

British Library Cataloguing in Publication Data

Data available

Library of Congress Cataloging in Publication Data
The institutional framework of European private law / edited by Fabrizio Cafaggi.
    p. cm. — (Collected courses of the Academy of European Law)
Includes bibliographical references and index.
ISBN 0–19–929604–9 (hardback : alk. paper)
 1. Civil law—European Union countries. 2. Conflict of laws—European Union countries.
I. Cafaggi, Fabrizio. II. Series.
  KJE995.I57 2006
  346.24—dc22   2005033313

Typeset by Newgen Imaging Systems (P) Ltd., Chennai, India
Printed in Great Britain
on acid-free paper by
Biddles Ltd., King's Lynn

ISBN 0–19–929604–9   978–0–19–929604–0

1 3 5 7 9 10 8 6 4 2

Contents

Acknowledgements

The initial project for this book was proposed to and accepted by the Academy of European Law at the European University Institute in Fiesole. The directors at that time, Gráinne de Búrca and Bruno de Witte, discussed the content and actively contributed to the success of the summer school of 2004. Students participating in that school joined the discussions and showed great interest and surprising awareness of the approach and its conceptual implications.

This book could not have been written without the continuing assistance and support of Barbara Ciomei. Her professional competence, and ability to organize the summer school and to coordinate the group of contributors have allowed me to concentrate on the scientific task in hand, and made enjoyable even those small organizational charges I have had to face. To her goes my profound gratitude.

Finally thanks also to my secretary Anna Coda, whose excellent assistance often made up for my own organizational lapses.

F. Cafaggi
Fiesole, August 2005

Table of Cases

European Court of Justice

Court of First Instance

European Court of Human Rights

National Courts

France

Cour de cassation

Trib gr inst Paris

Germany

Italy

Latvia

Netherlands

Spain

United Kingdom

United States of America

Tables of Legislation

EC Treaty

National Legislation

Estonia

France

Germany

Hungary

Russia

Spain

United Kingdom

United States of America

Notes on Contributors

Albertina Albors-Llorens is a Senior Lecturer in Law at the University of Cambridge. She is also Fellow and Tutor at Girton College, Cambridge. She specializes in European Union Law and Competition Law and is the author of two books: *Private Parties in EC Law* (1996) and *EC Competition Law and Policy* (2002). She has also written several articles and case notes on EC Competition Law, and on Judicial Review in European Community Law. In 2003, she was awarded a University of Cambridge Pilkington Prize for teaching excellence.

Fabrizio Cafaggi is Professor of Private Law at the University of Trento and holds the Chair of Comparative Law at the European University Institute, where he has taught courses on Private Law and Regulation and an Introduction to Comparative Law, focusing on codification. He is co-director of the European Private Law Forum and organized the 2004 Academy of European of Law summer school on Private Law and Regulation. He coordinates a research project with Horatia Muir Watt on governance and regulation in European private law, and another on the law and economics of Italian industrial districts within the framework of a European corporate governance project coordinated by Simon Deakin. His research interests focus on European private law, particularly on the role of soft law and self-regulation in European integration. Other research fields are local development; governance and network of firms; private actors, communities and social rights; law and economics. His most recent publications include: 'Gouvernance et responsabilité des régulateurs privés', 2 *Revue Internationale de Droit Economique* (2005), pp. 111–163; 'Organizational Loyalties and Models of Firm: Governance Design and Standard of Duties', in *Theoretical Inquires in Law*, Vol. 6 No. 2, July 2005, pp. 463–526; and (ed.) *Reframing Self-regulation in European Private Law*, Kluwer (forthcoming, 2006).

Angus Johnston is University Lecturer in Law at the University of Cambridge and Director of Studies in Law at Trinity Hall, Cambridge. His research focuses mainly on European law (including comparative and EC law), with particular emphasis on competition law, energy law and judicial and institutional aspects. His recent publications include (with A. Dashwood, eds) *The Future of the Judicial System of the European Union* (2001), (with S. Deakin and B. Markesinis) *Markesinis and Deakin's Tort Law* (5th edn, 2003), (with P. J. Slot) *Introduction to Competition Law* (forthcoming, 2006) and (with B. Markesinis and H. Unberath) *The German Law of Contract: A Comparative Treatise* (forthcoming, 2006).

Horatia Muir Watt is Professor of Private International and Comparative Law at the University of Paris I (Panthéon-Sorbonne). She prepared her doctorate in private international law (University of Paris II, 1985) and was admitted to the *agrégation* in 1986, following which she was appointed to the University of Tours, then the University of Paris XI, before joining Paris I in 1996. She is Deputy Director of the Comparative Law Center of Paris (UMR de Droit comparé, Paris I-CNRS) and Secretary General of the *Revue critique de droit international privé*, the leading law review on private international law in France. She directs the Masters program in Anglo-American Business Law and co-directs the Masters program in Global Business Law (Paris I/Institute of Political Science). She is a regular visitor to the University of Texas in Austin, where she teaches the Conflict of Laws. She lectured in July 2004 at the Hague Academy of International Law. Her course on 'Aspects économiques de droit international privé' was published in Vol. 307 of the *Recueil des Cours*.

Norbert Reich is Emeritus Professor of Civil, Commercial and EU Law at the University of Bremen (Germany) and former Rector of the Riga School of Law (RGSL). He was an editor of the *Journal of Consumer Policy* from 1975 until 2000, and the President of the International Academy of Consumer and Commercial law from 2000 to 2002. He has held several University positions in Germany, USA, France, the UK and Switzerland. In 2000, he was awarded a *doctor iuris honoris causae* from Helsinki University. He has published extensively on EU free movement, competition, civil rights and consumer protection law, comparative contract and tort law, and legal theory. He has worked regularly in various CEE and candidate countries and Russia on TACIS, PHARE and TWINNING projects. His most recent publication is *Understanding EU Law* (2nd edn, 2005).

Hannes Unberath is *Wissenschaftlicher Assistent* at the Institute of International Law, *Ludwig-Maximilians-Universität München*, and currently completing his *Habilitation* in the field of contract theory. His research interests are comparative law, conflict of laws, European law and jurisprudence. His most recent English language publications include *Transferred Loss* (2003); (with B. Markesinis) *The German Law of Torts* (4th edn, 2002); (with B. Markesinis and A. Johnston) *The German Law of Contract* (forthcoming, 2006); 'Comparative Law in the German Courts' in Canivet, Andenas, and Fairgrieve (eds), *Comparative Law before the Courts* (2004).

Walter van Gerven is Professor at the KU Leuven, where he taught Private and Commercial Law, European Community Law and Legal Theory, until 2000. He has been visiting professor at, among others, the universities of Chicago, Amsterdam, Paris II, Stanford, and King's College London. He is a Member, and Past President, of the Royal Academy of Sciences of Belgium, a Member of the Dutch Royal Academy of Sciences, and the European Academy of Sciences. He is a Doctor *honoris causa* of the University of Gent and an Honorary Bencher of Gray's Inn. From 1982 to 1988 he served as President of the Belgian Banking Commission, from 1988 to 1994 he was Advocate-General in the European Court of Justice, and in 1999 he served as a member of the Committee of Independent Experts investigating the European Commission. He is the author of several books and many articles on European Union law, private law and constitutional law. He is the General Editor of the series of case-books for the Common Law of Europe published by Hart Publishing, Oxford. His most recent book is *The European Union, a Polity of States and Peoples* (2005).

Stephen Weatherill is Jacques Delors Professor of EC Law in the University of Oxford, Deputy Director for European Law of the Institute of European and Comparative Law, and a Fellow of Somerville College. Before joining the Oxford Faculty, he held the Jean Monnet Chair of European Law at the University of Nottingham, and he has also previously held positions at the Universities of Manchester and Reading. He is the author of many books and journal articles in the general field of EU law. He is co-author of *Weatherill and Beaumont's EU Law* (3rd edn, 1999, with P. Beaumont), and author of *Law and Integration in the European Union* (1995), *EC Consumer Law and Policy* (1997), and *Cases and Materials on EU Law* (7th edn, 2005).

1

Introduction

FABRIZIO CAFAGGI

1. THE INSTITUTIONAL FRAMEWORK AND THE NEED FOR GOVERNANCE IN EUROPEAN PRIVATE LAW

This book was born out of a pressing need: to complement the existing rich and diverse scholarship on European private law (EPL) with reflections on the institutional framework around which EPL has been built and, more importantly, will grow in the future. While this has, in general, been mainly the task of constitutional lawyers, it is necessary for private lawyers to engage in this endeavour in order to explore the strong connection between the nature of rule-making and the content of EPL.

The institutional framework is composed of the set of institutions that affect the process through which private law is 'produced' at European and national level. There is an underlying methodological premise that should be made explicit: in the field of private law, the production process and the final product, i.e. the substantive rules, are linked in significant ways. The way in which rules are produced affects both their quality and their content. This is especially true if law-making is understood as a dynamic process, in which rules are not simply the result of a single legislative procedure but the outcome of continuing interaction between legal, political, and economic institutions. The formation of European private law is a process; it can be broken down for analytical purposes, but it should not be separated out into discrete, fixed stages. Accordingly, even the unlikely eventual codification of this body of law would be a merely relevant, yet not conclusive, part of the process.

Processes and products have always been related in the field of private law. The substantive rules of contract, property, civil liability, etc. have been affected by the procedures through which they were produced, and by the interaction between different institutions: those private parties, legislatures and courts competent to intervene. National legal traditions in the field of private law have, however, paid less attention recently to the importance of the institutional framework of their national private laws, for a number of different reasons. Perhaps the most important is that these frameworks are (perceived to be) relatively stable. However, significant changes in the institutional structure of western nation-states have strongly influenced the development of private law, in particular the role and the interpretation of private autonomy. These changes have been generated by internal modifications of the regulatory State and by globalization, the driving force behind many regulatory policies at the international level. Furthermore, in the European setting, the political, economic and legal changes that occurred in the last part of the twentieth century have completely redefined the institutional framework of private law in many new Member States. Hence there is a need to reconsider the relationship between private law and its institutional framework in Member States of the EU.

If this is true for national systems, it is even more the case in the context of the European framework, in which the institutional structure is diverse and unstable and the foundations and boundaries of private law are not well defined.[1] The important changes in regulatory strategies at the EU level in different fields, related to the traditional domains of private law, pose new challenges in terms of designing the institutional framework. The central and modernized role afforded to competition law, for example, makes necessary a re-evaluation of the interaction between the European system of competition law and the consolidation of EPL. Moreover, the accession of new Member States has imposed additional burdens on European and national institutions, and broadened the potential for differentiation as a result of the emergence of new public and private institutions.[2] Such challenges, however, should not be tackled with the simple tactic of centralization in order to increase total harmonization, but rather by focusing on the correlation between EPL and governance designs.

Similarly, those countries that have recently undergone important changes in both institutional and market design must pay close attention to the institutional framework developed in the context of EPL, as defined above. In particular, the role of national courts and regulators is essential in ensuring the effectiveness of legal reforms and the ability to coordinate between various national legal systems and the European one. To avoid discussing the role of European and national institutions in the production of private law rules would therefore be a mistake when engaging in the design of new EPL rules, particularly those of the Common Frame of Reference related to contract law.[3]

---

[1] See, from different perspectives, Study Group on Social Justice in European Private Law, 'Social Justice in European Contract Law: A Manifesto', 10 *ELJ* (2004) 653.

[2] The importance of the institutional framework for the implementation of community law is emphasized by N. Reich in Chap. 8, critically building on Emmert, 'Administrative and Court Reform in Central and Eastern Europe', 9 *ELJ* (2003) 288.

[3] See on the specific question of European contract law, the Commission's 2004 Communication, entitled 'European Contract Law and the Revision of the *Acquis*: The Way Forward', Brussels, 11 October 2004, COM (2004) 651 final (hereinafter 'The Way Forward'). 'The Way Forward' follows the Action Plan of 2003 COM (2003) 68 and the Resolution of the European Parliament of 2 September 2003. The Action Plan was a response to the observations made on the Communication of the Commission 2001. The debate dates back to 1989, when the European Parliament enacted a Resolution, on 26 May 1989, to bring the private law of the Member States into line, and then the following Resolution, of 6 May 1994, on the harmonization of certain sectors of private law. On the process and its goals see D. Staudenmayer, 'The Commission Action Plan on European Contract Law', *ERPL* (2003) 113.

At the moment, we clearly have different degrees of harmonization in the area of private law; differences that are even greater if we take the new Member States into account. This is more the result of legal and political constraints than the outcome of a deliberate strategy. Does such differentiation undermine the unity of private law systems? Should this value, particularly dear to the codified systems of continental Europe, be preserved? How, in the future, should we ensure the internal coherence, between the European and national levels, of different branches of private law?

Perhaps an even more radical question should be addressed. Does the category of private law constitute a useful device for identifying the system of legal relations among private parties, or is a new reconceptualization needed at the European level?[4] Answers to these questions are beyond the scope of this book, but the contributions presented here will help towards framing them. Important issues from this perspective are: (1) the relation between positive/negative integration and the creation of European private law; and (2) the balance among the different institutional components that contribute to the creation of EPL.

The link between the creation of EPL and the process of European legal integration through harmonization measures is quite evident, although European private law is certainly wider than European Community private law, encompassing also the *jus commune Europaeum*. Somewhat less explored is the link between the creation of EPL and negative integration. Negative integration often does not merely 'level the playing field', but can also require some regulatory intervention to re-define the institutional framework.[5]

The relationship between judicial and legislative harmonization has long been debated, and the future of the Europeanization of private law may depend heavily on the balance between the two. The role of the ECJ as a catalyst for harmonization has been strongly emphasized;[6] in particular, much research has focused on its

---

[4] The definitional debate has not only theoretical implications, but also extremely important institutional consequences for defining what should be harmonized, and how. For example, the extent to which regulatory law can be part of private law may affect the traditional partitioning employed in Member States' legal orders, and also the construction of EPL. In a more theoretical perspective, and mainly in relation to the Anglo-American world, see P. Cane, 'The Anatomy of Private Law Theory: A 25th Anniversary Essay', 25 *OJLS* (2005) 203; B. Zipursky, 'Philosophy of Private Law', in J. Coleman and S. Shapiro (eds), *The Oxford Handbook of Jurisprudence and Philosophy* (2002) 623; S. Waddams, *Dimensions of Private Law* (2003); E. Weinrib, *The Idea of Private Law* (1995).

[5] A clear illustration is provided by the link between Art. 28 and several fields of private law concerning contract and tort law, particularly the sale of goods and defective products. A voluminous literature has focused on the relationship between positive and negative integration and on the relationship between Arts. 95 and 28; however the effects of case-law applying Art. 28 to domestic contract and tort law outside the realm of a selling arrangement is still relatively unexplored. But see Muir Watt in this volume at Chap. 4.

[6] See G. De Búrca and J.H.H. Weiler, *The European Court of Justice* (2001); K. Alter, *Establishing the Supremacy of European Law: The Making of International Rule of Law in Europe* (2001); Alter, *The European Court and National Courts — doctrine and jurisprudence: legal change in its social context; explaining national court acceptance of European Court jurisprudence; a critical evaluation of theories of legal integration* (1995).

cooperation with national courts, through the use of, among other things, preliminary rulings, and convincing evidence in this regard has been uncovered.[7] Divergences between European and national laws have been monitored by national courts with the support of the European Court of Justice (ECJ), and often reconciled by means of interpretation.[8] It remains an open question whether the current system has been adequately constructed, or whether it needs to be strengthened and rendered more 'institutionalized', given the growing complexity of European private law.

Specific problems are posed by those areas, particularly significant in context of the generation of new private law Directives, where there is an alternative between judicial and administrative enforcement; or, as is more frequently the case, when both methods of enforcement are available but the modes of combining them are left to individual Member States. The principle of procedural autonomy and that of effectiveness may come into conflict. In legislation such as the Unfair Contract Terms Directive 93/13, the Product Liability Directive 85/374, the General Product Safety Directive 2001/95, or the more recent Unfair Trade Practices Directive 2005/29, the role of administrative bodies or even private regulators may be significant, not only in monitoring the implementation of legislation but also in clarifying whether implementing acts (legislative and governmental) and European legislation are in conformity. What kind of institutional arrangements are needed when not only the judiciary but also regulators must ensure the consistent and relatively homogeneous interpretation of the implementation Acts at national, or even subnational, level? What if implementation is realized through a longer regulatory chain going beyond the level of national legislation, involving independent regulatory agencies, as is often the case in regulated markets? Current mechanisms do not seem to be sufficient. The institutional framework of European private law needs to be re-engineered, taking into account the different contributing actors. The relationship between judges and regulators and the role of judicial review in the field of EPL has gained importance in recent years and more attention to these aspects should be paid when designing substantive rules of contract, civil liability and property at the European level.

In addition, the debate should focus on whether complementary means are needed to ensure *decentralized harmonization*, or at least better horizontal coordination among Member States' institutions. The need for coordination concerns not only vertical harmonization between European law and national systems in relation to enacted European legislation, but also coordination between unharmonized and indirectly harmonized fields that have been or can be strongly affected by processes

---

[7] See J.H.H. Weiler, *The Constitution of Europe* (1999); A. Stone Sweet, *The Judicial Construction of Europe* (2004). See also, for the connection between the role of Courts and comparative law, K. Lenaerts, 'Interlocking Legal Orders in the European Union and Comparative Law', 52 *ICLQ* (2003) 873.

[8] Recent ECJ judgments seem to redefine the allocation of tasks between national courts and the Court at Luxembourg, leaving more room to national courts than in the past. Such 'delegation' can lead to stronger divergences if national courts interpret the Directives differently, particularly when they may rely on specific circumstances without being able to harmonize the effects of their solutions.

and modes of harmonization (for example, business-to-business (B2B) contracts, tenancy law, and property law). Spill-over effects of harmonized measures are quite diffuse.[9] Most of them are still unintended and judicially-driven, but some are intentional and have been incorporated into national instruments. The recent reform of the German BGB, 'induced' by the necessity of coordination with European legislation, provides a good example.[10] Different, yet equally important, spill-overs have occurred in other Member States (e.g. France and Italy, amongst others), with the creation of consumer codes that aim to cover the whole field of consumer law. The phenomenon of spill-over is also very relevant in new Member States, where it is part of the more general process of legal reform.[11]

Together with *structural spill-overs*, where, for example, a piece of legislation dealing with consumer contracts becomes part of general contract law, we are witnessing *functional spill-overs*, in particular in relation to the regulatory functions of private law rules. These spill-overs need to be monitored and governed to further the goals of harmonization. The coordination of indirect harmonization is perhaps even more necessary than the coordination of the impact of harmonizing measures themselves.

Considerations related to the institutional framework are strictly linked to the role of governance in EPL. The need for a governance structure is related not only to: (1) the complexity of the systems of sources of law; but also to (2) the goal-oriented nature of EPL. I will examine these in turn.

(1) The Sources of Law The sources of private law, especially those of continental systems, have not thus far required a particular governance structure because they were relatively simple and often hierarchically structured. In a sense, hierarchy constituted a simplified governance device.[12] Even the administration of the relationship between mandatory rules and private autonomy, the classic partitioning of western national private law systems, has not required a particular governance structure, other than the judiciary. The main device employed to implement European legislation in Member States has been Directives; however, in the field of private law, particularly in relation to cooperation in civil and commercial matters and in international private law, the use of Regulations is also frequent.[13] Soft law has also been used to promote the adoption of relatively harmonized laws at State level in the field of private law, particularly in consumer and environmental law.[14] Private

---

[9] See van Gerven's contribution to this volume at Chap. 2.

[10] See Johnston and Unberath's contribution to this volume at Chap. 5.

[11] See Reich's contribution to this volume at Chap. 8.

[12] This is not to say that hierarchy does not require governance, only that it may be satisfied by a simpler structure.

[13] See Johnston and Unberath in this volume at Chap. 5. For an analysis of the different instruments employed to Europeanize private law, see Annex 1 to Communication from the Commission to the Council and the European Parliament on European Contract Law, COM (2001) 398 final.

[14] See, on these matters, L. Senden, *Soft Law in European Community Law* (2004); U. Morth (ed.), *Soft Law in Governance and Regulation: An Interdisciplinary Analysis* (2005).

regulation has developed either autonomously or in co-regulation systems, and it touches several fields from consumer contract law to advertising, and from product liability to environmental protection. It contributes significantly to the production of rules employed by private parties in their transactions.

The multiplication of sources of law and their increasingly pluralistic nature pose a problem of coordination that cannot be overcome purely by means of a non-hierarchical system of resolving conflicts between norms. The coordination of different layers through cooperation, unlike hierarchy, requires a governance structure. Changes have taken place both in the realm of public law sources concerning private law, and in the domain of private autonomy. Regarding the former, the phenomenon of multi-level law-making, the combination of hard and soft law, has reduced the ability to solve conflicts through hierarchy. As to the latter, the role of collective private autonomy has grown and different types of self-regulatory arrangements have been flourishing, both at the European and national levels.[15]

Internal changes have occurred, redefining the manner in which the subject matter of private law is partitioned. In the field of judicial protection, for example, the shift from internal market to cooperation in civil matters has caused important changes both in terms of substance but also in terms of sources.[16]

Multi-level law-making is the dominant feature of EPL. It implies the necessity to deal with several competing sources. It is the result of a competence system that should combine the goal of harmonization with that of preserving the 'integrity' and identity of each national legal system. Various combinations of law-making, monitoring, and enforcement will ensure decentralization and coordination among the different levels at which EPL is produced. Legislative changes and innovations, promoted at the European level, have to be adapted to existing legal systems, and also to new ones emerging in Central and Eastern Europe. The latter have grown out of an original combination of existing western legal traditions and the *acquis communautaire* as an autonomous legal formant. European private law has in these cases been a catalyst for legal reform and a device for market building.[17] The ways in which implementation takes place are relevant for the creation of EPL and the impact of Community law on national legal systems. Particularly in countries with

---

[15] For a broader perspective on this point, see F. Cafaggi, 'Le role des acteurs privés dans le processus de régulation: participation, autorégulation et régulation privée', 109 *Revue française d'administration publique* (2004) 23; F. Cafaggi, 'Gouvernance et responsabilité des régulateurs privées', *RIDE* (2005) 111.

[16] For an analysis of the implications in the area of consumer judicial protection, see H. Micklitz, N. Reich and S. Weatherill, 'EU Treaty Revision and Consumer Protection', 27 *JCP* (2004) 367, at 380 ff. See also N. Reich, *Understanding EU Law: Objectives, Principles and Methods of Community Law* (2003).

[17] On the concept of legal formant see R. Sacco, 'Legal Formants: a Dynamic Approach to Comparative Law', 39 *AJCL* (1991) 1 and 343. On these developments see the contribution of N. Reich to this volume at Chap. 8. On the role of the *acquis communautaire* as a formant of EPL, see R. Schulze, 'European Private Law and Existing EC Law', 1 *ERPL* (2005) 3; S. Grundmann, 'The Optional European Code on the Basis of the Acquis Communautaire—Starting Points and Trends', 10 *ELJ* (2004) 698. With reference to new Member States, see *infra* Chap. 8.

Civil Codes, the choice between modifying the Code and enacting special legislation often has substantive implications. The experience of new Member States shows that this choice has had more relevance there than in 'old' Member States since it has provided the opportunity to revise parts of the legal systems that had become obsolete.[18]

It is important to underline that multi-level law-making does not involve only legislative law-making but also judicial and regulatory rule-generation and, in many cases, law-finding.[19] Frequently, the Treaty refers back to the laws or to the general principles common to Member States in order to identify Community law. The sources of Community law are the common rules of Member States. The ECJ puts in place a multi-level system by means of gap-filling through law-finding.[20] The identification of Community law is therefore based on a difficult search for common rules, and an examination of the manner in which they are formulated.[21] The liability of both Community institutions and Member States for breach of Community law certainly provides one of the most illustrative examples of this.[22] A significant body of European tort law has been developed through the use of this methodology; as much as, if not more than, has been generated through EC Directives.[23] Often the formulation of European rules does not and cannot reflect the existing rules, but presupposes further elaboration through a sophisticated comparative analysis.[24] Comparative methodology implies not only information

---

[18] See Reich's contribution to this volume at Chap. 8.

[19] See in general B.S. Markesinis (ed.), *Law Making, Law Finding and Law Shaping* (1997).

[20] It has been claimed that a different attitude operates when the Court has to interpret what has already been interpreted by national courts acting as Community courts. See Lenaerts, *supra* note 7, at 894.

[21] Such a search is generally associated with the ECJ, but should characterize all European Institutions. See W. van Gerven, 'A Common Law for Europe: The Future Meeting the Past?', 9 *ERPL* (2001) 485, at 494 ff: 'The obligation to look for principles which are common to the law of the Member States should not only apply to the Court but also, and even in the first place to the Community legislature [. . .] The creation of a jus commune within the framework of EU an ECHR law, by virtue of general principles which the Member States or Contracting states have in common, is an ongoing process which goes hand in hand with, and receives its vigour from the ever-increasing economic and political integration of EU'.

[22] See the Opinion of Advocate General Tesauro in Case C-46/93 *Brasserie du Pêcheur* [1996] ECR I-1029, paras. 80–87. Many other examples of multi-level law-making in the area of private law can be provided. In some cases, substantive rules are defined at the European level (what constitutes a contract, when it is concluded, what are the rights and obligations), while remedies for violations and enforcing institutions are left to Member States, according to their legal traditions, provided they are effective.

[23] See W. van Gerven, 'Bridging the Unbridgeable: Community and National Tort Laws after Francovich and Brasserie', 45 *ICLQ* (1996) 507.

[24] W. van Gerven, 'Taking Art. 215(2) EC Treaty seriously', in J. Beatson and T. Tridimas (eds), *New Directions in European Public Law* (1998) 35; van Gerven, 'The Emergence of a Common European Law in the Area of Tort Law: the EU Contribution', in D. Fairgrieve, M. Andenas and J. Bell (eds), *Tort Liability of Public Authorities in a Comparative Perspective* (2002) 125; Lenaerts, *supra* note 7, at 878 and 887 ff. Lenaerts analyses the different possibilities regarding the search for common rules. He explores the issues arising when a uniform rule does not exist, focusing on cases in which national solutions are divergent or even contradictory. Several questions arise in this case, some concerning the meaning that should be given to the expression 'common rule or principle', others related to the institutional consequences created by the choice of one rule among several conflicting ones.

finding, but also an evaluative procedure for identifying commonalities and differences in order to extract the common principles or rules.[25] The improvement of law-finding procedures should be at the core of the institutional agenda concerning the Europeanization of private law.

Infringements proceedings and preliminary rulings represent additional patterns of multi-level judicial law-making. The ECJ's interventions to examine whether implementing legislation is effective have proved to be a means of designing the multi-level system, by forcing national courts to find the most effective solutions consistent with European legislation. The notions of contract invalidity, compensation in contract and tort, and redress may vary quite substantially across Member States' jurisdictions, and these differences may have an impact on harmonization strategies. In other circumstances, the liability regime remains undefined and is determined through judicial interpretation. Often there is a link between a certain remedy and a liability regime: for example, compensation can be associated with fault, or injunctions with strict liability. To intervene at the State level in order to alter remedies may imply consequences for the liability regime, in theory defined at the European level. Again, if national courts hand down different interpretations, it might be appropriate to make use of the intervention of the ECJ as a means to promote a more effective and sophisticated system of monitoring and adjustment.

Hence, EPL clearly operates—and will grow in the future—within a multi-level system.[26] Such architecture poses serious governance problems. The system is relatively complex and needs coordination, not only in terms of law-making, but also monitoring and enforcement. Horizontal cooperation in law-making is growing, but further and greater systematic integration of vertical and horizontal regulatory and judicial cooperation is needed when the method of harmonization is rule-finding instead of rule-making. Even more problematic is monitoring implementation, which, when seen in the light of the principle of effectiveness, should play a strategic role in the design of EPL. The relevance of the duty of loyal and sincere cooperation can certainly be enhanced, but the real question is related to the balance of power between different courts and the ways of solving conflicts arising from divergent interpretations.

Different contributions in this book (particularly those of van Gerven in the field of security regulation and Albors-Llorens in the field of competition) analyse existing

---

[25] See, on the role of comparative law as a tool to select best practices, F. Cafaggi, 'Una governance per il diritto europeo dei contratti', in F. Cafaggi (ed.), *Quale armonizzazione per il diritto europeo dei contratti?* (2003) 189.

[26] See G. De Búrca and B. De Witte, 'The Delimitation of Powers Between the EU and its Member States', in A. Arnull and D. Wincott (eds), *Accountability and Legitimacy in the European Union* (2002) 5; P. Von Bogdandy and J. Bast, 'The European Union's Vertical Order of Competences: the Current Law and Proposals for its Reform', 39 *CMLRev* (2002) 227; T. Baumé, 'Vers une clarification de la répartition des compétences entre l'Union et ses États Membres', 38 *Cahier de droit européens* (2003) 135; A. Dashwood, 'The relationship between the Member States and the European Union/European Community', 41 *CMLRev* (2004) 355; G. Berman, 'Competences of the Union', in T. Tridimas and P. Nebbia, *European Union Law for the Twenty-First Century: Rethinking the New Legal Order* (2004) 65.

governance designs aimed at coordinating different layers and functions (law-making, monitoring, and enforcement). Proposed solutions include extending the Lamfalussy scheme from regulatory to judicial cooperation (van Gerven) and other coordination devices based on the duty of loyal and sincere cooperation (Cafaggi).

(2) The Goal-oriented Nature of EPL The second reason why a governance system for EPL is required is associated with the goal-oriented nature of that body of law. Such an approach is mainly due to the necessity to provide adequate reasons for European (legislative) intervention.[27] Insofar as EPL is a set of rules with specified functions, it requires a governance system to ensure that these functions are pursued and the goals are achieved. To the extent that EPL is aimed at defining the legal infrastructure of an integrated European market coherent with existing constitutional values and based on social justice, the rules require a monitoring system to verify their effectiveness with regard to the goals they aim to achieve. Such monitoring should enable European institutions to readjust and modify the content of the rules or the coordination mechanisms in place when difficulties emerge. In national legal systems, in which such goals are absent or implicit, there has been less need to devise a governance structure for private law systems. Methodologies to verify that given rules are appropriate to the goals they are intended to pursue have been mainly developed through the use of the open method of coordination or regulatory impact evaluation. The question is whether analogous methodologies should operate in relation to traditional private law fields, and, if so, which modifications, if any, are required.

2. THE DIFFERENT DIMENSIONS OF EPL

It is useful to group the issues related to the EPL institutional framework into different categories dealing with: (A) the constitutional; (B) the institutional; and (C) the regulatory dimensions of EPL.

A. The Constitutional Dimensions of EPL

The definition of a constitutional dimension of EPL is itself a problematic issue.[28] It clearly goes beyond the text of the Treaty itself, and concerns the roles both of

---

[27] The goal-oriented nature of EPL fits quite well, as will be illustrated below, with the regulatory function of private law. But how is the creation of a full body of contract law compatible with the idea that these rules perform a function? To be sure, one could resort to the general function of the necessity to create the legal infrastructure of an integrated European market; then, however, it would be more appropriate to acknowledge the different intensity of the goal-oriented nature of European private law.

[28] See V. Zeno-Zencovich and N. Vardi, 'The Constitutional Basis of a European Private Law', in A. Hartkamp *et al.* (eds), *Towards a European Civil Code*, (3rd edn., 2004), at 205; C. Joerges, 'What is Left of the European Economic Constitution? A Melancholic Eulogy', *EUI WpL* 13/2004.

common national constitutional traditions and of fundamental rights.[29] These traditions are quite diverse and the identification of a common set of principles is a rather difficult enterprise.[30]

One aspect is certainly related to competence, given the particular structure of the EU. The contributions in this book present different approaches to and readings of Treaty provisions in relation to the legal bases of EPL, but they converge on the conclusion that no general competence concerning private law exists today. Competence is related to powers to intervene and to harmonize, their legal foundations and limits.[31] The issue has been hotly debated, particularly after the *Tobacco Advertising* judgment and the ECJ case-law that followed it, in which the Court made clear that the mere fact of disparity between legal rules is not sufficient to justify legislative intervention.[32]

The question of competence is not limited to the European level, but also impacts national levels. Even if, in the majority of cases, competence concerning private law is attributed to the State, in an increasing number of contexts a competing competence is also recognized at sub-national levels, posing both similar problems to those that exist between Europe and Member States, and entirely new problems as it forces coordination between more than two layers at once. The focus on competence is naturally related to the issue of legislative harmonization. A related question concerns the possibility that competence obstacles can be bypassed by using judicial instead of legislative harmonization. While it is important to recognize that judicial harmonization of private law can play a strategic role as much as, or, in certain fields, even more than legislative harmonization, it must also be pointed out that there are also constitutional limits to judicial harmonization.

One open question concerns the constitutional relevance of the diversity of legal systems and traditions in private law which affects modes of harmonization.[33] Once competence to intervene is found, the desirability of harmonization should be evaluated from different perspectives, among which is the preservation of diversity. Legal

---

[29] See Art. 6 of the EU Treaty.

[30] For a useful attempt to identify the role of the constitutional traditions of Member States in relation to the 2004 Constitution, see J. Ziller, 'La funcion de los conceptos constitucionales de los Estados miembros en la nueva constitucion para Europa', in M. Cartabia, B. de Witte and P. Perez Tremps (eds), *Constitucion Europea y Constituciones nacionales* (2005) 27.

[31] The question of competence is often addressed in national systems, particularly in those characterized by a federal structure.

[32] See, in this volume, the contributions of Weatherill, at Chap. 3, and van Gerven, at Chap. 2. The case-law is now voluminous, since the so-called *Tobacco Advertising* judgment: see Case C-376/98 *Germany v Council, Parliament and Commission* [2000] ECR I-8419; Case C-434/02 *Arnold André GmbH & Co KG v Landrat des Kreises Herfors* [2004] not yet reported, paras. 83–84; Case C-210/03 *Swedish Match AB and Swedish Match UK Ltd* v *Secretary of State for Health* [2003] not yet reported, paras. 76–77.

[33] See B. De Witte, D. Hanf and S. Prechal (eds), *The Many Faces of Differentiation in EU Law* (2001). In this volume, see, from different perspectives, the contributions from Weatherill, van Gerven and Muir Watt (at Chaps. 3, 2 and 4). See, specifically in relation to private law, H. Collins, 'European Private Law and the Cultural Identity of States', 3 *ERPL* (1995) 153.

diversity is not incompatible with integrated market-building to the extent that it is organized and coordinated.[34] Legal diversity affects not only law-making but also law-finding and interpretation; the presence of primarily judge-made legal systems in the area of private law poses important questions to be addressed when choosing means and modes of harmonization. Even when a rule is harmonized by means of a Directive or a Regulation, its implementation may be affected by the use of different judicial styles, which exist beyond the conventional common/civil law distinction.[35]

Does legal diversity, and in particular the legal diversity of private law rules, partly related to different national institutional frameworks, have a constitutional foundation? The affirmative answer is generally framed within the principle of subsidiarity, but perhaps this is too narrow and too vertical a view. Complementary principles may be suggested. The constitutional foundations of legal diversity and of its limits can also, for example, be grounded in the Treaty in relation to the protection of national identity and cultural diversity. Certainly national identity should also encompass legal identity (Article 5 EC).[36] Cultural diversity represents another source for a constitutional foundation of legal diversity.[37] To the extent that legal diversity is a subset of cultural diversity it should be protected.[38] This approach may have important institutional effects; for example, when evaluating an infringement concerning the transposition of Directives, the ECJ will have to consider more deeply whether the differences between the national text of the implementing measure and that of the

---

[34] Often this question has been discussed within the framework of the harmonization of private law. See Collins, *supra* note 33.

[35] See van Gerven's contribution to this volume at Chap. 2, and B. Markesinis (ed.), *The Gradual Convergence. Foreign Ideas, Foreign Influences and English Law on the Eve of the 21st Century* (1994); Markesinis, 'Studying Judicial Decisions in the Common Law and the Civil Law: A Good Way of Discovering Some of the Most Interesting Similarities that Exist Between these Legal Families', in M. Van Hoecke and F. Ost (eds), *The Harmonisation of European Private Law* (2000) 117.

[36] The protection of national identity is defined in Art. 17 of the Treaty. On the general principle and its ramifications in the Constitutional Treaty see L. Diez Picazo, 'Observaciones sobre la clàusula de identitad nacional', in Cartabia *et al.*, *supra* note 30, at 437.

[37] On the concept of legal cultures and legal traditions the volume of debate in comparative law is overwhelming. See, for different perspectives, A. Watson, 'Legal culture v. Legal tradition', and H. Patrick Glenn, 'Legal cultures and legal traditions', both in M. Van Hoecke (ed.), *Epistemology and Methodology of Comparative Law* (2004), at 1 and 7 respectively.

[38] On cultural diversity, see B. de Witte, 'The Value of Cultural Diversity', in M. Aziz and S. Millns (eds), *Values in the Constitution of Europe* (forthcoming) 2005. On the relationship between legal pluralism and EPL see K.H. Ladeur, 'Methodology and European Law—Can methodology change so as to cope with the multiplicity of the law?', in Van Hoecke and Ost (eds), *supra* note 35, 91. On the approach of constitutional pluralism, see N. Walker, 'The Idea of Constitutional Pluralism', 65 *MLR* (2002) 317; Walker, 'Europe's Constitutional Momentum and the Search for Polity Legitimacy', 3 *I-con* (2005) 218; M. Dorf and C. Sabel, 'A Constitution of Democratic Experimentalism,' 98 *Col L Rev* (1998) 267; O. Gerstenberg and C. Sabel, 'Directly-Deliberative Poliarchy: An Institutional Ideal for Europe', in C. Joerges and R. Dehousse (eds), *Good Governance in Europe's Integrated Market* (2002) 289; and G. Teubner, 'Societal Constitutionalism: Alternatives to State-Centred Constitutional Theory?', in C. Joerges, I.J. Sand and G. Teubner (eds), *Transnational Governance and Constitutionalism* (2004) 3. On the role of cultural identity in EPL, see Collins, *supra* note 33, at 153.

Directive can be justified in the light of the protection of legal identity. This value should affect not merely the choice of whether or not to harmonize but, once the decision to harmonize is taken, it can and should influence the modes of harmonization. This will include which instruments should be used when a choice is available; how much detail legislation should contain; and how many options should be left to the Member States when Directives or recommendations are used, etc.[39]

If the protection of legal diversity has a constitutional foundation, then the balance between harmonization and differentiation must be (re)defined. In this vein, the main question is whether a single strategy in the field of private law is desirable or whether different combinations should be defined for each area of EPL. Whether different levels of and devices for harmonization and the preservation of legal diversity may be used in contract, tort, property, family law, and in corporate and labour law cannot be decided once and for all. However, the implications of an approach based on the constitutional relevance of different legal identities would be manifold. It would, for example, affect the analysis of the implementation of Directives by Member States: whereas, at the moment, the examination is predominantly premised upon the (presumed) conflict between the interest in a harmonized and integrated legal system and the interests of individual States in protecting their discretion when implementing Directives, the recognition of a constitutional dimension of legal diversity should provide different grounds for justifying legislative and judicial choices that deviate from the model. Legal diversity in a coordinated framework can become an important cornerstone of European integration. Legal integration and the protection of legal diversity would both have constitutional foundations and could complement each other.

Different harmonizing strategies have to be confronted within specific sectors. Such choices have constitutional value. The alternative between minimum and complete harmonization, that between regulatory competition and regulatory coordination or a combination of the two, and the use of international private law and its relationship with the four freedoms are all matters of constitutional relevance in relation to EPL. They should be scrutinized, not only for the purpose of establishing whether or not they are formally compatible with the principles of subsidiarity and proportionality, but also their effectiveness in relation to the goal of harmonization and their ability to protect national identities and legal diversities.

The constitutional dimension is certainly influenced by the role of the four freedoms and that of competition law. Their impact, direct or indirect, on relationships among private parties cannot be disputed.[40] Once their relevance has been recognized, several issues have to be addressed: first, in relation to their influence on

---

[39] On these questions see the contributions to this book by Weatherill, and Johnston and Unberath at Chaps. 3 and 5.

[40] On competition law and the importance of *Courage* v *Crehan*, see N. Reich, 'The "Courage" Doctrine: Encouraging or Discouraging Compensation for Antitrust Injuries?', 42 *CMLR* (2005) 35; J. Stuyck, 'EC Competition Law After Modernisation: More than Ever in the Interest of Consumer', 28 *JCP* (2005) 1.

integration, whether they operate as harmonizing factors of European private law; secondly, in relation to the regulatory function of private law, whether they direct the developments of private law toward a regulatory function aimed at facilitating cross-border trade; and, thirdly, what the relationship is between four freedoms and fundamental rights in shaping EPL.

The constitutional dimension also affects the relationship between constitutional values and principles and EPL. In particular, it means that the Charter of Rights and national constitutional principles concerning fundamental rights and freedoms are brought to the very core of the foundations of this body of law.[41] The importance of fundamental rights in the realm of European law and particularly EPL has long been recognized by the Court of Justice, but not yet fully explored in academic debate.[42] The relationship between private law and fundamental rights is extremely complex and relatively differentiated in legal systems; and it presents challenging questions at the European level.[43] There are at least two different, complementary perspectives.

The first and more traditional of these looks at the effects that the protection of fundamental rights can produce on the content of substantive rules of private law. This is the perspective adopted by several legal systems in the field of contract, torts, and property. In this framework, the function of the principles of dignity, solidarity and equality (of opportunities or outcomes) have been explored in these three fields in many national legal systems.[44] The most plausible institutional implication of this perspective is that increased equal protection of fundamental rights might require higher levels of harmonization of substantive private law.[45] This perspective should, however, be partially corrected if the right to national legal identity is considered as part of the catalogue of fundamental rights.

The second perspective, less explored, examines the ways in which private law can be designed and employed to foster the protection of fundamental rights. Property,

[41] See Art. 6 of the EU Treaty.

[42] See Case 4/73 *Nold* v *Commission* [1974] ECR 491, in which the Court stated that it could not uphold measures incompatible with fundamental rights recognized and protected by the Constitutions of the Member States.

[43] One of the most debated questions is that of the horizontal effects of fundamental rights. On this question in relation to private law see M. Hesselink, 'The horizontal effects of social rights in European contract law', *Europa e diritto privato* (2003) 1; A. Colombi Ciacchi, 'Non-Legislative Harmonisation of Private Law Under the European Constitution: The Case of Unfair Suretyships', 3 *ERPL* (2005) 294, summarizing the rich German debate.

[44] A relevant example is provided by the English experience with the enactment of the Human Rights Act of 1998. However, the issue is relevant for the new Member States in which changes have taken place at the constitutional level and have affected the structure of private law.

[45] The harmonizing role of rights in different fields of private law has allowed the development of judicial harmonization in addition to legislative harmonization See, on these questions, W. van Gerven, 'Remedies for infringements of fundamental rights', 10 *EPL* (2002) 261; G. Comandé, 'Diritto privato europeo e diritti fondamentali', in G. Comandé (ed.), *Diritto privato europeo e diritti fondamentali* (2004) 21; O. Gerstenberg, 'Private Law and the New European Constitutional Settlement', 10 *ELJ* (2004) 766; Hesselink, *supra* note 43.

contract and tort may be seen as devices to improve the effectiveness of rights protection. Particularly in relation to rights to access goods and services or participatory rights, different designs of branches of private law may promote or undermine the protection of fundamental rights.[46] In other words, the manner in which private law rules are designed is not neutral when it comes to promoting the protection of fundamental rights. The institutional implications of this perspective refer more to the actual content of substantive rules than to their degree of harmonization.

Constitutional relevance, going beyond a traditional and hierarchical approach to the sources of law, can be attributed to the way in which Directives and Regulations regulate matters of constitutional value. Examples in this vein often refer to equality Directives. The temporary interruption of the adoption process for the Constitutional Treaty affects the legal relevance of the Charter and its binding character, but certainly does not undermine the importance of fundamental rights and freedoms in the consolidation of EPL. In this field, it would be highly desirable to develop a real test for the conformity of Regulations and Directives with the Charter, instead of providing a formal declaration of conformity without any specific evidence of the analysis developed by the European Institutions during the legislative process.

Certainly, there are elements specific to the constitutional foundations of EPL that should be taken into account. These include the multi-level structure of rule-making, rule finding and the regulatory function of Community law. These aspects can be better analysed within the institutional and regulatory dimensions of EPL.

B. The Institutional Dimensions of EPL

The constitutional dimension partly overlaps with the institutional dimension, although the two are far from coextensive. Many institutional questions can also be tackled at a subconstitutional level. The institutional dimension of EPL is built around the different roles of European and national institutions: in particular, modes of cooperation and, to a more limited extent, competition between legislators, courts, and regulators. It brings the governance perspective to centre stage. It broadens the perspective on competence, often focused on the alternative between existence or inexistence, by concentrating on the different modes by which the creation of the 'private law infrastructure' of a common market can be established. In particular, it is useful to focus on the institutional dimension of private autonomy as a substantive principle of EPL.

The institutional dimension is particularly relevant when we consider the following features:

(a) EPL is organized round a multi-level system involving at least four vertically determined layers, each one itself composed of several institutions:
  • International conventions;
  • European legislators, regulators and courts;

---

[46] See, from different perspectives, the Study Group on Social Justice in European Private Law, *supra* note 1, at 653.

- National legislators, regulators and courts;
- Regional legislators and regulators, for those systems that recognize regions or equivalent entities as having competence in private law.

(b) The strong interaction—in the field of law-making and to some extent monitoring—between public institutions and private actors, individual parties, and private regulators. Such interaction occurs at each level or layer, but also among actors operating at different levels, so that private national bodies can interact with European Institutions, and—*vice versa*—private European actors may interact with local, regional, or state institutions.

(c) The governance of the implementation process concerning direct and indirect harmonization, defined as follows:

- by 'direct harmonization' we mean the pursuit of explicit goals that harmonizing acts are meant to achieve in national legal systems;
- by 'indirect harmonization' we mean those harmonizing effects not directly caused by a legislative act, but by intentional or unintentional spill-overs. For example, indirect cross-sector harmonization occurs when a particular device is exported from one field (e.g. consumer law) into another (e.g. business law). Cross-national indirect harmonization occurs when there is circulation from one legal system to another by way of a European legislative Act or an ECJ judgment.[47]

(d) The institutional mechanisms aimed at preserving national legal identities in ways compatible with the goals of harmonization.

Here, I shall concentrate on the first two, as I have previously addressed the others at some length.[48] An institutional framework in the European context different from those operating in Member States has characterized the development of EPL. Recent developments driven both by internal changes, particularly enlargement, and by external factors have created the need for institutional reforms.[49] A new set of institutions is required; different from those used in Member States, but also from those employed thus far to generate the *acquis communautaire*.

The institutional dimension of EPL is strongly linked with European legal integration, and with different modes of harmonization. Harmonization has occurred through different institutional means, beyond the use of legislation.[50] On the one

[47] On the interplay between Community and comparative law, see W. van Gerven, 'Comparative Law in a Texture of Communitarization of National laws and Europeanization of Community Law', in D. O'Keeffe (ed.), *Liber Amicorum in Honour of Lord Slynn of Hadley, vol. 1, Judicial Review in the European Union* (2000) 433.

[48] See *supra* the introduction (Section 1) and the section on the constitutional dimension (Section 2.A).

[49] The accession of new members means that further reforms are necessary in order to govern legal systems with such diverse backgrounds.

[50] Even within legislative harmonization there have been several concurring strategies depending on the hierarchical nature (top-down or bottom-up), on completeness (minimum or total) and on the quality of rules (principles, detailed rules). These strategies may require different types of institutional framework to be implemented.

hand, there has been judicial harmonization: as noted above, the strategic role of the ECJ and national courts has long been recognized as a main driving force behind the creation of a European legal system.[51] In particular, it is important to emphasize again the role of preliminary rulings as an instrument of dialogue between the ECJ and national courts.[52] Judicial harmonization has occurred at the European level, whereas it has until now proved more difficult to achieve cooperation between national judiciaries, aimed at increasing the scope of 'bottom-up' harmonization.[53] Recent developments concerning judicial liability for failure to interpret domestic law according to European law may reinforce the potential importance of judicial harmonization of EPL.[54] The role and potential development of Article 10 EC are relevant to the future of judicial governance in this regard.

On the other hand, new modes of governance can contribute to harmonization while preserving legal diversity.[55] These modes are much more flexible and may be better suited to a landscape in which Member States have become much more diversified. Legislative harmonization does not constitute the only mode of governance of EPL. Lack of competence may forbid direct intervention, but, even in fields in which legislative competence exists, alternative solutions to harmonizing legislative

---

[51] Van Gerven, *supra* note 45, at 679; W. van Gerven, 'Of Rights, Remedies and Procedures', 37 *CMLR* (2000) 501; van Gerven, 'The ECJ Case-law as a Means of Unification of Private Law?', in Hartkamp *et al.*, *supra* note 28, at 117; Lenaerts, *supra* note 7; Weiler, *supra* note 7; De Búrca and Weiler, *supra* note 6.

[52] J. Weiler, 'The Transformation of Europe', 100 *Yale LJ* (1991) 2420; A.-M. Slaughter, A. Stone Sweet and J. Weiler (eds), *The European Courts and National Courts* (1998); also, in particular, W. Mattli and A.-M. Slaughter, 'The Role of National Courts in EC Legal Integration', in A.-M. Slaughter, A. Stone Sweet and J. Weiler (eds), *The European Court and National Courts: Doctrine and Jurisprudence* (1998) 253; Alter (1995), *supra* note 6, at 227. See also A. Stone Sweet and T.L. Brunell, 'Constructing a Supranational Constitution: Dispute Resolution and Governance in the European Community', 92 *American Political Science Review* (1998) 63. For an attempt to test the different explanations of the importance of preliminary rulings for European integration, see C.J. Carrubba and L. Murrah, 'Legal Integration and the Use of the Preliminary Ruling Process in the European Union', *International Organisation* (2005) 399, reaching the conclusion that current explanations do not necessarily diverge significantly.

[53] See, for some examples of judicial dialogue not necessarily resulting in judicial transplants, van Gerven's contribution to this volume at Chap. 2.

[54] The existence of a duty of the judiciary to apply EC law has long been recognized. See Case 92/78 *Simmental* v *Commission* [1979] ECR 777; Case 283/81 *CILFIT and others* v *Ministry of Health* [1983] ECR 3415; and Case C-106/89 *Marleasing SA* v *La commercial Internacional de Alimentacion SA* [1990] ECR I-4135. More recently, the Court has recognized State liability for the failure of judges to interpret domestic law according to European law. See *Gerhard Köbler* v *Republik of Osterreich* [2003] ECR I-10239; Case C-129/00 *Commission* v *Repubblica Italiana* [2000] not yet reported. Such a duty, supported by a liability sanction in case of failure, has the potential to become a significant driving force behind judicial harmonization. However, by the same token, judges could be held custodians of the European principle of legal diversity. It should also be mentioned that the Commission can open an infringement procedure in case of judicial misinterpretation. In this case, an opinion of the ECJ recognizing the infringement should force the Member State to take the most appropriate measures to comply with Art. 228(1). See, on these matters, L.S. Rossi and G. Di Federico, 'Case Note', 42 *CMLR* (2005) 829.

[55] On the role of new modes of governance in areas related to EPL, see J. Scott and D. Trubeck, 'Mind the Gap: Law and New Approaches to Governance in the European Union', 8 *ELJ* (2002) 1.

interventions may be employed if more effective. A clear example can be found in consumer law in which 'according to Article 153(3)(b)' measures to support, supplement, and monitor the policy can be pursued by Member States.[56]

The use of modified forms of the open method of coordination in the field of private law has been proposed as a potentially useful device for mutual learning and monitoring a coordinating set of national rules, whose diversity may create obstacles to the functioning of the internal market, even if these divergences do not reach the level required by Articles 94 and 95 EC for legislative intervention.[57] But even when legislative measures of harmonization are adopted in accordance with Articles 94 or 95, many factors can contribute to undermine the harmonizing goals, requiring constant monitoring and (non-)legislative adjustments.[58] Distinctions should be made between new modes of governance concerning rule-making and those focusing on monitoring and reporting.[59]

In the area of private law, particular relevance should be attributed to the different relationships between legislators, regulators and judges existing at national level. While, in order to ensure uniform application of Community law, States have been conceived of as unitary entities, regardless of their internal organization, in real life these differences matter for multi-level governance of EPL; and the case-law of the ECJ has begun to take this into account.[60] Instead of continuing to hold these differences irrelevant, it would be more useful to recognize them and take them explicitly into account when designing EPL rules, particularly if they are principle-based and need further specification at national level. The institutional dimension of EPL imposes consideration of the different national frameworks within which the harmonized rules will operate.

The institutional dimension of EPL is also affected by the different nature of private law rules, and in particular by both the distinction between legislation and private autonomy and, in the public domain, between legislators and regulators. It reflects different relationships between rules and rule-makers. The debate over EPL,

---

[56] Art. 153(3) states: 'The Community shall contribute to the attainment of the objectives referred to in paragraph 1 through:

(a) measures adopted pursuant to Art. 95 in the context of the completion of the internal market

(b) measures which support, supplement and monitor the policy pursued by the Member States.'

On the relationship between Arts. 95 and 153 see Micklitz, Reich and Weatherill, *supra* note 16, at 374.

[57] See on this point Cafaggi, *supra* note 25, at 202 and the references in para. 52 of the Action Plan of 2003. See also, from a different perspective, W. van Gerven in this volume, speaking of an open method of convergence (at Chap. 2).

[58] See on this point Cafaggi, *supra* note 25, at 204 ff.

[59] See on this point Cafaggi, *supra* note 25, at 202 ff.

[60] The ECJ has repeatedly reiterated the principle in relation to different areas, such as delegation and liability. On the liability issue, however, the tendency is to identify the liability of specific institutions, in particular concerning judges and executives. See, in this volume, the contribution from W. van Gerven at Chap. 2.

its desirability, forms and scope is mainly associated with the different sets of rules that populate private law: mandatory, default rules and private autonomy. The nature of the rules and the desirability and modes of harmonization are strongly correlated. They affect the institutional dimension, and particularly the interaction between different 'norm-producers'.

The role of private autonomy in private law, and especially contract law, has been a core principle of western European legal systems.[61] But what is the current function of private autonomy and what are its institutional implications? Which changes have occurred in the private spheres, modifying the boundaries and functions of private autonomy, private law and, consequently, its institutional dimensions? What is the relationship between harmonization, market integration, and private autonomy? And that between private autonomy and fundamental rights? Is there a difference between the concepts of private autonomy arising out of national legal traditions and that/those developed in the framework of EPL? Does the function of private autonomy differ in mature and emerging markets? Can a 'certain' exercise of private autonomy become an obstacle to the creation of an integrated European market? Should we limit the harmonization debate only to legislative and perhaps regulatory measures, or should we also compel private parties to exercise their private autonomy homogeneously in the pursuit of legal integration?

Mistaken implicit assumptions about private autonomy have influenced choices and modes of harmonization. In particular, the role of private autonomy may differ not only in highly structured markets that have existed for centuries, but also and perhaps more strongly in newly-built markets that have replaced other economic and political systems, as in the case in post-Communist countries. The relationship between private autonomy as a substantive principle of EPL and the different strategies of integration and differentiation is more complex than is currently recognized.

In the field of private law, recurring arguments in favour of harmonization have been related to the differences concerning mandatory rules in Member States and the problems they may cause for the creation of an integrated European market. Analogous reasoning is applied to international private law rules.[62] Often, however,

---

[61] See S. Grundman, W. Kerber and S. Weatherill, *Party Autonomy and the Role of Information in the Internal Market* (2001), and in particular S. Grundmann, W. Kerber and S. Weatherill, 'Party autonomy and the Role of Information in the Internal Market—An Overview' (at 1) and S. Muller Graff, 'Basic Freedoms: Extending Party Autonomy Across Borders' (at 133). See also S. Grundman and J. Stuyck, *An Academic Green Paper on European Contract Law* (2002). On the constitutional relevance of private autonomy at the European level, see C. Castronovo, 'Autonomia privata e Costituzione europea', in *Europa e diritto privato* (2005) 29; S. Mazzamuto, 'Note minime in tema di autonomia privata alla luce della Costituzione europea', *Europa e diritto privato* (2005) 51.

[62] See, for an illustration in relation to international private law rules taking into account ECJ case-law, H. Muir Watt, 'The Challenge of Market Integration for European Conflicts Theory', in Hartkamp *et al.*, *supra* note 28, at 191: 'Scrutiny under market freedoms may apply to any form of mandatory state regulation which is internationally enforceable under Articles 5 to 7 of the Rome Convention, including national measures implementing Community directives (as, for instance, in the *Arblade* and *Mazzoleni* cases) but does not apply to the choice-facilitating rules which fall within the scope of Art. 3 of the Rome

private law is mainly concerned with enabling rules. Such a circumstance weakens this rationale for unification, limiting harmonization to mandatory rules only. Moreover, this justification is based on the implicit assumption that private parties, interested in harmonizing the different legal systems, could use private autonomy to change diverging default rules for the purpose of harmonization. Such a conclusion is built on two, at least debatable, assumptions: the first is that private parties are interested in having a harmonized set of rules for the European market; the second, that different private actors would have similar or identical preferences about which rules, based on the exercise of private autonomy, should operate in any given circumstances. Even if the prevailing interests of contracting private parties were in favour of a uniform European set of rules, different private groups might have different interests and preferences; therefore, they might diverge over which set of rules they would like to govern an integrated European market.[63] Private autonomy is an abstraction that must be articulated if its institutional dimension is to be taken into account. Certainly, private autonomy cannot function as the sole catalyst for the harmonization of non-mandatory rules in the domain of private law.

If the idea that legal diversity is the result of different legal cultures is taken seriously, there is reason to believe that different contracting practices are the result not only of different legislative cultures, but also of different philosophies of private parties in exercising their private autonomy.[64] As noted previously, it may happen that the interests of contracting parties do not converge towards an integrated legally defined market.[65] From this perspective, the forced harmonization of private autonomy is unthinkable. On the contrary, voluntary coordination is both possible and desirable. The institutional question over different methods of exercising private autonomy concerns modes of coordination, and in particular the space that public institutions may have to facilitate the coordination of private spheres and frameworks for the purpose of combining harmonization and differentiation.[66] This conclusion holds even more true if we consider the power of private regulators to shape contractual practices.

Private autonomy, though still predominantly conceptualized as the basis of individual contracting, is at the core of the production of standardized contracts and contract rules (such as those in codes of conduct drafted by trade associations, for example). The most relevant form of private autonomy today is collective private

---

Convention. As the *Alsthom Atlantique* case shows, national rules within this latter category are not subject to scrutiny under fundamental freedoms. Thus the conflict rule governing transactions on the internal market draws a double dividing line: it demarcates the scope of free choice, as opposed to internationally mandatory regulation, while simultaneously ensuring the vertical allocation of competences between Community law, designed to cure market failures (consumer protection, competition law) and regulation at the lower Member State level, of the garden variety of contract law'.

 [63] See on this point Cafaggi, *supra* note 25, at 191 ff.
 [64] From a different perspective but similar conclusions see Teubner, *supra* note 38, at 3 ff.
 [65] See Cafaggi, *supra* note 25, at 191 ff.
 [66] See, in this perspective, 'The Way Forward', at para 2.3.

autonomy. Private autonomy, particularly when exercised to produce standard-form contracts, should be considered an important institutional component of EPL, and therefore analysed in its most important manifestations, such as, for example, that of private regulation.[67] From this perspective, obstacles to the creation of a competitive integrated European market can derive from an exercise of private autonomy creating barriers to trade, thus violating Articles 28 EC and 81 EC.[68]

In addition, it is important to ask to what extent, when viewed in the light of economic integration, can private autonomy become a privately produced semi-public good? Should different harmonization strategies also encompass the use of private autonomy as both a harmonizing and differentiating element in legal systems?

The role of regulators as 'private law' rule-makers, both at the European and national levels, has become extremely relevant due to two related factors: privatization and liberalization; and changes in regulatory techniques. This is certainly true for public regulators, and it is becoming more significant for private regulators.[69] Today, it would be impossible to define many areas of law—such as the law of privacy, the law of contract in utilities markets (both between firms and consumers and between firms themselves), the law of contract in securities regulation, and the law of torts in product liability and environmental protection—without considering the intervention of both public and private regulators. It would, however, also be impossible to define contract law in e-commerce without considering different forms of self-regulation that characterize the modes of transaction taking place on the internet.

The regulatory function of private law in relation to actions and transactions taking place on the internet is growing in importance. This is undoubtedly a global concern, yet different approaches have been adopted in Europe, USA and East Asia on whether, what and how to regulate. The manner in which technology has changed economic interactions has affected not only the content of private law rules, but also the regulatory function of international private law. The regulatory function of internet architecture influences the ways in which transactions take place on the web and requires specific rules.[70] Framework contracts and other general tools have been developed to operate on the internet. The formation of epistemic and economic communities of firms and consumers has translated into strong forms of private rule-making that affect both the modes and the content of transactions. The consequences of all this have yet to be revealed, but it is clear that consumer communities on the web, combining an epistemic and educational function with the

---

[67] See F. Cafaggi, *Self Regulation and European Contract Law* (forthcoming).

[68] According to the ECJ, Art. 28, unlike Art. 81 does not have direct horizontal effects, but creates duties for Member States. See Case C-265/95 *Commission* v *France* [1997] ECR I-6959 and Case C-453/99 *Courage* v *Crehan* [2001] ECR I-6297. Such an interpretation implies that Member States are guardians of the creation of barriers to trade by private actors, while the Community system is the guardian for the competition law perspective. I am indebted to A. Johnston for clarification on this point.

[69] See Cafaggi (2004), *supra* note 15, at 23 ff; and Cafaggi (2005), *supra* note 15, at 111 ff.

[70] See L. Lessig, *Code and Other Laws of Cyberspace* (1999).

expression of preferences, can radically alter the structure of contract law and of markets.[71] The evolution of EPL cannot seek to minimize the impact of technology on the design of the institutional framework. On the contrary, it should place technological development at the core of institutional evolution.

Regulators affect the production process of contract rules in different ways, depending on whether they are public or private or operate within a co-regulatory scheme; we must, however, take their activity into account when designing the institutional framework within which EPL is to be constructed. This question is separate from, but related to, that of the regulatory dimension of EPL. This regulatory function goes beyond the role performed by regulators, and may concern private law rules administered by a system of pure private autonomy. Within this framework, the importance of international private law should have a more relevant role to play.

The relationship between EPL and international private law has been explored by scholars, and yet has not received the attention it deserves in policy-making.[72] Not only has the former had a significant impact on the latter, but the challenges of harmonization pose the problem of the future relevance of international private law in the context of EPL.[73] Empirical evidence and theory show that, even in the context of harmonized rules, a system of international private law could remain strategically important. Its relevance and functions will depend on the modes and degrees of harmonization and on its combination with an organized system of differentiation.[74]

A footnote on languages and the institutional dimension of EPL. Institutions are composed of people and languages. The problem of language in the generation of EPL has not yet been adequately considered. The choice of one language to create new rules and its 'translation' into 20 or more others does not really address the comparative issue that has caused so many problems for the transposition of

---

[71] See C. Shapiro and H. Varian, *Information Rules* (1999).

[72] See Muir Watt in this volume at Chap. 4; Muir Watt, *Aspect économiques du droit international privé* (2005); Muir Watt, 'Choice of Law in Integrated and Interconnected Markets: A Matter of Political Economy', 9 *Colum. J. Eur. L.* 383. See also S. Grundmann, 'Internal Market Conflict of Laws: From Traditional Conflict of Laws to an Integrated Two Level Order', in A. Fichs, H. Muir Watt and E. Pataut (eds), *Les conflits de lois et le système juridique communautaire* (2004) 5; C. Joerges, 'The Challenges of Europeanization in the Realm of Private Law: A Plea for a New Legal Discipline', 24 *Duke Journal of Comparative and International Law* (2004) 149; and Joerges, 'The Impact of European Integration on Private Law: Reductionist Perceptions. True Conflicts and a New Constitutional Perspective', 3 *ELJ* (1997) 378; J. Basedow, 'The Communitarization of the Conflict of Laws under the Treaty of Amsterdam', 37 *CMLR* (2000) 687.

[73] See H. Muir Watt, 'The Challenge of Market Integration for European Conflicts Theory', in Hartkamp *et al.*, *supra* note 28, at 191 ff; Muir Watt, 'Experiences from Europe: Legal Diversity and the Internal Market', 39 *Texas International LJ* (2004) 429; G. Teubner and A. Fischer Lescano, 'Regime-Collision: How the Emergence of Private Governance Regimes Changes Global Legal Pluralism', 25 *Michigan Journal of International Law* (2004), 999; C. Joerges, 'Europeanisation as Process: Thoughts on the Europeanisation of Private Law', 11 *EPLR* (2005) 63, at 69.

[74] See Muir Watt's contribution to this volume, at Chap. 4.

Directives: the ability to use multiple legal languages to reconcile the goal of harmonization with that of preserving national or sub-national legal traditions. Multilinguism is not in itself the solution, but it is perhaps the beginning of a response. The use of several languages without the support of a strong comparative analysis of the impact of harmonized rules is question-begging. An adequate institutional framework for EPL should be supported by a comparative analysis engaging not only in an *ex ante* evaluation of the effects associated with the use of multilinguism to pursue harmonization and to preserve differentiation, but also in an *ex post* evaluation of the impact of harmonized rules in national or regional legal systems that maintain their own legal and everyday vocabularies.

C. The Regulatory Dimensions of EPL

The regulatory dimension of private law has been analysed from different perspectives.[75] In substantive terms, the different contributions in this book all address questions related to the regulatory functions of private law and the relationship between harmonization and regulation strategies. Some focus explicitly on the regulatory functions of private and international private law (Cafaggi, Albors-Llorens and Muir Watt). Others address this problem from a constitutional (Weatherill, Johnston and Unberath) or a governance (van Gerven) perspective. Others still view it from the perspective of the influence of EPL on new Member States (Reich).

While, at the national level, such an interpretation of private law is still strongly debated, consensus is growing regarding the regulatory function of EPL. This is partly due to the origins of legislative interventions, since the Directives on consumer protection have been justified primarily as a 'private law' response to market failures, but it is also linked to ECJ case-law, particularly when the Court has been asked to deal with internal private law measures in contrast to the four freedoms.[76] In a broad sense all private law rules may have regulatory scope if we include lowering transaction costs within their functions. Law-making itself can be interpreted in this light. It is, however, useful to maintain a narrower meaning of the regulatory function of private law-making. What are the signs that a particular set of private law rules has regulatory functions?

First, we must consider the scope of legislative intervention. The regulatory function of a private law rule can be identified if the legislative act is aimed at solving one or more market failures.[77] Market failures should be interpreted extensively to encompass also general phenomena such as market confidence-building, traditionally

---

[75] See the different contributions in C. Parker, C. Scott, N. Lacey, and J. Braithwaite (eds), *Regulating Law* (2004).

[76] See the contributions to this volume by Weatherill and Reich at Chaps. 3 and 8. See also S. Grundmann, 'The Structure of European Contract Law', 9 *ERPL* (2001) 505; and Grundmann *et al.*, *supra* note 61.

[77] See H. Collins, *Regulating Contracts* (1999); Parker *et al.*, *supra* note 75.

viewed as more of a consequence than a failure in itself. There may be different reasons for low levels of confidence in a European market, associated with contingent phenomena such as financial scandals or food epidemics. Often, a lack of consumer confidence or the danger of insufficient confidence has triggered, or at least has contributed to the enactment of, recent legislative interventions relating to consumer protection and financial markets (examples are the General Product Safety Directive, the Market Abuse Directive, Unfair Trade Practices Directive, etc.). Confidence-building is associated with a regulatory function, while the link with harmonization is not entirely clear.[78]

In a context in which an integrated European market is often missing, regulatory functions can often contribute to the creation of market integration over fragmentation.[79] This specificity of the European level broadens the regulatory functions of private law to incorporate legal integration and forces us to ask the following questions.

(a) How can specific designs of private law systems contribute to the integration of a European market independently of the use of harmonized rules? In other words, can substantive private law (i.e. the definition of contract, breach, the remedies) vary if the aim is to create an integrated market? If so, what are the specific features compatible with the aim of building an integrated market?

(b) How should the regulatory function of private law, concerning responses to market failures, be distinguished from that of market integration?[80]

Secondly, the nature of the rules themselves can assist in identifying a regulatory function. The mandatory nature of rules in question provides an important, and often decisive, indication that a regulatory function is present. It is not, however, true that a private law rule that is enabling in nature cannot have a regulatory function; it depends on the regulatory strategy it embodies. In particular, when the regulatory strategy associated with private law rules is not command and control, the rules of contract and even tort law may not be mandatory in nature, and yet they can pursue regulatory goals.[81] Examples can be found in the field of contract, as is the case with Directive 99/44 on Non-Conformity in the Sale of Goods, but also in tort and in environmental law.[82] More complex mechanisms in which mandatory laws can broaden the role of private autonomy can be found in disclosure rules.

---

[78] See Weatherill's contribution to this volume at Chap. 3, examining the role of confidence as legal basis and policy driver, and its relationship with the *Tobacco Advertising* judgment.

[79] On the interaction between regulatory goals and integration goals in the area of consumer law and policy, see S. Weatherill, *EC Consumer Law and Policy* (1997).

[80] On these questions see the contributions to this volume by Weatherill and Cafaggi, at Chaps. 3 and 6.

[81] See I. Ayres and R. Gertner, 'Filling Gaps in Incomplete Contracts: An Economic Theory of Default Rules', 99 *Yale LJ* (1989) 87. See also the essays included in 2 *Southern California Interdisciplinary Law Journal* (1993).

[82] See Grundmann, *supra* note 76, at 698.

The regulatory function in that case is aimed at reducing the impact of market failures on the exercise of private autonomy.[83]

An important role should be attributed to the different regulatory frameworks within which actions and transactions take place. The institutional environment of EPL is fairly complex and composed of several sets. Among these certainly two are worth mentioning.

> (1) The framework of regulated markets where contract law between firms themselves, and between firms and consumers, is strongly influenced by the regulator, its activity and the underlying regulatory goals.
> (2) The framework of technological regulation for transactions taking place on the web. As mentioned, the set of private rules that organize market participants has its own regulatory function, closely linked with that of the different rules concerning electronic transactions.

The different nature of the rules in private law has in the past affected harmonization strategies, distinguishing fields predominantly characterized by mandatory rules, subject to harmonization, and fields crowded with enabling rules, left to the discretion of Member States. The new generation of Directives seems to discard these differences, and encompass default rules as much as mandatory rules in the harmonizing strategy.[84] The interpretation of this trend is, however, ambiguous, and perhaps based on multiple rationales. The development of new regulatory strategies, based on consensual and cooperative instruments, suggests that one should distinguish between different branches of private law according to the mandatory or enabling nature of the rules in ways different from those employed in the past, and in some cases the distinction should be ignored altogether.[85]

In this framework, an important yet still unresolved question concerns the regulatory function of general clauses in contract law and civil liability and its effects on harmonization. The answer to this brings us back to considerations dealt with under institutional dimension above. While the relevance of general clauses for the development of EPL is clear, the question of whether they can play a harmonizing role or should instead reflect differences in legal systems remains unsettled.[86] Even more provocatively, one could imagine that general clauses could play an important role in preserving different identities of legal systems in conformity with some legal traditions that use them to juridify social practices.

---

[83] See K. Hopt, 'Disclosure Rules as a Primary Tool for Fostering Party Autonomy—Observations from a Functional and Comparative Perspective', and S. Grundmann and W. Kerber, 'Informational Intermediaries and Party Autonomy—The Examples of Securities and Insurance Markets', both in Grundmann *et al.*, *supra* note 61, 246 and 264 respectively.

[84] See the Directive on Non-Conformity in Sale of Goods, and the Directive on Electronic Commerce. On this question, see Grundmann, *supra* note 76.

[85] On new regulatory strategies and private law fields, see Parker *et al.*, *supra* note 75.

[86] See, for example, the debate concerning the role of good faith in the Unfair Contract Terms Directive.

The use of good faith, for example, is quite widespread in EPL, but the meanings attributed to this general clause are generally determined according to national legal traditions, which are significantly diverse.[87] If good faith is to play a regulatory role in the European legal system, but is interpreted differently in each Member State by judges and regulators, there is a risk of divergent regulatory policies operating through general clauses in contract law. Coordination can help to foster the regulatory function of general clauses and avoid undermining regulatory goals. In addition, there is growing awareness of the necessity to combine different strategies in regulating a field or, more often, an activity, such as advertising. The recent Directive 2005/29, on Unfair Trade Practices, provides a nice illustration of the regulatory mix that can be employed in order to improve the effectiveness of rules of private law concerning economic conduct.[88]

The regulatory functions of EPL certainly include private international law. Focusing on international private law sheds light on the allocation of regulatory power between States and individuals in different fields concerning goods and services, contracts, and torts.[89] Jurisdictional allocation by uniform international private law rules within a framework characterized by un- (or only partially-) harmonized rules can play a significant role in shaping legislative incentives to regulate cross-border relationships in compliance with economic freedoms. The clearest, but by no means the only, example is the use of international private law rules to administer regulatory competition.[90] This function poses several challenges to the discipline: perhaps most importantly, whether the regulatory function would shift the balance between the private and public dimensions of international private law, or whether the private dimension should simply be rethought in the light of the new or newly acknowledged regulatory functions.[91]

An important regulatory function is also played by competition law principles when applied to private law.[92] However, the role of competition law as a contributing factor to the Europeanization of private law goes beyond the regulatory

[87] See H. Collins, 'Good Faith in European Contract Law', 14 *OJLS* (1994) 229; G. Teubner, 'Legal Irritants: Good Faith in British Law or How Unifying Law Ends Up in New Divergences', 61 *MLR* (1998) 11; S. Whittaker and R. Zimmerman, *Good Faith in European Contract Law* (2000); M.W. Hesselink, *The New European Private Law: Essays on the Future of Private Law in Europe* (2000); and the SECOLA (Society of European Contract Law) contributions to the Paris Conference 2003. See also Reich's contribution to this volume, at Chap. 8.

[88] See H. Collins (ed.), *The Forthcoming EC Directive on Unfair Commercial Practices* (2004). See also the references to the role of the Office of Fair Trading in enforcing the UK's unfair contract terms rules in the contribution of Johnston and Unberath to this volume, at Chap. 5.

[89] See H. Muir Watt's contribution to this volume at Chap. 4.

[90] See A. Ogus, 'Competition Between National Legal Systems: A Contribution to Economic Analysis of Comparative Law', 48 *ICLQ* (1998) 405; W. Kerber, 'Interjurisdictional Competition within the European Union', *Fordham International LJ* (2000) 217.

[91] See Muir Watt, both in this volume at Chap. 4, and *supra* note 73, at 194, text and footnotes 16 ff.

[92] On the relation between competition and regulation in relation to the UK and European contexts, see T. Prosser, *The Limits of Competition Law: Markets and Public Services* (2005).

function. Explicit recognition of the link between standard contract terms and competition law has been recently made in a Communication of the Commission.[93] The existence of a set of norms concerning competition law in the Treaty suggests that if the correlation between competition law and EPL were to be fully exploited, the contribution of the former to the harmonization of the latter might be highly relevant.[94] *Courage* v *Crehan* is a good illustration of this interaction, and of its potential effects on European and on Member States' private law systems.[95] The interesting development is that the rationales for EPL legislation are moving from a purely negative perspective (the elimination of distortions of competition) to a more pro-active perspective (the promotion of competition).[96] Such developments can contribute to the creation of a pro-competitive private law system, both in contract, property and tort law, as is happening in the field of regulation.

3. THE STRUCTURE OF THE BOOK AND ITS CONTRIBUTIONS

The contributions to this book aim to address different questions concerning the institutional framework of EPL. Walter van Gerven's contribution focuses on the different components that should bring together the different legal systems that belong to the EU. After describing the route followed by the Commission in coming to the definition of a programme in EPL, van Gerven addresses the main features of judicial styles in different European traditions. On one hand, he points to the persisting differences in national legal systems related to codification and to the role of legislation; on the other, he describes the important changes towards convergence stimulated by the ECJ and the ECtHR. In particular, he notes how the law-making nature of judicial activity is becoming an 'institutional *acquis*' at the European level.

He proposes a normative conceptual distinction between approximation (result-oriented) and harmonization (purpose-oriented). He examines different means of approximation, starting with approximation through legislation, case-law, and general principles. After emphasizing the different wording in the Treaty and addressing the difference between harmonization and approximation, van Gerven recalls the

---

[93] See 'The Way Forward', para. 2.2.3.2, on the Guidelines on the relationship between the competition rules and EU-wide STC, at 7.

[94] See Albors-Llorens' contribution to this volume at Chap. 7, and also Stuyck, *supra* note 40.

[95] See Reich, *supra* note 40; Stuyck, *supra* note 40, at 1; W. van Gerven, 'Substantive Remedies for Private Enforcement of EC Antitrust Law before National Courts', in P. Ehlerman and I. Atanasiu (eds), *European Competition Law Annual* (2001) 53; A. Albors-Llorens, '*Courage* v. *Crehan*: Judicial Activism or Consistent Approach?', 61 *Cambridge LJ* (2002) 38; A. Komninos, 'New Prospects for Private Enforcement of EC Competition Law: *Courage* v. *Crehan* and the Community Right to Damages', 39 *CMLR* (2002) 447. See also Albors-Llorens' contribution to this volume at Chap. 7.

[96] On this question, see H. Micklitz, *Competitive Contract Law* (forthcoming); F. Cafaggi, 'Market Forms and Contract Remedies' (unpublished).

principal institutional differences between Articles 94 and 95 concerning legislative approximation in order to draw some important conclusions regarding potential constraints. In his opinion, while the use of Article 94 cannot lead to unification, given the necessity to use Directives, Article 95 does allow for codification.[97]

He then moves on to the judicial approximation that has also occurred for the interpretation of access to justice, employed by the ECtHR in relation to Articles 6 and 13, and endorsed by the ECJ in *Johnston* and *Heylens*. While providing different illustrations of judicial approximation, van Gerven highlights the case-law on State liability as the most prominent example.

He analyses the role of the ECJ and national courts as harmonizing institutions. He claims that the incremental nature of judicial activity prevents the task of harmonizing EPL being left to the courts. However, considerable differences exist between contract, competition, and tort law. He then proceeds to an examination of new modes of governance in relation to EPL. After recalling their main features, van Gerven focuses upon the OMC, highlighting its strengths and weaknesses. He proposes an open method of approximation of private law in combination with an institutionalized legislative and judicial process.

He identifies four different forms of convergence: (a) spill-over from one jurisdiction to another; (b) a mutual learning process between supranational and national courts; (c) benchmarking and good practices among regulators; and (d) learning and teaching processes. He concludes by proposing a new action plan for fostering convergence, divided into two parts: one focusing on practitioners of the law, particularly lawyers and judges, and the other on educational aspects. In the first part, emphasis should be placed on possible instruments for stimulating convergence of case-law by applying to the European judiciary a methodology analogous to that employed by regulators at level 3 in the Lamfalussy architecture. In the second, the development of European legal education should be fostered by re-organizing the curricula of law schools, revising teaching methods and producing new teaching materials.

Stephen Weatherill addresses the constitutional dimension of EPL. He focuses on the constitutional validity of the harmonization of private law. This is analyzed primarily from the perspective of competence, asking whether the EC legislature has 'surreptitiously' self-authorized an extension, thereby violating Article 5(1) EC. In relation to contract law, he provides a critique of the Commission's framing the issue of harmonization in terms of subsidiarity instead of competence. After stating that there is no general competence concerning either private law or market regulation, he goes on to identify the different legal bases, from that of consumer protection under Article 153 to judicial cooperation in civil matters under Article 65,

---

[97] '[A]pproximation on the basis of article 94 *cannot* lead to *unification* that is complete uniformity of national laws, whereas approximation on the basis of article 95 can lead to *unification*, and therefore also codification—by which I understand comprehensive binding legislation covering a whole area of the law; *provided*, however, that article 95 contains a sufficient legal basis to support such comprehensive legislation (emphasis added).' See van Gerven's contribution to this volume, at Chap. 2.

concentrating on the harmonization of laws for the creation of an integrated market in accordance with Articles 94 and 95. Weatherill suggests that it is problematic to find constitutional competence for the entire existing *acquis communataire* concerning private law, particularly on the basis of the *Tobacco Advertising* judgment and the case-law that followed it. He suggests that today it would prove much harder to provide legal justification for these decisions. On the other hand, he subscribes to the Commission's approach of leaving aside the question of competence in relation to the evolution of the Common Frame of Reference.

The creation of EPL has been partly associated with the promotion of an integrated internal market. After setting out the relationship between harmonization and market-building, Weatherill clarifies the connection between harmonization and regulation, including private law, pointing out that the harmonization of EPL has been associated with different forms of re-regulation. This regulatory function has been acknowledged not only by legislative institutions but also by the ECJ's case-law. The last part of Weatherill's contribution focuses upon the constitutional dimensions of market confidence as a basis for legislative intervention. After emphasizing the importance of confidence-building in both policy documents and legislative Acts, the author considers the different legal bases related to confidence-building and concludes that the rationale for it is ambiguous, as are its constitutional foundations.

Johnston and Unberath concentrate on the role of the ECJ and national courts in the creation of EPL. They explain that an important role is afforded to courts by the use of Directives in a multi-level system, given the room for discretion that such instruments leave to Member States, and the necessity to control the manner in which this is exercised. They suggest that the ECJ has developed three main devices for monitoring the process: limited direct effect; interpretation of national laws in conformity with Community law; and State liability for failure or incorrect implementation of Directives. They focus only on the first two.

In relation to direct effect, they subscribe to the case-law that denies direct effect for failed or incorrect implementation. Direct application of a Directive would eliminate the main purpose of the Directives as instruments in general: that is, to accommodate European legislation within the specificity of Member States and their legal systems. They stress the legal uncertainty that indirect vertical effect has caused in national legislation, and the burdens consequently placed on the ECJ.

The interpretation of national law in conformity with European legislation has proven to be an effective tool of judicially-driven legal integration. In *Von Colson* and subsequent case-law, the ECJ has both corrected inappropriate attempts at implementation and contributed to judicially harmonizing national legislation in compliance with the effectiveness principle. The authors recall certain institutional developments that have become part of the constitutional theory of private law: the discretion of national legislators leading to divergent implementation—in theory allowed by Directives—has been reduced by national courts through judicial interpretation, consistent with the principles set out in European legislation. However, they do point out the limits that national courts encounter when playing this role, associated with the different leeway that each legal system allows for judicial interpretation. They also illustrate the different attitudes of national courts, focusing particularly on Germany and the UK. In conclusion, they suggest that there are significant limits to the use of national courts as harmonizing agents by means of judicial interpretation, given the different legal principles that govern the interpretative processes and possibilities.

After analysing interpretation as a means of inducing private parties to act as involuntary agents of harmonization through national courts, Johnston and Unberath go on to examine the role of the Commission in infringement proceedings under Article 226. They examine the Unfair Contract Terms and Consumer Sale Directives to identify the actual and potential role that the ECJ has played and can play in relation to implementation. They show that the Court seems to have a fairly strict attitude towards Member States' discretion when transposing rules into the national context, and suggest some possible conflicts between the roles of the Court when hearing infringement proceedings and when performing its interpretative function in preliminary rulings. They conclude with a word of caution in relation to this view, and suggest that the potential of Directives would be better and more effectively exploited in the process of the Europeanization of private law. In the light of the additional administrative burden of policing the implementation of Directives, Regulations can often achieve better results in terms of harmonizing private law.

Muir Watt's essay focuses on the regulatory function of international private law and its disappearance from the debate concerning EPL. This contribution is divided into two parts. The first is devoted to the relationship between the country of origin principle and private law, and the second to the relationship between economic due process and conflict of laws.

Muir Watt analyses the role of international private law in relation to the four freedoms, criticizing the approach that favours only those rules endorsing the country of origin principle, and suggests that the freedoms are compatible with other rules of international private law, such as those endorsing the host country principles. She criticizes the suitability of mutual recognition in the field of private law because contract and tort rules are not territorial in scope. She distinguishes between goods and services, and underlines the difficulty in applying the product/marketing distinction (used by the ECJ in *Keck* in relation to goods) to services.

She examines the role of conflict of laws in torts and rejects the applicability of the principle of mutual recognition in tort law. In her opinion, such a principle, if applied to tort law, would mean that the country of origin principle would be applied, thereby causing a 'race to the bottom' of liability standards. She concludes that tort rules cannot be subject to mutual recognition without distorting the competitive process. She then proceeds to an analysis of conflict of law principles in contract. She distinguishes between default and mandatory rules; while in the case of the former, no conflict with economic freedoms can be envisaged, when the latter come into play a balancing test should be applied.

In the second part of her contribution, Muir Watt addresses the relationship between economic due process and conflict of laws rules. After noting the growing attention being paid to inter-State commerce clauses in the latter part of the last century, she addresses the interpretative question stemming from the clause: whether all regulations restraining cross-border trade should be invalidated, or merely those with discriminatory effect. She analyses the theory of economic due process and the main objections raised against it. Economic due process is interpreted as a means of controlling attempts by State regulations to externalize costs in a discriminatory manner. She then asks which rules of international private law are more consistent with such an (anti-discriminatory) interpretation of economic due process. After rejecting mutual recognition and case-by-case adjudication, she suggests the adoption of uniform conflict rules for torts and regulatory law. The use of uniform conflict of law rules is important for several reasons, among which are the ability to correct potential distortions introduced by regulatory competition, as the examples relating to the posting of workers and environmental pollution show. Muir Watt's proposal is to use the regulatory function of international private law rules to implement economic due process by avoiding or reacting to opportunistic use of regulatory competition devices.

Fabrizio Cafaggi's chapter concentrates on the relationship between civil liability and administrative regulation in EPL. After examining their historical evolution, he concludes that they have frequently complemented each other. Such complementarity has often been based on the need to integrate reciprocal insufficiencies. This happened, for example, at the end of the nineteenth century, when welfare regulation complemented civil liability for industrial accidents; and at the end of the twentieth century, when civil liability complemented economic de-regulation.

The normative thesis of this chapter is that civil liability and regulation, public and private, are functional complements to be used simultaneously in order to pursue homogeneous goals: higher consumer and environmental protection. While the approach is meant to have general application, the relationship is analysed in two fields: product safety and environmental protection. The descriptive claim is that, both at the European and national levels, there is insufficient coordination between civil liability and regulation. He advocates a more integrated approach in relation to: (a) *substantive rules*, i.e. product defectiveness, remedies in product and environmental liability; and (b) *institutions*, judges, public and private regulators, called upon to administer the two systems. To pursue a coordinated strategy institutional changes are required. A different functional partitioning between regulation and civil liability, in order to assess and manage risks associated with dangerous products and processes, is a necessary but insufficient step; a new institutional framework, designed to ensure that effective deterrence and just compensation occur, is also required. These are not only necessary components of European citizenship but also important requirements of an efficient integrated European market.

Cafaggi also emphasizes the importance of recognizing the liability of regulators in ensuring the effectiveness of regulatory strategies. He advocates greater coordination among national judiciaries in relation to product and environmental liability, based on the duty of loyal and sincere cooperation. In relation to general concepts, such as product safety and environmental pollution, harmonized judicial interpretation is particularly necessary, given the width of legislative definitions and the strategic function of national regulators and judges in specifying standards and monitoring compliance.

Albors-Llorens' contribution considers the role of competition and consumer law in the development of EPL. She looks firstly at the specific role of competition law, then at the interaction between consumer and competition law (suggesting that they exist in a relation of mutual influence), and finally their prospective functions in the evolution of EPL. She considers several consumer law Directives, pointing out the substantive references to competition law issues, but also highlighting the shifting attitudes of the Court towards control over unfairness, and comparing the *Océano Grupo* judgment with that in *Hofstatter*. She emphasizes in particular the interpretation of Article 3 of the Unfair Contract Terms Directive in relation to both Articles 81 and 82.

Her thesis is that competition law has played a significant role in the process of the Europeanization of private law, and she grounds this claim in Treaty provisions, secondary legislation, and the case-law of the ECJ. In relation to Treaty provisions, she stresses the correlation between the control of anti-competitive behaviour under Articles 81 and 82 and the Unfair Contract Terms Directives, emphasizing the different perspectives from which such control operates. Concerning secondary legislation, her focus on Regulation 1/2003 provides several references, both in relation to covenants not to compete and to coupling enforcement decentralization with uniform interpretation. The model envisaged in the Regulation could be employed in other areas of private law, in which the need to keep a decentralized enforcement structure should be combined with that of preserving integration goals. Albors-Llorens emphasizes the role of preliminary rulings as a coordinating mechanism, employed by the ECJ to implement the principles of procedural autonomy, non-discrimination, and effectiveness. She then explores the impact of *Courage* v *Crehan* on the principles of private law in Member States' legal systems, beginning with the specific questions posed by the English Court of Appeal concerning the relationship between the illegality of contracts and the right to compensation. In *Courage* a balance between European principles, compensation, national rules, and how such compensation could be granted seems to have been struck. The potential impact of *Courage* on private law systems is significant, but it still needs to be explored by national courts. After scrutinizing the different dimensions in which consumer interests are taken into account by competition law, Albors-Llorens concludes by suggesting that competition law can have a harmonizing effect on different areas of private law, and in particular contract law. She emphasizes the spill-over effects that principles developed in competition law may have, for example that of civil liability arising out of a violation of a competition law rule. She also points to the increasing references in consumer law Directives to the promotion of competition.

Norbert Reich's contribution addresses the changes in contract law in five new Member States (Poland, Hungary, Latvia, Estonia, and Lithuania), brought about by European legislation. He points out the main features of European contract law, in particular the core function of private autonomy, and limits associated with good faith and more broadly with general clauses. He states that the implementation process of European contract legislation has been very different and that it would be impossible to identify any one single model.

Despite the fact that all five countries were governed, until relatively recently, by socialist political systems, the impact of socialist ideology on legal systems has been very different in each, and thus their institutional frameworks are quite diverse. In some countries (the Baltic republics), there has been a process of recodification; in Poland and Hungary the old codes were retained. Reich classifies the different strategies in relation to the integration of European law and suggests that Estonia has adopted a monist approach; Latvia a dualist approach; Lithuania a parallel approach; Hungary a modified monist approach; and Poland a mixed approach.

He then moves to autonomy and analyses how the principle has been recognized in civil legislation. He deals principally with the role of good faith as a limit to the principle of autonomy. His focus is on the Unfair Contract Terms Directive and its implementation in the five new Member States. Different strategies have been used, both in relation to the content and to its application to business to business (B2B) transactions. In some cases, the good faith principle has been associated with reasonableness; in others, with the principle of equality. In some countries, the implementation of the Directive has been separated from the general regulation of standard contract terms, correlated to Unidroit principles (Lithuania); in others, it has been extended to business transactions (Hungary).

He then examines further issues of regulation and information, analysing relevant issues concerning the implementation of Directive 99/44. He focuses specifically on the expansion of the Directive's principles in general contract law, and how they have been received by the different Codes. He distinguishes between dualist and monist legal systems, claiming that dualist systems of contract law will have more problems than monist in implementing the Directive. Regarding information, systems differ between those in which the duty to inform is expressly regulated in the civil code, and those, less common, in which it is inferred from the general provision on pre-contractual liability.

Finally, Reich examines the relevance of spill-overs in new Member States, and emphasizes their importance, particularly in relation to rules originally applicable to consumers and then extended to B2B transactions. He compares 'law in the books' with 'law in action' in these new Member States, and concludes that the role of courts and administrations in implementing EPL is highly relevant in these countries, and that it must be considered when evaluating the process of implementation.

4. SOME THOUGHTS ON THE FUTURE DEVELOPMENT OF EPL

The design of the institutional framework of EPL is relevant to strategic choices concerning what and how to integrate. It is, however, also important to organize the differences in the legal systems of Member States. The enlargement process has meant that higher levels of flexibility are needed in order to pursue the goals of creating an integrated market and a cohesive polity. The need to respect national legal identities means that new mechanisms for coordination between the European institutions, and between them and the institutions of Member States, are required. The use of new modes of governance, and the revision of old ones, has become a necessity, given the importance of judicially-driven harmonization and unintentional spill-overs of harmonized rules into non-harmonized fields, in which no legislative competence exists. A combination of new and old modes of governance can allow a better balance to be struck between harmonization and differentiation.

When designing the Common Frame of Reference (CFR) or a coordinated strategy for risk control in relation to product safety, the multi-level institutional setting should play a considerably more important role than it has to date. The different contributions in this book illustrate that the choice of different substantive rules is, or should be, affected by the selection of an appropriate institutional framework. The implementation of a regulatory strategy in contract law based, for example, on coupling disclosure rules and private autonomy may be different from one articulated around the more traditional partitioning of mandatory/enabling rules, and hence may require different institutional arrangements. Similarly, in the field of product liability, different institutional settings are necessary if safety regulation is considered a functional complement or a functional equivalent of civil liability. The manner in which the role of judges is combined with that of regulators would be altered. More specifically, the function of judicial review may be very different.

The effectiveness of the Europeanization of private law depends to a high degree on an *ex ante* analysis of Member States' institutional backgrounds. They are somewhat diverse, and will remain so in the near future at least. If the design of the rules in Regulations and Directives does not take these differences sufficiently into account, the new legislation can prove to be ineffective or worse. As a consequence, the differences between Regulations and Directives should be re-articulated. The direct application of Regulations may be subjected to different conditions according to the institutional framework of each Member State. Directives should provide stronger correlation between the substantive rules and the different set of institutions employed to administer them at the national level. Acknowledging institutional diversity may help in reaching substantive homogeneity. Product safety regulation again provides a good example. The effectiveness of product liability Directives has been relatively heterogeneous in Member States, due to the different roles played by the judiciary. Adjusting liability regimes and remedies to these different backgrounds may help to bring about a more homogeneous level of product safety throughout Europe. Of course, institutional background should not be considered as an independent and non-modifiable variable. When possible and compatible with procedural autonomy, national institutions should change according to the new legislative objectives in order to better pursue the goals of integration and organized differentiation.

The process of the Europeanization of private law needs to be appropriately monitored to ensure that the *ex ante* defined goals meet with real implementation in each Member State. Compliance with European law cannot be limited to compliance with European rules, since the effectiveness of the latter largely depends upon the institutions that administer them. A goal-oriented system of EPL has to organize monitoring in relation to both rules and institutions. A lack of homogeneous application may sometimes depend on the content of the rule, or, at other times, on the bodies with the power to enforce it.

To extend the use of regulatory impact assessment (RIA) of regulatory choices in relation to EPL may be useful, but perhaps not sufficient.[98] The specificity of EPL and the central role of private autonomy create the need to tailor RIA techniques to the field. Empirical data about social and economic practices are needed. More European databases of court judgments, such as the CLAB for unfair contract terms, should be built up. The Commission should make an effort to promote large-scale information gathering and processing. This would provide a basis for the performance of impact analyses and *ex post* evaluations that would allow for better correlation between the content of rules and institutional design.

EPL is based not only on law-making but also on law-finding. This activity, today mainly performed by courts and academics and, when coordination is organized, by regulators, should be recognized as an integral part of the process of Europeanization. Explicit acknowledgement of law-finding as a source of European law requires more attention to the design of an appropriate set of procedures. The institutional framework of law-finding may in fact be significantly different from that associated with law-making; not because law-finding is a 'bottom-up' process while law-making is 'top down', but rather because law-finding presupposes a higher level of knowledge and coordination of the different legal systems involved, including private orderings.[99] Efforts should be made to proceduralize the search for common rules and principles in relation not only to judicial but also to regulatory law-finding. The search for common rules may also employ benchmarking and best practices selection, particularly when rules do not coincide or when they diverge. However, benchmarking should be organized differently in relation to judicial law-finding and regulatory law-finding. Furthermore, law-finding may require the complementarity of coordination and competition strategies. Law-finding does not only concern rules created in the past; it also defines incentives at national level to produce rules that can be employed at European level. Different benchmarking techniques for the search for European common rules may combine different doses of cooperation and competition among the legal systems in which the rule has to be found. In the short run, given the large diversity that currently exists among Member States, a higher

---

[98] On the most recent developments of RIA see the Regulatory Impact Analysis Inventory, 15 April 2004, drafted by the OECD, and available at www.oecd.org (last visited 30 August 2005).

[99] The evolution of law-making shows that the legislative process is developing new forms of coordination between different layers; and, certainly, more are needed at regional levels. Similarly, law-finding by the ECJ, when looking for common rules and principles, tends to be quite centralized, despite the attention paid to the work of national courts. This is particularly true in difficult cases in which legal orders are conflicting and not converging.

level of cooperation may be desirable in law-finding to ensure that all participants have powerful incentives to contribute to the creation and implementation processes of EPL.

The manner in which EPL is conceptually organized, its internal partitioning, will affect the organization of the institutional framework. To define the core and boundaries of contract, civil liability, property, and family law is not only a challenging intellectual enterprise, but also affects the shape of the institutional framework required for each field and for the overall body of EPL. Furthermore, it has become crucial, after the modernization process, not only to identify which role competition law should play in defining substantive rules, but also to draw the boundaries between competition and traditional private law domains such as contract law. The interaction between judges, operating as community courts in the field of private law, and national anti-trust authorities will be relevant in ensuring that harmonization goals are correctly pursued in the light of competition policies.

The aim of the book is to raise questions whose answers may help to increase the legitimacy of the process of Europeanizing private law and to make it more effective. The hope is that academic and political institutions will begin to focus on the institutional design of EPL to a much greater extent. This is at once an ambitious and challenging perspective, but one that could reduce, though certainly not eliminate, the risks of further separation between European institutions and European civil communities.

2

Bringing (Private) Laws Closer to Each Other at the European Level

WALTER VAN GERVEN

1. THE EFFORTS OF THE EU COMMISSION TO HARMONIZE CONTRACT LAW

In July 2001 the European Commission published a Communication on European contract law in which it outlined four options for future Community policy in the field. Those options were:

(i)   do nothing, that is, leave it to market forces how contract law at the European level would develop;
(ii) promote non-binding common contract principles leading to greater convergence of national laws;
(iii) improve the quality of existing legislation, particularly in the area of consumer law; or
(iv) adopt comprehensive and binding legislation at Community level.[1]

The Commission submitted its Communication to responses from governments, business, consumer organizations, legal practitioners, and academics, and received more than 180 reactions. It became clear that from private stakeholders there was considerable support for option (ii), and that an overwhelming majority supported option (iii). There was a majority *against* option (iv).[2] As for the institutions, the Council highlighted the need for greater coherence and improvement of the existing *acquis communautaire*, Parliament insisted on the need to pursue the harmonization of contract law with the aim of facilitating cross-border transactions, and the Economic and Social Committee advocated, on a mid-term basis, for an

---

[1] OJ 2001C 255/1. For a discussion and a formulation of my own viewpoint, see my article, 'Codifying European Private Law? Yes, If . . . !', 25 *EL Rev* (2000) 156–76.

[2] See Staudenmayer, 'The Commission Action Plan on European Contract Law', 11 *European Review of Private Law* (2003) 113, at 118. This corresponded with my own preference. See my article, *supra* note 1, which was also submitted, in a somewhat different form, as a response to the Commission's request for reactions.

opt-in uniform contract law which the parties could choose via a choice of law clause.[3]

In accordance with these reactions, the Commission adopted, in February 2003, a further Communication entitled 'A More Coherent European Contract Law—An Action Plan'.[4] In this new Communication, the Commission proposed the elaboration of a *common frame of reference*, which would enable it to increase *coherence* in the Community's 'specific-contract' *acquis* (mainly consumer law), and to provide best solutions in *common terminology* with regard to *concepts* and abstract terms (like 'contract' and 'damage') as well as with regard to applicable *rules* (as, for example, in the case of non-performance of contracts). In addition to the creation of such a framework, the Action Plan formulates two other proposals: one is to promote the drafting of EU-wide standard contract terms, and the second is to encourage the drafting of an optional code.[5]

The Commission's Communications are part of an ongoing process of European integration which has engaged a steadily growing number of States since the early 1950s. (The process started with six Member States, and now involves 25 Member States.) The result of this process is that a large body of uniform European legislation, laid down in Treaties, Regulations, and Directives, and judgments from Community Courts, has come into existence together with numerous implementing acts and judgments from national legislatures and courts concerning this uniform legislation. However, this legislation, and accompanying case-law, remains limited in scope, as it affects only those areas of the national legal systems for which the Member States have transferred jurisdiction to the European Community (now the European Union). In consequence, European Community law is 'sector-specific', and looks very much like 'patchwork',[6] incoherent as a whole and often internally inconsistent.[7] This is why the European Commission, in its Communications, proposed to bring more coherence in the existing *acquis communautaire*, mainly in the area of consumer law.

Obviously, the most radical method of achieving coherence and consistency is to enact comprehensive codification covering all Member State laws in a particular area of the law, that is to extend the European harmonization process, now covering primarily cross-border aspects, also to encompass intra-State aspects of that particular area. Thus, for example, it might be desired to enact a comprehensive European Consumer Act which covers the whole area of consumer legislation, regardless of

---

[3] Staudenmayer, *supra* note 2, at 114–17.

[4] OJ 2003 C 63/1.

[5] Staudenmayer, *supra* note 2, at 124–7. In October 2004, the Commission issued a third communication in which it set out the follow-up to the 2003 Action Plan: COM(2004)651 final.

[6] See, in addition to the article referred to *supra*, in note 2, van Gerven, 'Comparative Law in a Texture of Communitarization of National Laws and Europeanization of Community Law', in D. O'Keeffe (ed.), *Liber Amicorum in Honour of Lord Slynn of Hadley*, Vol. I, *Judicial Review in the European Union* (2000) at 433–45.

[7] E.g., see Staudenmayer, *supra* note 2, at 118–20.

cross-border effects or, even broader, to enact a comprehensive European Contract Law covering the whole of general and specific contract law, irrespective of whether it relates to inter-State or intra-State transactions. The difficulty with this method is that the EU legislature (i.e. the European Parliament and the European Council of Ministers, acting jointly, on a proposal from the European Commission, on the basis of Article 95 EC) currently has no jurisdiction to enact fully comprehensive and binding legislation because of the limited transfer of competences by the Member States to the EU.[8] It surely has no jurisdiction, therefore, to extend the codification process to even greater areas of private law than contract law, such as tort law, property law, or even family law (as was suggested by the Council in its response to the 2001 Communication of the Commission).[9]

As a result, the most secure way to enact such comprehensive legislation is to resort to an international agreement between the Member States, or some of them. In order to become effective, such an agreement requires ratification by each of the Member States in accordance with their constitutional requirements—that is, with the involvement of their national parliaments (if not of the electorate in a referendum). Even then, it is unlikely that the contracting Member States will be allowed to make use of the Community institutions and procedures in order to implement the agreement and, particularly, of the Community courts and the preliminary procedure of Article 234 EC in order to interpret the agreement provisions in a uniform manner.[10]

All of this raises the following question: how much uniformity do we really need in matters of private law? That is, in the words of the Preamble to the draft Constitution for Europe, how 'united' do we need Europe to be, and how far do we need to go in restricting its (legal) 'diversity'? Put in historical terms, should we pay heed to Montesquieu's warning when, having analysed the laws of various countries, he concluded that, although all laws referred to the same principles of justice, it was better to preserve diversity in laws and forms of government and religion, given the large diversity of historical experience, cultural tradition, and geographical location?

---

[8] That follows from the ECJ's judgment in Case C-376/98, *Federal Republic of Germany* v *European Parliament and Council of the European Union* [2000] ECR I-8419. See further my articles *supra*, in note 1, and *infra*, in note 28. See, however, for a different opinion, J. Haas, *La responsabilité de l'entreprise en Europe* (2004), at 114–18. In subsequent judgments, the ECJ has clarified and refined its case-law, most recently in its judgments of 14 December 2004 in Case C-434/02, *Arnold André GmbH & Co. KG* v *Landrat des Kreises Herford* (not yet reported); and in Case C-210/03, *Swedish Match AB* v *Secretary for Health* (not yet reported). In those cases the Court continues to state that, in the absence of differences between Member States' laws which are such as to obstruct the fundamental freedoms and thus have a direct effect on the functioning of the internal market, a mere finding of disparities between national laws is not sufficient to have recourse to Art. 95 EC (at paras. 30 and 29 respectively).

[9] See Council Report of 16 November 2001 (available at http://register.consilium.eu.int/pdf.en/01/st12/12735enl.pdf), at point 28(e).

[10] See further De Witte, 'Chameleonic Member States: Differentiation by Means of Partial and Parallel International Agreements', in B. De Witte, D. Hanf, and S. Prechal (eds), *The Many Faces of Differentiation in EU Law* (2001), at 231, 255–6 and 260–6.

Or should we rather follow Condorcet who, 30 years later, in his commentary on Montesquieu's *Esprit des Lois*, wrote that 'a good law must be good for all men, as a true proposition is true for all'.[11] The controversy should remind us of the fact that 'uniformity' is not necessarily better than 'diversity'; a view also implied in Article 151(1) EC, which makes it an obligation for the Community 'to contribute to the flowering of the cultures of the Member States, while respecting their national and regional diversity [but] at the same time bringing the common cultural heritage to the fore'.[12]

2. EUROPE'S BACKGROUND OF LEGAL DIVERSITY

Within the European Union, uniformity of laws finds its limitation in the diversity of legal cultures and legal mentalities. There are indeed considerable differences in style between the European legal systems (mainly between the Common Law, the Romanistic, and the Germanic legal families) which were set in stone as a result of the codification movement in the nineteenth century. That movement was closely linked with the emergence of strong nation-States on the European continent, and saw codification as a symbol of national pride and independence.[13]

A. Differences in Style and Mentality

The basic difference in legal mentality between the three major legal families has been admirably described by R.C. Van Caenegem, Professor Emeritus at the University of Ghent, in his Goodhart lectures held in Cambridge in 1984–1985.[14] In these lectures, published under the title 'Judges, Legislators and Professors', Van Caenegem compares the peculiarities of English, French, and German law, the first being judge-made law, the second shaped by legislation, and the third bearing the imprint of scholarly, Pandectist, learning—hence the title of his book.

Any person who wonders whether these differences in legal mentality still exist need only compare judgments of the House of Lords with those of the French *Cour de cassation* and of the German *Bundesgerichtshof*. Only in a common law system is it possible for a judge to say in his decision that '[t]he state of a man's mind is as much a fact as the state of his digestion'[15] or, more prosaically (and more recently),

---

[11] Quoted by Todorov, 'Right to Intervene or Duty to Assist?', in N. Owen (ed.), *Human Rights, Human Wrongs*, Oxford Amnesty Lectures 2001 (2002), at 29, 41–2.

[12] In favour of a large amount of diversity, see e.g. Beale, 'Finding the Remaining Traps Instead of Unifying Contract Law', in S. Grundmann and J. Stuyck (eds), *An Academic Green Paper on European Contract Law* (2002), at 67–72.

[13] See van Gerven, *supra* note 1, and 'A Common Law for Europe: The Future Meeting the Past?', 9 *European Review of Private Law* (2001) 485.

[14] *Judges, Legislators and Professors, Chapters in European Legal History* (1987).

[15] Quoted by Markesinis, 'A Matter of Style', 118 *LQR* (1994) 607, at 608, from *Edgington v Fitzmaurice* (1885) 29 Ch D 459, at 483, *per* Bowen LJ.

is it possible for a Law Lord to express himself on a delicate issue of 'wrongful life' in the following terms: 'I have not consulted my fellow travellers on the London Underground but I am firmly of the view that an overwhelming number . . . would answer the question with an emphatic No'.[16] By contrast, who would contradict the famous American judge Cardozo when he describes the decisional practice of German judges as 'march[ing] at times to pitiless conclusions under the prod of a remorseless logic which is supposed to leave no alternative'.[17] And, as Cartesian as French judges may be, that does not show in the cryptic judgments of the *Cour de Cassation* which, following the style of legislative pronouncements, expresses its opinion with a minimum of justification or explanation. All in all, English judgments continue to reflect spoken language from a judge sitting on the bench, whilst German judgments continue to resemble highly reasoned academic legal writings, and French judgments continue to be formulated in the same authoritative way as statutes promulgated by a legislature. Each of these judicial styles reflects the mentality characteristic of the 'Judges, Legislators and Professors', in Van Caenegem's legal narrative, that is, characteristic of, respectively, judge-made law, codified law, and scholarly law. These characteristics are the result of deep-rooted differences between the three legal traditions embodied in *case*-oriented English law, *rule*-oriented French law, and *concept*-oriented German law.

To be sure, legal mentalities and methodologies change with the times, certainly now that States from the three large legal families (and from the Nordic countries) have become EU members,[18] and are therefore subjected to the same body of Community legislation and case-law. Thus, for example, since World War II, UK courts have become increasingly 'purposive' in their practice of statutory interpretation, a change which has been, and will surely be, strengthened now that UK judges are becoming more and more familiar with the teleological approach applied by the Community Courts (and by the European Human Rights Court).[19] In the same vein, UK courts have changed their attitude to the use of extrinsic materials, more specifically Parliamentary materials,[20] just as they have started to discuss the work of living academics in their judgments. The latter may seem to be merely anecdotal, but it points to a more fundamental change in the perception of legal authority—that is, legal authority which is no longer based solely on official recognition, in statutes or by the judiciary, but now also depends, as in Germany, on natural authority derived

[16] Lord Steyn in *Macfarlane* v *Tayside Health Board*, in excerpt in W. van Gerven, J. Lever, and P. Larouche, *Cases, Materials and Text on National, Supranational and International Tort Law* (2002), 92–6 at 96.

[17] Quoted by Markesinis, *supra* note 15, who also observes at 609 that German judges quote much academic literature in their judgments.

[18] On the impact of the most recent enlargement, see Norbert Reich's contribution to this book at Chap. 8.

[19] See I. McLeod, *Legal Method* (3rd edn, 1999), at 261–6, and 327 ff., where it is pointed out that the British version so far remains more conservative.

[20] *Ibid.*, at 294–300, referring to the judgment of the House of Lords in *Pepper* v *Hart* [1993] 1 All ER 42.

from the quality of learning in extra-judicial writings.[21] On the contrary, in the European continental legal systems, the rule-making or normative function of courts, mainly of supreme courts, is increasingly, and openly, being recognized. This trend is stimulated by the creativity displayed in the pioneering case-law of the European Courts, i.e. the European Court of Justice (ECJ) and the European Court of Human Rights (ECtHR).[22]

One of the consequences of these differences in legal styles and mentalities is the attitude that the three legal systems adopt *vis-à-vis* binding legislation and, more specifically, as regards the desirability of codification. As Zweigert and Kötz recall in their *Introduction to Comparative Law*,[23] statutes enacted by Parliament play a different role in the development of English law as compared to that played by statutes on the Continent. The reason, obviously, is the prominent part which English judges have fulfilled in recording and developing the unwritten common law which, until the nineteenth century, caused the legislative activity to be regarded 'as necessary only to counteract some specific social or economic mischief'. Indeed '[w]ith their practical empiricism and habit of going step by step from case to case the English would have regarded as dangerous and unnatural to prescribe the outcome of comparable cases in advance by making general regulations to cover the whole area of life . . .'. Accordingly, 'English statutes were originally sporadic *ad hoc* enactments which as legal sources had much less force than the unwritten Common Law . . .'.[24] Actually, this reserved attitude to statute law also explains why statutes must be narrowly construed, since they are deviations from the common law, and must be drafted as precisely as possible. It may also explain why the piecemeal approach of European Community law might be felt to be less worrisome in the UK than on the Continent.

The lesser role, historically, of statute law in common law countries is undoubtedly at the origin of the reluctance of common lawyers to adopt comprehensive legislation, and to accept general principles or concepts underlying comprehensive legislation.[25] Indeed, when solving a legal problem, common lawyers will not search

---

[21] Thus Peter Birks introduced a colloquium on *Learning and Lawmaking* held on 11 January 2003 in All Souls College, Oxford.

[22] That normative function of the judiciary was, e.g., acknowledged in the ECJ's landmark judgment in *Brasserie du Pêcheur and Factortame*, where the Court held that the principle of State liability for breaches of Community law causing prejudice to individuals could also be relied on against breaches committed by a national legislature proper (Joined Cases C-46 and 48/93, [1996] ECR I-1029). In holding thus, the Court rejected the argument of the German government that such ruling cannot be made by a court of law, and stated bluntly that, in a large number of Member States, State liability has been regulated through case-law (recs. 24 and 30).

[23] K. Zweigert and H. Kötz, *An Introduction to Comparative Law* (trans. A. Weir, 3rd edn, 1998), at 265 ff.

[24] *Ibid.*, at 265.

[25] That has not prevented codification from having had in England a passionate defender in the person of Jeremy Bentham, who strongly promoted codification (a word coined by him) in the name of 'cognoscibility'. Bentham indeed felt 'that a law embalmed in thousands of cases spread over many

for general principles or even rules from which the solution can be derived. They will rather look to cases that can be used as a precedent by reason of having been decided in similar circumstances or, on the contrary, that can be discarded as precedents for having been decided in situations that must be distinguished from the case to be decided now. Accordingly, the prevailing paradigm in the common law is not some precept of equal treatment of comparable situations in light of a general rule or principle, but rather the need to treat plaintiffs equally, for reasons of natural justice and equity, in the specific circumstances of the case.[26] However, here too the common law and the continental legal systems have come closer to each other in recent decades, equity considerations now also playing an important part in the reasoning of continental courts and considerations of legal certainty not being totally absent from the mind of common lawyers.

All of the above shows the lesser enthusiasm, if not reluctance, of common lawyers to embrace codified law,[27] an element to be taken into account in assessing the need to enact comprehensive legislation at the European level. Surely, that should not prevent the enactment of specific Acts covering a large area of Community law if that is required for reasons of coherent and uniform application of Community law in the Member States—and provided that there is a legal basis for it in the Community Treaties. Nor should it stand in the way of the European Commission's concern, as reflected in its 2003 Communication, to develop a common framework of reference, *provided* that it is not a purely abstract, 'concept'- or 'rule'-oriented framework, but also a practical, 'solution'-oriented framework of reference (and teaching).[28]

---

centuries could not be cognoscible to the people'. See Van Caenegem, *supra* note 14, at 47, where, in the following pages, it is analysed why, despite Bentham's plea, codification has nevertheless failed to make headway in England.

[26] A typical example is the judgment of the House of Lords, *per* Lord Goff, in *White* v *Jones* ([1995] 1 All ER 691, HL) where a claim in damages was granted to frustrated beneficiaries of a will that was not drawn up because of the negligence of the solicitor, who had failed to make an appointment with the testator in time (the testator died while the solicitor was on holiday). After a thorough analysis of English case-law and of German legal theories, Lord Goff came to the conclusion that there was a lacuna in English law that needed to be filled in order to produce practical justice. On that basis he, and with him the majority (two Law Lords dissenting), accepted that the claim of the frustrated beneficiaries was to be granted. See the excerpts in van Gerven *et al.*, *supra* note 16, at 219–23.

[27] To deal with the increasing flood of decided cases which makes the law unmanageable in a large jurisdiction like the United States, case-law has been compiled in so-called 'Restatements'. However, these restatements of the law do not have more weight with the American courts than a leading textbook (which is not very much): thus Zweigert and Kötz, *supra* note 23, at 251–2. The authors also refer to the Uniform Commercial Code, which Code has served as a model for the State legislatures, and was finally adopted in all States of the USA, albeit with reservations or alterations in some States. The Code is very much the work of Professor Carl Llewellyn, and proves that, in the right circumstances, academics may play a role in convincing State legislatures voluntarily to accept comprehensive legislation prepared by a group of external experts.

[28] See further van Gerven, 'A Common Framework of Reference *and* Teaching', 1 *European J Legal Education* (2004) 1.

B. Differences in Teaching Methods

The basic differences in style between the common law and the civil law traditions are not responsible merely for different attitudes to legislation and codification; they are also responsible for different approaches to teaching methods and teaching materials.

As is well known, contrary to the prevalent style of teaching on the European Continent, which is one of formal and scholarly lectures, Anglo-American teaching (with the emphasis on American) is based on the so-called 'case method', introduced by Dean Langdell of Harvard University in the second half of the nineteenth century, and since then adopted under the influence of the American Bar Association in all leading American law schools.[29] The basic idea behind the 'case method' is that the rules of law should be presented to the student in the context of decided cases, an approach to teaching which fully corresponds with the emphasis laid in the Common Law on the judicial development of the law. Whereas the method of 'formal lecturing' is supported by text-books in which the rules of the law are described and commented on, the 'case method' is supported by case-books in which the leading judicial decisions are reproduced and followed up by a large number of questions put to the students by the author of the book. The case method is less systematically applied in the UK than in the USA, but many English books, used in law schools, contain a large number of excerpts from cases and other legal sources, such as statutes or legal writings, followed by questions.[30] Again, the distinction between common law and civil law countries tends to be less significant today than it used to be. On the continent, too, especially in countries like Belgium and the Netherlands, formal lecturing and case-oriented seminar meetings are essential parts of the curriculum, and a large amount of case material is put at the disposal of students, often at the initiative of faculty members who have taken an LL.M degree in the USA or the UK, and are therefore familiar with the case method.[31]

The case method of teaching and the use of case-books (and other source-books) in that context are essential elements in studying the law, which, in the end, turns on applying legal rules to concrete situations, and solving conflicts when rules are not complied with voluntarily in a particular instance. Looking at the law 'top down' (that is, looking at the rules to find solutions and applying them to the facts of the case) is surely one aspect of legal training. However it must be accompanied by looking at the law 'bottom up' (that is, by looking at decided cases to see how rules work out in the field, and whether they lead to acceptable solutions in comparable cases). In that regard, the case method is an essential part of the learning process,

---

[29] See Zweigert and Kötz, *supra* note 23, at 244–5.

[30] See, for instance, in the field of contract law, H.G. Beale *et al.*, *Contract Cases and Materials* (3rd edn, 1995); S. Wheeler and J. Shaw, *Contract Law, Cases, Materials and Commentary* (1994).

[31] For example, at the KU Leuven, a large majority of the professors have taken a degree, and/or have taught, at one of the top American law schools.

and has been recognized as such not only in common law countries but also in other jurisdictions.[32]

It follows from the foregoing, first, that codification is not a paradigm that the EU Member States have in common, and that even the phenomenon of law-making through legislation is not perceived in the same way in all the Member States' legal systems, and, secondly, that law-making through judicial activity is traditionally as much a source of law as law-making through statutory activity. This is also the case in the Community because of the constitutional importance that judgments of the Community Courts, primarily of the ECJ, enjoy when they interpret Treaty provisions in a way that is also binding upon the Community legislature. And, indeed, as we will see, approximation through the case-law of the Community Courts will often have the same effect as approximation by way of legislation in the form of Directives.

3. APPROXIMATION OF LAWS WITHIN THE EUROPEAN UNION

In this part, I will first discuss (at A and B) the main avenues through which laws in general, and private laws in particular, are traditionally approximated under the European Union's first pillar, i.e. the European Community. I will then discuss (at C) the impact of the so-called 'new modes of governance' on the Community's approximation process.

A. Harmonization through Legislation, Case-law, and General Principles

I. Legislation

In the original version of the EEC (now EC) Treaty, the term 'harmonize' was used in Article 99 (now 93) only in relation to indirect taxes. In all other matters 'approximation' was used, in Article 100 EEC (now 94 EC) Treaty, as the generic term for 'bringing together' ('rapprocher') by way of Directives those Member State 'laws, regulations or administrative provisions' which, in the absence of approximation, would 'directly affect the establishment or functioning of the common market'. Later, with the incorporation, by the 1987 Single European Act, of Article 100a EEC (now 95 EC) Treaty, the term 'harmonization' became used as a synonym for approximation (see Article 95(4) and (5) EC). The latter term was however still

---

[32] No less a person than the famous German scholar Rudolf von Jhering wrote in 1881 that he had 'always believed that [he] could introduce his students more effectively to the law by paying special attention in his lectures to its casuistry', adding that '[n]obody who has had any experience as an examiner will doubt that a student is only able truly to comprehend those ideas which he can conceptualise in the concrete form of actual cases': taken from the Introduction to his book, *Zivilrechtsfälle ohne Entscheidungen* (4th edn, 1881), at 5, quoted by Markesinis, 'Bridging Legal Cultures' [1993] *Israël L Rev* 363, at 374.

used in the title of the chapter that now comprises Articles 94–97 EC Treaty.[33] In contrast to Article 94 EC, Article 95(1) EC deals with the approximation through measures 'of the provisions laid down by law, regulation or administrative action in the Member States which have as their object the establishment and functioning of the internal market'.

Accordingly, whereas approximation on the basis of Article 94 EC *must* occur through Directives, approximation on the basis of Article 95 EC *can* occur through measures generally—which can be *either* Directives *or* Regulations. As is well known, Directives are defined in Article 249, first paragraph, EC, as being 'binding as to the result to be achieved, upon each Member State to which it is addressed, but . . . [leaving] to the national authorities the choice of form and methods', whereas a regulation is defined in the second paragraph of Article 249 EC as '[having] general application . . . [being] binding in its entirety and directly applicable in all Member States'. In other words, approximation on the basis of Article 94 cannot lead to unification, that is complete uniformity of national laws; whereas approximation on the basis of Article 95 can lead to unification, and therefore also to codification— by which I understand comprehensive binding legislation covering a whole area of the law—*provided*, however, that Article 95 EC contains a sufficient legal basis to support such comprehensive legislation. As pointed out previously, according to the prevailing case-law of the ECJ, that is the case only if the disparities between the national rules in that area of the law are such that the threat to the establishment or functioning of the internal market resulting therefrom amounts to more than an abstract risk. Indeed, of itself, Article 95 EC does not, in the words of the ECJ, contain 'a general power to regulate the internal market'.[34]

The foregoing does not prevent Article 95 EC from being used (along with other, more specific Treaty provisions, such as Articles 40, 41, 49, and 83 EC, or with the supplementary clause of Article 308 (ex 235) EC) to harmonize Member States' provisions in numerous areas of the law. This is mainly in areas where coercive legal provisions were established to protect interests, of a public or a private nature, that in all or several Member States were regarded as deserving of special protection: thus, for instance, as regards private law, in the areas of consumer protection, industrial and commercial property, company law, financial services (banking, insurance, securities), worker protection, public procurement, and electronic commerce.[35] All

---

[33] In the original text of the EEC Treaty, the term 'harmonize' was consistently used in the four original languages: '*harmonisieren*', '*harmoniser*', '*armonnizzare*', and '*harmoniseren*'. For 'approximation' less consistent terms were used: '*rapprochement*', '*Angleichung*', '*ravvicinamento*', and '*nader tot elkaar brengen*'.

[34] See the judgment of the ECJ in *Germany* v *European Parliament and Council, supra* note 8, at recs. 83 and 84: 'a mere finding of disparities between national rules and of the abstract risk of obstacles to the exercise of fundamental [economic] freedoms or of distortions of competition liable to result there from, [is not] sufficient to justify the choice of Article [95] as a legal basis'. The judgment was confirmed in later case-law, be it in slightly different words, most recently in the December 2004 judgments in *Arnold* and *Swedish Match, supra* note 8.

[35] For an exhaustive enumeration in the field of contract law, see Annex I to the July 2001 Communication of the Commission on European Contract Law, *supra* note 1. See also the Annex (more

this has given rise to a large body of sector-specific Community law, mostly Directives (and therefore to be implemented by national laws), that is called the Community's '*acquis communautaire*'.

II. Case-law and general principles

Allthough they are synonyms, approximation and harmonization have a different emphasis: the emphasis of the first is on *result*, that of the second on *purpose*. While harmonization refers to legislation that is intended to do away with disparities, approximation refers to the result achieved, i.e. that legal systems come closer to each other. The latter, 'result', need not necessarily be the fruit of a deliberate legislative effort to harmonize, as it can also be the consequence of incremental development of the law through case-law. Approximation through case-law has occurred, for example, as regards judicial remedies that the ECJ has required Member States' authorities, including national courts, to make available to individuals who need to enforce their Community rights. The overarching principle in that regard is the fundamental right of access to court, laid down in Articles 6 and 13 of the ECHR, which the ECJ has embraced in its case-law, particularly in *Johnston* and in *Heylens*.[36] As a result, in the 1980s and 1990s, the ECJ's doctrine of direct effect was metamorphosed into a doctrine of effective judicial protection aimed at achieving a sufficient level of uniform application of Community law throughout the Member States.[37] The new doctrine has led to the emergence of the specific remedies of compensation, restitution, and interim relief, in addition to the general remedy of setting aside national measures. All in all, it has allowed individuals to obtain adequate and relatively uniform judicial relief throughout the Community in enforcing their Community rights before Community and national courts.[38]

By far the most instructive example of judicial approximation is the case-law of the Community courts concerning the *liability* of Community institutions, and of Member State authorities, to compensate for breaches of Community law causing damage to individuals. The doctrine has been created with the help of 'general principles common to the laws of the Member States' which, according to Article 288(2) EC, govern the non-contractual liability of Community institutions as well as, according to the Court's *Francovich* case-law, the liability of Member States' authorities for breaches of Community law. Since for both liability regimes inspiration is

than 10 pages long) to Müller-Graff, 'EC Directives as a Means of Private Law Unification', in A. Hartkamp *et al.* (eds), *Towards a European Civil Code* (3rd edn, 2004), at 77–100.

[36] Case 22/84, *Johnston* v *Chief Constable RUC* [1986] ECR 1651, at rec. 18; Case 222/86, *UNECTEF* v *Heylens* [1987] ECR 4097, at rec. 14.

[37] See van Gerven 'Bridging the Gap between Community and National Laws: Towards a Principle of Legal Remedies?', 32 *CML Rev* (1995) 679.

[38] See van Gerven, 'Of Rights, Remedies and Procedures', 37 *CML Rev* (2000) 501. For a further analysis see Eilmansberger, 'The Relationship between Rights and Remedies in EC Law: In Search of the Missing Link', 41 *CML Rev* (2004) 1199.

drawn from general principles common to the laws of the Member States, it is not surprising that, 'in the absence of particular justification, both regimes are subjected to the same rules'.[39]

In the case-law of the courts, principles which the Member States have in common play a crucial role in the approximation of the Community and national legal orders, particularly so because it is, to a large extent, for the courts themselves to fashion the principle concerned in the way they want. Naturally, no-one holds the view that, for a principle to be common, it must exist in all of the Member States. That would have been difficult at the outset, with only six Member States, and it would now be virtually impossible in a Community of 25 Member States. To be common, it is surely enough that the 'principle' be accepted by the prevailing opinion in a sufficiently large number of Member States in which the issue concerned has arisen in similar terms. Moreover, a principle need not be expressed as a precise rule and may refer to a maxim, even an unwritten one, or a concept with a considerable degree of abstraction which, in specific cases, will or may result in similar solutions.

Given this broad understanding, it is clear, for example, that the three conditions for non-contractual liability to arise under both Article 288 EC and under *Francovich* (i.e., illegality (with some ingredients of objective, and even subjective, fault), occurrence of damage, and causation) are principles that are common to the laws of the Member States. The same holds true for the consequence which liability entails, i.e., that adequate, if not full, reparation must be made for the injury caused, insofar as it is sustained by a plaintiff belonging to the group of persons that the infringed rule is intended to protect. A less conspicuous example of a truly common principle is the rule adopted by the ECJ according to which *Francovich* liability may also arise if the breach of Community law is attributable to a Member State's legislator, as was acknowledged in *Brasserie*,[40] or to a Member State's court, as was decided in *Köbler*.[41] No support could be found in the laws of the Member States, particularly not for the first finding.[42] The ECJ seems to recognize this, as it relies for justification not on a general principle found in the Member States' legal systems, but on the rule of international law according to which a State 'must be viewed as a single entity, irrespective of whether the breach . . . is attributable to the legislature, the judiciary or the executive'.[43]

---

[39] Joined Cases C-46 and 48/93, *Brasserie du Pêcheur and Factortame, supra* note 22, at rec. 42, and Case C-352/98P, *Bergaderm* [2000] ECR I-5291, at recs. 39–44. For a full and comprehensive account of European liability law, see W. Wurmnest, *Grundzüge eines europäischen Haftungsrecht* (2003).

[40] *Supra* note 22.

[41] Case C-224/01, *Köbler* v *Austria* [2003] ECR I-10239. For a comment, see Classen, 41 *CML Rev* (2004) 813. For a critical view, see Wattel, 'Köbler, CILFIT and Welthgrove: We Can't Go On Meeting Like This', 41 *CML Rev* (2004) 177.

[42] See van Gerven *et al.*, *supra* note 16, at 392. As for the second finding, the Court noted, referring to the Opinion of Léger AG, that 'the application of the principle . . . to judicial decisions has been accepted in one or another form by most of the Member States, . . . even if subject only to restrictive and varying conditions' (at rec. 48 of the *Köbler* judgment).

[43] See rec. 35 of the *Brasserie* judgment, *supra* note 22.

III. Cross-fertilization

An interesting feature of approximation, whether through case-law or through statute law, in each case with the help of general principles, is that it entails an on-going process of cross-fertilization, back and forth. Finding general principles that the legal systems of the Member States have in common is indeed the result, for courts and legislatures, of a dialectical interaction between national laws and Community law. Such interaction is made possible by the fact that, within the European institutions, lawyers from all Member States work closely together, so that 'law-making' and 'solution-finding' are unavoidably activities in which all national legal backgrounds play a role. That is most obvious, of course, in the case of normative legal instruments, which will become part of the positive law of the Member States. However, it also occurs in the preparation of judgments of the Community Courts (and the Opinions of Advocates General) where all legal systems of the Member States are, so to speak, omnipresent in the minds of those involved, including Court members, legal secretaries, researchers, and translators. Moreover, when new or important issues arise, internal memoranda will be prepared by the Court's research department in which the legal systems of the Member States are thoroughly analysed. After the Advocate General's Opinion has been submitted and the Court's judgment has been delivered, both documents will be published in the official languages of the Community, and subsequently used in proceedings before domestic courts. They will also be extensively discussed and analysed in scholarly writings throughout (and outside) the Community. All these factors have the result that Community legislation and case-law are the outcome *and* the source of a long process of cross-fertilization, back and forth, between the national legal orders and the Community legal order. In that context approximation of legal systems and, more importantly, of legal mentalities is part of an ongoing process.

Interaction and cross-fertilization between courts is not a one-way street, and Community law is not set in stone. In other words, even when a rule or solution of Community law has been firmly established, it may still undergo developments on the national scene. An illustration thereof, in the area of State liability, is the re-allocation of *Francovich* liability away from the central State towards the regional divisions of a Member State, as was allowed, within limits, in the ECJ's judgment in *Konle*.[44] Clearly, that judgment reflects difficulties, arising especially in federalized Member States, when it comes to determining which division of a State (*Land* or region) is responsible, including financially, for a particular breach of Community law. As advocated by some,[45] the *Konle* ruling might in the future also be relied on to alter the liability of the legislator proper, this time away from the legislative towards the executive branch. That may occur in instances where the executive could, and should, have used its competence to 'correct' the failure of 'its' legislator to comply with

---

[44] Case C-302/97, *Konle v Austria* [1999] ECR I-3099, at rec. 62.

[45] See Anagnostaras, 'The Allocation of Responsibility in State Liability Actions for Breach of Community Law: a Modern Gordian Knot?', 25 *EL Rev* [2000] 139, at 142 ff.

Community law—a tendency already recognized in the Court's judgment in *Brinkmann*.[46] It shows how national legal systems continue to play a role in shaping established Community law, and more particularly, in this instance, how their reluctance to impose direct liability on the legislator proper may lead to a 'mellowing down'[47] of that liability, not with respect to the principle as such, but in terms of ultimate responsibility for its financial consequences. A precedent for reallocation of *Francovich* liability from legislature to executive can be found in the '*règlement écran*' theory of French administrative law, according to which the administration is held to be at fault (thus breaking the causal link with the legislature's fault) when it implements a legislative measure that was adopted in violation of Community law.[48]

Interaction between courts is not always congenial, as is illustrated by the dilemma which Member States' constitutional courts faced when asked by the ECJ to award precedence to Community law, even over and against their States' Constitutions. The conflict, dubbed by some as '*une guerre des juges*', culminated with the judgment of the German Constitutional Court in the *Brunner* case, in which Paul Kirchhof stated bluntly: '*Wir haben nur die Aufgabe, einem Herren zu dienen, nämlich dem deutschen Grundgesetz*'.[49] In the end however, it has been recognized by all sides that a conflict should and can be avoided 'through mutual respect and through "cooperation" '. For indeed:

European law would lose its roots and its power to grow by being made autonomous and separate from the Member States, whereas in the close interweaving with Member States' constitutions it gains its identity in a unitary origin and a unitary future . . .[50]

---

[46] Case C-319/96, *Brinkmann Tabakfabriken* [1998] ECR I-5255. See also the comment by Anagnostaras, *supra* note 45. Also when that does not occur, that same result is already achieved now if national law prescribes that an action in damages against the State for breach of Community law by the legislator proper must be brought against the Minister of Justice as the legal representative of the State in legal matters: thus under Belgian law, as illustrated by a judgment of the Brussels Court of Appeal of 5 January 2000 [2002] *Rechtsk Weekbl.* 1103. The same holds true for liability incurred as a result of violations of Community law by national courts, where the action in damages will obviously not be brought against the court itself, nor against the judicial branch of government as a whole, but against the executive government. As regards violations by the judiciary, there are, moreover, reasons relating to the independence of the judiciary to recommend that solution, as was acknowledged by the ECJ in *Köbler, supra* note 41, at rec. 42.

[47] The term is taken from Tridimas's article, 'Liability for Breach of Community Law: Growing Up and Mellowing Down', in D. Fairgrieve, M. Andenas, and J. Bell (eds), *Tort Liability of Public Authorities in Comparative Perspective* (2002), at 149–81.

[48] For excerpts from, and references to, relevant case-law, see van Gerven *et al., supra* note 16, at 380–3. See also Anagnostaras, *supra* note 45.

[49] In English translation: 'We have only one master to serve: the German Constitution'. See Judgment of 12 October 1993, *Treaty of Maastricht*, 89 BVerfGE 155; excerpts in English in 31 *CML Rev* (1994) 251. For a comment, see M. Herdegen, 'Maastricht and the German Constitutional Court: Constitutional Restraints for an Ever Closer Union', 31 *CML Rev* (1994) 251. For a full account of this '*guerre des juges*' in different Member States, see M. Claes, *The National Courts' Mandate in the European Constitution* (2005), at 323 ff.

[50] Paul Kirchhof (former judge of the German Constitutional Court) in 'The Balance of Powers between National and European Institutions', 5 *ELJ* (1999) 225, at 227–8.

Or, in the words of another author:

[t]he doctrine of supremacy of Community law is not to be confused with any kind of all purpose subordination of Member State law to Community law . . . . [T]he most appropriate analysis of the relations of legal systems is pluralistic rather than monistic, and interactive rather than hierarchical . . .[51]

B. Approximation of Private Laws

For brevity's sake, I will discuss here only the three areas of private law on which the impact of EC law is most visible: consumer law, competition law, and financial services.[52]

I. Consumer protection and general contract law

The impact of the European harmonization process on private law varies consider-ably from one area of the law to another. As mentioned previously, in the field of contract law, approximation often occurs in order to facilitate harmonization of coer-cive national laws intended to protect private interests of weaker parties, such as con-sumers, workers, or users of financial services. The result is the emergence of sector-specific Community laws, mainly Directives, and of implementing national rules which are similar but not identical. The situation is far from ideal: the separate Directives are not always consistent with each other; they do not cover the whole field of consumer protection and are conceived from a viewpoint of promoting the internal market freedoms, in that they regard consumers as economic agents who should use their legal rights to make the internal market function properly.[53] That does not, however, in the words of an impartial expert, prevent:

European Consumer Contract Law rules seen altogether form[ing] a relatively close body of rules which mirror the major policy problems of the last two decades [and are of a nature] to identify elements of [a] new paradigm in contract law theory . . . which is not bound [to cover] consumer law alone.[54]

That, indeed, seems to be the way forward: on the one hand, as suggested by the Commission in its 2001 Communication on European Contract Law,[55] to make

[51] N. MacCormick, *Questioning Sovereignty* (1999), at 117–21.

[52] For an enumeration of other areas, and a discussion in the context of an emerging European private law, see, *inter alia*, P.-C. Müller-Graff (ed.), *Gemeinsames Privatrecht in der Europäischen Gemeinschaft* (2nd edn, 1999). See also *supra* note 35.

[53] For a critical view, see Howells and Wilhelmsson, 'The EC Consumer Law: Has It Come of Age?', 28 *EL Rev* (2003) 370, where the recent 2001/2002 Commission documents on EU consumer protection are discussed, at 372–5.

[54] Micklitz, 'Competitive Contract Law—An Emerging Concept in European Contract Law?', at page 6 of a paper presented in draft form at the 12th Biennial Meeting in Riga, 11–14 August 2004, of the International Academy of Commercial and Consumer Law.

[55] *Supra* note 1. See also *supra* note 5, where the Commission's follow-up Communication of November 2004 is mentioned. In that Communication, the Commission clarifies the role which the

the existing Community rules (and, if possible, the implementing national rules) more consistent, and to complete and modernize them, and, on the other hand, to let the existing *acquis* act as a forerunner in modernizing contract law in general.[56] In that regard several elements can be drawn from European consumer law (and from other parts of the Community *acquis* in the area of contract, e.g. financial services) which can be used to renew the foundations of contract law in general. They relate, for example, to the pre-contractual duties of a supplier to give information; the type of information to be given to the other contracting party and to potential purchasers under an all-embracing transparency principle; fairness as a tool to control the substance of contract and access to market; and post-contractual cancellation rights and the availability of adequate legal protection mechanisms.[57]

The task of modernizing (and harmonizing) contract law in general cannot be left to the Community and national courts, because of the incremental nature of judge-made law and, moreover, in the case of the Community Courts, because of the limited jurisdiction they, like the other European institutions, have in the area of private law (as in other non-economic areas).

A few examples illustrate this incremental approach in the harmonization of national contract law. First, see the ECJ's judgment in *Dekker*, where it ruled that an employer's refusal to employ a woman on grounds of her pregnancy constituted unlawful sex discrimination, in the sense of Equal Treatment Directive 76/207.[58] Article 6 of that Directive requires Member States to introduce measures allowing victims of unequal treatment to pursue their claims by judicial process. Although the Directive leaves Member States free to choose the sanction with which to penalize an infringement, when a Member State opts for a sanction forming part of the rules on civil liability, it may not, according to the judgment, apply these rules so as to make the victim's claim subject to a requirement of fault or to a defence of justification by the other party, with the result that the plaintiff may not obtain full redress. Whilst *Dekker* illustrates how Community law principles can affect the freedom to contract, the Court's judgment in *Marleasing* shows how Community law principles can also affect—but again incrementally only—the conditions that must be fulfilled in order to conclude a valid contract.[59] The decision is well known: it relates to the interpretation of the first Company Law Directive which did not include 'illicit cause' as a ground of nullity. The Court was asked by a Spanish court whether the defendant company could nevertheless be declared null and void on the basis of provisions of the Spanish Civil code invalidating contracts that have an illicit cause. The Court answered in the negative, holding that the national court was obliged 'as far as possible' to interpret national law, even when it predated the

---

Common Frame of Reference, set out in the 2003 Action Plan (referred to *supra* note 4), can play in improving the present and future '*acquis*': at 2–5.

[56] Micklitz, *supra* note 54, at 6.
[57] On all these points, see *ibid.*
[58] Case C-177/88, *Dekker* v *Stichting voor Jong Volwassenen* [1990] ECR I-3941.
[59] Case C-106/89, *Marleasing* v *La Commercial Internacionale* [1990] ECR I-4135.

Directive, in light of the wording and the purpose of the Directive. Consequently, since the Directive enumerates the grounds for annulling companies falling within it in a limitative way, the 'illicit cause' provision of the Civil Code was, if at all possible, to be construed accordingly.

In yet another judgment, *Unilever Italia*,[60] the performance of contracts between individuals was at stake. In that case, Italian food labelling rules had not been notified to the Commission in accordance with Directive 83/189, although they were such as to hinder inter-State commerce. As a result, in the Court's view, the Italian rules were to be held 'ineffective', and the defence of the purchaser that it need not accept and pay for goods not labelled in accordance with the Italian rules had therefore to be dismissed by the national court. The judgment makes it clear that, although horizontal direct effect of Directives is not recognized by the ECJ, failure of a state to comply with a Directive may nevertheless have an impact on the application of national contract laws between individuals.[61] In another case, *Bacardi-Martini*, the issue of third party interference with a contract concluded between others was raised before a national court, and a preliminary question was submitted to the Court of Justice. Although the preliminary reference was held by the Court to be inadmissible,[62] the facts of the case are interesting enough to be mentioned. The case concerned a contract between Newcastle United Football Club and Dorna, pursuant to which Dorna was appointed to sell and display advertisements at football matches. Dorna had agreed to sell advertising space to Bacardi-Martini but, when Newcastle found out that the match would be broadcast in France, where such advertising was prohibited, it requested that Dorna remove the advertisement. Bacardi-Martini brought an action for damages against Newcastle, claiming that the latter's interference with the contract could not be justified by French legislation which, in its view, was incompatible with Article 49 EC (freedom of services). Since the Court declined to answer the preliminary question, the issue remained unresolved.

The foregoing shows how little harmonization is to be expected from the case-law of the ECJ in the area of general contract.[63] That is different from the position with tort laws which, as we will see later, can be used by individuals as a judicial remedy before national courts when their Community rights have been violated.

II. Competition law and judicial remedies

As pointed out previously,[64] the case-law of the Community Courts concerning non-contractual liability applies particularly to breaches committed by EC institutions

---

[60] Case C-443/98, *Unilever Italia* v *Central Food* [2000] ECR I-7535.

[61] For a comment, see Weatherill, 'Breach of Directives and Breach of Contract', 26 *EL Rev* (2001) 177.

[62] Case C-318/00, [2003] ECR I-905.

[63] See further my comments on the ECJ's judgment in Joined Cases C-240 to C-244/98, *Océano Gruppo* [2000] ECR I-4941, in 'The ECJ Case-law as a Means of Unification of Private Law?', in Hartkamp *et al.* (eds), *supra* note 35, 101, at 118–21.

[64] *Supra*, text accompanying note 39 and ff.

and Member States' authorities and thus relates essentially to public law, not private law.[65] However, in *Courage* v *Crehan*,[66] a case concerning private undertakings in breach of Article 81 EC prohibiting cartel agreements, the ECJ decided that the remedy of compensation must also be made available to individuals when the breach of their Community right derives from a provision such as Article 81 (or 82) EC that imposes a direct obligation on another individual.[67] Recalling that Article 81 EC constitutes a fundamental provision for the functioning of the internal market, and that it produces direct effects in relations between individuals, the Court concluded, as regards the principle of liability, that '[t]he full effectiveness of Article 8[1] of the Treaty and, in particular, the practical effect of the prohibition laid down [in the first paragraph thereof] would be put at risk if it were not open to any individual to claim damages for loss caused to him by contract or by conduct liable to restrict or distort competition'.[68] The judgment is of crucial importance for the development of national rules providing a remedy, in tort *or* contract, giving compensation for harm caused by one private person to another.[69] It will be for the Court to flesh out the principle of such 'private law' liability in future referrals for preliminary rulings by national courts.[70]

Actually, in *Courage* v *Crehan* itself the Court began to give guidance to the referring court (the English Court of Appeal) on whether relief by way of compensation was also available to a contracting party who had agreed to a contract prohibited by Article 81 EC. In contrast to the situation under English law, the Court of Justice held that there should not 'be any absolute bar to such an action' in the applicable national law.[71] The Court added, however, that, subject to the principles of equivalence (between Community law and similar national law claims) and of effectiveness (not making Community law claims practically impossible or excessively difficult), its ruling should not prevent a national legal system 'from taking steps' that the protection of the rights guaranteed by Community law does not entail the unjust enrichment of those who enjoy them'.[72] Nor, the Court went on to say, should it prevent national law 'from denying a party who is found to bear significant

---

[65] That is at least so from the viewpoint of Member States which have legal systems with different tort law regimes for public and private persons or entities.

[66] Case C-453/99, [2001] ECR I-6297.

[67] As the ECJ had held in Case 127/73, *BRT* [1974] ECR 51.

[68] At rec. 26 of the judgment, *supra* note 66.

[69] In addition to compensation, there are other remedies, such as nullity (*cf.* Art. 81(2) EC), restitution, and interim relief, which, however, will not be discussed in the present context. On these other remedies, see my paper, 'Substantive Remedies for the Private Enforcement of EC Antitrust Rules before National Courts', in C.-D. Ehlermann and I. Atanasiu (eds), *European Competition Law Annual 2001: Effective Private Enforcement of EC Antitrust Law* (2003), 53, at 54–7 and 63–6.

[70] For a thorough analysis of the judgment, see Komninos, 'New Prospects for Private Enforcement of EC Competition Law: *Courage* v *Crehan* and the Community Right to Damages', 39 *CML Rev* (2002) 447–87.

[71] At rec. 28 of the judgment.

[72] At recs. 29 and 30.

responsibility for the distortion of competition the right to obtain damages from the other contracting party', for which the Court refers to 'a principle which is recognised in most of the legal systems of the Member States', according to which 'a litigant should not profit from his own unlawful conduct, where this is proven'.[73]

The litigation before the referring court concerned a dispute between two contracting parties, with the effect that the ECJ's preliminary ruling focused on contractual performance. However, in his Opinion, Advocate-General Mischo indicated that the 'individuals who can benefit from [the] protection [from harmful effects which an agreement prohibited by Article 81 EC, and therefore automatically void, may create] are, of course, primarily third parties, that is to say consumers and competitors who are adversely affected by a prohibited agreement'.[74] In other words, the Court's ruling obliging the Member States' legal systems to provide in a remedy by way of compensation, applies to both contractual and non-contractual liability—and, indeed, in its judgment, the Court clearly treats the contractual situation as a specific application of a more general rule.[75] The ECJ would have had the opportunity to shed more light on this crucial question if it had not dismissed a preliminary question, for lack of factual and legal information necessary to answer it, that had been referred to it by the Justice of the Peace of Bitonto in Italy.[76] One of many questions put to the Court in a case dealing with a cartel agreement in the insurance sector was whether an infringement of Articles 81 and 82 EC implied 'an obligation on the part of the person committing it to compensate *end users*, and all those who demonstrate that they have suffered any injury . . .' (emphasis added).

We will have to wait for another case to discover the correct answer as to who can be beneficiaries of compensation. However, in its *Muñoz* judgment,[77] the ECJ has given some further clarification, albeit not in the context of competition law, with regard to remedies available to private plaintiffs, more particularly competitors of the person committing a breach of Community law. In that judgment, the Court, referring to *Courage*, repeated—now in the case of a (directly applicable) Regulation containing quality standards for grapes—that civil proceedings must be made available to private parties to enforce their Community rights, adding that this also applies when public authorities have been charged to supervise and check the enforcement of the Regulation. However, in order to grant a competitor the right to initiate (not further specified) civil proceedings, the Court carefully examined

---

[73] At recs. 30–31. In the following recs. 33–35, the Court then enumerates a number of factors which a national court should take into consideration in applying that principle, e.g. the fact that the party asking for damages was the stronger party in terms of negotiating the contract.

[74] Opinion at [2001] ECR I-6300, recs. 37 and 38.

[75] See rec. 24 of the judgment, *supra* note 66, according to which 'any individual', even when he is a contracting party, should be allowed to claim damages under the laws of the Member States.

[76] Order of the Court of 11 February 2004 in Joined Cases C-438, C-439, C-509/03 and C-2/04, *Cannito* [2004] ECR I-1605.

[77] Case C-253/00, *Muñoz and Superior Fruiticola* [2002] ECR I-7289.

whether the Regulation was intended to safeguard the economic interests of traders. It thus avoided the question whether the Regulation was also intended to protect consumer interests.[78]

When the ECJ is asked to flesh out the principle of liability of private parties for breaches of Community law, it can (and most likely will, at least in cases where non-contractual liability is at stake) draw inspiration from its Article 288 and *Francovich* case-law.[79] In doing so, it should, obviously, take account of the 'private law' nature of the obligations breached in the case of Articles 81 and 82. Thus, for example, when confronted with the question of which breach suffices to create liability, the Court will probably not be able to apply its case-law on wide discretion, which is a common situation for public authorities, particularly for legislatures, but not for private parties having violated Articles 81 or 82 EC. Since those provisions contain precise prohibitions which, moreover, have been interpreted in numerous court judgments, *unlawful* conduct on the part of the undertaking concerned should suffice to find a breach, leaving little space even for any criterion of culpability.[80]

However, when, in the context of private relations, clarification is sought regarding the notions of causation and damages, and the duty of reparation, the Court may indeed draw inspiration from its Article 288 and/or *Francovich* case-law. Thus, the Court decided in its Article 288 case-law that *causality* is deemed to exist when the link between the violation and the injury sustained is 'direct, immediate and exclusive',[81] and has not been broken by an intervening cause, such as contributory negligence.[82] As for the notion of *damage*, guidance can be found in the Court's

---

[78] See further Biondi's comment on the case in 40 *CML Rev* (2003) 1241.

[79] *Supra* text accompanying note 39. In *Courage* v *Crehan, supra* note 66, the Court referred to earlier case-law when it stated that a national court should be allowed to avoid unjust enrichment on the part of the plaintiff, or to prevent a plaintiff from making a profit from his own unlawful conduct. The Court referred more specifically to Case 238/78, *Ireks-Arkady* [1979] ECR 2955, at rec. 14, for the first principle, and to Case 39/72, *Commission* v *Italy* [1973] ECR 101, at rec. 10, for the second principle.

[80] As regards State liability, the Court, in earlier case-law, quoted some circumstances that a national court should take into account when looking for liability to arise, all of them, however, in instances of an authority having a large margin of discretion: see rec. 56 of *Brasserie, supra* note 22. Where that is not the case, a mere infringement of the rule may suffice: see Joined Cases C-178, 179, 188–190, *Dillenkofer* [1996] ECR I-4845, at recs. 24–29. In *Courage* v *Crehan, supra* note 66, the ECJ did not have to resolve the issue, stating nevertheless, in rec. 35, that the conditions for application of Art. 81 (or 82) EC must not necessarily be the same as for the application of certain civil law consequences. The Court made it clear, however, that, in the context of contractual relations, one party may bear more responsibility towards the other than *vice versa*.

[81] See further Toth, 'The Concepts of Damage and Causality as Elements of Non-contractual Liability', in T. Heukels and A. McDonnell (eds), *The Action for Damages in Community Law* (1997), at 179, 186, where it is specified at 193 ff. that the cause should not be too remote and not too broad and unspecific, and that an intervening cause may be positive or negative.

[82] That point was confirmed in *Brasserie*, where the Court held it to be a general principle which the legal systems of the Member States have in common, that 'the national court may inquire whether the injured party showed reasonable diligence in order to avoid the loss or damage or limit its extent and whether, in particular, [it] availed [it]self in time of all the legal remedies available to [it]'. See recs. 84 and 85 of the judgment, *supra* note 22.

'Article 288 EC' judgments in *Mulder* v *Council*[83] and *Mulder* v *Commission*,[84] where issues of burden of proof, heads of damage, and the assessment thereof, and the award of pre- and post-judgment interest were explicitly dealt with.

In future cases, the question may arise whether there should also be liability following breaches of Treaty provisions to which the Court has attached 'some horizontal' direct effect, even though they do not contain precise obligations for private parties. Thus, for instance, Article 39 (ex 48) EC, which was discussed in *Angonese*,[85] a case concerning an Italian with German as his mother tongue who was refused access to an examination for employment by a private savings bank. The reason given for the refusal was that the applicant was not allowed to prove his knowledge of Italian by means other than a certificate issued by the provincial authority of Bolzano in Italy.[86]

III. Financial services and framework legislation

In July 2000, the ECOFIN Council decided on the establishment and terms of reference of a Committee of Wise Men, under the chairmanship of Alexandre Lamfalussy. The Committee's task was to analyse the shortcomings of the current framework of the European securities markets. In February 2001, the Committee brought out a report in which it proposed a legislative process intended to speed up the regulatory process as regards financial markets, and to allow the regulatory system to react speedily to changing market conditions. The Report was adopted on 23 March 2001 by the European Council at its summit meeting in Stockholm, and was endorsed by the European Parliament.[87] The Process (commonly called the 'Lamfalussy Process') is centred on a four-level approach, the novelty consisting in adding to the ordinary legislative process (level 1) two intermediate levels (levels 2 and 3), each supported by a new committee (ECS and CESR[88]) and creating an

---

[83] Joined Cases C-104/89 and C-37/90, *Mulder et al* v *Council and Commission* [1992] ECR I-3061 (interlocutory judgment).

[84] Joined Cases C-104/89 and C-37/90, *Mulder et al* v *Council and Commission* [2000] ECR I-203 (definitive judgment).

[85] Case C-281/98, *Angonese* [2000] ECR I-4139, at recs. 29–36. In that judgment, as in previous judgments, horizontal effect was acknowledged by the Court in the specific context of rules emanating from private actors 'to regulate in a collective manner' gainful employment or provision of services: at rec. 31.

[86] The Court decided that the practice amounted to unlawful discrimination on the basis of nationality (at recs. 45–46). It is interesting to note that M. Angonese's action before the referring judge aimed at the annulment of the unlawful condition and damages because of a loss of chance (of being engaged): at rec. 13.

[87] On all this, see Sáinz de Vicuña, 'The Legal Integration of Financial Markets of the Euro Area' [2001] *European Business L Rev* 223, at 228.

[88] In the European Securities Committee (ECS) high-level Member State officials are represented, whilst in the Committee of European Securities Regulators the national supervisory authorities are represented.

inter-institutional monitoring group (IIMG) with the task of assessing whether the process works, and to identify emerging bottlenecks.[89]

The four-level legislative approach is as follows. At level 1 framework legislation is adopted by the Community institutions in conformity with the co-decision procedure. At level 2 the Commission adopts Directives or Regulations laying down technical details to implement level 1 legislation, in view of which it consults the ECS and takes the advice of the CESR, which must prepare its advice in consultation with market participants, end-users, and consumers. The Commission acts under the supervision of the European Parliament to ensure that the proposed measures do not go beyond the level of implementation. At level 3, the CESR works on joint interpretation recommendations, consistent guidelines to facilitate day-to-day implementation of Community rules in the respective Member States, and common (but not binding) standards in areas not covered by Community legislation. At level 4 the Commission oversees the compliance of Member States' laws with Community legislation, and if necessary takes legal action before the ECJ.

The four-level approach has many advantages.

(i) Level 1 legislation remains limited to framework principles, making it easier for the three institutions (Commission, Parliament, and Council) to adopt the legislative measure by co-decision (Article 251 EC), possibly even by means of a fast-track procedure, that is, when, after a single reading of the Commission proposal in the European Parliament, the Council approves all amendments proposed by Parliament or Parliament agrees not to propose amendments (or to put forward only those which it knows will be accepted by the Council) (Article 251(2) EC).

(ii) Level 2 implementing legislation, set out in either a Regulation (which shortens the procedure) or a Directive issued by the Commission, contains mere 'technical' rules on which Member States have been consulted in the ESC and national regulators have given their advice in CESR. Enacting basic legislation at level 1 and relegating detail to level 2 makes it easier for the Commission to adapt the rules to changing circumstances.

(iii) At level 3, national regulators assembled in the CESR are to co-ordinate the implementation and interpretation of (level 1 and level 2) EU legislation in the Member States in a coherent and consistent manner. Through peer review, they will compare regulatory practices with a view to preventing inconsistent or incorrect practices occurring in the course of application.

---

[89] The Group is composed of six external members, two for each institution. The committee published a first interim report in May 2003, a second interim report in December 2003, and published its third report—the last within the group's present mandate—on 17 November 2004. See also *infra* note 149. For a brief description of the Committee, see van Gerven, 'IIMG—The Inter-institutional Monitoring Group' [2003] *European Banking & Financial LJ* 265–8.

(iv) At level 4 devices should be found to assist the Commission in its task of uncovering specific cases of incorrect implementation by national regulators, and of making them comply. It is characteristic of the Lamfalussy Process that, at each level, broad consultation with a large variety of interested parties is organized and followed up.[90]

So far, the so-called Lamfalussy Process has been followed with regard to four directives: the Market Abuse Directive, the Prospectus Directive, the Investment Services Directive, and the Directive on Transparency Obligations for Security Issuers.[91] So far, level 1 Directives have been put in place in accordance with Article 251 EC—once, in the case of the Transparency Directive, by a fast-track procedure (because of imminent parliamentary elections). Moreover, level 2 legislation has been enacted by the Commission for two Directives, i.e. the Market Abuse and the Prospectus Directives, consisting altogether of three implementing Directives and two implementing Regulations. Furthermore, much thought has been given, mainly by CESR, to the way in which level 3 implementation in the Member States should take place, and by the Commission and private actors, to how compliance with Community legislation should be secured at level 4. Three reports have been published by the IIMG on the successes and the difficulties of the process.[92]

In its last report the IIMG found that, all in all, the process had indeed speeded up the legislative process at Community level and, moreover, had considerably enhanced the transparency, and quality, of the legislative process. However, it is still too early to know whether Member States will act faster and more consistently in implementing level 1 and level 2 Community legislation than is the case in other areas.[93] Leaving that question aside, the Lamfalussy Process is innovative, in that it incorporates all stages of the legislative process, i.e. at both the Community and national levels, into one process that is strongly supported by a committee of national regulators (CESR) and closely supervised by a monitoring committee (IIMC) on behalf of the three Community institutions. As the procedure appears to be effective, it will probably be extended to other financial services sectors.

---

[90] For a description and analysis of the Lamfalussy Process, see Moloney, 'New Frontiers in EC Capital Markets: from Market Construction to Market Regulation', 40 *CML Rev* (2003) 809–43. also Ooppenholle, 'Reflections on Regulatory Developments in the European Union', [2004] *European Banking & Financial LJ* 5–41.

[91] See Annex 4 to the third report of the IIMG, *supra* note 89.

[92] In its first interim report, *supra* note 89, the monitoring committee revealed the criteria which it will use in assessing the work of the institutions and of the CESR, and identified the issues (e.g. parallel work on levels 1 and 2; still too much detail in level 1 legislation; use of Regulations or of Directives at level 2; methods and quality of consultation) as well as some bottlenecks (e.g. impact of parliamentary elections in 2004; effect of sunset clause limiting the time period given the Commission for the adoption of level 2 legislation). The committee also analysed the complaints from market participants and from the institutions with regard to transparency and public consultation. In its second and third reports, the committee followed up all of these points as well as others.

[93] On all this see the third report, *supra* note 89. See also *infra* text accompanying note 146 ff.

Moreover, in Article I-36 of the draft Constitution, the distinction between framework enactments containing essential elements of the proposed Union at level 1 and delegated enactments that contain non-essential elements at level 2 has been turned into a general legislative instrument within the doctrine of hierarchy of norms.

C. Coordination Taking over from Harmonization in Certain Areas

With the extension of the Community's powers to areas in which the Member States do not wish to abandon too many of their sovereign rights, more instances have arisen in which the Community legislature is explicitly prohibited from harmonizing Member State laws. These are areas in which, in the terminology of Article I-17 of the proposed Constitution, the Union may carry out only 'supporting, coordinating or complementary action'. For these areas, the institutions may adopt binding acts which, however, 'shall not entail harmonisation of Member States' laws or regulations' (Article I-12(5)). Currently, prohibitions of this kind are found in Articles 149(4), 150(4), 151(4), and 152(4) EC concerning, respectively, education, vocational training, culture and public health. Moreover, in areas where policy takes over from law, harmonization of laws is replaced by coordination of policies. In that respect, so-called new modes of governance, namely the open method of co-ordination (OMC) and voluntary accords with and by private actors, have taken over from the traditional modes of governance, known as the 'Community method'. It is characteristic of such new modes of governance, that they are:

guided by (1) the principles of voluntarism—that is, non-binding targets and soft law, without formal sanctions; (2) subsidiarity—that is, measures are decided by member states or private actors; and (3) inclusion—that is, the actors concerned participate in defining the policy goals and the instruments to be applied.[94]

The new modes of governance relate mainly to social policies of employment, retirement pensions and social inclusion,[95] where convergence of objectives, not harmonization of rules, is at the centre. The most prominent of these new modes is the Open Method of Coordination which will be described hereinafter, first in general and then in connection with coordination of national private laws. Coordination of laws is used here as a concept comprising harmonization or approximation—either through legislation (Directives or Regulations) or through case-law—but is not limited to it.[96] It refers to the broader phenomenon of convergence which

---

[94] Héritier, 'New Modes of Governance in Europe: Increasing Political Capacity and Policy Effectiveness?', in T.A. Börzel and R.A. Cichowski (eds), *The State of the European Union* (2003), at 105, 106.

[95] On the use of the new modes in the area of social exclusion (fighting poverty), see Armstrong, 'Tackling Social Exclusion through OMC: Reshaping the Boundaries of European Governance', in *ibid.*, at 170–94.

[96] As pointed out *supra*, in the text accompanying notes 33 and 34, in the EC Treaty harmonization of laws is used as a synonym for approximation of laws: see the heading above, and the wording of Arts. 94 and 95 EC. Approximation can result in unification of national laws when Regulations are used

will be described in Section 4. As we will see there, convergence is a generic name comprising both the approximation of laws through an institutionalized (legislative or judicial) process and the growing together of legal systems as a result of voluntary action, or even spontaneous behaviour, on the part of legislatures, regulators or courts.[97]

I. The Open Method of Coordination (OMC)

The OMC was already applied 'avant la lettre', in the Maastricht Treaty for the coordination of the economic policies of Member States (Articles 98–99 EC), and was used again in the Amsterdam Treaty with regard to employment policies (Articles 125–130). The method

implies that member governments should agree to define certain policy purposes or problems as matters of 'common concern', whereas the actual choice of effective policies should
remain a national responsibility. Its core is an iterative procedure, beginning with a report
from the Commission to the European Council, which is followed by guidelines of the
Council based on a proposal from the Commission. In response to these guidelines, member governments will present annual 'national action plans' and reports on measures taken—
which will then be evaluated in the light of comparative benchmarks by the Commission
and a permanent committee of senior civil servants—leading to new guidelines, or specific
recommendations of the Council. These evaluations will feed into the next iteration of annual
reports and guidelines, but may also lead to the adoption of specific recommendations of the
Council to individual member states.[98]

Harmonization of Member State laws and regulations is explicitly excluded (Article 129). The method is confirmed in Article I-15 of the draft Constitution.[99]

The new methods of governance and the open method of coordination in particular are expected to enhance political capacity (reaching decisions without

to approximate national rules (as is possible under Art. 95, but not under Art. 94). When Directives are
used (as is possible under both Arts. 94 and 95) no unification in the full sense of the word can be
achieved, as circumscribed in Art. 249 EC).

[97] In the United States convergence in the field of constitutional law is sometimes called 'generic
constitutional law'. It has been described as follows: 'The interconnectedness of federal constitutional
law to other bodies of law illustrates a broader phenomenon of constitutional adjudication. To expound
a constitution—any constitution—is to draw upon and contribute to a body of principle, practice, and
precedent that transcends jurisdictional boundaries. Communalities emerge across jurisdictions because
constitutional law develops within a web of reciprocal influences, in response to shared theoretical and
practical challenges. These communalities are at points so thick and prominent that the result may fairly
be described as *generic constitutional law* . . .': see Law, 'Generic Constitutional Law', 89 *Minnesota L
Rev* (2005) 652–742, at 659.

[98] Scharpf, 'Legitimate Diversity: the New Challenge of European Integration' in Borzel and
Cichowski, *supra* note 94, at 79, 101.

[99] New governance is in contrast with the traditional model of EC constitutionalism and contains,
as such, a number of potential tensions. See de Búrca, 'The Constitutional Challenge of New Governance
in the European Union', 28 *EL Rev* (2003) 814–39.

long negotiations and greater support of all involved) as well as policy effectiveness
(greater problem-solving capacity with a view to achieving the defined policy target,
no imposition of majority view).[100] It is too early for a definitive evaluation, but
the potential and the limitations of the method seem to be quite clear. On the one
hand, Member States remain in control of their own policy choices, and remain
capable of responding to the diversity of national economics and preferences, but are
nevertheless put in a position, through the monitoring process, to learn from their
neighbours. On the other hand, it is uncertain whether, in the absence of effective
sanctions, 'shaming governments' will be enough of an incentive, and the policies
adopted will remain vulnerable to all the legal constraints which the 'acquis communautaire' of market integration, liberalization and competition imposes on
mainly accession States.[101]

Both these limitations might perhaps be alleviated if the open method could be employed
in the implementation of framework directives which, though legally binding, allow more
room for the discretion of national policy makers than is normally true of EU directives.[102]

The OMC constitutes a new form of governance which stands between the
Community method of integration based on binding legal rules and the instrument
of intergovernmental cooperation between Member States.[103] It is a mode of governance that is particularly suited to areas where the Community and the Member
States share competences, with the result that there is no legal basis in the Treaties
that is broad enough for the Union institutions to cover a whole policy area alone.
Three areas have been identified in which the method is particularly useful:

where the subject matter touches closely on national identity or culture, where the national
arrangements are so diverse and/or complex that harmonisation would be out of proportion
to the objective and where the Member States are not ready to embrace common legislation
immediately but do have the political will to take very concrete steps towards an identified
common objective.[104]

II. *Towards an open method of approximation of private law*

The OMC can be applied in areas in which the Community has only limited
jurisdiction, i.e. competences that it shares with the Member States as, for example,
in the field of consumer protection, or that are of a merely supportive or coordinating nature as, for example, in the field of education or vocational training. It
could also be used in areas for which the Community has no general jurisdiction,
as with regard to private law. In matters of limited jurisdiction, the method can be

---

[100] Héritier, *supra* note 94, at 107 ff.

[101] See Scharpf, *supra* note 98, at 102.

[102] *Ibid.*

[103] Fletcher, 'EU Governance Techniques in the Creation of a Common European Policy on
Immigration and Asylum', 9 *European Public Law* (2003) 533, at 551.

[104] *Ibid.*, at 552.

set up as a framework of cooperation between Community institutions and Member State authorities and with the involvement of private actors. The scope of such framework could be extended to all matters for which any of the participants have any competence, allowing all those involved to work out a global action plan at the supra-national and national levels and to agree on common targets and on methods of screening results and monitoring the functioning of the process. Under such a global action plan, tasks are assigned to the participants, public and private, each of whom assumes the responsibility for carrying out his task by whatever means available to him within his sphere of competence.

Within such an OMC framework, Member States and Community institutions, and private actors, can agree more specifically on:

(i) fixing goals, guidelines and timetables;
(ii) laying down benchmarks and comparing best practices, taking into account national preferences;
(iii) encouraging mutual learning processes; and
(iv) establishing reporting and monitoring mechanisms to assess progress.[105]

As mentioned above, the open method of coordination is most appropriate in situations where large cultural diversities exist, thus making full harmonization or unification premature, or out of proportion to the effort to be deployed, or where Member States, although not yet prepared to establish a high degree of uniformity through binding legislation, are willing to attain some convergence by laying down common standards or guidelines by methods of soft law.[106]

The OMC may also be useful in areas where the Community has no competence to regulate, but where the Member States are prepared to act jointly at their own initiative, however with the involvement of the Commission. It seems that, in such instances, the Commission may, in its capacity of 'motor of European integration' (*cf.* Article 211, second hyphen, EC), follow up such request with a view to preparing the ground for subsequent legislation by way of soft law acts, such as informative communications,[107] and may even, when the matter is taken further, coordinate the process in a general fashion. That is at least the case when the European Parliament or the European Council has passed a resolution to that

---

[105] The OMC and the instruments involved in it were explicitly recognized as a form of governance at the 2000 Lisbon European Council: see further Fletcher, *supra* note 103, at 551.

[106] On soft law, see Senden and Prechal, 'Differentiation in and through Community Soft Law', in De Witte *et al.* (eds), *supra* note 10, at 181–99, and the exhaustive study by Linda Senden, quoted in note 107.

[107] It remains a controversial question how far the Commission may go in adopting non-binding (i.e. soft law) acts, more specifically whether it may issue informative communications to institutions other than the European Parliament and the Council in areas for which there is no legal basis in the Treaty. See further L. Senden, *Soft Law in European Community Law* (2004), at 291–320, who is of the opinion (rightly, I think) that the Commission, in 'its role as the motor of European integration' (recognized in Art. 211, second hyphen, EC), may 'by the adoption of non-binding acts . . . pave the way for future Community [proposals for] legislation' (at 479).

effect[108] (as occurred in matters of private law) calling on the Commission to draw up a preparatory study.[109] The purpose of such a study, which is normally addressed to the European Parliament and the Council of Ministers, is to ascertain the reaction of these legislative institutions, and that of the Member States and their parliaments, and to discover whether the political will exists to go ahead, and on which legal basis—and eventually to use Article 308 EC as a (controversial) legal basis.

In this context, it should be clear that, under the method of open coordination, not only should the contribution of the European Parliament be sought but also that of the national parliaments, whenever policy decisions have to be taken which are likely to touch on cultural differences. Indeed, in such matters, the early involvement of parliaments, both at Community and national levels, is absolutely indispensable to impregnating the project with democratic legitimacy. All this does not, of course, rule out that, once the final product of cooperation needs the enactment of comprehensive and binding codification, it will be necessary to find a legal basis, or create a new one when Article 308 EC does not suffice (under that Article the EU Council of Ministers can only act unanimously). If no such legal basis exists, and a new one is not created, an international agreement between the Member States (or some of them) will be the only way out.[110]

The Commission's 2003 Action Plan concerning a more coherent European Contract Law,[111] referred to at the beginning of this chapter, is clearly a first step in the direction of applying the OMC in the field of private law. It is only a first step, however, as it is laid down for only one field of private law, i.e. contract law, but, more importantly, because it is drafted from an exclusive legislative approach,[112] that is reflecting the conviction that *uniformity* is the prevailing paradigm for making private law converge, and neglecting the positive aspects of *diversity* in the field of private law.[113] Moreover, the Action Plan totally ignores the educational dimension, that is, how university curricula can be fashioned and lawyers can be educated to make approximation of private laws succeed in actual practice—which is not an easy task considering the huge differences that exist between legal mentalities and styles in the Member States, as well as in teaching methods, as described at the beginning of this chapter.[114] Education is however a matter for which the Community

---

[108] On the effect of declarations, conclusions, and resolutions (of the Council mainly), see Senden, *supra* note 107, at 193 ff.

[109] For references, see the resolutions of the European Parliament and the conclusions of the European Council mentioned under I-2 and 3 of the Communication from the Commission to the Council and the European Parliament on European Contract Law, COM(2001)398 final.

[110] On the legal status of such 'ancillary' Treaties not based on the EC (or EU) Treaty, see De Witte, *supra* note 10, at 255 ff.

[111] OJ 2003 C 63/1, *supra* note 4, and accompanying text.

[112] See further van Gerven, *supra* note 28, 1–15.

[113] On the positive value of legal diversity, see Beale, *supra* note 12, at 70. As for public law, see P. Beaumont, C. Lyons, and N. Walker (eds), *Convergence and Divergence in European Public Law* (2002).

[114] See van Gerven, *supra* note 28.

has been granted (supportive and supplementing) competences, with the express purpose (among others) of 'developing the European dimension in education' (see Article 149(2) EC).

4. CONVERGENCE OF LAWS WITHIN AND OUTSIDE THE EUROPEAN UNION

As appears from Articles 94 and 95 EC, *approximation* of laws, through Directives or Regulations (i.e., by way of harmonization or unification), refers to the bringing together of national laws, in the context of Community law, as a result of concerted action within the framework of an institutionalized legislative process.[115] However, in Community law, approximation of laws is also the result of case-law of the Community courts, i.e. of an institutionalized judicial process.[116] *Convergence*, by contrast, is here understood, as already mentioned, as a generic term comprising two components, i.e. approximation through an institutionalized (legislative or judicial) process and the growing together of rules through voluntary or even spontaneous action—and therefore not necessarily occurring because of a legal obligation but perhaps for reasons of consistency, natural justice, or simply convenience. Taken in this broad meaning, convergence refers to a global phenomenon that transcends different legal orders within and outside the geographic borders of the European Union.

Hereinafter, I will describe different forms of convergence in terminology that is normally used to define the open method of coordination—to which convergence, in its second component, is related by its characteristics of voluntarism, good practices and mutual learning.[117] On the basis of this terminology, I will describe convergence as a matter of spill-over from one jurisdiction or part of the law into another (at A); as a mutual learning process among supranational and national courts (at B); as a matter of benchmarking and good practices between regulators (at C); and as a learning and teaching process (at D).

A. Spill-over from One Part of the Law, or from One Jurisdiction, into Another

Spill-over occurs in various situations. Within the EU Member States, it refers to the impact which EC law has *indirectly* on the laws of Member States, as a result of legislative, regulatory, or judicial action of national authorities in areas which do not fall within the sphere of EC law—and which therefore remain outside the framework of

---

[115] See also *supra* the text accompanying notes 33 and 34, and *supra* note 96.
[116] See further van Gerven, 'Harmonization of Private Law: Do we Need it?', 41 *CML Rev* (2004) 505–32, at 515 ff.
[117] *Supra* text accompanying note 94.

the EC's official harmonization process and are not directly affected by it. In other words, this form of spill-over consists in transplanting or transposing a legal instrument or measure from one part of national law (one that *is* affected by Community law) into another part of the same national law (that *is not* affected by Community law). The need for such 'transposition' is felt because of the fact that harmonization measures, in areas falling within the sphere of EC law, constitute, more often than not, patchwork legislation as a result of the limited competences which Member States have conferred upon the European legislature (Articles 5 and 7 EC).[118] This limited conferral of competences causes parts or branches of national laws which were coherent before harmonization occurred to fall, as a result of harmonization, into two different sets of rules within the same State and within the same area: one for trans-border transactions governed by EC law and one for local transactions governed by purely national law. An example is anti-competitive behaviour, which is regulated by EC competition rules (Articles 81 and 82 EC) when cartel agreements or abuses of dominant position affect inter-State commerce, but is regulated by national competition rules when only intra-State commerce is affected.

To restore coherence within their Member State many national legislatures have attempted to make their national laws conform as closely as possible to the European rules, allowing their authorities and courts, in the example of competition law, to benefit from rulings issued by European regulators and courts in similar factual situations. Belgian, Dutch and UK laws are an illustration of such convergence which is brought about voluntarily—for reasons of consistency and good management—and not on the basis of some obligation of transposition (which is applicable only within the realm of Community law).[119] Interestingly enough, this type of legislative convergence is not limited to relations among the EU and its Member States. It also occurs in relations of the EU with third countries, and thus by spill-over from one jurisdiction into another jurisdiction. This is the case with Switzerland, where the Federal Council decided in 1988 voluntarily to bring Swiss legislation with international application into line with EU standards.[120] The same is true for the few remaining EFTA countries: there, however, on the basis of an obligation that these States have undertaken as regards the EU.[121]

Convergence by way of spill-over from one part of the law into another within the same Member State can also be the result of judicial action. A famous English case is *M* v *Home Office* concerning an application for judicial review of the Home

[118] See further van Gerven, *supra* note 6, at 435–9.

[119] The spill-over effect of Community competition rules occurred also in the new (2004) Member States many of which have reformed their national competition laws with a view to accession by incorporating the European competition rules almost literally into their internal national law: see Schwarze, 'Enlargement, The European Constitution, and Administrative Law', 53 *ICLQ* (2004) 969, at 976–7.

[120] See Breitenmoser, 'Sectoral Agreements between the EEC and Switzerland: Contents and Context', 40 *CML Rev* (2003) 1137–86.

[121] See Baudenbacher, 'The EFTA Court—An Example of the Judicialisation of International Economic Law', 28 *EL Rev* (2003) 880–99.

Secretary's decision to deport a citizen of Zaïre claiming refugee status in the UK. The judgment of the House of Lords in that case came after the ECJ had ruled in *Factortame I* that 'the full effectiveness of Community law would be . . . impaired if a rule of national law could prevent a court seized of a dispute governed by Community law from granting interim relief [against the Crown] . . .'[122] In his leading speech for the House, Lord Woolf referred to the 'unhappy situation' whereby 'while a citizen is entitled to obtain injunctive relief (including interim relief) against the Crown or an officer of the Crown to protect his interests under Community law he cannot do so in respect of his other interests which may be just as important.'[123] Speaking for the House of Lords, Lord Woolf concluded that 'it would be most regrettable if an approach which is inconsistent with that which exists in Community law should be allowed to persist if this is not strictly necessary.'[124] As a result, the House of Lords held that also in a purely internal situation there would be jurisdiction to bring an action against the Crown.[125]

B. Mutual Learning between Courts

As mentioned elsewhere,[126] convergence is often the result of the development of common principles of law in a continuing process of cross-fertilization between the Community and the Member States' legal orders. This process has taken place, notably, in the field of administrative law.[127] Recently, however, more concrete examples of direct mutual learning between courts of law have come to the fore. Two prominent examples are the relationship between the ECJ and the ECtHR, and the comparative method used by the House of Lords in filling gaps in its own legal system.

I. ECJ and ECtHR: avoiding a collision course

As long as the EU has not acceded to the ECHR, as envisaged in Article I-9(2) of the draft Constitution, the ECtHR has no competence to examine the compatibility

---

[122] Case C-213/89, *R* v *Secretary of State for Transport*, ex parte *Factortame Ltd and others* [1990] ECR I-2433, rec. 21.

[123] [1993] 3 WLR 433, at 448. See further Anthony, 'Community Law and the Development of UK Administrative Law: Delimiting the "Spill-Over" Effect', 4 *European Public Law* (1998) 253–76, at 262.

[124] [1993] 3 WLR 433, at 463.

[125] S. Douglas-Scott, *Constitutional Law of the European Union* (2002), at 337.

[126] See *supra* text preceding note 43 and van Gerven 'The Emergence of a Common European Law in the Area of Tort Law: the EU Contribution', in Fairgrieve *et al.*, *supra* note 47, 125, at 131–40. On the (much more limited) interaction between the ECtHR and the national courts, see the report of Heringa, on 'Existing Forms of Interaction: their Potential and their Limits', submitted at a seminar at the Strasbourg Court of 9–10 Sept. 2002, which is available from the website of the Council of Europe.

[127] See primarily J. Schwarze, *European Administrative Law* (1992) (translation of an earlier book in German, *Europäisches Verwaltungsrecht* (1988), 2 vols). See also, more recently, from the same author, 'The Convergence of the Administrative Laws of the EU Member States', 4 *European Public Law* (1998) 191, and *supra* note 119.

of Community acts with the ECHR (only the ECJ has jurisdiction over the EU institutions[128]). However, it does have competence over the EU Member States, even when they act in their capacity as EU Member States in the preparation of Community legislation. This can lead to delicate jurisdictional questions, the more so because there has been an increasing trend for applicants to bring proceedings before the ECtHR against all Member States in circumstances in which applicants feel that an act attributable to the Community has infringed their rights.[129] Obviously, concurrent jurisdiction contains the risk of conflicting decisions between the two supranational courts.[130] For example, in the *Emesa Sugar* litigation before the ECJ,[131] the applicant relied before the Court of Justice on the *Vermeulen* judgment of the ECtHR[132] in order to argue that the lack of opportunity to reply to the Advocate-General's Opinion constituted a violation of the right to adversarial proceedings laid down in Article 6(1) ECHR. In its decision the ECJ ruled that the *Vermeulen* case-law of the ECtHR (concerning the Procurator General before the Belgian Court of cassation) was not transposable to the Opinion of the Court's Advocates General because of 'the organic and the functional link between the Advocate General and the Court'.[133]

Having regard to the ECtHR's well-established case-law, it was not at all certain that the Strasbourg court was going to agree with the Luxembourg court at the occasion of later litigation. The answer came with the judgment of the ECtHR in *Kress* v *France*.[134] In that case the applicant alleged a violation of Article 6(1) ECHR in that she could not, before the French *Conseil d'État*, inspect the submissions of the *Commissaire du Gouvernement* before they were made at the hearing and that she was unable to address the court in reply after he had spoken. On this point of law, the Court ruled that there were sufficient other safeguards to ensure compliance with the principle of adversarial proceedings. These included the fact that the applicant could ask the Commissioner, before the hearing, to indicate the general tenor of his submissions; that she had taken the available opportunity to reply to the submissions by memorandum before the judges' final deliberations; and that the procedure of the *Conseil d'État* provided that, when appropriate, the presiding judge would adjourn to allow the applicant to present arguments.

---

[128] See further W. van Gerven, *The European Union. A Polity of States and Peoples* (2005) (in comparison with the U.S.).

[129] See further Hamsen, 'National Responsibility for European Community Acts under the European Convention on Human Rights: Recasting the Accession Debate', 7 *European Public Law* (2001) 625, at 641 ff.

[130] See P. Craig and G. De Búrca, *EU Law, Text, Cases and Materials* (3rd edn, 2004), at 367–8.

[131] Case C-17/98, *Emesa Sugar* v *Aruba*, Order of 4 February 2000 [2000] ECR I-665. For the judgment on the merits of the case, see [Judgment of 8 February] [2000] ECR I-675.

[132] *Vermeulen* v *Belgium* [1996] R &D I, 224.

[133] Order in *Emesa Sugar*, *supra* note 131, at rec. 16; see also the two preceding recs.

[134] Judgment of the ECtHR of 7 June 2001 in App. no. 39594/98. For a short overview, see Human Rights Survey, 27 *EL Rev* (2002) HR/134–5.

Interestingly enough, in *Emesa Sugar* as well as in *Kress*, both the ECJ and the ECtHR were careful to quote the other court's case-law, showing that both courts wished to avoid conflicting judgments.[135] That was confirmed in two recent cases[136] in which the ECJ was asked either to grant leave to an applicant to submit written observations following the Opinion of the Advocate General, or to order the reopening of the oral procedure. The ECJ dismissed both claims, being careful to remain within the limits of the ECtHR's judgment in *Kress*. It dismissed the first request because the Court's Rules of Procedure made no provision for it, and dismissed the second request pointing out that it had all information necessary to answer the preliminary question before it.

It appears from the foregoing (and other) judgments that the two supranational courts are well aware of the risk of divergences in their case-law and are keen to learn from each other, and to ensure as much convergence as possible when interpreting the provisions of the ECHR within their own jurisdictions.[137]

II. Member States' courts comparing notes

Two recent decisions of the House of Lords indicate how convergence between judicial decisions can be achieved through mutual learning. Both decisions relate to the law of obligations. In the first decision convergence does not lie in the outcome of the case but in the way of reasoning; in the second decision, convergence lies in the outcome. In the first judgment, in *Macfarlane* v *Tayside Health Board*,[138] the question arose whether parents who already had four children could claim damages in negligence for the cost of maintaining until majority a fifth healthy child born despite a vasectomy which the father had undergone in the defendant's clinic. The House of Lords held that the mother's claim to obtain damages for pain, suffering and distress relating to the pregnancy and birth should proceed to trial, but dismissed the claim for compensation for the cost of raising the child.

Interestingly enough, two of the Law Lords who expressed their opinion on the issue gave different reasons for concluding that the defendant Health Board had no

---

[135] *Emesa Sugar* defended its case also before the ECtHR, this time against the Netherlands: App. no. 62023/00. However, the Strasbourg Court declared the case inadmissible, holding that the facts relating to matters of taxation (customs duties) fell outside the scope of Art. 6 of the ECHR which concerns only disputes about the determination of 'civil rights and obligations': Judgment of 13 January 2005. Also in that judgment the Strasbourg Court, in relating the facts of the case, quoted extensively from the ECJ's Order of 4 February (referred to *supra* note 131).

[136] See the judgments of 14 December 2004 in *Arnold* and *Swedish Match*, *supra* note 8 (at recs. 24–27 and 22–25).

[137] On the concurrent jurisdiction between the two supranational courts, and the divergences in the case-law of the two courts, see Craig and De Búrca, *supra* note 130, at 365–8.

[138] [2000] SC(HL) 10 Excerpts from the speeches of Lord Slynn and Lord Steyn are reproduced in van Gerven *et al.*, *supra* note 16, at 92–6. For an overview of UK law, see Lord Rodger of Earlsferry, 'Wrongful Birth in United Kingdom Law', in S.C.J.J. Kortmann and B.C.J. Hamel (eds), *Wrongful Birth and Wrongful Life* (2004), at 43–52.

duty of care to the parents with regard to the cost of maintenance. For Lord Slynn, the reason for the non-existence of a duty was the lack of proximity between the physician and the parents as regards that head of damage. In so doing, he avoided basing his judgment on public policy factors ('just, fair and reasonable'). On the other hand, Lord Steyn analysed the case from the point of view of distributive justice, which is concerned with the just distribution of burdens and losses among members of society. He concluded that it would not be morally acceptable, relying on principles of justice, to grant compensation for cost of maintenance. In reaching his conclusion, Lord Slynn referred (among other material, much from Commonwealth countries) to the judgment of the Dutch Hoge Raad of 21 February 1997 (of which he was informed through the case-book on torts where the judgment was excerpted and discussed).[139] In that judgment the Dutch Supreme Court, deviating from a strongly-reasoned Opinion of its Advocate General J. Vranken, granted the parents' claim, also with regard to the cost of maintenance, in a similar factual and legal context. Although the Supreme Courts differed in their judgments on the facts, they examined the same kind of arguments, many of an ethical nature, but attached different weight to the arguments for and against.

The difference in legal reasoning, but not in outcome, between the judgments of Lords Slynn and Steyn in *Macfarlane*, and the difference in outcome, and in legal reasoning, between the Dutch Supreme Court and its Advocate-General Vranken illustrate how the same legal rules and concepts may, within the same legal system, lead to different solutions. It is therefore unsurprising that the House of Lords and the Dutch Supreme Court can also come to opposite solutions. However, the interesting point is how both these courts and their members, in reaching similar or different solutions, did so on the basis of underlying value judgments and of legal arguments that may be the same or different and, when they are the same, are sometimes differently evaluated. The lesson to be learned from this is how relative legal concepts and rules are in the face of underlying ethical, social or ethical considerations, and that mutual learning between judges from different legal systems can take place notwithstanding differences in rules or concepts.

The second judgment in point is the decision of the House of Lords in *Fairchild* v *Glenhave*.[140] The case concerns the issue of double or multiple causation, that is whether a victim who has suffered a legal wrong can obtain compensation for harm caused by one of several possible persons (all having acted in breach of duty), even though it has not been possible for the plaintiff to prove which of those people was the real culprit. The harm consisted in contracting mesothelioma from inhaling asbestos during the victim's employment at different times by two employers.

---

[139] The judgment was already reproduced and discussed in the first (and short) edition of van Gerven *et al.* (1998), at 161–5. In the second (and enlarged) edition, *supra* note 16, the judgment is reproduced and discussed at 133–6. For a later wrongful birth case (relating, however, to a handicapped child: Kelly) decided by the Dutch Hoge Raad, see judgment of 18 March 2005 [2005] RvdW 42 and [2005] JOL 162 with the Opinion of Procurator General Hartkamp.

[140] The judgment, of 20 June 2002, concerns three joined cases.

In his leading speech Lord Bingham put the issue in a wider perspective, examining not only immediate judicial precedents but also wider case-law from other jurisdictions, including civil law jurisdictions, mainly Germany and the Netherlands. In that respect, he referred to Christian von Bar *The Common European Law of Torts*, to Markesinis and Unberath *The German Law of Torts*, and to the case-book on *National, Supranational and International Tort Law*, co-authored by Jeremy Lever QC and Pierre Larouche.[141] In a long quotation from the case-book, Lord Bingham noted that it said that it was unfortunate that the House of Lords had, in the past, retreated from earlier case-law at a time when laws in other countries were converging on the point of law at issue—that is accepting liability in the case of multiple causation.[142]

At the end of an extensive and thorough overview of case-law in many Commonwealth and European countries, Lord Bingham made the following remark, which deserves to be quoted in full:

This survey shows, as would be expected, that though the problem underlying cases such as the present is universal the response is not. Hence also the intensity of academic discussion . . . But it appears that in most of the jurisdictions considered the problem of attribution [of legal responsibility to multiple causes] would not, on the facts such as those of the present cases, be a fatal objection to a plaintiff's claim . . . Development of the law in this country cannot of course depend on a head-count of decisions and codes adopted in other countries around the world, often against a background of different rules and traditions. The law must be developed coherently, in accordance with principle, so as to serve, even-handedly, the ends of justice. If, however, a decision is given in this country which offends one's basic sense of justice, and if consideration of international sources suggests that a different and more acceptable decision would be given in most other jurisdictions, whatever their legal tradition, this must prompt anxious review of the decision in question.

On the basis of these arguments Lord Bingham, and with him the House of Lords, allowed the plaintiff to obtain compensation.[143]

Mutual learning is not a monopoly of the House of Lords. Supreme courts of other Member States are also engaged in comparative jurisprudence. However, because of differences in style, they may be less tempted to do so openly. Indeed, as pointed out previously,[144] the legal style of French or German judgments is less apt than that of British ones to incorporate arguments and solutions borrowed from other legal systems. That does not mean, however, that supreme courts of other Member States do not make use of comparative research when deciding controversial issues. An example of the latter is a judgment of the French Cour de cassation in *Epoux Brachot* v *Banque Worms* in which the Court introduced into French law

---

[141] Paras. 23 and 25. The case-book on tort law is referred to *supra* note 16.

[142] The quotations in Lord Bingham's speech are taken from *ibid.*, 441, 461, and 465. In the quotation from von Bar's book, reference is made to a well-known decision from the Dutch Hoge Raad, known as the *DES daughters* case, which is also excerpted and commented on in *ibid.*, at 447–52.

[143] The quotation is in para. 32, the conclusion in paras. 34 and 35 of Lord Bingham's speech.

[144] See text *supra* accompanying notes 15 ff.

a new procedural remedy in insolvency proceedings.[145] Actually, a considerable amount of comparative research in view of judicial decision-making in concrete cases (within the realm of Community law) is contained in comparative notes composed by the research department of the ECJ—which, unfortunately, are not published but kept in the Court's archives.

C. Spreading Good Practices Between Regulators

Cooperation between regulators of the now 25 Member States is an essential ingredient of the so-called Lamfalussy Process on the regulation of European securities markets. As pointed out above,[146] under that process two committees (i.e. the European Securities Committee (ESC) and the Committee of European Securities Regulators (CESR)) have been set up. It is one of the tasks of the latter to strengthen cooperation between national regulators to ensure consistent and equivalent implementation of level 1 (framework) and level 2 (implementation) Community legislation in all the Member States (level 3). In its own words:

CESR should fulfil this role by producing administrative guidelines, interpretation recommendations, common standards, peer reviews and comparisons of regulatory practice to improve enforcement of the legislation concerned.[147]

The CESR proposes to pursue this objective through three different avenues: coordinated implementation of EU law in the Member States; regulatory convergence; and supervisory convergence.

In this context, 'regulatory convergence' is the most important. In the words of the CESR, this:

is the process of creating common rules. The legitimacy of the role of CESR at level 3 comes from the fact that CESR members take individual decisions on a daily basis that create jurisprudence. This bottom up approach relates to the normative nature of concrete decision making activities of the legislators. . . . [I]n an integrated market, the jurisprudence created by supervisors produces effects that cannot be limited to national jurisdictions and therefore must be faced at EU level. . . . [On the basis of that jurisprudence] the members of CESR will introduce . . . guidance, recommendations and standards in their regulatory practices on a voluntary basis.[148]

Regulatory convergence, as conceived of by the CESR, is a powerful instrument for making national regulations and practices converge in the area of financial services.

---

[145] Cass. Civ. 1ere, 19 Nov. 2002, with the Opinion of Sainte-Rose AG, annotated by Chaillé de Néré, [2002] *JCP* II 10,201; see also the annotation by Khairallah, [2003] *D* 797. For further comment, see Muir Watt, 'Injunctive Relief in the French Courts: a Case of Legal Borrowing', 62 *CLJ* (2003), 573. I am grateful to Dr. Patrick Späth, Berlin, who drew my attention to this case-law.

[146] See also *supra* the text accompanying note 87 ff, and the articles referred to *supra* note 90.

[147] *The Role of CESR at 'Level 3' under the Lamfalussy Process*, Consultation Paper 2004 (ref: CESR/04–104b).

[148] *Ibid.*, at 7–8.

It illustrates how convergence may be put to use, in the hands of national regulators, to lay down uniform rules and standards on the basis of good practices, benchmarking and peer review. Although not binding, these rules and standards are complied with voluntarily through mutual confidence between regulators and are applied by these regulators, in consultation with private actors, to relations between producers and users of financial services occurring within their jurisdiction. It is true that this method is not without danger from the viewpoint of political accountability and the rule of law, and 'the multiplication of non-binding rules at Level 3 should not lead to a grey area where legal certainty is absent and political accountability is unclear.'[149] Indeed:

soft law has its limits. As it is not legally binding, it cannot be relied on by private actors. Nor can it be directly submitted to judicial scrutiny by courts of law at national or Community level. And it may affect the institutional balance between institutions at those levels.[150]

However, applied with circumspection, it may be a powerful instrument for ensuring the consistency of Community law in the Member States.

D. Educating Lawyers and Preparing Learning and Teaching Materials

It is not the place here to repeat what has been written elsewhere,[151] namely that the best way to promote convergence (as a support for Community legislation and case-law) is to educate open-minded young lawyers and to prepare materials which can be used by teachers (and students) throughout the Union, but also by judges and other practitioners who want to study, and draw benefit from, other legal systems. The materials most apt for learning and understanding a legal system are case-books (and other source-books)[152] which, in a European context, focus on *actual* cases decided by national and supranational (ECU and ECtHR) courts and legislatures, and compare the various legal orders in order to discover common traits and explain differences at the pan-European level. Such a 'bottom-up' approach is needed to supplement, and support, more concept- and rule-oriented approaches.

In concrete terms, the different stages of that approach can be described as follows, taking tort law as an example.[153] First, material (i.e. judgments in the first place, but also statutory rules and excerpts from academic writings) is collected from

---

[149] Thus the Inter-Institutional Monitoring Group, *Third Report Monitoring the Lamfalussy Process*, Brussels, 17 November 2004, at 28 (available at http://europa.eu.int/comm/internal_market/securities/monitoring/thirdreport/2004-11-monitoring en.pdf?).

[150] *Ibid.*, at 29. See also, on the (weak) legal basis of CESR, 27–8.

[151] In the article referred to *supra* note 28.

[152] The famous German scholar Rudolf von Jhering wrote in 1881: 'Nobody who has had any experience as an examiner will doubt that a student is only able truly to comprehend those ideas which he can conceptualise in the concrete form of actual cases': quoted by Markesinis, *supra* note 32, at 374.

[153] See *supra* note 16, for the reference to the case-book devoted to this branch of the law.

national legal orders. This should include as many as possible, but at least one for each of the four large families (that is including the Nordic countries). Relevant material from the two supranational and international legal orders should also be gathered. The material is selected by reason of its similarity in the factual and legal context of the concrete situation, and is grouped around ten or more selected themes of tort law. Secondly, the material is placed in the context of the legal system to which it belongs, identifying the procedural, constitutional and political peculiarities of that legal system, and describing the place that the excerpted material takes in the legal system and the contribution it can make to convergence or integration in the wider context of European integration. Thirdly, the role that abstract concepts, general principles and specific rules play in reaching the specific judicial or statutory solution in the excerpted material is examined and defined, and compared with the role these elements play in the other legal systems. Fourthly, the impact of meta-legal or meta-judicial considerations, often of an ethical, sociological, economic or political nature, on the (judicial or statutory) decision-making process is analysed in connection with the excerpted material and compared with the impact these considerations may have on material from the other systems.

Producing and using a case-book is not an easy matter—more difficult in my experience than writing or using a textbook—but it is worth the effort: it allows the author and the reader to reach a level of understanding which cannot be reached when reading a textbook, however well-written it may be. This is because learning the law through cases demonstrates how rules operate in a concrete situation that looks familiar to the reader because, if the cases are chosen from daily life (and similar daily life cases exist in all legal systems), they are fully recognizable to him or her. Fully to understand the case, the author and reader will have to cope with the peculiarities of the system from which the case is drawn. Moreover, they must try to familiarize themselves with the legal position adopted, and the arguments used, by the litigating parties and with the legal reasoning and arguments which induced the court and/or legislator to decide the case or adopt the rule as it did. That is a question of not just understanding the legal reasoning, but also the underlying interests and value judgments which led the court or legislator to choose one solution over another that could have been reached under a different line of reasoning.

5. TOWARDS AN ACTION PLAN APPLYING THE OPEN METHOD OF CONVERGENCE IN THE AREA OF PRIVATE (AND PUBLIC) LAW

So far, the European Commission has focused its harmonization efforts in the area of private law on contract law in general.[154] That in itself is a remarkable choice: general

---

[154] See the text *supra* accompanying note 1 ff. The Commission's efforts were a follow-up to O. Lando and H. Beale (eds), *Principles of European Contract Law*, Parts I, II and III, prepared by the

contract law is supplementary law that can be set aside by contracting parties when they wish to do so; moreover it has not been the object of much creative case-law on the part of the Community courts.[155] From that viewpoint, tort law might have been a better choice in the field of private law.[156] However that may be, as a result of public consultation, the Commission has abandoned its original idea of unifying general contract law, and has now opted for a common framework of reference, and an optional code—which is more in line with the principle of party autonomy in the field of contract law. Obviously, one of the reasons for this policy change is the absence, in EC law, of a legal basis for regulating contractual relations in general.[157] This lack of a general competence requires the Community legislature to focus on specific subjects (mainly consumer law) over which the Community has only limited (and often incoherent) competences and, as mentioned above,[158] this is responsible for the 'patchwork' character of Community legislation in the field of private law as well as of the case-law of the Community and national courts (already incremental by nature) interpreting EC legislation and national laws implementing it.

Having said that, uniformity of laws should not be an objective in itself, as it is not of itself a higher good than diversity. It is important to remember the huge diversity between the legal families within the EU, which exists not only with regard to content but also, and even more so, with regard to style and mentalities, including a legal system's attitude towards the phenomenon of codification. Therefore, taking into account the difficulty of the task, uniformity, unification and harmonization should occur only when there is good justification for it.[159] Within the framework of EC law, such justification for uniformity consists mainly in the necessity to create and operate an internal market with a (sufficiently) level playing ground—which implies the elimination of concrete legal impediments in the Member State laws. More particularly, and apart from the requirement to set aside such specific legal impediments (in accordance with the ECJ's case-law), there will, as a general rule, be no justification for harmonizing matters which touch closely on national identity or culture, or other matters of national interest for which Member States are not (yet) prepared to adopt common legislation. To bring those matters closer to each other, more appropriate instruments than the traditional

Commission on European Contract Law (a private initiative). Parts I and II were published in 2000, Part III in 2003.

[155] See van Gerven, *supra* note 63, at 113–21.

[156] Or administrative law, then in the area of public law, see Schwarze, 'The Convergence of the Administrative Laws of the EU Member States', *supra* note 127. Also tort law has been the subject of study groups working on principles; in particular the European Group on Tort Law (European Centre of Tort and Insurance Law, Vienna) which published the result of its activities in May 2005: *Principles of European Tort Law, Text and Commentary* (2005).

[157] See further van Gerven, 'Codifying European Private Law? Yes if . . . !', *supra* note 1.

[158] See *supra* text accompanying note 118.

[159] Compare Art. 151 EC where the Community institutions are invited to 'contribute to the flowering of the cultures of the Member States, while respecting their national and regional diversity and at the same time bringing the common cultural heritage to the fore'.

method of binding legislation should be put in place. Among these new instruments—so-called new modes of governance—the open method of coordination is of particular importance.[160]

As explained in Part 4, the open method of coordination is a mode of governance which is based on voluntary cooperation between all parties concerned (public and private, at the national, supranational and international levels) who are included in a transparent and openly organized policy making process, and involved in its implementation tailored to the needs of the different Member States. Its objective is not, in the first place, to issue binding legislative acts but rather to fix targets, guidelines, and timetables for achieving the goals set, to establish qualitative indicators and benchmarks based on best practices and examples, and to organize periodic monitoring, evaluation and peer review as part of an ongoing mutual learning process.[161] Based as it is on close cooperation between the EU institutions and the Member States, the method can also be used in areas for which the EU institutions have competence only to carry out actions to support, coordinate, or supplement the actions of the Member States. It can even be used in areas over which the EU has no specific competence, but in which the EU Commission has been authorized by the other institutions and the Member States' representatives to act 'as a motor of European integration . . . and to pave the way for future Community legislation'[162]— that is, for the event that a new legal basis will be created by Treaty amendment (or a change in the case-law of the ECJ).

The concept of convergence corresponds in the legal field to the method of coordination in the field of governance and can be made part of the latter. As seen above, it refers to the coming together of legal systems not only as a result of legal or judicial harmonization processes but also, and mainly, as a result of voluntary cooperation between, or spontaneous action among, legislators, judges, regulators and academics. It has in common with the method of coordination the fact that it is based on voluntarism and the inclusion of all actors concerned. Moreover, the forms of convergence that have been identified and described above consist basically of similar processes of mutual learning and following good practices which are at play in the open method of coordination—a method which tries to steer the process of convergence by means of flexible soft law instruments rather than by the traditional instruments which are characteristic of the formal legislative or judicial harmonization procedures.

What convergence in the area of private law needs is an Action Plan steering the mutual learning process in a more visible and more systematic manner than has happened so far. Such plan would have two parts, one focusing on practitioners of the law, judges in the first place, and the other focusing on educational aspects. As for the first part, the Action Plan should contain an outline of how to stimulate

---

[160] See the text accompanying Fletcher's article, *supra* note 103.

[161] The method was explicitly recognized as a form of governance at the March 2000 Lisbon European Council: see *ibid.*, at 551.

[162] See *supra* note 107.

convergence in the case of law courts through mutual learning techniques, identifying a number of subjects and pilot projects and offering sufficient resources to allow judges and other practising lawyers to meet regularly in working sessions, to allow them to communicate and to exchange decisions in a common working language and to look for best solutions. Obviously, academics should be able to participate, but the emphasis would not be on legislation but rather on case-law in the context of European integration (not unlike what regulators of financial markets do within the framework of CESR in view of bringing national regulations closer to each other[163]). The objective would be to compare solutions and find similarities notwithstanding conceptual differences. As for the second (educational) part of the Action Plan, it should seek to promote convergence in the longer term by developing, in the terminology of Article 149(2) EC 'the European dimension in education' building further on the Bologna reforms, now however:

(i)   to reorganize the curricula of law schools in a less national and a more European perspective;
(ii)   to revise teaching methods to allow more space for a less doctrinal approach in countries where that approach has been neglected; and
(iii) to develop teaching materials that can be used in master programmes throughout the EU.

The Action Plan should not replace the existing common frame of reference but complement it by emphasizing that the 'top-down' approach (i.e. the rule- and concept-oriented approach) should be supplemented by the 'bottom-up' approach (i.e. the solution-oriented approach) and that legal education is as (or even more) instrumental in making European legal systems converge as harmonization or unification of laws can ever be. The latter objective in particular is of crucial importance, as was highlighted by the German legal historian, Professor Coing, who, as early as 1978,[164] emphasized:

The immense role academic learning has had in the formation of our common legal heritage, in the Middle heritage [should this be 'Middle Ages'?] as well as in the Age of the Enlightenment. It was academic training based on European ideas that created a class of lawyers animated by the same ideas, and it was the European lawyer who preceded the European law. This is the point, I think, at which our academic responsibility begins . . . The curricula of our law schools must not be restricted to the study of national law, and not even to national law combined with a certain seasoning of comparative law. What is necessary . . . is a curriculum where the basic courses present the national law in the context of those legal ideas which are present in the legislation of different nations, that is, against the background of the principle and institutions which the European nations have in common.

Thirty years later, this message has yet to be taken seriously.

---

163 See *supra*, text accompanying notes 146 ff.
164 Coing, 'European Common Law: Historical Foundations', in M. Cappelletti (ed.), *New Perspectives for a Common Law of Europe* (1978) 31, at 44.

3

European Private Law
and the Constitutional Dimension

STEPHEN WEATHERILL

1. INTRODUCTION

Normative conclusions about what one may want from European private law may be confronted by awkward questions about the scope of available competence. Article 5(1) EC stipulates that the EC operates only within the limits set by its founding Treaties, and there is no general legislative competence attributed to it to act in the field of private law. In practice, the apparently barren constitutional landscape is irrigated by the generous approach taken to the scope of the functionally broad competence to harmonize granted by the EC Treaty. Private law has therefore been the subject of a significant degree of intervention by the EC. There are, however, important questions that must be addressed about the constitutional validity of what has been done in the area of private law in the name of harmonization; and these questions are pertinent not only to assessment of past legislative practice but also to understanding what may be done in future, in particular in the light of the Commission's preoccupation with the future of European contract law. This contribution addresses the constitutional dimension of European private law, with particular emphasis on the patterns of legislative harmonization. It is underpinned by the conviction that there are some important ambiguities that deserve exploration.

2. RELEVANT COMPETENCES ATTRIBUTED BY THE TREATY

Although it may be intuitively appealing to assume that an integrated market for Europe inevitably brings with it an integrated regulatory strategy underpinning that market, the EC Treaty does not provide for this. Article 5(1) EC declares that 'The Community shall act within the limits of the powers conferred upon it by this Treaty and of the objectives assigned to it therein.' This is commonly referred to as the principle of 'attributed competence'. The EC has no general regulatory competence and it cannot 'self-authorize' an increase in its own competence. It may act in the areas in which the Member States have granted it a mandate. Extension of the grant rests with the Member States acting at times of periodic Treaty revision. Article 5(1) was formally introduced into the EC Treaty by the Maastricht Treaty with effect from 1993 but, as a general statement of the law of Treaties, it has always been a foundation stone of the EC's constitutional order.

There is no competence to be found in the Treaty which confers any general authorization on the EC to operate in the field of private law. There are, however, particular legal bases that can feasibly be exploited to adopt legislation that touches private law. One is found in Article 153(3)(b), which provides that the Community may adopt measures which support, supplement and monitor the policy pursued by the Member States in order to promote the interests of consumers and to ensure a high level of consumer protection. This was an innovation of the Treaty of Maastricht, so it has been available as a legislative competence only since 1993. Judicial cooperation in civil matters may be pursued by reliance on Articles 61–65 EC. This has a pedigree in the EC Treaty which goes back only as far as the Treaty of Amsterdam, so the key date here is 1999. Both legal bases have been employed for the making of legislation affecting private law. Neither has been the source of anything remotely as significant as the body of EC rules that has been made, and continues to be made, pursuant to a legislative competence that has been on the EC's permitted list ever since the founding of the system in the 1950s. This is the competence to harmonize laws in support of defined economic ends.

True, it is not only legislative harmonization that transports the EC into the realms of private law. EC competition law intimately affects private law by requiring that contracts which fall foul of its demands be treated as unenforceable.[1] In some circumstances the rules governing free movement in the Treaty affect private law, especially those (such as the law governing free movement of persons) which the European Court has interpreted to be capable of direct application to the activities of private parties.[2] Directives that pursue effective market management by requiring Member States to notify draft technical rules to the Commission may impact directly on patterns of contractual responsibility determined before national courts—where States fail to meet their obligations of notification.[3] The gender equality rules and, more recently, the wider equality rules covering *inter alia* race and sexual orientation have an important impact on private relations.[4] But it is (what are today) Articles 94 and 95 EC that have been of paramount importance in the shaping of a legislative *acquis* relevant to private law. The harmonization

---

[1] Art. 81(2) EC.

[2] See e.g. Case C-415/93, *URBSFA* v *Bosman* [1995] ECR I-4921; Case C-281/98, *Roman Angonese* [2000] ECR I-4139.

[3] Case C-443/98, *Unilever Italia SpA* [2000] ECR I-7535; Case C-159/00, *Sapod Audic* [2002] ECR I-5031. See Weatherill, 'Breach of Directives and Breach of Contract', 26 *EL Rev* (2001) 177.

[4] Directive 2000/43, OJ 2000 L 180/22; Directive 2000/78, OJ 2000 L 303/16.

programme has 'spilled over' to exert a powerful impact on private law even though the relevant Treaty provisions do not explicitly recognize their capacity to affect private law. And it is the body of harmonized rules affecting private law that have generated an increasingly vigorous, even hostile, debate about the value and validity of an EC contribution to private law.[5] This chapter does not address the criticism that EC harmonization is economically superfluous or, even worse, damaging, although there is a growing and important literature that engages with the costs and benefits of setting centralized rules in preference to preserving local autonomy, choice and room for regulatory experimentation.[6] Nor does this chapter tackle the deeply important debate about whether harmonization is antagonistic to Europe's cherished diversity or even a pointless bureaucratic exercise in seeking to bring together what is irretrievably culturally separate, although there is here a fascinatingly inviting inquiry into whether harmonization is a worthy exercise in quelling harmful disharmony or rather a cunningly alluring camouflage for an intolerant process of bleaching Europe clean of difference.[7] The focus of this chapter is the constitutional dimension. What is the scope of the EC's competence to act in the field of private law, with particular reference to the programme of legislative harmonization? The inquiry is located, as it deserves to be, in the wider context of the prevailing preoccupation to find a better model in the European Union for balancing the virtues and vices of centralization against those of local autonomy and diversity.

3. THE LEGISLATIVE *ACQUIS* SUMMARIZED

The following list identifies a selection of the most high-profile measures adopted under the programme of legislative harmonization which affect private law.

---

[5] For an attempt to provide a systematic framework for understanding the type of objections that have been raised see Weatherill, 'Why Object to the Harmonization of Private Law by the EC?', 12 *Euro Rev Private Law* (2004) 633.

[6] E.g. Wagner, 'The Economics of Harmonization: the Case of Contract Law', 39 *CML Rev* (2002) 995; Van den Bergh, 'Forced Harmonization of Contract Law in Europe: Not to be Continued', in S. Grundmann and J. Stuyck (eds), *An Academic Green Paper on European Contract Law* (2002); Faure, 'Toward a Harmonized Tort Law in Europe? An Economic Perspective', 8 *MJ* (2001) 339. For a more extended exploration, see E.-M. Kieninger, *Wettbewerb der Privatrechtsordnungen im Europäischen Binnenmarkt—Studien zur Privatrechtskoordinierung in der Europäischen Union auf den Gebieten des Gesellschafts- und Vertragsrechts* (2002).

[7] A rich mix of disagreement may be found in e.g. Legrand, 'European Legal Systems are not Converging', 45 *ICLQ* (1996) 52; Hage, 'Legal Reasoning and Legal Integration', 10 *MJ* (2003) 67; Zeno-Zencovich, 'The European Civil Code, European Legal Traditions and Neo-positivism', 6 *Euro Rev Private Law* (1998) 349; van Gerven, 'Harmonization of Private Law: Do We Need It?', 41 *CML Rev* (2004) 505; Truilhé-Marengo, 'Towards a European Law of Contracts', 10 *ELJ* (2004) 463; Collins, 'European Private Law and the Cultural Identity of States', 3 *Euro Rev Private Law* (1995) 353; Paasilehto, 'Legal Cultural Obstacles to the Harmonisation of European Private Law', in V. Heiskanen and K. Kulovesi (eds), *Function and Future of European Law* (1999); Wilhelmsson, 'Private Law in the EU: Harmonized or Fragmented Europeanisation?', 11 *Euro Rev Private Law* (2002) 77.

- The 'Product Liability Directive': Council Directive 85/374 on the approximation of the laws, regulations and administrative provisions of the Member States concerning liability for defective products; Directive 99/34 of the Parliament and the Council amending Council Directive 85/374 on the approximation of the laws, regulations and administrative provisions of the Member States concerning liability for defective products.[8]
- Council Directive 86/653 on the co-ordination of the laws of the Member States relating to self-employed commercial agents.[9]
- The 'Doorstep Selling Directive': Council Directive 85/577 to protect the consumer in respect of contracts negotiated away from business premises.[10]
- Council Directive 87/102 for the approximation of the laws, regulations and administrative provision of the Member States concerning consumer credit; Council Directive 90/88 amending Directive 87/102; Directive 98/7 of the Parliament and the Council amending Directive 87/102.[11]
- Council Directive 90/314 on package travel, package holidays and package tours.[12]
- Council Directive 93/13 on unfair terms in consumer contracts.[13]
- Directive 94/47 of the Parliament and Council on the protection of purchasers in respect of certain aspects of contracts relating to the purchase of the right to use immovable properties on a timeshare basis.[14]
- Directive 97/7 of the Parliament and Council on the protection of consumers in respect of distance contracts.[15]
- Directive 99/44 of the Parliament and Council on certain aspects of the sale of consumer goods and associated guarantees.[16]
- Directive on 'electronic commerce': Directive 2000/31 of the Parliament and Council on certain legal aspects of information society services, in particular electronic commerce, in the Internal Market.[17]
- Directive 2000/35 of the Parliament and Council on combating late payment in commercial transactions.[18]
- Directive 2002/65 of the Parliament and the Council concerning the distance marketing of consumer financial services (and amending Council Directive 90/619 and Directives 97/7 and 98/27).[19]

---

[8] OJ 1985 L 10/29, OJ 1999 L 141/20.
[9] OJ 1986 L 382/17.
[10] OJ 1985 L 372/31.
[11] OJ 1987 L 42/48, OJ 1990 L 61/14, OJ 1998 L 101/17.
[12] OJ 1990 L 158/59.
[13] OJ 1993 L 95/29.
[14] OJ 1994 L 280/83.
[15] OJ 1997 L 144/19.
[16] OJ 1999 L 171/12.
[17] OJ 2000 L 178/1.
[18] OJ 2000 L 200/35.
[19] OJ 2002 L 271/16.

It can be seen that most of the older measures were adopted by the Council alone, in accordance with the applicable legislative procedure prior to the entry into force of the Single European Act in 1987. More recent measures have been adopted under (what is now) the Article 251 'co-decision' procedure, which has become the normal method of legislating in the EC and which involves both Parliament and Council. But all are measures of harmonization. All depict harmonization of laws in the relevant areas as necessary to further the cause of market integration in Europe. And insofar as the relevant areas subjected to the discipline of harmonization are private law, then the consequence is a species of European private law. The majority of the measures on the list involve consumer contract law, but some concern commercial contract law; and the 'Product Liability' Directive, at the top of the list, is not about contract law at all. Put together, these measures of legislative harmonization represent a sizeable body of influence exerted by the EC legislature in the sphere of private law.

The matter does not end with the legislature. The European Court, allowed the opportunity to interpret measures of harmonization, has on occasion chosen to do so in a strikingly expansive, even intrusive, manner. A helpful illustration is provided by *Océano Grupo Editorial SA* v *Rocio Murciano Quintero*.[20] This concerns the interpretation of Directive 93/13, which harmonizes laws controlling the use of unfair terms in consumer contracts. The European Court was asked by a Spanish court if a national court is empowered to consider of its own motion whether a term is unfair within the meaning of Directive 93/13 on unfair terms in consumer contracts. The Court took the view that effective protection of the consumer may be attained only if the national court acknowledges that it has such a power to evaluate terms of this kind of its own motion. The Court was accordingly prepared to use the harmonization Directive as a springboard to interpret rules of civil procedure relevant to the vindication of consumer rights.[21] Subsequently, in *Freiburger Kommunalbauten* v *Hofstetter*,[22] the Court made clear its readiness to interpret 'general criteria' found in a harmonization Directive. And in *Simone Leitner*[23] the Court ruled that Directive 90/314 on package travel implicitly recognizes the existence of a right to compensation for non-material damage. The Directive did not make this explicit. However, the Court observed that the Directive's purpose of eliminating disparities between national laws in the area would be advanced by bringing rules governing compensation for non-material damage within its scope; and it added that compensation for non-material damage arising from the loss of enjoyment of a holiday is of particular importance to consumers.[24] The general message holds

---

[20] Cases C-240 to C-244/98, [2000] ECR I-4941.

[21] See similarly Case C-473/00, *Cofidis SA* [2002] ECR I-10875.

[22] Case C-237/02, judgment of 1 April 2004.

[23] Case C-168/00, [2002] ECR I-2631.

[24] For a critical account of the Court's sense of adventure, see annotation of the case by Roth, 40 *CML Rev* (2003) 937.

that the programme of legislative harmonization may be broad in its scope, and may be broadened yet further by judicial interpretation.[25]

4. HARMONIZATION—LAW, PRACTICE AND MYTH

The constitutional background needs to be spelled out more fully. In the growth of the harmonization programme there is a gap between what was said by the legislature and what was really intended.

A. Integration and Re-regulation

The original Treaty of Rome included a provision which provided:

. . . for the approximation of such provisions laid down by law, regulation or administrative action in member states as directly affect the establishment or functioning of the common market.

This was Article 100 EEC, and it is today Article 94 EC (in consequence of the Amsterdam Treaty's re-numbering of the EC Treaty effective from 1999). This legislative power is subject to a requirement of unanimity in the Council. It was used during the 1970s and early part of the 1980s as the basis for a number of the above-mentioned pieces of secondary legislation that harmonized national laws.

After the entry into force of the Single European Act (SEA) in 1987, a new provision inserted by the SEA began to be used to harmonize national laws in the field of, *inter alia*, consumer contract law. This was Article 100a, and it is today (after amendment) Article 95. It provides for the adoption of measures:

. . . for the approximation of the provisions laid down by law, regulation or administrative action in member states which have as their object the establishing and functioning of the internal market.

Nothing has turned on the difference between a common market (Article 94) and an internal market (Article 95), and in practice Article 95 (ex 100a) has largely superseded Article 94 (ex 100) as an instrument of harmonization. Harmonization

---

[25] An attempt to develop a more systematic account of when the Court is and should be ready to provide detailed interpretation is provided by Gerstenberg, 'Private Law and the New European Constitutional Settlement', *ELJ* (2004) 766, at 782–6. For discussion of where the process may or may not lead, see Teubner, 'Legal Irritants: Good Faith in British Law or How Unifying Law Ends Up in New Divergences', 61 *MLR* (1998) 11; Berger, 'Harmonization of European Contract Law: the Influence of Comparative Law', 50 *ICLQ* (2001) 877; Whittaker, 'Unfair Contract Terms, Public Services and the Construction of a European Conception of Contract', 116 *LQR* (2001) 95; Van Hoecke, 'Deep Level Comparative Law', *EUI Working Paper Law No. 2002/13* (Florence, 2002); Pozzo, 'Harmonization of European Contract Law and the Need of Creating a Common Terminology', 11 *Euro Rev Private Law* (2003) 754.

legislation adopted pursuant to Article 95 (ex 100a) requires only a 'qualified majority vote' (QMV) among the Member States acting in Council, coupled to the support of the Parliament. Article 95 (ex 100a) is the legal base of the above-mentioned harmonization measures made after 1 July 1987.

The Directives harmonize national laws in the name of promoting the establishment or functioning of the common or internal market, but—insofar as the national measures subjected to the discipline of harmonization fall within the field of private law—they also contribute to the shaping of a European private law of sorts. This 'dual function' is central to the character of the programme of harmonization. Variation between national laws is typically portrayed as an impediment to the smooth functioning of the market, prompting a need for harmonization at Community level: 'common rules for a common market'. The EC unavoidably assumes the function of setting its own—common—rules. Community laws come into existence in order to integrate the market, but their incidental effect is additionally to regulate it—or more pertinently to 're-regulate' it, in the sense that the Community is not acting as a *de novo* regulator but rather is responding to the pre-existing diverse regulatory choices among the Member States. So harmonization sets common rules for the European market but it also involves a choice of the appropriate common standard of (re-)regulatory protection.

The purpose of measures of legislative harmonization is not simply to prise open markets but also to serve the interests of parties intended to enjoy regulatory protection, and this has been granted vivid confirmation by the Court. It has accepted that harmonization Directives are apt to produce *rights* held by those envisaged as enjoying regulatory protection—consumers, most prominently—in the event that a Member State fails to put in place the envisaged regime.[26] The Court has also nourished the capacity of measures of legislative harmonization to promote the consumer interest by ruling that derogations from Community rules for the protection of consumers must be interpreted strictly.[27] The Treaty superstructure itself confirms that harmonization is not a technical exercise in market-making. It is not simply a question of creating common rules. The *quality* of the 're-regulatory' environment established at EC level is constitutionally relevant, as is made clear by the associations between market integration and regulatory protection upon which provisions such as Articles 95(3), 6 and 153(2) EC insist.[28] This has generated interest in making sense of the thematic connections that bind together the EC's

---

[26] E.g. Case C-91/92, *Paola Faccini Dori* [1994] ECR I-3325; Cases C-178/94 *et al*, *Dillenkofer* [1996] ECR I-4845.

[27] Case C-203/99, *Veedfald* [2001] ECR I-3569, para. 15; Case C-481/99, *Heininger* [2001] ECR I-9945.

[28] See also Art. 38 EU Charter. This is non-binding, although this will change if the Treaty establishing a Constitution enters into force (*infra*), when it will become Art. II-98. This will not, however, firm up the admittedly aspirational character which weakens its likely legal force: *cf.* Kiss, 'Environmental and Consumer Protection', Chap. 10 in S. Peers and A. Ward (eds), *The EU Charter of Fundamental Rights: Politics, Law and Policy* (2004).

interventions into private law. Harmonization 'spills over' to provoke new academic sub-disciplines, as commentators have debated the weight and merits of principles and techniques that pervade the *acquis* such as information disclosure, party autonomy and inquiry into substantive unfairness.[29] The phenomenon extends far beyond private law, for the harmonization programme acts as an engine driving the 'Europeanization' of many policy sectors that are in explicit terms subject to only a limited interventionist competence granted by the EC Treaty.[30] The general lesson is that a programme presented as an exercise in securing market freedom inevitably involves a sustained commitment to rule-making.[31] Integration is tied to re-regulation.

B. The Secret Life of Harmonization

But it is time to look below the surface. There are plenty of harmonization measures that are obviously based on the perception that legislative diversity damaged integration, and that, in matters such as (for example) specifications for machine parts, safety of pharmaceuticals and composition of chemicals, a common market did indeed require common rules. But does this logic extend to harmonization of rules governing consumer credit? Or unfair terms in consumer contracts? Or consumer sales? The allegation is that several Directives have been adopted pursuant to the Treaty-conferred competence to harmonize with no serious expectation that they would advance the process of market integration. Is the legislative *acquis*

---

[29] E.g.—and by no means adopting the same outlook—Micklitz, 'Principles of Social Justice in European Private Law', 19 *YEL* (1999–2000) 167; Weatherill, 'Consumer Policy', in P. Craig and G. de Búrca (eds), *The Evolution of EU Law* (1999); Stuyck, 'European Consumer Law after the Treaty of Amsterdam: Consumer Policy in or beyond the Internal Market?', 37 *CML* Rev (2000) 367; Howells and Wilhelmsson, 'EC Consumer Law: Has It Come of Age?', 28 *EL Rev* (2003) 370; N. Reich and H.-W. Micklitz, *Europäisches Verbraucherrecht* (2003); R. Schulze and G. Ajani (eds), *Gemeinsame Prinzipen des Europäisches Privatrechts* (2003); S. Grundmann, W. Kerber, and S. Weatherill, *Party Autonomy and the Role of Information in the Internal Market* (2001); Grundmann, 'The Structure of European Contract Law', 9 *Euro Rev Private Law* (2001) 505; Grundmann, 'Information, Party Autonomy and Economic Agents in European Contract Law', 39 *CML Rev* (2002) 269; Micklitz, 'De la Nécessité d'une Nouvelle Conception pour le Développement du Droit de la Consommation dans la Communauté Européenne', in J. Calais-Auloy (ed.), *Liber amicorum Jean Calais-Auloy, Études de droit de la consummation* (2004); Special Issue, 'The Protection of the Weak Party in a Harmonised European Contract Law', 27/3 *JCP* (2004) (ed. Weatherill); H. Rösler, *Europäisches Konsumentenvertragsrecht* (2004); K. Riesenhuber, *Europäisches Vertragsrecht* (2003); Sixto A. Sánchez Lorenzo, *Derecho Privado Europeo* (2002).

[30] E.g. on environmental law see J. Scott, *EC Environmental Law* (1998); J. Jans, *European Environmental Law* (2000), esp. Chs. I and III; on labour market regulation and social policy more generally see J. Kenner, *EU Employment Law: From Rome to Amsterdam and Beyond* (2003); T. Hervey, *European Social Law and Policy* (1998); C. Barnard, *EC Employment Law* (2000); on family law, see Caracciolo di Torella and Masselot, 'Under Construction: EU Family Law', 29 *EL Rev* (2004) 32; on health care law, see Hervey, 'Mapping the Contours of European Union Health Care and Policy', 8 *Euro Public Law* (2002) 69.

[31] M. Egan, *Constructing a European Market* (2001).

affecting private law an example of the EC legislature surreptitiously 'self-authorizing' an extension of its own competence, contrary to the fundamental principle of attribution found in Article 5(1) EC?

The background context to the harmonization programme affecting private law is embedded in the sphere of consumer policy. It is dominated by the political commitment to the establishment of a consumer protection programme for the EC. At the 'Paris Summit' in October 1972 the Member States expressed a general desire to broaden the appeal of the Community beyond economic affairs and into the social sphere. As one element in this policy, the heads of State and government called for the submission of a programme of consumer protection policy. The soft law initiative that emerged from this new political atmosphere was the first in a lengthy series which continues today. It was the Council Resolution of 14 April 1975 on a preliminary programme of the European Economic Community for a consumer protection and information policy.[32] This Resolution constituted the formal inauguration of a consumer protection and information policy for the Community. The Annex, a 'Preliminary Programme of the European Economic Community for a Consumer Protection and Information Policy', provides a relatively extended assertion of the place of the consumer interest in Community law. Point 3 encapsulates consumer interests in a statement of five basic rights:

(a) the right to protection of health and safety;
(b) the right to protection of economic interests;
(c) the right of redress;
(d) the right to information and education; and
(e) the right of representation (the right to be heard).

This is doubtless politically important. But the Treaty did not reflect this generously broad conception of the EC's mission. Consumer protection was not a legislative competence explicitly granted to the EC by its Treaty, and at the time there was no appetite for amending the Treaty. The gap between, on the one hand, the visible political commitment to shape a consumer policy for the EC and, on the other, the deficient constitutional foundation provided by the Treaty was to be bridged by an ambitious interpretation of the scope of existing legislative competences. Point 4 of the 1975 Resolution provided an immediate reminder that, in conformity with the formal terms of the EC Treaty as they stood at the time, there is no consumer protection policy which exists independently of other Community policies. Consumer policy will be amplified '. . . by action under specific Community policies such as the economic, common agricultural, social, environment, transport and energy policies as well as by the approximation of laws, all of which affect the consumer's position . . .' Here, then, the principle of attributed competence now contained in Article 5(1) EC came to the fore in the admission that consumer policy could not be treated in itself as falling within the Community's legislative gift. But

[32] OJ 1975 C 92/1.

the constitutional sensitivities of the matter detained few observers.[33] The stream of soft law instruments asserting the importance of an EC consumer policy continued to flow. The 1975 Resolution on the preliminary programme was followed in 1981 by the (similarly motivated) Council Resolution of 19 May 1981 on a second programme of the European Economic Community for a consumer protection and information policy.[34] The third Council Resolution, of 23 June 1986, concerning the future orientation of the policy of the European Economic Community for the protection and promotion of consumer interests was expressed within the context of internal market policy[35] and in December 1986, the Council adopted a Resolution on the integration of consumer policy in the other common policies.[36] The pattern for what would later become the Consumer Protection Title inserted into the Treaty by the Maastricht Treaty was being set. The 'rights' discourse is today reflected in Article 153(1) and the integration principle is embedded in Article 153(2).

These soft law Resolutions issued during the 1970s and 1980s were accompanied by an increasingly solid block of legislative material. These were harmonization Directives. They largely affected consumer contract law, and they provided the flagship of the European private law fleet. The key point of current relevance is that some of the legislative *acquis* affecting private law was *presented* as a contribution to improving the process of economic integration in order to cloak the measures with constitutional respectability, while in political reality it was a reflection of the eagerness to shape an EC consumer policy, affecting *inter alia* private law, particularly contract law.

One of the more blatant examples of this type of unconvincing, even 'impure', harmonization is provided by Directive 85/577 on 'doorstep selling'.[37] It was based on Article 100 EC (now Article 94). The Preamble states that the practice of doorstep selling is the subject of different rules in different Member States. This is perfectly true. The Preamble then proceeds to declare that 'any disparity between such legislation may directly affect the functioning of the common market'. This is rather less obviously true, and the claim is not supported by any evidence. The Directive then proceeds to establish a European-level regulation of the phenomenon by requiring *inter alia* that the consumer be permitted a minimum seven-day cooling-off period within which to withdraw from an agreed transaction. The use of the phrase 'any disparity between such legislation may directly affect the functioning of the common market' in the Directive's Preamble reflects the need to pay respect to

---

[33] Among the few examples on record of anxiety at the time, see the House of Lords Select Committee on the European Communities (22nd Report, 1977–78); Close 'The Legal Basis for the Consumer Protection Programme of the EEC and Priorities for Action', 8 *EL Rev* (1983) 221.

[34] OJ 1981 C 133/1.

[35] OJ 1986 C 167/1.

[36] OJ 1987 C 3/1.

[37] OJ 1985 L 372/31, *supra* note 10.

the fundamental constitutional principle found in Article 5(1) EC that the Community can act only where its Treaty equips it with competence. The language of (what was) Article 100 is borrowed to invest the Doorstep Selling Directive with constitutional respectability. But in fact the political environment demonstrates the ease with which the principle of attributed competence may be subverted. The Preamble also makes reference to Council Resolutions of 1975 and 1981 on consumer protection and information policy[38] and observes that consumers may be 'unprepared' in negotiations for contracts away from business premises. This gives the political game away. It was plain that the Member States, as explained, were committed to developing a richer texture to EC policy-making, beyond mere trade integration in the narrow sense. In the absence at the time of any formal Treaty revision giving effect to these wider aspirations by extending the list of available legislative competences, harmonization was used as the chosen route. At this time, prior to the entry into force of the Single European Act, the Member States were required to act unanimously to adopt such legislation. Given unanimity in Council, as was the case for measures such as that governing 'doorstep selling', constitutional niceties tended to sink from view.

The governments of the Member States were fully aware and entirely content with the tendencies to use the functionally broad Treaty competence governing harmonization to invade wider areas of (apparently) national competence, including consumer contract law, but touching other areas too.[39] This was not 'Brussels' imposing unwelcome new rules, although it was often deftly and mendaciously presented as such, this was political elites in the Member States participating cheerfully in exploitation of the EC's lawmaking system as a source of constitutionally questionable intervention. What is at stake here is what has been labelled 'competence creep'.[40]

It strays close to an expansion in the EC's competence achieved not by Treaty revision, but by over-ambition practised by the EC's legislative institutions. This is in principle entirely impermissible, for it subverts the constitutional constraint of attributed competence, now found in Article 5(1) EC, and in doing so it tends to impoverish democratic structures within Member State political life. But, given unanimity in Council, this (to put it politely) 'constitutionally adventurous' rationale for harmonization has pumped a number of measures relating to private law through the EC's legislative process.

---

[38] *Supra* notes 32, 34.

[39] *Cf.* the literature cited *supra* note 30.

[40] The literature is vast and, in parts, characterized by disagreement, or at least different points of emphasis. *Cf.* e.g. Weiler, 'The Transformation of Europe', 100 *Yale LJ* (1991) 2403; Pollack, 'Creeping Competence: The Expanding Agenda of the European Community', 14 *J Public Policy* (1994) 95; A. Moravscik, *The Choice for Europe* (1999); H. Wallace and W. Wallace, *Policy-Making in the European Union* (2000); A. Stone Sweet, W. Sandholtz, and N. Fligstein (eds), *The Institutionalisation of Europe* (2001); Special Issue, 'Dynamics of Formal and Informal Institutional Change in the EU', 10 *J European Public Policy* (2003, Number 6).

This is *not* to suggest that the whole programme of harmonization is lacking in purpose or incapable of intellectual systematization. Indeed, its peculiar evolution demands that attention be paid to teasing out its expectations and influence, and academics have cheerfully taken on that task.[41] However, it was inevitable that this 'creeping centralization' would attract discontent, especially as it became ever more visible to surprised national private lawyers. Indeed if principles such as information disclosure, party autonomy and, even more remarkable, inquiry into substantive unfairness are identified as embedded in European private law, they become imbued with a constitutionalized force,[42] which adds a huge extra dimension to the debate about the importance of achieving a satisfactory balance between the EC's capacity for dynamic growth and its perceived tendency to undermine the principle of attributed competence contained in Article 5(1) EC through inadequately justified legislative centralization.

5. THE RISE OF 'COMPETENCE SENSITIVITY'

There is much to criticize in the intransparent and ill-defined pattern of competence allocation made by the EC Treaty.[43] Nevertheless the scars of 'competence sensitivity' have been visible in the Treaty for some time. For example, EC action in the fields of culture and public health is defined by Articles 151 and 152 EC respectively as supplementary to State action. Harmonization of laws pursuant to these provisions is explicitly excluded. Article 153(3)(b) on consumer protection, a Maastricht innovation, is similarly tightly confined. Articles 176, 137 and 153 EC, governing competence to legislate in the fields of environmental protection, social policy and consumer protection respectively, stipulate that national measures that are stricter than the agreed Community standard are permitted. The Member States added new competences to the EC's list in the Single European Act and at Maastricht but they carefully calculated the textual limits they would impose. 'Subsidiarity', of course is a label capturing a general mood of acute anxiety concerning the need to think

---

[41] See the sources at *supra* note 29.

[42] *Cf.* Joerges, 'European Challenges to Private Law: on False Dichotomies, True Conflicts and the Need for a Constitutional Perspective', 18 *Legal Studies* (1998) 146; Study Group on Social Justice in European Private Law, 'Social Justice in European Contract Law: a Manifesto', 10 *ELJ* (2004) 653.

[43] Dashwood, 'The Relationship between the Member States and the European Union/European Community', 41 *CML Rev* (2004) 355; Von Bogdandy and Bast, 'The European Union's Vertical Order of Competences: the Current Law and Proposals for its Reform', 39 *CML Rev* (2002) 227; De Búrca and de Witte, 'The Delimitation of Powers between the EU and its Member States', Chap. 12 in A. Arnull and D. Wincott (eds), *Accountability and Legitimacy in the European Union* (2002); Mayer, 'Die Drei Dimensionen der Europäischen Kompetenzdebatte', WHI-Paper 2/02 (Walter Hallstein Institut, available via www.whi-berlin.de); Michel, 'Le Défi de la Repartition des Compétences', 38 *CDE* (2003) 17; Hanf and Baumé, 'Vers une Clarification de la Répartition des Compétences entre l'Union et ses Etats Membres?', 38 *CDE* (2003) 135.

more closely about just *why* the EC should act rather than leaving a matter to be handled at national level, although subsidiarity's operational utility in guiding decisions in particular cases *via* its specifically legal manifestation in Article 5(2) EC is unimpressive.

'Competence sensitivity' is reflected in Article 95 EC by the managed derogation procedure found in Articles 95(4) *et seq*[44] and by the small number of functional exceptions on which Article 95(2) insists. But Article 95(1) EC remains remarkably broad in scope, and it allows a generous legislative mandate to the Council (acting by qualified majority voting (QMV)) allied with the Parliament. How could one argue effectively against its use? There is, as Koen Lenaerts famously remarked, 'no nucleus of sovereignty that the Member States can invoke, as such, against the Community'.[45]

The lurking anxiety that harmonization had, in short, gone too far—too far as a basis for an assertion of centralizing Community competence and too far as an incursion into national private law—was always likely eventually to force its way to the surface once the voting rule in Council was altered from unanimity to QMV. This occurred in 1987 on the entry into force of the Single European Act. Thereafter a Member State opposed to a proposed measure of harmonization could not simply veto it. It could vote against it but, if in a sufficiently small minority in Council, the Member State could find itself outvoted and bound by legislation adopted pursuant to Article 95 (ex 100a) to which it was opposed.

The temptation to proceed to the Court and argue that the legislation was invalid as an improper exercise of the competence to harmonize laws is obvious. It took time for such litigation to occur, not least because it remains the case that most measures are supported by unanimity in Council even where this is not formally required. But in 2000 the Court was provided with the opportunity to clarify its view of the scope of legislative harmonization granted by the Treaty in the *Tobacco Advertising* judgment. This judgment is of the highest significance to understanding the permissible reach of Article 95 as a vehicle for advancing *inter alia* private lawmaking under the cover of the harmonization programme. It is of central importance that the Court asserted a constitutional reading of the limits of the scope of the Treaty-conferred competence to harmonize laws, notwithstanding past practice that had placed the matter in the gift of the EC's political institutions, most significantly a unanimity-driven Council.

6. HARMONIZATION AND CONSTITUTIONAL SENSITIVITY

In *Tobacco Advertising* (more properly, *Germany* v *Parliament and Council*[46]) the Court was invited to annul Directive 98/43 on the advertising of tobacco products.

---

[44] See for analysis De Sadeleer, 'Procedures for Derogations from the Principle of Approximation of Laws under Article 95 EC', 40 *CML Rev* (2003) 889.

[45] Lenaerts, 'Constitutionalism and the Many Faces of Federalism', 38 *AJCL* (1990) 205, 220.

[46] Case C-376/98, [2000] ECR I-8419.

The measure had been adopted as a measure of harmonization directed at integrating goods and services markets and was based on Articles 100a, 57(2) and 66 (now 95, 47(2) and 55). Germany had opposed the measure but had been outvoted in Council. Here, then, was the bite of QMV. But Germany persuaded the Court to annul the Directive. So Germany, having lost the political debate, was rescued by resort to arguments based on the constitutional limits imposed on the EC.[47]

The Court observed that:

> the measures referred to in Article 100a(1) [now Article 95(1) EC] of the Treaty are intended to improve the conditions for the establishment and functioning of the internal market. To construe that article as meaning that it vests in the Community legislature a general power to regulate the internal market would not only be contrary to the express wording of the provisions cited above [Articles 3c and 7a EC, now 3(1)(c) and 14 respectively] but would also be incompatible with the principle embodied in Article 3b of the EC Treaty [now Article 5 EC] that the powers of the Community are limited to those specifically conferred on it.[48]

The Treaty confers no competence to harmonize *per se*: the competence is more limited than that and is, in short, tied to the process of market-building. Accordingly, 'curing' legal diversity *per se* will evidently not do as an adequate basis for intervention founded on Article 95 EC. The EC measure must work harder in the service of market integration. This is not new, as a matter of principle. What is new is the opportunity taken by the Court to explore precisely where the limits of legislative harmonization might lie. The essence of the test established by the Court in this case and the small number that have followed in its wake[49] holds that a measure of harmonization must actually contribute to eliminating obstacles to the free movement of goods or to the freedom to provide services, or to removing appreciable distortions of competition.

If a measure fails to cross this threshold, it must seek its legal basis elsewhere in the Treaty. The 'Tobacco Advertising' Directive was not regarded as a valid exercise of the competence to harmonize laws because much of its content was directed at the suppression of advertising on products such as ashtrays, billboards and parasols for use in street cafés, where the contribution to the establishment and functioning of an internal market was minimal. The implication of the judgment was that the measure was in truth concerned with public health protection, and that even though the EC Treaty grants a competence in that field, the relevant provision (i.e. Article

---

[47] Usher, 'Annotation', 38 *CML Rev* (2001) 1519; Hervey, 'Community and National Competence in Health after Tobacco Advertising', 38 *CML Rev* (2001) 1421; Khanna, 'The Defeat of the European Tobacco Advertising Directive: a Blow for Health', 20 *YEL* (2001) 113; Tridimas and Tridimas, 'The European Court of Justice and the Annulment of the Tobacco Advertisement Directive', 14 *Euro J Law & Economics* (2002) 171.

[48] Para. 83; see also paras. 106–107.

[49] Case C-377/98, *Netherlands* v *Council* [2001] ECR I-7079; Case C-491/01, *R* v *Secretary of State*, ex parte *BAT and Imperial Tobacco* [2002] ECR I-11543; Cases C-465/00 *et al.*, *Rechnungshof* v *Osterrreichischer Rundfunk et al.* [2003] ECR I-4989.

152 EC) expressly excludes harmonization of laws. It would not have been constitutionally sturdy enough to support this Directive.

National laws may be the subject of a valid measure of harmonization, thereby generating a 're-regulatory' rule of EC law, provided that the measure of harmonization actually contributes to eliminating obstacles to the free movement of goods or to the freedom to provide services, or to removing appreciable distortions of competition. If that threshold is not crossed, the EC's competence to act in the field must be sought elsewhere. For consumer law, for example, one may look to Article 153(3)(b), a Maastricht innovation, but that stretches only to 'measures which support, supplement and monitor the policy pursued by the Member States'. This falls short of a competence to set harmonized rules. Private law may be affected by measures in the field of judicial co-operation in civil matters adopted pursuant to Article 65 EC—but here too an explicit linkage to the proper functioning of the internal market is asserted by the Treaty provision. 'Competence sensitivity' abounds.

It is fundamentally important to appreciate that in the *Tobacco Advertising* judgment the Court does *not* deny that public health policy and concern for consumer protection may legitimately inform the shaping of the harmonization programme. Quite the reverse. The Court insists that such concerns form a constituent part of the Community's other policies, including market-making pursued in the name of harmonization.[50] This follows from the directions in favour of policy integration found in Articles 95(3), 152(1) and 153(2) EC. This means *inter alia* that in principle the Community is able, by harmonization, to adopt a re-regulatory standard that restricts or even forbids particular forms of trading practice throughout the territory of the EU.[51] The Court's point is that the threshold of a required sufficient contribution to the improvement of the conditions for the establishment and functioning of the internal market must be crossed *before* the competence to harmonize exists and *before* the values of *inter alia* a high level of consumer protection may—and must—play their part in shaping the content of the harmonized regime.

As a general observation *Tobacco Advertising* injects a shadow of 'competence anxiety' into exploration of the scope of the harmonization programme. Harmonization has become a more contested process.[52] In fact, *Tobacco Advertising* injects 'competence anxiety' into a number of sectors remote from the judgment's particular concern and it has already become a rich source of speculation about the constitutional validity of existing rules and proposed initiatives.[53]

---

[50] *Cf.* paras. 78, 88 of *Tobacco Advertising*, *supra* note 46; para. 62 of *Ex parte BAT*, *supra* note 49.

[51] *Cf.* paras. 98, 117 of *Tobacco Advertising*, *supra* note 46.

[52] Weatherill, 'Why Harmonise?', in P. Tridimas and P. Nebbia (eds), *European Union Law for the Twenty-First Century: Rethinking the New Legal Order* (2004), ii.

[53] E.g. Katsirea, 'Why the European Broadcasting Quota should be Abolished', 28 *EL Rev* (2003) 190; Moloney, 'New Frontiers in EC Capital Markets Law: From Market Construction to Market Regulation', 40 *CML Rev* (2003) 809.

The message of *Tobacco Advertising* is readily transplanted from harmonization affecting public health to harmonization affecting private law. Do all the older measures of harmonization concerning consumer contract law comply with the Court's test? Many were adopted at a time when sensitivity to the limits of the EC's attributed competence lay buried beneath the political force of unanimity in Council, and before the vocabulary which the Court now attaches to the definition of the limits of Article 95 had been concocted. Directive 85/577 on 'doorstep selling' was mentioned above.[54] It is plain that the threshold for reliance on the Treaty as a basis for harmonization which is envisaged by the Court in *Tobacco Advertising* is a good deal higher than that with which compliance is asserted in that measure. The historical explanation for this lack of congruence is readily explained. The key to the functional expansion of the harmonization programme lies in the political willingness of the Member States acting unanimously in Council to treat the relevant Treaty provisions as little short of the *carte blanche* to harmonize which, as a matter of constitutional principle, the Treaty never declared them to be. This is *not* to say that because the reasons given for the older generation of consumer protection Directives do not reach the rigorous standards demanded by the Court in *Tobacco Advertising* no adequate reasons—by the standards of October 2000—could be found. It is only to observe that previously no effort was made to provide a justification for compliance with the requirements of the Treaty provisions governing harmonization that was more sophisticated than mere repetition of the relevant words, simply because there was no political or, in practice, legal need for such conscientiousness. If the Member States in Council agreed, there was adopted legislation. If they did not, there was none. The task now is to rethink whether the older generation of Directives could satisfy the benchmark set by the Court in *Tobacco Advertising*, in part to determine whether the measures will stand if attacked, as may occur indirectly via proceedings before national courts even though direct actions before the European Court are, of course, time-barred. But the principal purpose for considering this issue lies in mapping the future.

7. THE TREATY ESTABLISHING A CONSTITUTION FOR EUROPE

One should note *en passant* that these tensions and sensitivities about competence were on the agenda in the recent debates about the re-shaping of the EU, but that they have emphatically not been 'solved' by the agreed new texts. These are enduring problems.

According to the Laeken Declaration, agreed by the Heads of State and Government of the Member States in December 2001:

. . . the important thing is to clarify, simplify and adjust the division of competence between the Union and the Member States . . . there is the question of how to ensure that a redefined

---

[54] *Supra* note 37.

division of competence does not lead to a creeping expansion of the competence of the Union . . . How are we to ensure at the same time that the European dynamic does not come to a halt? . . . Should Articles 95 and 308 of the Treaty be reviewed for this purpose in the light of the *acquis jurisprudentiel*?

This identified issue of 'competence sensitivity' concerning *inter alia* harmonization pursuant to Article 95 therefore found its way on to the agenda of the Convention on the 'Future of Europe' which held its inaugural session under the Chairmanship of Valery Giscard d'Estaing in February 2002. In fact, Articles 95 and 308 were the only explicitly listed Treaty provisions to be found in the whole of the Laeken Declaration.

Competence was therefore one of the issues that attracted a great deal of attention at the Convention.[55] There were voices raised at the Convention on the Future of Europe in favour of tighter drafting or even elimination of these provisions as motors of 'competence creep',[56] but the majority concluded this would unduly harm the EU's capacity for effective problem-solving. Both provisions were retained in the June 2003 draft agreed by the Convention and both are retained in the text signed in Rome in October 2004. The successor to Article 308 is Article I-18, and the successor to Article 95 is Article III-172. No attempt has been made to alter their wording in order to clarify the scope of the competence to harmonize laws. In fact, as a general observation the dominant concern at the Convention was to secure clarification of the key organizing principles governing competence, not a radical setting aside of the essence of the current arrangements.[57] Reorganization is largely confined to presentation, not substance. The governing provisions on *Union Competences* are contained in Title III of the final text and comprise Articles I-11 to I-18.[58]

Given this textual conservatism, the ambiguous status of the scope of the competence to harmonize will remain a hot topic for debate, unchanged by the

---

[55] For discussion of the progress of the debate see Weatherill, 'Competence Creep and Competence Control', 23 *YEL* (2004) 1–55.

[56] E.g. CONV 291/02, 24 Sept. 2002 (Heathcoat-Amory); WD 14–WG V 7, Aug. 2002 (Heathcoat-Amory, Working Group on Complementary Competencies).

[57] For inquiry specific to consumer policy see Micklitz, Reich, and Weatherill, 'EU Treaty Revision and Consumer Protection', 27 *JCP* (2004) 367.

[58] See among a vast and growing literature e.g. Craig, 'Competence: Clarity, Conferral, Containment and Consideration', 29 *EL Rev* (2004) 323; Wuermeling, 'Kalamität Kompetenz: Zur Abgrenzung der Zuständigkeiten in dem Verfassungsentwurf des EU-Konvents' [2004] *Europarecht* 216; Kokott and Rüth, 'The European Convention and its Draft Treaty Establishing a Constitution for Europe: Appropriate Answers to the Laeken Questions?', 40 *CML Rev* (2003) 1315; Dougan, 'The Convention's Draft Constitutional Treaty: a "Tidying-up Exercise" that Needs some Tidying Up of its Own', Federal Trust Paper 27/03, Aug. 2003 (available at www.fedtrust.co.uk); P. Steinberg, 'A Tentative Survey of the Innovations of the Constitution for Europe that Might Impact upon National Constitutional Law', WHI-Paper 14/03 (Walter Hallstein Institut, available at www.whi-berlin.de); Dashwood, 'The Relationship between the Member States and the European Union/European Community', 41 *CML Rev* (2004) 355; Davies, 'The Post-Laeken Division of Competences', 28 *EL Rev* (2003) 686.

entry into force of the Treaty establishing a Constitution for Europe (should that occur). However, the new Treaty is not wholly devoid of innovation. The institutional context has been adjusted. In 2001 Alain Lamassoure grumbled that 'No European institution is in reality willing to comply with the principle of subsidiarity'.[59] Against this background assumption that the existing institutional culture of the EU tends to mute criticism of expansive use of EU competences, an innovative Protocol allocates a formal status to national Parliaments in monitoring the exercise of competences. It is hoped that this will freshen the supervisory system. National Parliaments are empowered to issue a 'reasoned opinion' objecting to Commission legislative proposals, which forces formal Commission re-consideration provided at least one-third of national Parliaments are involved. However, this applies to legislative proposals only where the existence of competence is claimed under Article I-18(2) ('flexibility', the successor to Article 308) and where a violation of the subsidiarity principle is alleged. So this procedure does not cover use of the legal base authorizing harmonization except in so far as the issue of compliance with the subsidiarity principle is raised. It is submitted that this is regrettable.[60] At the very least the Laeken-inspired twinning of what are now Articles 95 and 308 EC, and will become Articles III-172 and I-18 EU, should have been retained. Both are prime suspects in the crime of 'competence creep,[61] and both should be monitored in the same way. However, as a general observation, the involvement of national Parliaments holds out the enticing prospect of a more lively debate about the relative virtues and vices of centralization and preservation of local autonomy in the context of the EU lawmaking process.

In reflecting on these tensions, the Opinion of Advocate General Fennelly in *Tobacco Advertising* is worth recalling.

The legal basis invoked by the Advertising Directive relates to the internal market. The Community's internal market competence is not limited, a priori, by any reserved domain of Member State power. It is a horizontal competence, whose exercise displaces national regulatory competence in the field addressed. Judicial review of the exercise of such a competence is a delicate and complex matter. On the one hand, unduly restrained judicial review might permit the Community institutions to enjoy, in effect, general or unlimited legislative power, contrary to the principle that the Community only enjoys those limited competences, however extensive, which have been conferred on it by the Treaty with a view to the attainment of specified objectives. This could permit the Community to encroach impermissibly on the powers of the Member States. On the other hand, the Court cannot, in principle, restrict the legitimate performance by the Community legislator of its task of removing barriers and distortions to trade in goods and services. It is the task of the Court,

---

[59] Alain Lamassoure MEP (and subsequently Conventioneer), in evidence given to the Scottish Parliament's European Committee on 30 October 2001 (available at: www.scottish.parliament.uk/ S1/official_report/cttee/europe-01/eu01-1202.htm#Col1211). (SP Paper 466, 'The Governance of the European Union and the Future of Europe', Session 1 (2001).)

[60] Weatherill, 'Better Competence Monitoring', 30 *EL Rev* (2005) 23–41.

[61] *Supra* note 40.

as the repository of the trust and confidence of the Community institutions, the Member States and the citizens of the Union, to perform this difficult function of upholding the constitutional division of powers between the Community and the Member States on the basis of objective criteria.

Controlling centralization is crucial in sustaining legitimacy. This is true of a great many political systems.[62] And, in the EU, the Treaty establishing a Constitution will make it no less important—and no easier.

8. EUROPEAN CONTRACT LAW—THE SHAPE OF THE DEBATE

The Commission's thinking on the issue of private law and the matter of 'competence sensitivity' is illuminatingly cautious.

In July 2001 the Commission issued a Communication on European Contract Law.[63] This was designed to generate a debate about the proper shape of an EC supplement to existing long-established systems of contract law in the Member States. Most of all, the 2001 Communication promised a willingness on the part of the Commission to reflect critically on the desirability of maintaining the hitherto fragmented, patchwork, model of lawmaking in the field at EC level.

Four options were floated (although they were not mutually exclusive). The first option was no EC action. This was based on the perception that the capacity of markets to achieve self-correction without legal intervention should not be underestimated. The second option centred on the promotion of the development of common contract law principles leading to greater convergence of national laws. There would be Commission support for research into comparative law. The third option was to improve the quality of legislation already in place. The current legislative *acquis* is marked by odd inconsistencies, such as the lack of uniform length fixed for 'cooling off' periods in the consumer Directives, and by a general absence of common definitions for key phrases. The fourth and most ambitious option was the adoption of new comprehensive legislation at EC level, taking the form of a European code that could either replace national law or co-exist with it as an optional instrument. This fourth option was advanced with great caution.

The 2001 Communication attracted a great deal of attention.[64] This was hardly surprising. The Commission's Communication signalled a clear readiness to engage with the question of how far the EC should reach into the field of private law.

---

[62] *Cf.* K. Nicolaidis and R. Howse (eds), *The Federal Vision: Legitimacy and Levels of Governance in the United States and the European Union* (2001).

[63] COM(2001)398.

[64] E.g. Grundmann and Stuyck, *supra* note 6; Staudenmayer, 'The Commission Communication on European Contract Law and the Future Prospects', 51 *ICLQ* (2002) 673; Special Issue of *European Review of Private Law* (2002), vol. 10/1; van Gerven, 'Codifying European Private Law? Yes, if . . . !', 27 *EL Rev* (2002) 156; Weatherill, 'The European Commission's Green Paper on European Contract Law: Context, Content and Constitutionality', 24 *JCP* (2001) 339.

It served as a focus for a debate that had been brewing for most of the decade since Directive 93/13 on unfair terms in consumer contracts had ignited a general concern among private lawyers to think more critically about the impact of the EC.

In February 2003 a follow-up emerged from the Commission. This was the Action Plan on a more coherent European Contract Law.[65] This revealed the outcome of the process of consultation. The Commission, having digested the feedback received from the 2001 Communication, had moved towards a preference for solutions that fall between the extremes of inaction and comprehensive intervention. The planned way forward was located in a combination of options 2 and 3 from the 2001 menu. The sector-specific approach to legislation is to be maintained, with additions proposed only where a need is convincingly demonstrated. In addition, a mix of regulatory and non-regulatory measures will be used to increase the coherence of the EC contract law *acquis*. The Action Plan refers to problems associated with the current absence of comprehensive definitions of abstract notions such as 'damage', which may lead to inconsistencies in application at national level. The Commission airs the idea of developing a 'common frame of reference' for European contract law principles. This would provide a pool of expertise on which jurists could draw in seeking to resolve difficulties and ambiguities in the interpretation of EC measures relevant to contract law. The Commission also proposes that the elaboration of EU-wide general contract law terms should be encouraged. A further (tentatively expressed) idea involves the drawing up of an optional instrument which parties may choose to use in order to facilitate the process of cross-border contracting. It would exist in parallel to national contract law systems. In the 2003 Action Plan the Commission is non-committal on a number of aspects of its optional instrument, including the type of legal instrument that would be used. The Commission invited further comment.

Like its 2001 predecessor, the 2003 Action Plan attracted a torrent of comment.[66] Again, this was scarcely surprising, as the debate about the future of European contract law was intensifying.

In October 2004 the Commission, having absorbed feedback on the 2003 Action Plan, issued a third document in the series. This was 'European Contract Law and the revision of the *acquis*: the way forward'.[67] It sets out the three measures suggested by the 2003 Action Plan and uses them to map the 'way forward' for European Contract Law. First, improving the quality of the EC contract law *acquis*. The central role of a proposed Common Frame of Reference (CFR) is confirmed. This is to be

---

[65] COM(2003)68, 12 February 2003.

[66] E.g. Karsten and Sinai, 'The Action Plan on European Contract Law: Perspectives for the Future', 26 *JCP* (2003) 159; Von Bar and Swann, 'Response to the Action Plan on European Contract Law', 11 *Euro Rev Private Law* (2003) 595; Staudenmayer, 'The Commission Action Plan on European Contract Law', 11 *Euro Rev Private Law* (2003) 11; Blair and Brent, 'A Single European Law of Contract?', 15 *Euro Bus Law Rev* (2004) 5.

[67] COM(2004)651 (available at http://europa.eu.int/comm/consumers/cons_int/safe_shop/ fair_bus_ pract/cont_law/communication2004_en.htm).

the subject of elaboration, with 2009 foreseen as a target date for its adoption. Expert researchers will be funded by the Commission and a supporting network of stakeholder experts on the Common Frame of Reference is to be assembled. A first meeting of Member State experts was held in early December 2004.[68] Stakeholders (drawn from among business, professional and consumer interests) had their first meeting two weeks later.[69] The intent is to sustain an intensive dialogue about the shape of the CFR, involving close attention to the practical value of the instrument. It is ultimately the Commission itself that will be responsible, following a further round of consultation, for choosing the eventual shape and content of the CFR. The Commission's stated perception in the October 2004 Communication is that the aim will be to identify 'best solutions', and account will be taken of national practice, the EC *acquis* and relevant international instruments, albeit that the CFR is to be fit for the EC's specific requirements (2004 Communication, p.11). It would set out common fundamental principles of contract law, including guidance on where exceptions could be required. Although it is envisaged as a non-binding instrument, the 'CFR' is plainly intended to become influential in the drafting and interpretation of legislative measures relevant to contract law.

As a second measure the promotion of the use of EU-wide standard terms and conditions is also promised, in line with the idea floated in the 2003 Action Plan. This would be driven by private parties. The Commission would not prepare the standard terms, but rather would merely seek to act as facilitator, for example by hosting a website on which information could be shared. The third measure, concerning the viability of an optional instrument in European contract law, co-existing with national law, is again the subject of discussion in the 2004 Communication, albeit of a brief and inconclusive nature. The Commission promises to continue to reflect on 'the opportuneness of such an instrument' (2004 Communication, p.8).

The October 2004 document also refers to perceived failings of a minimum model of rule-making (2004 Communication, p.3). This conforms to the general concerns currently expressed by the Commission about the fragmenting effect of a model of minimum rule-making and its intention to press for maximum harmonization in order to drive forward market integration more vigorously. The criticism that minimum harmonization deprives the market of a uniform legal pattern had already been aired in the 2003 Communication,[70] and recent consumer policy documents, including the Commission's Consumer Policy Programme for 2002–2006, reveal a growing preference for full or maximum harmonization, identifying this to be in both the commercial and the consumer interest.[71] It is by no means uncontroversial to contend that the consumer is best served by a model

[68] See http://europa.eu.int/comm/consumers/cons_int/safe_shop/fair_bus_pract/cont_law/wshop 122004_en.htm.

[69] See http://europa.eu.int/comm/consumers/cons_int/safe_shop/fair_bus_pract/cont_law/ cfr_15122004_en.htm.

[70] Paras. 24, 50, *supra* note 65.

[71] COM(02)208, OJ 2002 C 137/2.

which excludes the possibility of stricter rules being introduced to meet local concerns.[72] The 2004 Communication's confirmation that this policy preference is to be used in the re-thinking of European contract law seems likely to fuel this intensifying debate.

This, and in particular the CFR, is fascinating stuff. The CFR could be seen as an exercise in applied comparative law, designed to nourish a dynamic process of co-ordinated learning in Europe. The Commission's concern is conspicuously to move away from orthodox notions of legislative harmonization. But who wants it?[73] Will it truly generate 'a significantly higher degree of coherence in European contract law'?[74] How desirable is that, and what may be lost in the quest for coherence? Is there an emphasis on the contribution of the CFR to economic growth in preference to wider distributional concerns?[75]

And—the concern of this chapter—what of competence?

9. EUROPEAN CONTRACT LAW—QUESTIONS OF LEGAL COMPETENCE

The 'competence sensitivity' injected by *Tobacco Advertising* now pervades the Commission's thinking about the future of European contract law. In the documents issued in 2001, 2003 and 2004 the debate is not simply about what *should* be done by the EC in the field of contract law. It is also about what—constitutionally— *can* be done. But this dimension, although visible, is kept as an undercurrent.

A. 'Competence Sensitivity' Glimpsed

The constitutional dimension was addressed only briefly in the 2001 Communication, although it is plain that the shadow of the *Tobacco Advertising* ruling has been cast over the Commission's thinking. The Communication calls explicitly for information on whether diversity between national contract laws

---

[72] *Cf.* Wilhelmsson, 'The Abuse of the "Confident Consumer" as a Justification for EC Consumer Law', 27 *J Consumer Policy* (2004) 317; Micklitz, 'De la Nécessité d'une Nouvelle Conception pour le Développement du Droit de la Consommation dans la Communauté Européenne', in J. Calais-Auloy (ed.), *Liber amicorum Jean Calais-Auloy, Études de droit de la consommation* (2004); Dougan, 'Vive La Différence? Exploring the Legal Framework for Reflexive Harmonisation within the Single European Market', 1 *Annual of German and European Law* (2002) 113.

[73] *Cf.* Hesselink, 'The Politics of European Contract Law: Who Has an Interest in What Kind of Contract Law for Europe?', Chap. 12 in Grundmann and Stuyck, *supra* note 6; Hesselink, 'The Politics of a European Civil Code', 10 *ELJ* (2004) 675.

[74] Staudenmayer, 'The Place of Consumer Contract Law within the Process on European Contract Law', 27 *JCP* (2004) 269, at 277. See also, in vigorously positive vein, Karsten and Petri, 'Towards a Handbook on European Contract Law and Beyond', 28 *JCP* (2005) 31–51.

[75] *Cf.* Study Group on Social Justice in European Private Law, 'Social Justice in European Contract Law: a Manifesto', 10 *ELJ* (2004) 653.

'directly or indirectly obstructs the functioning of the internal market, and if so to what extent', with a view to considering appropriate action by the EC's institutions.[76] The Commission is actively seeking to uncover areas in which the internal market is malfunctioning because of deficiencies in the existing bloc of harmonized contract law. It aspires to a newly focused and empirically driven search for problems with the existing pattern[77] and, from the constitutional perspective, it wants hard—Court-proof—data to underpin any claim to competence under the Treaty to shape an EC contract law. The Communication addresses these issues predominantly in the language of subsidiarity (Article 5(2) EC) rather than attributed competence (Article 5(1) EC)—which is constitutionally a mistake[78]—but the general perception that justification for EC intervention must be found and carefully explained holds good. The mood is different from the relatively carefree attitude to competence taken in the consumer contract law Directives adopted in the 1980s. In part, this is because prior to the entry into force of the Single European Act in 1987 the voting rule in Council was unanimity, which meant that the presence of political consensus was the practical be all and end all of any decision on whether to legislate. Today, the rise of qualified majority voting in Council throws up the possibility of outvoted minorities converting political defeat in Council into a constitutional challenge before the Court—precisely as occurred in *Tobacco Advertising* itself. It is also to be hoped that the Commission's new painstaking concern to spell out exactly why it suspects an EC intervention may be required is part of a process of wider and more open-minded dialogue with affected parties, including the academic community.

The 2003 Action Plan's intention to improve the quality of the *acquis* ensured that the scope of the competence to harmonize laws pursuant to Article 95 remains a live issue.[79] Once again the constitutional dimension is not explored in depth in the Commission's Communication, but once again it is undoubtedly relevant and once again the Commission nods in its direction. The Action Plan insists on having unearthed 'implications for the internal market' arising from legal diversity, drawing a distinction for these purposes between the impact of mandatory and non-mandatory rules of national law.[80]

The October 2004 Communication, 'European Contract Law and the revision of the *acquis*: the way forward'[81] maintains the trend. The awkward questions of

[76] Paras. 23–33, 72 of the 2001 Communication, *supra* note 63.

[77] *Cf.* in this vein, Grundmann and Stuyck, *supra* note 6, including relevant contributions *inter alia* by Beale, 'Finding the Remaining Traps instead of Unifying Contract Law', Collins, 'Transaction Costs and Subsidiarity in European Contract Law', and Schwartze, 'Design for an Empirical Data Investigation into the Impact of Existing Law Harmonization'.

[78] Weatherill, *supra* note 58.

[79] Kenny, 'The 2003 Action Plan on European Contract Law: is the Commission Running Wild?', 28 *EL Rev* (2003) 538; Weatherill, 'European Contract Law: Taking The Heat out of Questions of Competence', 15 *Euro Business L Rev* (2004) 23.

[80] Part 3.2, paras. 25–51; also para. 14. The Annex to the Communication provides a detailed account of responses to the 2001 Communication received by the Commission.

[81] COM(2004)651, *supra* note 67.

competence lurk beneath the discussion and are visible to the trained eye, but the Commission studiously avoids aggressive engagement with the matter. Issues of competence are merely glimpsed. The goal of eliminating internal market barriers is explicitly associated with review of the consumer-related harmonization *acquis* (2004 Communication, p.3). The question is asked: is the level of harmonization sufficient to eliminate internal market barriers and distortions of competition for business and consumers? (2004 Communication, p.4). The debate is therefore to be conducted with respect for the 'problem of competence' but the Commission studiously places the question '*should* we do this?' much higher up the agenda than the question 'are we competent to do this?' Similarly the Communication ends with a very brief remark on the legal base of an 'optional instrument, which is illuminatingly open-ended. Articles 308, 95 and 65 EC are cited, but the Commission observes (2004 Communication, pp.21–22) that the question of legal base is tied to those concerning legal form, content and scope. Accordingly reflection on the question of legal base can be left to be addressed 'within a larger debate on the parameters of an optional instrument'.

B. Explaining the Commission's Caution

Why does the Commission prefer to set aside detailed inquiry into matters of competence in these communications?

The principal reason is a perfectly good reason: if the Commission had included an extended treatment of available legal competence in its 2001 Communication, it would doubtless have faced the protest that it was revealing a predilection for those options which most seriously engage the issue of competence, which are at the more ambitious end of the scale and involve the adoption of binding legislation. In order to avoid an imbalanced debate the Commission may have acted wisely in striving to maintain an open-minded focus on what is normatively desirable in the field of EC contract law. Only later will it address questions of competence in detail—if that proves even necessary. As the debate has developed it has become apparent that in at least some respects the increased attention given to 'softer' forms of activity in the 2003 and 2004 documents (such as the non-binding common frame of reference) has in any event served to take some of the heat out of the debate about available competence.[82] This positive attitude towards the virtue of soft law has close associations with the much broader agenda for change in how the EU operates mapped out by the Commission in its 2001 White Paper on Governance.[83] It is, moreover, doubtless difficult to attack a process involving experts and stakeholders that seems so scientifically respectable.

---

[82] Weatherill, *supra* note 79.

[83] *European Governance: a White Paper*, COM(2001)428. For a more general survey of departures from 'classic Community method' see Scott and Trubek, 'Mind the Gap: Law and New Approaches to Governance in the European Union', 8 *ELJ* (2002) 1.

Another reason for the Commission's preference not to engage deeply with questions of competence is that the answers are very far from being clear. It is easy to identify that the vocabulary used by the Court in *Tobacco Advertising* imperils the validity of some of the older measures harmonizing consumer contract law. But that is by no means the end of the story. At the time of their adoption, those Directives were not buttressed by constitutionally sophisticated analysis, because there was no practical need for such flourishes. Unanimity among the Member States was the guarantee of adoption. It does not follow that were these Directives to be re-considered today they could not be shown to meet the demands of Article 95; it follows only that their proponents would need to work harder. Moreover, it is far from settled just how the scope of Article 95 post-*Tobacco Advertising* should be defined. Legislative practice suggests that there is more to Article 95 than simply the elimination of obstacles to trade and the removal of appreciable distortions of competition. Directive 99/44 on certain aspects of the sale of consumer goods and associated guarantees, based on (what is now) Article 95 EC provides in its Preamble that:

Whereas the creation of a common set of minimum rules of consumer law, valid no matter where goods are purchased within the Community, will strengthen consumer confidence and enable consumers to make the most of the internal market . . .

This 'confidence-building' rationale for harmonization was foreshadowed in the Preamble to Directive 93/13 on unfair terms in consumer contracts. Underpinning this debate is the awkward question whether a market for Europe can adequately be made by eliminating perceived trade barriers or whether a more aggressive commitment to centralized regulation designed to tackle the uncertainties in the market consequent on trade liberalization is required. This is considered more fully below.

A third and final reason in favour of allowing the competence question to keep a low profile pending attention to substantive concerns arises because of the possibility of Treaty revision. When the Commission launched its inquiry into contract law in 2001 it was perfectly possible that Treaty revision would change the constitutional ground rules. There is a good case to be made in favour of setting to one side concerns regarding constitutional hurdles that might in any event prove temporary. However, as explained above, it is now apparent that Treaty revision will not change the rules, at least in the medium term.

10. OUTSTANDING AMBIGUITIES—WHAT MAKES A MARKET?

In 2001 the Commission stated that 'Ensuring consumers are confident in shopping across borders is as important for making the internal market work as is making it easier for businesses to sell across borders'.[84] In fact this confidence-building

---

[84] Commission report on the Action Plan for Consumer Policy of 1999–2001, COM(01)486, at 11.

perspective has been scattered across many policy documents in recent years.[85] In the Commission Communication of May 2003 entitled *Internal Market Strategy, Priorities 2003–2006* it is stated that:

Free movement of goods (and services) in the Internal Market is above all based on confidence. Confidence of businesses that they can sell their products on the basis of a clear and predictable regulatory framework. Confidence of Member States' administrations that the rules are respected in practice throughout the EU and that the competent authorities in other Member States will take appropriate action when this is not the case. And, of course, consumers' confidence in their rights and that the products they buy are safe and respect the environment . . .[86]

More significantly, this perspective is visible in legislative practice too. Regulation 2560/01 on cross-border payments in euros[87] is based on Article 95 and contains in its Preamble the claim that:

The fact that the level of charges for cross-border payments continues to remain higher than the level of charges for internal payments is hampering cross-border trade and therefore constitutes an obstacle to the proper functioning of the internal market. This is also likely to affect confidence in the euro. Therefore, in order to facilitate the functioning of the internal market, it is necessary to ensure that charges for cross-border payments in euro are the same as charges for payments made in euro within a Member State, which will also bolster confidence in the euro.

Of more direct relevance to contract law, Directive 99/44 on certain aspects of the sale of consumer goods and associated guarantees, also based on (what is now) Article 95 EC,[88] asserts in its Preamble that:

Whereas the creation of a common set of minimum rules of consumer law, valid no matter where goods are purchased within the Community, will strengthen consumer confidence and enable consumers to make the most of the internal market . . .

A comparable assertion of the role of legal rights in promoting consumer confidence may be found in the Preamble to Directive 93/13 on unfair terms in consumer contracts.[89] The attention here is focused on making markets not from the viewpoint of the supplier, the issue at stake in *Tobacco Advertising*, but rather from the viewpoint of the consumer.

The claim that confidence among consumers in the viability of shopping across borders is relevant to making the internal market a reality is convincing. Its potential

---

[85] See also e.g. Commission Communication, 'Better Monitoring of the Application of Community Law', COM(2002)725; Commission Communication, 'Consumer Policy Strategy 2002–2006', COM(2002)208, e.g. para. 2.3.3.

[86] COM(2003)238 final.

[87] OJ 2001 L 344/13.

[88] *Supra* note 16.

[89] *Supra* note 13.

application to the case of European contract law is obvious.[90] But many questions remain. One plausible view is that these broader 'confidence-inducing' rationales for harmonizing laws represent a dimension to Article 95 that was simply not at stake in *Tobacco Advertising* and which is therefore not ruled out by that judgment. So one may take the view that 'confidence building' constitutes a distinct paradigm of harmonized lawmaking which lies beyond the fact pattern of *Tobacco Advertising* and is untouched by it. An alternative—and frankly no less plausible—view is that *Tobacco Advertising* is aimed at suppressing precisely such woolly, open-ended claims to assert legislative competence pursuant to Article 95. Accordingly examples of legislative practice which rely upon this rationale are vulnerable to annulment should a court ever be asked to consider their validity, and it is no basis for future harmonization initiatives. Another approach is to question whether Article 28 and Article 95 are two sides of the same coin. Some national rules of private law fall outwith Article 28.[91] They are not trade barriers and the State is not called on to justify them. But can the EC then harmonize these areas pursuant to Article 95? It is not clear. For some, a reading of Article 95 which refuses to extend its use beyond mere reaction to barriers to trade falling within the reach of Article 28 creates the risk of a 'problematic one-sidedness for Community law'.[92] A response to this may be to accept that the Treaty *is* one-sided.

A sub-theme in this debate asks whether it is in any event plausible to regard legislative harmonization as an effective method in boosting the consumer's confidence in crossing borders to shop. Linguistic variation and impeded access to justice may be much more serious hindrances than the absence of minimum legal rights promised on paper.[93] And should one in any event take account of different expectations among consumers in different jurisdictions, different cultural milieux? Empirical evidence of the extent to which legal regulation generates confidence in new markets would be useful, although hard to gather.[94] Such data would be potentially germane to an assessment of whether a particular Community initiative crosses the threshold of constitutionality by making an actual contribution to inducing cross-border mobility.

---

[90] *Cf.* Basedow, 'A Common Contract Law for the Common Market', 33 *CML Rev* (1996) 1169.

[91] *Cf.* Case C-339/89, *Alsthom Atlantique SA* [1991] ECR I-107; Case C-93/92, *CMC Motorradcenter* [1993] ECR I-5009. Both cases are factually unusual, but may be best read as having partially paved the way to the imminent re-shaping of Art. 28 EC effected by the Court in Cases C-267 and 268/91, *Keck and Mithouard* [1993] ECR I-6097.

[92] Von Bogdandy and Bast, 'The EU's Vertical Order of Competences: the Current Law and Proposals for its Reform', 39 *CML Rev* (2002) 227, at 245. See also Davies, 'Can Selling Arrangements be Harmonized?', 30 *EL Rev* (2005) 370.

[93] Wilhelmsson, 'The Abuse of the Confident Consumer as a Justification for EC Consumer Law', 27 *J Consumer Policy* (2004) 317. *Cf.*, also robustly dismissing the 'confidence-building' perspective, Goode, 'Contract and Commercial Law: the Logic and Limits of Harmonisation', *Ius Commune Lectures of European Private Law No 8* (METRO, Maastricht, June 2003).

[94] *Cf.* in another sector Moloney, 'Confidence and Competence: the Conundrum of EC Capital Markets Law', 4(2) *J Corporate Law Studies* (2004) 1.

The matter remains deeply ambiguous but it is of central importance in understanding the proper scope of Article 95 EC. Without pretending that the law currently offers sturdy support for this perspective, an argument is pitched in the following terms. Without a reliable pattern of legal rights 'on paper' the consumer will not treat the internal market as trustworthy or viable and will retreat to the relative security of local purchasing. The argument is therefore not that without harmonized legal protection the internal market will work unfairly; it is instead that without harmonized legal protection the internal market will never even come into existence in accordance with the pattern mapped by Article 14 EC. So Article 95 is available only for measures that contribute to the establishment and functioning of the internal market, while wider regulatory ambitions must be pursued under other provisions which are textually more narrowly drawn (such as Article 153(3)(b)). But breeding confidence among consumers is essential to the establishment and functioning of the internal market. This can be validly achieved by the creation of harmonized legal protection, albeit that inquiry into the genuine contribution of such legal rules to promoting confidence must be conducted by the legislature. The 'consumer confidence' argument should not simply be the new motor of 'competence creep' for the harmonization programme.

In conclusion, the Commission's development of European contract law raises some intriguing and, as yet, timidly addressed questions about constitutional propriety. The *constitutional* significance of the confidence-building rationale for introducing harmonized laws is ambiguous, and this issue will continue to bubble close to the surface. What is needed to make a market? Article 14 and Article 95 of the EC Treaty do not provide satisfactory answers. These open-ended questions carry a deep constitutional resonance for the future of European private law.

4

Integration and Diversity: The Conflict of Laws as a Regulatory Tool

HORATIA MUIR WATT

Regulatory Techniques and the Conflict of Laws European integration requires appropriate regulatory strategies and new tools of multi-level governance, in the fields both of public and private law.[1] In the latter area, which essentially covers the law applicable to cross-border contracts and torts,[2] substantive uni-fication, whether in the form of a code or a more modest 'common frame of

---

[1] For a varied sample of the already rich reflection on the changes affecting methods and strategies of regulation in the context of globalization or regional integration, see Aman, 'Globalization, Democracy and the Need for a New Administrative Law', 10 *Ind J Glob L Stud* (2003) 125; Black, 'Decentring Regulation: Understanding the Role of Regulation and Self-Regulation in a Post-Regulatory World', 54 *Current Legal Problems* (2001) 103; Cafaggi, 'Le rôle des acteurs privés dans les processus de régulation: participation, autorégulation et régulation privée', 109 *Revue fr. d'admin publique* (2004) 23; Collins, 'Regulating Contract Law', in C. Parker, C. Scott, N. Lacey, and J. Braithwaite, *Regulating Law* (2004), 23; Freeman, 'The Private Role in Public Governance', 75 *New York Univ L Rev* (2000) 1; Glaeser and Scheifer, 'The Rise of the Regulatory State' [2003] *Journal of Econ. Lit.* 401; Majone, 'The Rise of the Regulatory State in Europe' [1994] *West European Politics* 77; Michalet, 'Les métamorphoses de la mon-dialisation, une approche économique', in Credimi Colloquium (dir. by E. Loquin and C. Kessedjian), *La mondialisation du droit* (2000), 11–25; Scott, 'Analysing Regulatory Space: Framented Resources and Institutional Design' [2001] *Public Law* 329; Schwarcz, 'Private Ordering', 97 *Nw U L Rev* (2002) 319; Teubner, 'After Legal Instrumentalism? Strategic Models of Post-Regulatory Law', in G. Teubner (ed.), *Dilemmas of Law in the Welfare State* (1988), 299.

[2] We will not attempt here to pin down a distinction which is notoriously problematic (see Merryman, 'The Public Law–Private Law Distinction in European and American law, 17 *Forum of Public Law* (1968) 3; Kennedy, 'The Stages of Decline of the Public/Private Distinction', 130 *U Pa L Rev* (1982) 1423; Glendon, 'The Sources of Law in a Changing Legal Order', 17 *Creighton L Rev* (1983) 663; M. Loughlin, *The Idea of Public Law* (2004); Harlow, 'Public and Private Law: Definition without Distinction', 43 *MLR* (1980) 241. For the purposes of this chapter, it will be taken that rules of contract and tort which concern horizontal relationships between individuals are private law, and that product quality norms or administrative authorizations, which concern the vertical relationship between indi-viduals and the State, are public. It is quite clear, however, that these labels are misleading, and that rules of contract and tort can obviously serve as regulatory tools as a substitute for administrative or public law (see, for an interesting demonstration on this point, Gkoutisinis, 'Free Movement of Services in the EC Treaty and the Law of Contractual Obligations Relating to Banking and Financial Services', 41 *CML Rev* (2004) 119; Collins, *supra* note 1).

reference',[3] may well be as much a 'discredited option' as it is in the field of product quality rules for goods or administrative authorizations for services.[4] The recitals which accompany the Commission's recent proposal for a Directive on Services in the Internal Market[5] contain, under the title 'a combination of regulatory techniques', what might be seen as a policy statement on the importance of methodological pluralism in this respect. They announce the concurrent use, in the regulation of service activities, of the country of origin principle, derogations from that principle, mutual assistance among national authorities, targeted harmonization, and alternative methods of regulation, including codes of conduct. While this pluralistic approach to the regulation of cross-border services is certainly interesting in itself and worthy of further exploration, it is noteworthy that the conflict of laws seems to have disappeared from the scene, or rather, appears to have been absorbed by the principle of mutual recognition. This chapter focuses on the reasons why the disappearance of the conflict of laws as a regulatory technique in its own right in the field of private law is problematic.

The Conflict of Laws and Economic Due Process Indeed, a close scrutiny of the case-law of the ECJ concerning the requirements of the economic freedoms in cases of conflict between national regulations, norms or policies, suggests that issues of private law arising in relation to cross-border services do not always fit into the territorial scheme which underlies mutual recognition and the country of origin principle. The latter are both designed to operate in the field of public law, where they allow legal diversity to be maintained, while encouraging regulatory competition.[6]

---

[3] Communication from the Commission to the European Parliament and the Council: A More Coherent European Contract Law—An Action Plan, COM(2003)68 final at 4. The Action Plan seems to have abandoned the radical option of a code, at least for the time being. Instead, the measures proposed are: the improvement of existing Community law; an elaboration of a common frame of reference to enhance coherence; the encouragement of various professional or consumer associations to draw up standard contracts; and further reflection on a possible optional instrument covering the whole field of contract law (*id.*, at 15–24). The perceived need to reduce or eradicate transaction costs generated by legal diversity appears to be central to the Commission's position. On the reason why the whole idea of a common frame of reference is misleading, see The Study Group on Social Justice in European Contract Law, 'Social Justice in European Contract Law: A Manifesto', 10 *ELJ* (2004) 653; Collins, 'Discovering the Implicit Dimensions of Contracts' (with Campbell), in D. Campbell, H. Collins, and J. Wightman (eds), *Implicit Dimension of Contract: Discrete, Relational, and Network Contracts* (2003), 25; Kennedy, 'The Political Stakes in "Merely Technical" Issues of Contract Law' [2001] *E Rev Priv L* 7.

[4] See S. Weatherill and P. Beaumont, *EU Law* (1998); for the Commission's 'new approach', which accepts diversity, see *Completing the Internal Market: White Paper from the Commission to the European Council*, COM(85)310.

[5] See the Council's proposed 2004 Directive on services in the internal market (2004/0001, COM(2004)2 final/3), and see in particular Recital # b, at 8, 'A Combination of Regulatory Techniques'.

[6] On the competitive paradigm underlying European integration, see J. Snell, *Goods and Services in EC Law. A Study of the Relationships between the Freedoms* (2002); Kerber, 'Interjurisdictional Competition within the European Union', 23 *Fordham Internat'l L J* (2000) 217.

However, on issues of private law, differences in legal rules which may appear to distort the playing field from the standpoint of economic operators cannot be dealt with satisfactorily simply by distributing legislative jurisdiction according to a territorial model. This is due to the fact that provisions or principles of private law may well be designed to govern conduct, events or relationships which occur outside, or independantly, of State lines. In the United States, under the Commerce clause, regulation which claims to affect out-of-state interests will be subjected to a balancing test. According to one reading of the requirements of the federal Constitution on this point, the real issue behind extraterritoriality is 'economic due process', or, in slightly different terms, avoiding cost externalization to the detriment of categories of interests which are not represented in the domestic political process.[7] From a European perspective, Miguel Poiares Maduro has suggested that the quest for economic due process might, similarly, be the appropriate parameter for judicial control of national rules under the fundamental economic freedoms in Community law.[8] Taking this idea a step further, this chapter argues that economic due process should also provide the foundation for the conflict of private laws relating to cross-border activities, particularly in the field of services, where the territorial scheme applicable to rules of public law is unsatisfactory. In this case, the conflict of laws would perform an important regulatory function,[9] asserting its place among various other techniques and strategies which now contribute to the governance of diversity.[10] The aim of this chapter is to verify this regulatory potential of the conflict of laws. The research will be conducted in two parts. First, it must be explained why the country of origin principle and mutual recognition are irrelevant for issues of private law (Part 1). It will then be submitted that the conflict of laws may be used to implement economic due process in the field of tort and contract (Part 2).

[7] Eule, 'Laying the Dormant Commerce Clause to Rest', 91 *Yale LJ* (1982) 425; Goldsmith and Sykes, 'The Internet and the Dormant Commerce Clause', 110 *Yale LJ* (2001) 785.

[8] See M. Poiares Maduro, *We the Court* (1998) and 'Harmony and Dissonance in Free Movement', in W.H. Roth and M. Andenas (eds), *Services and Free Movement in EC Law* (2002), 41.

[9] See Wai, 'Transnational Liftoff and Juridical Touchdown: The Regulatory Function of Private International Law in a Global Age', 40 *Colum J Transnat'l L* (2002) 209; Trachtmann, 'International Regulatory Competition, Externalization and Jurisidiction', 34 *Harv Internat'l L J* (2003) 47; and by the same author, 'Conflict of Laws and Accuracy in the Allocation of Government Responsibilities', 26 *Vand J Transnat'l L* (1994) 975 and 'Economic Analysis of Prescriptive Jurisdiction' [2001] 42 *Virginia J Int'l L* 1; Garcimartin Alferez, 'Regulatory Competition: A Private International Law Approach', 8 *E J Law & Econ* (1999) 251; Grundmann, 'The Structure of European Contract Law', 4 *Eur Rev Priv L* (2001) 505.

[10] These may be mutual recognition in the field of public law, or self-regulation as a desirable alternative to legislation, or indeed, on points such as consumer protection, where targeted harmonization appears necessary.

1. THE COUNTRY OF ORIGIN PRINCIPLE AND PRIVATE LAW

A. Territoriality, Public Law and Regulatory Competition

Mutual Recognition and Public Law Mutual recognition is essentially about rules of public law—or, since the label is ambiguous,[11] rules about administrative authorizations, prudential supervision, or product quality. It heralds the spectacular end of the 'public law taboo' in intra-Community situations.[12] While the most remarkable examples can probably be found in harmonized areas, for instance, in the Directives on financial services, under which rules of the home country governing authorizations and prudential supervision of banks must be recognized and, if necessary, implemented,[13] by the courts of other, host, Member States, the ECJ's interpretation of the fundamental freedoms in the field of cross-border supply of products and services give effect to the same idea in the absence of substantive harmonization. Thus, under *Keck*,[14] the free movement of goods requires the importing country to recognize the product rules of the country of origin. This essentially entails accepting foreign goods as they were manufactured, and refraining from imposing further requirements relating to product quality or packaging. Subjecting a given imported item to a second set of regulations hinders its market access, since it is at a disadvantage as compared with domestic goods which can be sold after satisfying only one regulatory burden. This is why, once the item has crossed the frontier, the importing State may require compliance only to marketing rules—to which the item has not previously been subjected, and which do not entail a change of form or content, thereby involving no double regulatory burden. Now well established for goods (if not always easy to implement),[15] this allocation of regulatory competences between the exporting State and the host State gives rise to considerable difficulties as to the requirements of market access in the field of services.[16] This is precisely where mutual recognition and the conflict of laws appear, in the main, to cross swords. It is also where the ECJ's case-law appears less legible and

[11] See *supra* note 2.

[12] On the spectacular change entailed by mutual recogniton in the area of public law, see Radicati di Brozolo, 'Libre circulation dans la CE et règles de confli', [1993] *RCDIP* 401.

[13] See Snell, *supra* note 6, 97–8, noting that host State authorites are entitled to check that imported goods and services comply with the product rules of the home country (assuming that similar checks are carried out on domestic products). In litigation, this result could already be obtained under Art. 7(1) of the Rome Convention, at least before the courts of countries which agree to give effect to this provision. For those such as the UK and Germany which do not, the duty to ensure that foreign mandatory rules are complied with involves a more considerable change.

[14] Joined Cases C-267 and C-268/91, *Keck and Mithouard* [1993] ECR I-6097.

[15] The frontier between product and marketing rules may be problematic in some cases, for instance, as far as advertising is concerned. While clearly a marketing technique, advertising may also be part of the product itself, so that applying host country rules may mean modifying the product itself: see e.g. Case C-368/95, *Familia Press* [1997] ECR I-3689.

[16] See the various contributions to Roth and Andenas, *supra* note 8.

gives rise to considerable debate. To help clarify the relationship between mutual recognition and the conflict of laws in the field of services, it is useful to emphasize two points. The first concerns the economics of mutual recognition. The second point relates to the relevance of the public law/private law distinction to the scope of the country of origin principle.

The Economics of Mutual Recognition   The extent to which the dynamics of the internal market rest on regulatory competition in the field of public law has been emphasized by Wolfgang Kerber,[17] who demonstrates that competition for public goods in general is the inevitable result of the conjunction of subsidiarity, on the one hand, and the economic freedoms on the other: States are no longer monopolistic suppliers of public goods, since they are subject to competition sparked off by mobile firms and capital. That the competitive paradigm is at work behind the fundamental freedoms is also clear in the field of freedom of secondary establishment. Under the ECJ's recent case-law, companies are free to take advantage of the whole range of legal regimes on offer throughout the Community, wherever their seat is located or their business conducted.[18] This development, which in practice puts an end to the 'real seat' theory (at least insofar as it is used by the host State to refuse recognition to companies with no economic connection with the place of incorporation) has not been well received in Member States, where the market for corporate charters is perceived to give rise to a race to the bottom, particularly at the expense of worker participation in corporate decision-making. However, the ECJ's response to this concern has, in essence, been to point out that Member States are free to adopt a uniform model,[19] but that in the absence of sufficient political will on this point, it is up to the market alone to decide between the competing models of corporate governance.[20] Each Member State is required to mutually recognize the company law of the others, by refraining to impose additional requirements on companies incorporated in other countries which choose to set up a secondary establishment within their territory.[21]

The Scope of the Country of Origin Principle: Goods and Services   In a similar fashion, the dynamics of the market for goods and services is harnessed to the

[17] See *supra* note 6.

[18] This is the *Centros, Überseering, Inspire Art* line of cases: see Cases C-212/97, [1999] ECR I-1459, C-208/00, [2002] ECR I-9919, and C-167/01, [2003] ECR I-10155.

[19] See the Opinion of Alber AG, at point 139. On the reasons for which the new European company does not solve the regulatory competition problem, see Magnier, 'La société européenne en question', [2004] *RCDIP* 555.

[20] Considering the market as an alternative form of regulation is obviously, however, a choice in itself. The choice by certain States of the 'real seat' as the connecting factor is precisely designed to regulate competition by requiring an economic link with the State of incorporation.

[21] Under the *Inspire Art* ruling, *supra* note 18, the host State is prevented from imposing mandatory policies of domestic company law even to 'pseudo-foreign' companies, whose activity is entirely domestic.

mutual recognition of competitive advantages acquired under the law of the country of origin. Whether a given legal regime survives in the internal market will depend solely on consumer choice, which works in this context as a functional substitute for mobility. Mutual recognition thus ensures, here again, that the market alone decides on the success of the respective legal regimes, which is why the importing State must refrain from hampering free movement by imposing its own standards on foreign products or services. Understanding the economics of mutual recognition helps define the scope of the country of origin principle, and specifically how to identify those rules of the country of origin of a product or service which need to be mutually recognized, in order for foreign products and services to maintain their competitive advantage when offered simultaneously to domestic consumers. The 'Sunday trading saga' seemed at one point to suggest that freely moving goods carried around all the rules which impacted on the conditions in which they were made available in their country of origin, even if it meant forcing the shops of host States to open on a Sunday![22] Under such an approach, there would also be no reason to exclude from the scope of mutual recognition rules of law relevant to the production process, such as environmental or labour law, under which a product was manufactured or a service initially conceived. This result is clearly excessive— at least, it has never been contemplated as a necessary component of the internal market.

The Different Ways in which Regulatory Competition Operates Jukka Snell has shown that regulatory competition in fact takes place in different ways for different rules, and such differences must be taken into account in the design of mutual recognition.[23] If *Keck* distinguishes product and marketing rules, it is because competition operates differently for each of these categories. While competition between product rules (quality and presentation of products) takes place when consumers vote with their purses, marketing rules (such as whether shops are open on a Sunday, whether billboard advertising is allowed, etc.) are more likely to weigh on decisions made in light of the location (many might prefer to live in a quiet neighbourhood rather than one in which Sunday trading and billboard advertising are unrestricted). As Snell rightly points out, allowing mutual recognition of such rules of the country of manufacture along with the free movement of products would mean that there would be nowhere left to live where Sundays were quiet, billboards prohibited, etc.; the host country must therefore be allowed to respond to local preferences and should not be required to mutually recognize the country of origin's rules.[24] In the same way, production rules, such as labour or environmental law, influence the locational decisions of firms, which must be allowed to choose the

---

[22] See Case C-145/88, *Torfaen Borough Council* v *B & Q plc* [1989] ECR I-3851. On the 'saga', see Poiares Maduro, 'Harmony and Dissonance in Free Movement', *supra* note 8, 51.

[23] See *supra* note 6.

[24] In other words, mutual recognition is self-defeating if it does not give the host State the means to protect its own policies in certain cases. For a similar idea in the context of American federalism, see

most advantageous regime on offer; imposing mutual recognition on the host country would, there again, be self-defeating and undermine the economic dynamics of the internal market.

Implications: Market Access and Reverse Discrimination This analysis implies not only that the distinction in *Keck* between product and marketing rules is economically sound, but that restriction to market access in the field of goods, limited to product rules, should be defined by reference to a 'double burden' test. However, recent case-law, particularly in the field of services, has appeared to deviate from this line, either by reverting to what appears to be a purely deregulatory stance, using a 'market access' test without reference to duplication of regulations,[25] or by using the economic freedoms to eliminate reverse discrimination.[26] As Jukka Snell has shown, neither solution is compatible with a regulatory competition reading of the freedoms.[27] On the one hand, what violates the fundamental freedoms is not that the freely moving goods should be subject to regulation of some sorts, but that their competitive advantage be destroyed by making them subject to a double set of regulations pursuing similar ends. On the other, the content of the product rules in the exporting State is indifferent, since it is part of the regulatory make-up of the product and contributes to its comparative advantage—or disadvantage. If it happens to be inefficiently restrictive, it is up to citizen pressure in the form of voice or exit to bring about change; once again, the analysis goes, the market should be allowed to regulate. However, before concluding too hastily that the Court has radically modified its policy as far as the function of the freedoms is concerned,[28] by reverting to a pre-*Keck* state of affairs, it may be useful to ask how rules of private law fit into the picture. Cross-border service cases, such as *Alpine Investments*,[29] in which the Court seems to have adopted a market access rule without reference to regulatory duplication, tend to concern the application of internationally mandatory rules of contract law, which do not fit into the *Keck*-like territorial scheme designed for product rules. The real problem may then be the type of rules which are involved in free movement of services cases.

B. The Problem with Cross-Border Services

Rules with Extraterritorial Scope The difficulty which arose in *Alpine Investments* concerned rules of a specific nature and scope. These were internationally mandatory

Rosen, 'Extraterritoriality and Political Heterogeneity in American Federalism', 150 *U Penn LR* (2002) 855.

[25] As in Case C-415/93, *Bosman* [1995] ECR I-4921.

[26] As in Case C-384/93, *Alpine Investments* [1995] ECR I-1141.

[27] See *supra* note 6, 91 ff.

[28] For the considerable debate on this point, see the various contributions to Roth and Andenas, *supra* note 8.

[29] See Case C-384/93, *supra* note 26.

rules which prohibited certain aggressive forms of marketing. Although it is difficult to label them as either public or private, or to characterize them as market regulation rather than as contract law,[30] it is clear that these rules were problematic because they claimed to apply extraterritorially, to relationships between a domestic service provider and potential foreign customers. In other words, unlike the rules of public law envisaged by *Keck*, such rules did not fit into territorial compartments. Indeed, product quality rules apply naturally to goods manufactured within the territory of the home State, but do not claim to apply to goods manufactured elsewhere. Mutual recognition merely prohibits the host State from duplicating requirements already imposed on imported products, but it does not modify the natural scope—or at least the scope claimed—of the law either of the exporting country or of the host State. The analogy between mutual recognition and the recognition of vested rights has already been emphasized;[31] both presuppose that the various laws have a territorial scope and merely require of the recognizing State an acceptance of the operation of foreign law, as if it were a fact or a *fait accompli*. However, contract law does not fit into this scheme, precisely because it is not designed to apply exclusively to relationships which are located within a given territory. Rules applicable to contracts for the cross-border provision of services do not stop at the border, but embrace the whole relationship (as in *Alpine Investments*, where the Dutch prohibition of cold-calling either applied or did not apply to cross-border relationships involving foreign investors, but could hardly stop in the middle!).

Services and the Double Burden Test The debate as to whether the *Keck* ruling and its progeny are relevant to cross-border services often ignores the fact that there are two types of situation in which the territorial scheme present in *Keck* is not problematic in this context. First, as it is often pointed out, the service itself is less freqently regulated than the service-provider, of whom various authorizations or professional qualifications are often required in order to allow access to the local market.[32] In *Sager*[33] it was ruled that no further requirements can be imposed on the provider in view of market access in the other Member States, in accordance with the double burden test; mutual recognition of authorizations or professional qualifications as required by the country of origin protects the comparative advantage of the service as it is provided there. Secondly, it can happen that, because of a change in the place where the service is performed, the provider is subjected to

---

[30] The Dutch government claimed that the rules were designed to protect confidence in the national market, rather than to protect resident consumers specifically. It is obviously not for the ECJ to second-guess the objectives of the national rule. Under the proportionality test, however, the Court may judge the scope claimed by the rule to be excessive, given the objective pursued.

[31] G. Rossolillo, *Mutuo riconoscimento e techniche conflittuali* (2002).

[32] Snell and Andenas, 'Exploring the Outer Limits: Restrictions on the Free Movement of Goods and Services', in Roth and Andenas, *supra* note 8, 75 ff.

[33] Case C-76/90, [1991] ECR I-4221.

two successive sets of public or administrative regulations with equivalent goals, particularly in the capacity of employer. This is what happened in the line of cases regarding cross-border posting of workers: *Van der Elst, Arblade, Mazzoleni, Rush Portuguesa*.[34] Requirements of the country of posting relating to such issues as social security were deemed inapplicable to the extent that the provider–employer had fulfilled equivalent obligations in the country of origin. In such instances, the pattern is that of a *conflit mobile*: the internal market is fragmented and the free provision of services impeded simply because different laws of territorial scope come into play successively in respect of the same service, even when none of these laws pursue any protectionist goals. On the other hand, in accordance with the *Keck rationale*, once market access has been secured, nothing prevents the application of public law rules within the host country, as long as they are equally applicable to domestic service providers.[35] The non-economic policies of Member States impacting on the performance of services can be maintained in all their diversity when they do not affect market access by imposing a double burden.

The Cross-border Nature of Services But this territorial allocation of jurisdiction as between host country and country of origin encounters its limits in the cross-border nature of the relationship between service provider and customer.[36] In *Alpine Investments*, the ECJ rejected the double burden test, preferring to consider the impact of the contested national provision on the provider's market access. Thus, an internationally mandatory rule of the country of origin prohibiting a firm from marketing financial products by telephone (cold-calling), is considered as restraining market access to the extent that it claims to apply even when potential customers are abroad and the means employed are legal under the local domestic law. This test has been criticized as having a conclusionary ring about it.[37] Moreover, where, as in this case, the disqualified rule is that of the home country, it raises the question both of the status of rules relating to the marketing of services (insofar as *Keck* had excluded product marketing rules from the scope of Article 28 EC), and that of reverse discrimination.[38] On both these points, it might appear that the economic *rationale* of mutual recognition has been lost from view. Indeed, if the aim

[34] See Cases C-43/93, [1994] ECR I-3803 (*Vander Elst*); C-369 & 379/96, [1999] ECR I-8453 (*Arblade*); C-165/98, [2001] ECR I-2189 (*Mazzoleni*); and C-113/89, [1990] ECR I-1417 (*Rush Portuguesa*). On this line of case-law, see Pataut, 'Lois de police et ordre juridique comunautaire', in A. Fuchs, H. Muir Watt, and E. Pataut (eds), *Les conflits de lois et le système juridique communautaire* (2004), 122.

[35] A *de minimis* test is sometimes used to justify the exclusion from the scope of the freedom to provide cross-border services of provisions whose link with free movement is too indirect, as for instance in Case C-379/92, *Peralta* [1994] ECR I-3453.

[36] This results directly from the text of Art. 49 EC. See, too, on this point the Opinion of Lenz AG in *ibid*.

[37] See Snell and Andenas, *supra* note 32, 122.

[38] See *supra* 'Implications: Market Access and Reverse Discrimination'.

is to stimulate regulatory competition by maintaining the comparative advantage of goods and services produced in various legal environments,[39] the case in which the law of the country of origin is more demanding with regard to the conduct of its service providers than that of the host country should be strictly indifferent in respect of the exercise of the economic freedoms. In the same way, by excluding marketing rules from the scope of the freedoms, *Keck* had channelled their application to cases where the operation of the law of the host State would result in depriving an imported product of its comparative advantage—which is of course not the case where the more restrictive rule is in force in the country of origin.

The Problem with Internationally Mandatory Rules of Contract Law

Admittedly, much of the difficulty which affects the interpretation of *Alpine Investments* is linked to the scope claimed by the Dutch mandatory rule, which extended its prohibition of aggressive or intrusive marketing methods to cases involving foreign customers. This claim to extraterritorial effect was justified by the Dutch government by reference to the idea that that the rule was designed to regulate the domestic market and not merely to protect local consumers. This interpretation of the reach of the rule is in itself questionable, and it would certainly have been more reasonable to consider it as a rule of investor protection applicable to consumers habitually resident in the Netherlands.[40] However, beyond these issues of interpretation of national law which are not in the province of the ECJ, the case illustrates the difficulty of adjusting the pattern designed for territorial rules of public law to legislation relating to the provision of cross-border services. Whether such legislation is labelled 'regulatory' or 'private', since it impacts on an intrinsically international relationship, its application cannot stop at the border.[41] Although similar difficulties can obviously arise in respect of cross-border sales of goods, the fact that services are essentially processes[42] explains why their provision crystallizes on performance, through the relationship between the provider and the customer. The

---

[39] This analysis is challenged by Roth, 'The European Court of Justice's Case-law on Freedom to Provide Services: Is *Keck* Relevant?', in Roth and Andenas, *supra* notes 8, 9, which maintains that the aim of the freedoms is to ensure a level playing field between private actors, and not to promote regulatory competiton. But to the extent that the diversity of legal regimes and the regulatory competition to which it gives rise are the means by which the comparative advantage of firms can be upheld, the only issue which is really at stake here is that of reverse discrimination.

[40] Although it would then be seen to concern the pre-contractual relationship between the parties, it would appear to come within the scope of Art. 5 of the Rome Convention.

[41] On the distinction between internationally mandatory rules of private law, generally protective of the weaker party and applicable by reason of the protected party's residence, and rules of public law, which are generally territorial in scope, see Nuyts, 'L'application des lois de police dans l'espace (Réflexions au départ du droit belge de la distribution commerciale et du droit communautaire)' [1999] *RCDIP* 31.

[42] On this definition, see Snell and Andenas, *supra* note 32, 75; Gkoutisinis, *supra* note 2, 129 ff., emphasizing that services usually have a non-legal content, so that quality requirements are directed at the provider.

distinction between rules relating to the product itself and those concerning its marketing, which is cardinal to the allocation of regulatory competences under *Keck*, is irrelevant unless the service is in some way provided through a middle man in the host country.[43]

Lack of Relevance of the Territorial Scheme Thus, unlike the free movement of goods, the cross-border provision of services is necessarily grafted upon an international relationship. Correlatively, the laws which apply to it are frequently extraterritorial in effect, insofar as they apprehend, globally, the whole of the contractual relationship which supports the service. Whether they are rules of consumer protection designed to ensure the integrity of consent, or rules which define imperatively the content of certain contractual terms, or mandatory rules regulating the marketing of a service as characterized in *Alpine Investments*, and whether they come from the country of origin as in the latter case, or more frequently, from the host country, they concern the relationship between provider and customer in its cross-border dimension. From a different perspective, it could be said that this relationship implicates the concurrent jurisdiction of the State of origin and the host country to govern the relationship, which cannot be neatly divided up between them as can the different steps involved in the international sale of goods. This is why, structurally, the intra-Community provision of services does not lend itself to the geographical and chronological pattern on which mutual recognition of product rules is based.[44] Occulted by the territorial scope of public law and product regulation, the difficulty raised by the concurrent and overlapping reach of applicable laws (which is the very definition of the conflict of laws in the field of private law!) reappears. The laws of the country of origin and the host State cannot be shared out in time and space as in the case of a '*conflit mobile*' or the international recognition of vested rights.[45] Their respective claims to govern the relationship are simultaneous and call to be allocated according to more appropriate parameters than those which a purely territorial principle can provide. If the comparative advantage of a service is to be recognized and protected, the law of the country of origin, which presided over the initial conception of the service, should arguably play an important role; but its application will come up against the equally legitimate claim of the law of the host country, which will frequently be concerned with protecting the customer. And as *Alpine Investments* shows, the conflict of laws, supposedly

---

[43] Hatzopolous, 'Recent Developments of the Case Law of the ECJ in the Field of Services', 37 *CML Rev* 431 (2000); Gkoutisinis (*supra* note 2, 131) maintains that real cross-border services which do not involve one party moving physically to the other's country are rare in practice, outside financial services. However, the services of the information society belong to this category. These are governed by the Electronic Commerce Directive (2000/31) OJ 2000 L178/01.

[44] See Tison, 'Unravelling the General Good Exception', in Roth and Andenas, *supra* note 8, 321, esp. at 333.

[45] On this analogy, see Rossolillo, *supra* note 31.

detrimental to the harmonious functioning of the internal market, will often be maintained in the name of the general good.[46]

The Specificity of Legal Products However, it is sometimes argued that the country of origin principle remains relevant in instances where the content of the service is specifically legal, as in the field of insurance or financial services, insofar as the very definition of the product results directly from legal rules governing the contractual relationship between provider and customer.[47] To apply the host country's law would automatically impede free movement of the service, which should therefore be treated under mutual recognition in the same way as public or technical rules. Indeed, since the essence of the service is indissociable from the governing law, its redefinition in the host country through the application of different rules certainly impacts on its market access. The double burden test would therefore apply here to provisions concerning the formation or the content of a private law relationship—in particular, internationally mandatory laws regulating contracts. There would then be a distinction as to the operation of the country of origin principle, between 'mass' services, with a legal content, and the others, usually individualized and non-legal (such as hair-cutting)—these are the types of activity to which the proposed Services Directive applies. For these, a certain adjustment to the host environment would be acceptable, since the content of the service is not pre-determined before the conclusion of the particular service contract; thus, the application of the law of the host State would not act to fragment the internal market.[48]

Of Noise Levels and Legal Environment However, even when the service is not a specifically legal product, the economics of the country of origin principle seem to suggest that it must be accessible in the host country in the same terms as in the provider's own environment, in which it was conceived or shaped, and which constitutes its specifically comparative advantage. Andenas and Snell's example of the noise levels applicable to the performance of a rock band is a good one.[49] The competitive advantage of the 'loudest band in Europe' is lost if the sound levels of the host country apply—although, very conceivably, they would be justified under the general good exception. The Electronic Commerce Directive confirms this idea by extending the scope of the country of origin principle, which naturally governs the access of providers to the market for on-line service activities, to the conditions in which those activities are exercised, which appear to cover various rules including

---

[46] On the content and function of the general good exception in this context, see O'Leary and Martin, 'Judicially-Created Exceptions to the Free Provision of Services', in Roth and Andenas, *supra* note 8, at 163 and 174.

[47] *Cf.* Tison, *supra* note 44, at 364. Thus the applicable provisions include rules of private law governing the contractual relationship.

[48] Roth, *supra* note 39, at 18.

[49] Snell and Andenas, *supra* note 32, at 113.

their liability in tort. The real difficulty, as we shall see, is to determine exactly what would be included in the legal environment of a service, especially when one considers issues ranging from noise levels to private law. Be that as it may, if there is a real difference between legal services and the others, it probably concerns economies of scale more than anything else, since large scale exporters of services, such as financial institutions, may legitimately want to be able to count on the applicability of one governing law when exercising a transfrontier activity unless they choose otherwise—but this is in fact the result reached by the Rome Convention itself, to the extent at least that the applicable rules of substantive law are not already harmonized.[50]

The Perennial Conflict of Private Laws[51] Therefore the legal content of the product does not really modify the nature of the problem raised by cross-border services, which resides, rather, in the simultaneous vocations of the laws of the host State and the country of origin to govern the relationship between provider and customer established in different countries. Where the latter is a consumer, frequently protective mandatory rules will provide for a certain protective formalism in view of the conclusion of the contract, or indeed determine the content of the relationship between consumer and provider. When, in the absence of harmonization, the level of protection provided by the host country and the country of origin is unequal,[52] the chances are that a restrictive rule of the host country, however restrictive of the provider's freedom, will be maintained under the general good exception (subject to proportionality). Although the fact pattern was slightly different, this is exactly what happened in *Alpine Investments*: the more restrictive rule (here, of the country of origin) was initially disqualified as impeding market access, but in the end legal diversity was maintained in the name of the public policy interests it was attempting to protect. Identifying an obstacle to trade is therefore not enough to eliminate the conflict of private laws which arise in the course of the provision of a cross-border service.[53] So how should these be dealt with?

[50] Considerations of economies of scale often lead to targeted harmonization. In this respect, the Electronic Commerce Directive emphasizes the insecurity which diversity supposedly generates for mass on-line service providers, even when the services involved, such as the providing of on-line access, are not specifically or exclusively legal.

[51] The expression evokes the title of an article by O'Hara, 'Economics, Public Choice and the Perennial Conflict of Laws', 90 *Georgetown LJ* (2002) 941. Here, it just means that conflicts of laws always tend to reappear despite efforts to smooth them out of the way.

[52] On the difficult question of the applicability of stricter rules laid down on the basis of a Community Directive in the host State, see Grundmann, 'Internal Market Conflict of Laws. From Traditional Conflict of Laws to an Integrated Two Level Order', in Fuchs, Muir Watt, and Pataut, *supra* note 34, at 5.

[53] In the case of insurance and financial products, the problem raised by legal diversity has been solved by harmonization of rules at a level deemed to provide adequate protection for the customer or consumer of the service.

C. The Conflict of Private Laws

The Conflict of Laws and the Economic Freedoms The issue of the impact of the
economic freedoms on the conflict of laws has fostered an intense debate in the past
decade.[54] It was sparked by the suggestion that the freedoms operate as a 'hidden
conflict rule',[55] meaning, in practice, that any principle of private international law
(whether a conflict rule, a mandatory or procedural rule of the forum, the public
policy exception, etc.) which renders applicable a law other than that of the country of origin of the provider of a good or service would itself be disqualified as an
impediment to free movement. Such an approach would lead to the formulation of
a vast country of origin principle, which would prevail over all discordant rules.
Today, however, a consensus seems to be emerging to the effect that rather than
requiring the law of the country of origin to apply systematically to all aspects of
cross-border economic activities,[56] the freedoms merely signify that, whatever the
substantive law applicable under the conflict rules of the forum (generally those of
the host country[57]), its content should not be restrictive of free movement. This
means examining point by point the content of the applicable law, and setting aside

---

[54] For a sample of the vast literature on this question see Basedow, 'Der kollisonrechtlichte Gehalt
der produktfreiheiten im europäischen Binnemarket: favor offerentis' [1995] *RabelZ* 1; Fallon, 'Les conflits de lois et de juridictions dans un espace économique intégré—L'expérience de la Communauté
européenne', 253 *RCADI* (1995) 279; Gkoutisinis, 'Free Movement of Services in the EC Treaty and the
Law of Contractual Obligations Relating to Banking and Financial Services', 41 *CML Rev* (2004) 119;
Heuzé, 'De la compétence de la loi du pays d'origine en matière contractuelle ou l'anti-droit européen',
in *Mélanges P. Lagarde* (2004); Idot, 'L'incidence du droit communautaire sur le droit international privé',
248 *Le droit international privé communautaire: émergence et incidences, Peties Affiches* (2002), 27; Jessurun
d'Oliveira, 'The EU and a Metamorphosis of Private International Law', in *Reform and Development of
Private International Law. Essays in Honour of Sir Peter North*, ed. J. Fawcett (2002), at 111–36; Jobard-
Bachellier, 'L'acquis communautaire du droit international privé des conflits de lois', in J.S. Bergé and
M.N. Niboyet (eds), *La réception du droit communautaire en droit privé des Etats membres* (2003),
185–206; T. Kadner Graziano, *Gemeineuropäisches Internationales Privatrecht* (2002), 687; Kohler, 'Der
europäische Justizraum für Zivilsachen und das Gemeinschaftskollisionsrecht' [2003] *IPRax* 401–11;
Muir Watt, 'Choice of Law in Integrated and Interconnected Markets: a Matter of Political Economy',
9 *Col J Eur L* (2003) 383–410; P. Picone, *Diritto internazionale privato e diritto comunitario* (2004);
Radicati di Brozolo, 'Libre circulation dans la CE et règles de conflit' [1993] *RCDIP* 401; Rigaux, 'La
méthode des conflits de lois en droit européen', *Mélanges Dutoit* (2002), 243–56; Rossolillo, *supra* note
31; Spindler, 'Herkunftslandprinzip und Kollisionsrecht—Binnenmarktintegration ohne Harmonisierung?'
[2002] *RabelsZ* 633–709; Tebbens, 'Les conflits de lois en matière de publicité déloyale à l'épreuve du
droit communautaire' [1994] *RCDIP* 451; Tison, 'Unravelling the General Good Exception: The Case
of Financial Services', in Roth and Andenas, *supra* note 8. at 321; Wilderspin and Lewis, 'Les relations
entre le droit communautaire et les règles de conflits de lois des Etats membres' [2002] *RCDIP* 1; see
too the various contributions in Fuchs, Muir Watt, and Pataut, *supra* note 34.

[55] On the concept of hidden conflict rules, see Basedow, *supra* note 54.

[56] See Lagarde, *supra* note 54. This thesis 'has practically no support today': at 287.

[57] In cases of tort, the applicable law will very often be the law of the place where the harm occurred
(this is the general principle under the proposed Rome II Regulation of 22 July 2003, COM(2003)427
final, on which see *infra* 'Designing the Conflict Rule').

any aspect of it deemed to impede free movement. The country of origin principle would thus take the form of a more modest 'exception of mutual recognition',[58] which appears to be more in harmony with the case-law of the Court of Luxembourg.[59]

The Real Issue However, framed as an alternative between these two possible modes of operation of Community law (by way of an exception of non-conformity or a rule allocating jurisdiction?), this debate misses the real issue, which is to determine the circumstances in which the applicable substantive law can be deemed to impede free movement. If, by extending the double burden test designed for rules of public law, a rule of private (say, tort or contract) law is to be considered to be contrary to the freedoms every time it imposes on the operator constraints which do not exist under the law of the country of origin, the distinction between the exception of mutual recognition and a hidden conflict rule is of little import. The difference between the two approaches is meaningful only if the freedoms are not restricted by the difference *per se* (by definition unfavourable to the provider) between the practical result which would be reached by the courts of the country of origin and those of the host country. If the freedoms were affected every time the host country rule is unfavourable to the provider, this would mean setting aside the law applicable in the host country in cases where harm occurred there; in other words, this would be equivalent to formulating one vast conflict rule in favour of the law of the country of origin.[60] Such an approach would be both excessive, as going far beyond the requirements of the economics of free movement, and retrograde, as it would lead to ignoring the various objectives of private international law in the field of tort—among which some may well be required to maintain the harmony of the internal market itself.[61] Indeed, if these are the requirements of mutual recognition, then the conflict rule of the forum would be called upon to operate only in cases

---

[58] See Fallon and Meusen, 'Le commerce électronique, la Directive 2000/31 CE et le droit international privé' [2002] *RCDIP* 435, esp. at 487.

[59] Under the judicial reading of the fundamental freedoms, the grounds on which the disqualified rule is applicable do not matter (it may have been designated by a conflict of laws rule, but it may also be an internationally mandatory rule of the forum, or be applicable under the exception of public policy, for example), as is its national origin (it is difficult to see why it should be the law of a Member State: see however *contra*, Tebbens, *supra* note 54, at 476), its characterization as public or private (the distinction between public and private law, being diversely accepted and interpreted among the Member States, cannot serve as a parameter: see Case C-20/92, *Hubbard* [1995] ECR I-3777), and even the fact that it implements a rule of Community secondary law (a rule resulting from a Directive can be considered as an impediment to free movement, as can a provision of national law made applicable by a uniform European conflict rule).

[60] See Cachard, 'Le domaine coordonné par la Directive sur le commerce électronique et le droit international privé' [2004] *RDAI* 161, at 173.

[61] An excellent illustration can be found in the 'Rome II' proposal on the law applicable to non-contractual obligations (22 July 2003, COM(2003)427 final), which clearly pursues such regulatory goals within the internal market. Yet the main connecting factor is the place of the harm, generally the host country.

of 'false conflict', since any true difference between the country of origin and the host country will work systematically to the advantage of the former.

Mutual Recognition and the Reach of Private Law In this respect, if the generalization of the country of origin principle seems to be an unsatisfactory parameter when applied to the obligations of economic operators in the field of private law, it is because the allocatory function of mutual recognition is unadapted to this field. By hunting down the cases in which the operator would be subjected to a double burden by reason of the cross-border nature of its activity, mutual recognition gives effect in the host country to territorial rules of the country of origin, through a mechanism similar to the recognition of vested rights; but in the field of private law, the rules of the country of origin cannot easily be tidied away under the double burden test since they are not systemtically territorial in scope.[62] Is this not precisely the reason why the vested rights doctrine, with its territorial foundations, was unable to provide a credible theory of the conflict of laws? Thus a proper understanding of the effect of the economic freedoms in the field of private law means determining when the application of a rule of private law can be considered as restrictive of market access in the host country: in the way the Dutch mandatory rule was disqualified in *Alpine Investments*. The question concerns all the sources of the law of obligations, essentially tort (1) and contract (2).

I. Conflicts of laws in tort

Mutual Recognition of Tort Rules? Whether the requirements of mutual recognition apply to rules of tort law is at the heart of the debate on the future of the conflict of laws within the internal market. The question is whether, in assessing the liability of a supplier of goods or services for harm caused in the importing or host State, the courts of that State may apply a law other (and, by definition, more restrictive[63]) than the law of the provider's home country.[64] First presented as a

---

[62] The rhetoric of *levelling the playing field* is common to all free trade systems. Here, as elsewhere, it is misleading, since it creates an optical illusion (see, in the context of the WTO, Cass and Boltuck, 'Antidumping and Countervailing Duty Law: The Mirage of Equitable International Competition', in J.N. Bhagwaty and R.E. Hudec (eds), *Fair Trade and Harmonisation*, vol. 2, *Legal Analysis* (MIT Press, 1997), 351; see also, in the context of the Commerce Clause, Rosen, 'Extraterritoriality and Political Heterogeneity in American Federalism', 150 *U Penn L Rev* (2002) 855, at 962.

[63] The freedom to provide cross-border services will be invoked, practically, in cases in which the host State's law is more restrictive than that of the home State. This is why, for practical purposes, there is no real difference between the principle of origin, deemed to contain a complete conflict of laws rule in favour of the law of the host State, and the concept of an 'exception of mutual recognition', which would merely set aside rules of the host State when they impeded free movement (on the concept of an exception of mutual recognition, see Fallon and Meusen, 'Le commerce électronique, la Directive 2000/31 CE et le droit international privé' [2002] *RCDIP* 435. Under either system, the law of the country of origin prevails in cases of true conflict.

[64] See Wilderspin and Lewis, *supra* note 54.

implicit requirement of the fundamental freedoms, the thesis according to which more restrictive liability rules in the host country would restrict free movement gained credit from the 'internal market clause' in the 2000/31 Electronic Commerce Directive. This includes within the scope of the country of origin principle all issues relating to both access and exercise of activities through an electronic medium, to the exclusion, however, of products liability.

Deregulatory Thesis Problematic However, to accept that freedom to provide a service is inhibited whenever the provider's liability under the law applicable before the courts of the (host) country where the harm occurred is less favourable to the provider than the law of the home country, implies that in every case, effect must be given to the most liberal rule. In other words, this would produce a deregulatory effect similar to the state of affairs induced by *Dassonville* and *Cassis de Dijon* in the field of public law and technical norms—before *Keck* laid down that the economic freedoms are involved only to the extent that market access is restricted, and that free movement is not impeded by the sole fact that the provider is subject to more restrictive rules in the host country. As long as these apply after market access has been obtained, they are indifferent to the freedoms.[65]

Equivalence in Private Law The deregulatory effect of extending the country of origin principle to the field of tort law would be exacerbated by the fact that ascertaining whether the law of the host State is less favourable to the provider would necessarily take place point by point, without taking account of the global balance of interests achieved within a given system. For example, the law applicable in the host country might retain a lighter standard of care than the one applicable in the provider's home country, but might, on the other hand, provide for a longer delay of prescription or limitation. If one were to reason as in the field of public law, for instance concerning an administrative formality applicable to imported goods, one would have to conclude that the more generous statute of limitation, considered in isolation from the other elements which constitute the legal regime of the tort, would be considered as an impediment to free movement if the tort victim's action would have been barred by a statute of limitation before the courts of the country of origin. Now, if mutual recognition in the field of public law rests, like the conflict of laws, on a presumption that both laws are subtantially equivalent, this presumption operates in very different ways for public law or technical norms, and

---

[65] See Keck and Mithouard, *supra* note 14. The distinction made here between product and marketing rules is designed to reduce the interference of Community law in policy choices of Member States when free movement is not directly involved. The *Dassonville–Cassis de Dijon* line of cases had favoured a more expansive, deregulatory reading of the fundamental freedoms (see Poiares Maduro, 'Harmony and Dissonance', *supra* note. 8, esp. at 46). See too the Opinion of Tesauro AG in the *Hunermund* case (Case C-292/92, *R Hunermund* v *Landesapothekerkammer Baden-Württemberg* [1993] ECR I-6787), emphasizing that the goal of Art. 28 is to eliminate national measures which fragment the unity of the market, and not to promote free trade). Similar dualism can be found in the reading of the Commerce Clause in the United States (see Eule, *supra* note 7).

private law. In the former field, regulatory equivalence is presumed rule by rule, so that, in principle, application of the law of the host country will be redundant. On the other hand, in private law, the presumption operates globally. What is presumed to be interchangeable are whole systems of interconnected rules, which are delineated by the different conceptual categories of the conflict of laws. This is why it does not make sense to dismantle the applicable law by separating the various parts of a whole.[66] In the above example, prescription or limitation should not be considered in isolation of the balance achieved through the whole system of rules applicable in the field of tort.

The Internal Market Clause Despite the credit which the Electronic Commerce Directive appears to have given the country of origin principle in the field of tort, signals from recent secondary law are decidedly ambiguous. Indeed, the real significance of the internal market clause in that Directive is questionable.[67] If some commentators understand it as conferring an internationally mandatory nature on the rules of the country of origin comprised within the coordinated field,[68] others maintain that the reference to the law of the country of origin operates, in the manner of the foreign court theory, as an inclusive reference to the 'competent legal order'.[69] Under the latter reading, the parameter of an impediment to free movement would be the concrete result obtaining before the courts or other authorities of the country of origin, including the operation of its private international law, rather then merely the substantive law of that country.[70] Indeed, it is difficult to see why the country of origin should renounce its own conflict rules if they themselves are

---

[66] On this point, see Wilderspin and Lewis, *supra* note 54, at 35.

[67] In any case, given the uniform rules contained in the Directive, relating on the liability of service providers in connection with infomation stocked or diffused on the web, it is difficult to imagine what other sorts of factual situations involving the liability of service providers of the 'information society' are effectively covered by the country of origin principle.

[68] See the demonstration by Hellner, 'The Country of Origin Principle in the E-Commerce Directive: A Conflict with Conflict of Laws?', in Fuchs, Muir Watt, and Pataut (eds), *supra* note 34, at 205.

[69] Within the meaning defined by Picone, 'La méthode de la référence à l'ordre juridique compétent en droit international privé' [1986] II *RCADI* 229.

[70] Since the Directive states that it does not lay down 'additional rules of private international law', the advantage of the proposed interpretation is that it would be in keeping with the text itself. It would suffice to take the reference to the law of the country of origin as including the whole legal order of that country; on the other hand, if that same expression were read as meaning the substantive law of the country of origin, it would involve considerable modifications to the current solutions of the conflict of laws. From the point of view of the host country, it is clear that the internal market clause does not require systematic application of the law of the country of origin, but merely leads to setting aside the applicable substantive law if its content impedes free movement. Therefore, the question which the courts of the host country must ask in the event of litigation concerning the liability of an on-line service provider is exactly the same as under primary EC law; the only difference concerns the motives of general good which might justify maintaining a given impediment, which are much more restricted within the coordinated field than under primary law, in the ECJ's case-law. However, see Cachard, *supra* note 60, at 169, who believes that primary law prevails in any case under the ruling in Case 247/84, *Motte* [1985]

designed to pursue other ends than the protection of the provider.[71] Moreover, impediments to free movement are to be determined with reference to the way in which the service was shaped in the country in which it originated.[72] To include tort rules within the scope of the coordinated field is to recognize that such rules impact upon the locational decisions of providers.[73] If this is so, there is no reason not to take account of the way in which tort rules are actually implemented by the courts of the country of origin, insofar as they are considered as part of the legal environment which constitutes a competitive advantage for the provider.

Lax Tort Rules as Competitive Advantage? However, to consider tort rules as a competitive advantage to be mutually recognized, meaning that applying more demanding host country rules would restrict market access, would imply that such rules are an integral part of the product or service provided, of which they would be a sort of accessory. But if such analysis is conceivable in an efficient market, that is, say, as far as consumers of a product are concerned, who pay a price for the legal guarantees or warranties made available if the product is defective or harmful,[74] the remedy of third parties who suffer collateral damage in the course of performance of a service[75] cannot be considered as part of the price of the product. In other words, as Jurgen Basedow has put it, economic freedom to put a product or service on the market does not imply freedom to cause damage thereby.[76] Moreover, in the case of a harm occurring in the host country, one might consider either that the harm occurred after market access was acquired, so that the tort rule is excluded from the scope of the freedoms under the *Keck* rationale, or, in slightly different terms, that the conditions and extent of civil liability are part of the legal environment of

---

ECR 3887). But if the sole difference between the provisions or solutions respectively applicable in the country of origin and in the host country is not enough to constitute a restriction, then there must be some way of determining in which cases a given substantive law constitutes an impediment to free movement. This is precisely where the difficulties arise.

[71] On this point, see Wilderspin and Lewis, *supra* note 54.

[72] Of course, one may well challenge the idea that tort law conditions the content of a product or service, but then it is the very presence of tort law within the coordinated field which is problematic.

[73] The real issue is, as we shall see, whether in fact tort rules influence locational decisions of firms, which in turn sparks legislative competition.

[74] In an efficient market, the price will reflect the legal guarantees and warranties applicable in case of damage to and by the product. However, this fact does not necessarily lead to the country of origin principle in the field of product liability: see Posner, 'Preface: Market Torts—Choice of Law Defaults', in M. Whincop and M. Keyes, *Policy and Pragmatism in the Conflict of Laws* (2001), esp. at 81.

[75] Such as in cases of defamation or unfair competition (to remain in the field of on-line services).

[76] *Supra* note 54, at 37 ff. See the critique on this point by Wilderspin and Lewis, *supra* note 54, at 11, for whom the fundamental freedoms include a right of access to the courts. However, these issues are not on the same level. It is perfectly natural that free movement should comprise a non-discriminatory access to an appropriate forum; indeed, this requirement also results, in the United States, from 'due process' and 'full faith and credit'. But this does not necessarily point to the application of any particular legal system.

the host country to which the foreign provider must adapt.[77] To reason differently would be to exempt the provider from any obligation under the laws of the host country once market access has been acquired, which is clearly non-sensical. This is indeed why, in *Peralta*,[78] implementation of a public law rule of environmental protection was considered as having only an indirect link with the freedom of the service provider, who was subjected to criminal sanctions for non-compliance.

The Risk of Competitive Distortions But perhaps more importantly, the recent proposal for a Directive on Services in the Internal Market expressly excludes from the scope of the country of origin principle the issue of non-contractual liability in connection with physical or material damage suffered by a person as a result of the service provider's activities during its temporary presence in the host country.[79] While no explanation of this exclusion is given, it is clear that any other solution would deprive the conflict of laws of the regulatory function that has recently been reinforced by the proposed Rome II Regulation on the law applicable to extra-contractual obligations.[80] It has been pointed out that creating a manufacturer's haven by applying the country of origin principle in the field of tort would be likely to encourage a race to the bottom in standards of liability in order to attract investment,[81] and would transform the fundamental freedom to provide products or services in other Member States into an immunity from liability or even a positive right to cause harm there.[82] If one refers to Jukka Snell's analysis of the way in which competition takes place for different categories of rules, it seems clear that tort rules cannot be subject to mutual recognition without distorting the competitive process.

Rules of Conduct v Loss Allocation It is true that the ruling in *Inspire Art*[83] seems to indicate that host country rules applicable to the liability of company administrators in case of company insolvency were impediments to the freedom of secondary establishment. However, these rules, applicable to pseudo-foreign companies, were designed to compensate for the absence of a minimum capital requirement under the law of the place of incorporation. What was in fact at stake here was not the extent or the conditions of company officer liability, but the local rule of

[77] On the extent of the adjustment required of the foreign provider to the local legal environment, see Roth, *supra* note 39, at 18.

[78] *Supra* note 35.

[79] *Supra* note 5. See Art. 17(23). Recital 46 explains that an 'accident involving a person' covers physical or material injury suffered by that person.

[80] See *supra* 'The Problem with Internationally Mandatory Rules of Law' and *infra* 'Designing the Conflict Rule'.

[81] See Wilderspin and Lewis, *supra* note 54, at 18; Heuzé, *supra* note 54, note 29.

[82] See Basedow, *supra* note 54.

[83] Case C-167/01, *supra* note 18.

company law which such liability was designed to sanction. Now, this distinction between the norm whose violation is invoked, and the conditions and extent of the defendant's liability in tort, is enlightening. Indeed, in most of the examples considered in the context of free movement of goods and services, the country of origin principle concerns conduct rules which apply territorially, and not loss-distribution rules. A good illustration can be found in the field of advertising (which can be considered as a service in its own right, or as a marketing method for products[84]). Where a method, such as comparative advertising, which is legal in the country of origin, is 'exported' to the host country, where it is illegal, the issue is whether the prohibitive rule in the host country restrains market access.[85] According to an influential analysis by H.T. Tebbens, the conformity of a particular conduct with the law of the country of origin serves as a datum before the courts of the host country when implementing the law of the place of the affected market (generally the substantive law of the host country itself).[86] In other words, this is the distinction, brought to light by American functionalism between loss allocation rules and rules of conduct,[87] the latter being taken into consideration as datum by the court when evaluating the defendant's conduct. It may therefore be contrary to the principle of origin to assess the legality of the conduct of an advertiser otherwise than according to the rules of the country of origin.[88] However the possibility for the courts to consider the rules applicable at the place of conduct is in fact already integrated into the conflict even when the governing law is the law of the place where the harm occurred, or, in the case of unfair competition, the law of the affected market.[89]

II. Conflict of laws in contract

Market Access and Party Autonomy The first issue which arises as to the relationship between the economic freedoms and contract is whether rules of contract

---

[84] On the importance of this distinction in order to understand the ECJ's case-law in this field, see da Cruz Vilaça, 'On the Application of *Keck* in the Field of Free Provision of Services', in Roth and Andenas (eds), *supra* note 8, at 25 ff., esp. 37.

[85] A rule restricting methods of advertising available to a service provider in the host country can impede market access. This conclusion is confirmed by secondary law (see Tebbens, *supra* note 54, at 469, emphasizing that the 'new generation' of Directives since 1986, for example on cross-border television broadcasting or on financial services, all presuppose that an advertising activity legal in one Member State must be accepted elsewhere). However, one may also wonder to what extent certain advertising methods actually contribute to locational decisions of consumers, justifying the application of the host State's law (see *supra* 'The Different Ways in which Regulatory Competition Operates').

[86] See *supra* note 54, at 478.

[87] See Symeonides, 'The American Choice of Law Revolution in the Courts: Today and Tomorrow', 298 *RCADI* (2003) 13.

[88] See Tebbens, *supra* note 54, at 469.

[89] This conclusion is valid whether the requirement is imposed by an administrative authority or its violation alleged in support of a private action in tort (on this point, see *ibid.*). This is the reason for which the fact that tort law generally bears a label of private law is insufficient in itself to exempt it from

law which, under the Rome Convention, belong to the scope of party autonomy, may be considered as impediments to free movement.[90] In the *Althsom Atlantique* case, it was considered, obiter, that the possibility for the parties to choose the applicable law disqualified in this respect the more restrictive rule of the law governing the contract.[91] Although it has been pointed out that *Althsom* was handed down before *Keck*, it is hard to see why the solution would change.[92] Indeed, similarly, party freedom has been exempted from the scope of the internal market clause by the Electronic Commerce Directive. In addition to the fact that it is difficult to see how an operator could complain of being subjected to a restriction which the operator had the power to remove contractually,[93] the importance given to party autonomy in the dynamics of the internal market hardly argues in favour of a restriction of freedom of choice in the name of the economic freedoms.[94] Obviously, it is perfectly legitimate that large-scale product or service providers may want to rely on the applicability of a given law; the issue of economies of scale must be taken seriously.[95] But, as seen above, the Rome Convention already responds precisely to this need. Simply, under Article 3 of that Convention, the chosen law is not necessarily that of the provider's country of origin, which functions merely as a default rule. Moreover, the ECJ's case-law does not support the idea that rules of contract law subject to party autonomy can inhibit free movement. Admittedly, the *SETTG (Greek tourist guides)* case[96] characterizes a provision of Greek law as just such an impediment insofar as it subjected tourist guides to a status of employees, governed by Greek law; it is argued that the host country's contract law was thus considered as inhibiting market access.[97] However, it has been rightly pointed out that what is at stake here is a failure by Greece to mutually recognize the status of independent guides qualified in other Member States.[98] The example cannot be used to show

the scope of the freedoms. The problem is less to determine who is party to the litigation (see Wilderspin and Lewis, *supra* note 54, 33), than to look at the function of each rule.

[90] On the issue whether liberalization of choice of forum clauses subtracts from the imperativity of market regulation, see Nuyts, *supra* note 41; Radicati di Brozolo, 'Mondialisation, Juridiction, Arbitrage: Vers des règles d'application semi-nécessaire?' [2003] *RCDIP* 1; Muir Watt, 'Aspects économiques du droit international privé', RCADI 2004, t307, at 119.

[91] Case C-339/89, [1991] ECR I-107.

[92] See Gkoutisinis, *supra* note 2.

[93] See Tison, *supra* note 54, at 373.

[94] See Grundmann, 'The Structure of European Private Law', 4 *ERPL* (2001) 505, showing that the whole structure of EC contract law is dependent upon the distinction between rules which come under Arts. 5, 6, and 7 of the Rome Convention, on the one hand, and those which are within the scope of Art. 3 on the other.

[95] On taking transaction costs seriously, see Collins, 'Transaction Costs and Subsidiarity in European Contract Law', in S. Grundmann and J. Stuyck (eds), *An Academic Green Paper on European Contract Law* (2002), at 268 and see *supra* 'Of Noise Levels and Legal Environment'.

[96] Case C-398/95, [1997] ECR I-3091.

[97] See Roth, *supra* note 39, at 17.

[98] See Gkoutisinis, *supra* note 2, at 158.

that the Court considers provisions of contract law as being of a nature to impede free movement.[99]

Internationally Mandatory Rules If one sets aside the issue of consumer protection in the host State—which, in non-harmonized areas, is clearly likely to restrict free movement, but is as obviously justifiable under the general good exception—internationally mandatory rules affecting the conclusion or the content of the relationship between the service provider and the beneficiary, as in *Alpine Investments*, are directly concerned by the requirements of the economic freedoms. When these are not public law rules of strictly territorial effect, but regulations englobing the whole of the contractual relationship, such as rules of investor protection, the extraterritorial scope of these laws creates specific difficulties, as they do not fit into the territorial pattern on which mutual recognition rests. However, in all such cases, as *Alpine Investments* suggests, these provisions which carry mandatory social policies may all benefit, here again, from the general good exception.[100] At the most, the proportionality test may encourage regulatory self-discipline on the part of national legislators as far as the scope of the rule and the means employed to implement its ends are concerned.[101] In other words, as far as the field of private law is concerned, the economic freedoms principally come into play in presence of mandatory rules of contract law, whose extraterritorial effect will give rise to a balancing test.

Balancing Interestingly, the difficulty of applying a territorial scheme to provisions designed to apply extraterritorially, particularly those which claim to regulate out-of-State conduct under the 'effects' test, has also arisen in the United States, under the dormant Commerce Clause. The Clause has been held to prohibit statutes which are extraterritorial *per se*.[102] However, according to an alternative reading, borne out by recent case-law, the only reason to stigmatize extraterritoriality is when it accompanies a violation of economic due process:[103] it is not the fact that a State statute applies to events or persons outside its own constituency that burdens interstate commerce, but the circumstance that when it does so, it may impose undue costs on out-of-State interests. The requirements of interstate commerce then boil down to the application of a balancing test designed to detect illegitimate exportation of

---

[99] At the most, this example emphasizes that, in order to determine whether a specific provision of the substantive applicable law is or is not an impediment to free movement, the formal distinction between private or civil law and market regulation is unhelpful.

[100] This is the case under the Electronic Commerce Directive, *supra* note 43, where consumer protection appears among the motives of general good which can still be invoked within the coordinated field, and among the issues excluded from the coordinated field.

[101] On the application of the requirements of proportionality to the scope of internationally mandatory rules, see Nuyts, *supra* note 41.

[102] See Goldsmith and Sykes, *supra* note 7.

[103] See Eule, *supra* note 7.

costs, in the end not dissimilar to the proportionality test applied under the general good exception in Community law, which finally 'saved' the Dutch rule in *Alpine Investments*. In both contexts, it is clear that the double burden criterion gives way to a balancing test when the rule alleged to restrict market access claims an extraterritorial scope. This may explain why the ECJ reverted to an autonomous market access test[104] in the field of cross-border services, where the applicable rules do not fit the territorial scheme conceived for rules of public law. Be that as it may, in many cases, as in *Alpine Investments*, the restrictive rules will survive the balancing test. Under this test, the requirement of proportionality is designed to prevent legislative over-reaching, and has little to do with mutual recognition. Thus it seems legitimate to ask whether the idea that the economic freedoms require eliminating provisions of either private or regulatory law which claim to apply extraterritorially does not create a false perspective. Similarly, in the American context, Mark Rosen believes that the principles of federalism do not necessarily require 'tidying up' conflicting laws, in particular by giving priority to the law of the territorial State.[105] This may well be a promising path to explore as far as regulatory provisions carrying non-economic policies of Member States are concerned.

2. ECONOMIC DUE PROCESS AND THE CONFLICT OF LAWS

A. The Idea of Economic Due Process

A Process-based Approach to the Requirements of Inter-State Commerce
Rehabilitated as an important judicial tool in the last quarter of a century,[106] the Commerce Clause has also become the focus of debate relating to methods of constitutional interpretation, raising the question of whether or not the federal Constitution should be read as a charter of economic freedoms.[107] While one vision attempts to inject a liberal or deregulatory ideology into the constitutional fabric,[108] another advocates a radically different, process-based approach, principally concerned with integrity of the democratic process, investing the judge-interpretor with the mission of 'reinforcing representativity'.[109] In respect of the significance of the

---

[104] That is, distinct from the duplicatory burden test. That the rationale of the double burden test is to ensure market access was already clear in *Dassonville* (Case 8/74, [1974] ECR 837) and *Cassis de Dijon* (Case 120/78, [1979] ECR 649).

[105] *Supra* note 62, stating that '. . . concurrent jurisdiction is a natural and acceptable byproduct of a federal system of meaningfully empowered states' (at 951).

[106] As observed in 1980 by Eule, *supra* note 7, the renewal is now confirmed in the field of litigation concerning cyberspace: see Goldsmith and Sykes, *supra* note 7.

[107] On this debate, see Posner, 'The Constitution as an Economic Document', 56 *Geo. Washington L R* (1987) 4.

[108] See B. Siegan, *Economic Liberties and the Constitution* (1980); R. Epstein, *Takings: Private Property and the Power of Eminent Domain* (1985) and 'Towards a Revitalization of the Contract Clause', 51 *U Chi L Rev* (1984) 703.

[109] V. J. Ely, *Democracy and Distrust: A Theory of Judicial Review* (1980); Eule, *supra* note 7.

Commerce Clause, the issue is whether any regulation which restricts free cross-border trade calls to be invalidated, or whether the goal of the Clause is to ensure that measures which are likely to affect out-of-State conduct do not discriminate against interests which are not represented in the domestic political process.[110] The comparison with the debate over the function of the economic freedoms in Community law is immediately apparent, since here again a free trade or deregulatory reading of the freedoms confronts an approach which tends to favour legal diversity, including on the level of regulatory policy, as long as such diversity is not used to fragment the internal market.

True or False Balancing of Interests   Since the important *Pike* case,[111] federal courts proceed ostensibly to a balancing of interests, comparing the local benefits of national legislative measures perceived to restrict cross-border trade, and the negative effects of such restrictions. This approach is undoubtedly inspired by a free trade ideal, which implies that there is a distinct federal interest in the fluidity of cross-border commercial exchange, free from inhibitions from local regulation. However, the identification of such a federal interest is denounced by the partisans of a process-based approach as a myth,[112] far from real judicial practice.[113] On the one hand, the argument goes, if the initial policy behind the Commerce Clause was to eradicate State protectionism which threatened national unity, there was no reason to believe that the founders had intended to inject a free trade or *laissez-faire* ideal into the fabric of the Constitution.[114] On the other hand, it is difficult to see what form a judicial inquiry into 'discrimination against the interests of cross-border trade' could actually take. The latter expression is described by one writer as a 'red herring' among the motives of the cases handed down under the Commerce Clause.[115] Moreover, it is argued, the metamorphosis of the federal system itself discredits the deregulatory reading of the Constitution. This is because supposing it was once vested with a practical reality, judicial protection of a federal interest in the freedom of cross-border trade is significant only in a political context in which the principal threat of decentralized decision-making for the economic coherence of the national market resides in local protectionism.[116] However, today, the federal legislator has become far more interventionist, not hesitating to subordinate freedom

---

[110] See *ibid.*

[111] See *Pike* v *Bruce Church, Inc.*, 297 US 137 (1970).

[112] See Eule, *supra* note 7, at 439.

[113] See Regan, 'Judicial Review of Member State Regulation of Trade Within a Federal or Quasi-Federal System: Protectionism and Balancing, Da Capo', 99 *Mich LR* (2000) 1853.

[114] See Eule, *supra* note 7, at 435.

[115] Including in the *Pike* decision itself: see Regan, *supra* note 113. The writer denounces the danger of balancing free trade with other incommensurable values, such as protection of public health or environment. Eule (*supra* note 7) also shows that pure 'ends-balancing' does not in fact occur, and that the courts look rather for proportionality of means.

[116] The Commerce Clause was drafted in a context of commercial warfare between the different states of the Union: see Eule, *supra* note 7, at 430.

of commerce to other ends.[117] The main danger inherent in the federal structure for interests which are not purely internal to the various States lies elsewhere, in the lack of representativity of out-of-State interests in the local decision-making process.[118] The initial justification of the Commerce Clause having dissolved, the time has come to adopt an alternative, process-based model.[119]

Objections   Focusing on the integrity of process rather than product,[120] the economic due process model is designed to hunt down a specific kind of discrimination—the one which the courts tend to identify as being directed against the federal interest in cross-border trade itself—which consists in exporting or externalizing costs to the detriment of foreign interests which are not represented in the domestic legislative process. Insofar as it proposes a new paradigm against which to consider both horizontal and vertical conflicts of laws or interests, it has been the subject of considerable controversy. Similar debate has arisen in Europe since a European writer envisaged the transplantation of this idea into Community law.[121] While its exact effect on national measures affecting cross-border economic relationships no doubt needs to be explored further, it is also clear that the objections levelled against a process-based reading of the requirements of inter-State trade or the economic freedoms are not always properly targeted; and when criticism is justified, it points more to a refinement of the theory rather than to an outright rejection. In this respct, three main objections have been directed against the economic due process theory. First, specific protection of out-of-State economic interests would be redundant, since such interests are already vicariously represented through their local counterparts.[122] Secondly, such a model requires scrutinizing the decision-making processes in the various States, which would be excessively intrusive, overstating the requirements of the unity of the national market.[123] Lastly, paradoxically, economic due process is accused of promoting a neo-liberal ideology which would support a right of individual operators to be free of State restrictions.[124]

---

[117]   This contributes to reactivate the Commerce Clause in its positive function. See the examples cited in *ibid.* at 432, emphasizing its 'virtually limitless uses'. For the writer, it is both undesirable and anachronistic to confer on the courts a function identical to that of the legislator under the Commerce Clause. This explanation of the historical contingency of the Commerce Clause is interesting, since a similar argument is invoked in connection with the function of the fundamental freedoms in Community law (see Poiares Maduro, 'Harmony and Dissonance in Free Movement', *supra* note 8, at 41 ff.).

[118]   See Eule, *supra* note 7.

[119]   According to certain writers, it could be found in the Privileges and Immunities Clause (*ibid.*). According to this Clause, 'The citizens of each State shall be entitled to all Privileges and Immunities of Citizens in the several States'. It would need to be extended however to legal persons (excluded by *Paul* v *Virginia*, 75 U.S. 168, 1868).

[120]   See Eule, *supra* note. 7, 428: 'preserve process rather than protect products'.

[121]   See Poiares Maduro, *We the Court*, *supra* note 8, Chap. 3.

[122]   See Regan, *supra* note 113, at 1857 ff.; Snell and Andenas, *supra* note 32, at 106.

[123]   This critique is formulated by Roth, *supra* note 39, at 8.

[124]   *Ibid.*

Vicarious Representation The first criticism, and the most sophisticated, is formulated by Donald Regan,[125] then reiterated in the Community context by Snell and Andenas.[126] It consists in showing, from the pespective of an economic analysis of the legislative process, that if all the domestic interests affected by the measure are effectively represented, then there is no distortion to be feared as far as unrepresented, foreign, interests are concerned. There is therefore no need for the courts to give virtual expression to such foreign interests supposedly excluded from the legislative process. The explanation lies in the idea of indirect or vicarious representation, according to which a measure which is efficient from a local perspective can also be reputed to be globally optimal. Let us suppose, for example, that a State taxes sales of plastic products whose manufacture creates an environmental risk. This decision to tax, which obliges consumers of the product to internalize its ecological cost, results from a balance achieved, on a local level, between the interests of consumers as a group and those of the environment, represented through environmental lobbies. If this decision is efficient, it is so necessarily on a global level in respect of interests not represented in the political process, and thus there is no reason for the courts to intervene to protect say, foreign manufacturers of plastic goods. Any measure which attempted to discriminate against such interests—for example, by imposing an excessively heavy tax—would also be contrary to the interests of local consumers, whose voices are heard in the local process. As long as the local consumers are properly represented, there can be no risk of discrimination to the detriment of foreign manufacturers.[127] Thus, so the argument goes, there is a phenomenon of global/local equivalence.

The Problem of Exporting Costs This demonstration is perfectly convincing as long as foreign interests, such as those of the plastic manufacturers in the above example, are effectively represented through local interests, here those of local consumers. But it is no longer relevant when out-of-State interests are not relayed locally—which is precisely the case when costs are exported. For example, if the same State decides to subsidize the production of various plastic items, in the knowledge that the toxic smoke created in the course of manufacturing is blown downwind to a neighbouring State, it is quite possible that there is no vicarious representation of the interests of foreign residents indisposed by the smoke in the local decision-making process.[128]

---

[125] See Regan, *supra* note 113, at 1857.

[126] *Supra* note 32.

[127] Of course, the result might well be unfavourable to that category of interests, but it would be the fruit of democratic process and not of unfair discrimination.

[128] Regan accepts that his analysis would not be the same in a case of trans-frontier externalities, but considers that the law designed to react against such harmful effects would not be a 'trade regulation'. It is true that the desire of residents of a neighbouring State to have a clean environment are not (or not necessarily) commercial interests. But it seems to imply a very restrictive vision of the Commerce Clause to exclude them.

An Economic Approach to Conflicting Legislation It is this very question of cost externalization in the course of decentralized decision-making which is at the heart of economic due process. Exporting costs and lack of democratic representativity are really only two ways of describing the same situation.[129] They both represent, from two complementary angles, the risk that a decentralized political structure entails for the economic unity of the common market. That there is common ground between these two perspectives has been claimed by Jack Goldsmith and Alan Sykes, who suggest that the process-based argument should be incorporated into an economic analysis of the function of the Commerce Clause. To this end, the two authors give particular thought to litigation in connection with the constitutionality of State regulation of on-line activities, where there is a certain perception among courts that any claim to extraterritorial effect would be illegal *per se*. Quite clearly, the libertarian ideology of the internet has much to do with this approach.[130] State measures designed to sanction conduct which takes place through a foreign website accessible to local internauts have been struck down because of their claim to reach conduct outside the state boundaries. For example, in *American Libraries* v *Pataki*,[131] the unconstitutionality of a New York statute prohibiting certain pornographic contents is linked to the extraterritorial effect of the statute, from which the court induces, directly, the existence of an excessive burden for inter-State commerce. In particular, the obligation to conform simultaneously to multiple regulations, among which the most restrictive is bound to prevail, is considered prohibitive for on-line economic operators. However, since it is difficult to see why the requirements of the federal Constitution must differ according to whether the local regulation concerns conduct which takes place in real or cyber space, and since nothing hitherto has prevented a service provider from having to comply with the local regulations of each State in which the performance of the service takes place, it is not entirely clear, even given the exacerbated risk of different law applying simultaneously to activities conducted over the internet, why an on-line operator should be entirely free from the same contraints.[132] This line of case-law thus invites further exploration both of the cases in which the ubiquity of the web justifies specific rules for multi-State torts, and, in real space, of the circumstances in which a national provision which attaches effects to out-of-State conduct should be invalidated.

Calibrated Corrective Action The idea developed by Goldsmith and Sykes in this respect is that those extraterritorial provisions which appear to be problematic under

---

[129] See Levmore, 'Interstate Exploitation and Judicial Intervention', 69 *Va L Rev* (1983) 563.

[130] On the incidence of a libertarian ideology of the internet on its normative architecture, see Reidenberg, '*Yahoo!* and Democracy on the Internet', 42 *Jurimetrics J* (2002) 261.

[131] 969 F. Supp. 160 (SDNY 1997).

[132] On the existence, even under Community law, of such an obligation on the part of the operator to adapt to the local normative environment of the host country: see *supra* 'The Specificity of Legal Products'.

the Commerce Clause are always designed in turn to correct cross-border externalities resulting from the content of the laws of other States. For example, in *American Libraries*, the State of New York sought to protect various categories of its local population against the effects, perceived to be harmful, of free on-line access to pornographic content on websites operating from a neighbouring State. Such corrective action is not illegitimate in itself, but is the natural consequence of legal and cultural diversity within the federal system, which requires that States have the means to protect their own legislative policies against the risk of their being emptied of significance through citizen mobility—or the ubiquity of the internet. On the other hand, such action may be excessive; the State which seeks to protect itself against perceived externalities, not being able to see the benefits of the offending legislation, will tend to over-regulate instead of adopting a global perspective in which its drawbacks of the legislation are balanced against its positive effects.[133] This is why there is a need for a mechanism by virtue of which such defensive action is calibrated. The risk to be avoided is that an excessive reaction will in turn impose excessive costs on out-of-State operators. This would be the case, for example, if in protecting its citizens against pornography or hate speech on the Internet, a State prohibition were to paralyse the activities of operators acting in a legal environment where freedom of expression is valued above other values. The *Yahoo!* case, in which a French court required that offending web pages be made inaccessible in France, while accepting that such activity, tortious (and indeed criminal) under French law, was legal elsewhere, provides a remarkable illustration of just such an effort of self-discipline.[134] Indeed, this is where economic due process reappears: at risk here are interests affected by a State measure which are not vicariously represented in the legislative process. The extraterritorial effect of the measure merely invites the court to see whether, by targeting foreign interests or activities, a given State regulation does not carry an undue exportation of costs.

Solidarity and Proportionality Once established, the link between an approach which focuses on the democratic integrity of decsion-making processes and the control of cost externalization, the other criticisms directed against the model of economic due process dissolve. Hunting down distortions of the legislative process through cases of local bias does not make the Commerce Clause fundamentally different from other more traditional constitutional tools which require solidarity or mutual respect in a context of legal diversity. No more than in respect of political due process, it is not on economic due process's agenda to second-guess policy choices

---

[133] For an attempt to construct a conflicts system in the field of economic law on the global consideration of costs and benefits generated by a given operation, see Guzman, 'Conflicts of Laws: New Foundations', 90 *Geo LJ* (2002) 333.

[134] Trib. gr. inst. Paris, *UEJF et LICRA* v *Yahoo! Inc*, 20 November 2000 (www.juriscom.net/txt/jurisfr/cti/tgiparis20001120.pdf); see also *Yahoo! Inc.* v *La Ligue Contre le Racisme et l'Antisémitisme*, 145 F. Supp 2d 1168 (ND Cal, 2001); Reidenberg, '*Yahoo!* and Democracy on the Internet', 42 *Jurimetrics J* (2002) 261.

or check the functioning of the political instances of the various States. Indeed, the means by which it is proposed to verify the integrity of the legislative process leading to the adoption of a State measure alleged to be discriminatory is none other than a proportionality test concerning the means set in motion to attain the relevant goal of general interest. In other words, the regulating State will have to show that although the criticized measure affects unrepresented out-of-State interests, it does not pursue a protectionist goal in doing so, as evidenced by the choice of the means used to implement it, which must be proportionate to the aim pursued and must be the least restrictive available.[135]

Disproportionality and Extraterritorial Reach Among the points from which disproportion can be induced, suggesting legislative over-reaching or exportation of costs, figures the reach of the rule. An excessively defined scope could be the sign that the measure imposes disproportionate costs on outsiders. Once again, the Commerce Clause does not differ fundamentally on this point from other more traditional tools. Thus, in *BMW* v *Gore*, it was the Due Process Clause which justified the reduction of award of punitive damages handed down by the courts of Alabama in a products liability case.[136] Formally, the cause of the unconstitutionality lay in the fact that the conduct which the award was designed to punish had taken place outside the State. However, from an economic perspective, the real difficulty was the circumstance that the award imposed costs on consumers nationwide via the rise in price of the product on the national market, while the benefit remained purely local.[137] Alabama was exporting the cost of the punitive award obtained by a local citizen to consumers nationwide.[138] The imbalance was all the more evident that, moreover, the damages were designed to punish the defendant for conduct which had occurred in other States, whose citizens however had no share in the prize. This resulted in a capture of resources to the detriment of buyers nationally, incompatible with federalist principles. Now, if one compares this situation with the tools used by Community law to check national measures affecting the internal market, it is clear that it is more enlightening to see them as means of curbing unilateralism rather than to attempt to express the corrective action of the

---

[135] This is why Roth is right to say that the function of the economic freedoms is no way to remedy institutional defects in Member States (Roth, *supra* note 39). The model proposed here is indeed specifically designed, contrary to the fears of the same writer, to avoid balancing national interests and free trade. It does not carry a libertarian agenda!

[136] *BMW* v *Gore*, 116 S Ct 1589 (1996). The Supreme Court, which had hitherto refrained from interfering with punitive damages awards (each community must express its own sense of outrage), intervened here for the first time in the name of due process, to moderate a clearly excessive award made by an Alabama jury.

[137] On this analysis, see Rubin, Calfee, and Grady, 'BMW v. Gore: Mitigating the Punitive Economics of Punitive Damages' [1007] *Supreme Court L Rev.* 179; Krauss, 'Product Liability and Game Theory: One More Trip to the Choice of Law Well', [2002] *BYUL Rev* 759.

[138] Rules which provide for the jurisdiction of the courts of the state of the victim exacerbate this risk of exporting costs on out-of-State defendants.

economic freedoms in terms of eliminating impediments to cross-border trade.[139] But once it is accepted that good management of legal diversity means defining a reasonable scope for national measures given the end pursued, one is close to formulating a functional conflict of laws principle. It is therefore time to ask whether uniform conflict rules in fields of tort and regulatory law could serve to canalize externalities in an integrated economic environment. Far preferable to enclosing the conflicts which arise in these fields within the territorial scheme of mutual recognition, more foreseeable than a case-by-case balancing test, uniform conflict rules devised to serve the needs of economic due process could constitute a cardinal tool for the governance of legal diversity within the internal market.

B. Channelling Externalities through Uniform Conflict Rules

Regulatory Conflict Rules? Although it has received little attention, dwarfed as it is by the current debate on codification of private law or the relationship between mutual recognition and the conflict of laws, such a development is in fact already taking place. In areas where an unlevel playing-field is perceived to distort competition between firms,[140] appropriate conflict rules are being put into place in order to correct these distortions, while leaving each national system free to pursue its own economic or social policies through diverse substantive rules. Interestingly, the specifically regulatory function of these new conflict rules induces a profound change in the way they are designed; rather than attaching an appropriate connecting factor to an abstract category of issues, the rule identifies the risk of distortion and seeks the best way to correct it. The conflict of laws is generally neglected in discussion across the Atlantic concerning the limits of the competitive model and the means to rectify distortions resulting from cross-border externalities; usually, economic federalism concludes that centralized substantive legislation is the only way out.[141] At the same time, as we have seen, various constitutional tools have been developed judicially, in order to prevent over-reaching or the exporting of costs by the various States, without challenging the principle of decentralized decision-making. The concept of 'market-preserving federalism' gives expression to the idea that States are free to use their legislative powers as they think fit, except to fragment

---

[139] Through the balancing of interests to which it finally gave rise, the *Alpine Investments* case, *supra* note 26, comes close to this.

[140] Distortion of competition between firms is the result of distorted competition between legislators. Unless one considers that firms should not have to assume transaction costs linked to diversity, as the European Commission seems to do (see *supra* 'Regulatory Techniques and the Conflict of Laws'), it is less the difference between national laws that is objectionable than the distortions created by these differences, particularly in the form of a race to the bottom, usually generated by large differences in levels of protective legislation.

[141] On the conclusions of the Tiebout model in this respect, see Bratton and McCahery, 'The New Economics of Jurisdictional Competition: Devolutionary Federalism in a Second Best World', 86 *Georgetown LJ* (1997) 201.

or distort the common market.[142] While neither Full Faith and Credit nor Due Process have turned out to be particularly effective in this function,[143] the Commerce Clause now appears as a powerful break on diverse forms of State unilateralism.[144] The uniform conflict rules newly developed within the European Community incorporate similar checks on Member State opportunism, under the more manageable form of uniform conflict of law rules.[145]

Regulatory Dumping The two instances in which the Community now has a specifically regulatory conflict are characterized by an important risk of legislative dumping. This is the situation in which a State adopts a legislation which is more lax than that of other States, in the knowledge that the interests which a more stringent regulation would protect are outside its own territory. If the effects of the legislation are nevertheless felt outside the State, the risk is that the price of a more lax legislation is then borne by out-of-State interests, while its benefits are exclusively local. Such a risk is particularly important in the field of labour law and environmental protection, which is precisely where new conflict rules have emerged as regulatory tools.[146] Thus under Community law, the battle waged against social dumping in the relationship between high- and low-wage States, through adequate formulation of conflict of laws principles, reveals a tool which can be used, if necessary in conjunction with other measures such as minimal or targeted harmonization, in order to exert a calibrated check on the temptation to export costs. In the field of environmental protection, the proposed 'Rome II' Regulation on the law applicable to extra-contractual obligations, which is applicable to torts occurring outside the Community, suggests that even in the absence of harmonization, a careful allocation of legislative jurisdiction can contribute extensively to eliminating distortions induced by regulatory competition.

I. Posting of workers

Social Dumping The first example, which concerns the posting of workers within the Community, shows how the conflict of laws can be used to counter cross-border 'regulatory dumping' in the field of labour law. Although many aspects of labour law are now harmonized on a Community level, minimum wages are not.[147] Under

---

[142] See Weingast, 'The Economic Role of Political Institutions: Market Preserving Federalism and Economic Development', 11 *J Law, Econ & Org* (1995) 1, and the discussion in Rodden and Rose-Ackerman, 'Does Federalism Preserve Markets?', 83 *Va L Rev* (1997) 1521.

[143] See R. Weintraub, *Commentary on the Conflict of Laws* (4th edn., 2001), at 624.

[144] Too powerful, perhaps, when used to stigmatize extraterritoriality as a general rule? See on this point, Goldsmith and Sykes, *supra* note 7.

[145] On the issue of how far rules not based on content are nevertheless compatible with a functional approach to choice of law, see Symeonides, *supra* note 87.

[146] These two fields are also particularly problematic in the context of the global economy, when no corrective mechanism is available (see *infra* 'Conclusion').

[147] For an excellent overview of harmonized aspects, see Moreau, 'Le détachement des travailleurs effectuant une prestation de services dans l'Union européenne' [1996] *JDI* 889.

the Rome Convention, in the absence of party choice, employment contracts are governed by the law of the place where the work is habitually performed, even when the worker is posted temporarily to another country. This rule, which, in theoretical terms, eliminates the *'conflit mobile'*,[148] gave rise to a practice in the area of construction contracts whereby contractors in low-wage states, such as Portugal, were able to benefit from a considerable competitive advantage by posting workers to high-wage States. The posted workers continued to be subject to the lower wages of their country of habitual employment. Directive No 96/71 of 16 December 1996 on the posting of workers within the Community[149] was designed to put an end to this practice, the idea being that cross-border exchange of workers should be designed to encourage the sharing of particular professional expertise developed in different Member States, but not to create an unhealthy competition on costs.[150] Under this Directive, the worker benefits from the (higher) wage of the place of posting. Specific provision is also made for the case where the worker is posted within the Community from outside—a situation which would normally be subject, once again, to the conflict rule of the Rome Convention, with a similar risk of regulatory dumping from non-Member States with lower standards.[151] Seen as a regulatory tool, the mechanism put into place by the Directive calls for further explanation.

Article 6(2) of the Rome Convention The problem of social dumping between Member States is targeted by the 1996 Directive. One can see that the risk of a regulatory race to the bottom was exacerbated here by the existence of a wide disparity between the levels of protection offered across the Community. Indeed, the difficulty that the Directive sought to overcome had its source in the differences between the laws applicable to minimum wages, particularly in the construction sector.[152] Portuguese firms, in particular, enjoyed a considerable competititive advantage in respect of the prices they could charge for construction work, because

[148] That is, the difficulty which arises when a connecting factor (e.g. the place of performance) is displaced from one country to another.

[149] On the French statute implementing the Directive, see Robin, 'L'application du droit social français aux entreprises prestataires de services établies à l'étranger' [1994] *Droit social* 127. On the problem of social dumping, see G. and A. Lyon-Caen, *Droit social international et européen* 7th edn, 1991), no. 270; A. Lyon-Caen, 'Droit social et droit de la concurrence', in *Mélanges Jean Savatier* (1992), 331; Moreau, *supra* note 147.

[150] See Moreau, *supra* note 147.

[151] In pre-Directive cases, this difficulty could of course be remedied by applying the mandatory rules of the place of posting under Art. 7 of the Rome Convention and subject to a proportionality test. However, unless the forum agrees to apply foreign mandatory rules under Art. 7(1), practically, this remedy supposes that the worker has access to a forum at the place of posting—which is not provided for under the Brussels Convention. The Directive itself introduces such a forum, thereby reinforcing the credibility of the substantive protection it provides.

[152] The building sector is the main target of the Directive. Moreover, minimum wages are the main point of divergence in a field which is otherwise largely harmonized: see Moreau, *supra* note 147, at 891.

they were able to send temporary, low-paid manpower to building sites in other Member States which paid higher wages. Such a result was expressly condoned by the Rome Convention on the law applicable to contractual obligations, whose Article 6-2(a) excludes the *conflit mobile* (that is, a change in the applicable law) in cases where the worker is posted temporarily to another State. The worker thus remains subject to the law of the place where the work is habitually performed, even when its content is less favourable than that of the place of posting.[153] This provides an excellent illustration of the fact that an undiscriminating application of the country of origin principle may itself generate a deleterious race to the bottom, made possible in this instance by the mobility of the workforce.[154] A practice grew up involving intra-Community temporary transfer of workers not only as means of optimizing the employment of specialized manpower throughout the Community, which is particularly desirable within multinational firms, but also and perhaps above all, as a result of competition based not on quality but on costs, given the ready access to a mobile, unqualified and low-paid workforce.[155]

***Introducing the* 'Conflit Mobile'** The 1996 Directive seeks to remedy this situation by giving the posted worker[156] the benefit of the law of the place of posting[157] on a certain number of points, including minimum wages.[158] This benefit is made more effective by giving the worker the right to access the courts of the place of posting, notwithstanding the lack of any similar basis of juridiction in the Brussels Convention and without prejudice of the worker's right to use any of the other fora put into place by this Convention.[159] As emphasized by Marie-Ange Moreau,

---

[153] Unless the parties have chosen a law more favourable to the worker, and in the absence of a closer connection to another law (Art. 6(1) and (2)(b) *in fine*, of the Rome Convention on the law applicable to contractual obligations).

[154] On the fact that regulatory competition takes place in different ways for different rules, so that to give excessive scope to the country of origin principle can distort competition instead of encouraging it, see Snell and Andenas, *supra* note 32.

[155] See Moreau, *supra* note 147, at 898.

[156] On the definition of temporary posting, see *ibid.*, 893. Intra-group posting is comprised within this definition, the aim being to avoid allowing sophisticated techniques of social engineering to interfere with the protection provided. On the other hand, the requirement that the posting should take place on behalf of another firm excludes certain cases of cross-border provision of services which benefit from free movement under the EC Treaty (*ibid.*, 894).

[157] In cases of conflict between the Rome Convention and the Directive, the latter prevails by virtue of Art. 20 of the Convention.

[158] The other core aspects of worker protection are already harmonized for the most part. In harmonized areas, the question arises therefore whether the worker should continue to benefit from the law of the place of posting, when it is more generous than the Community 'floor' applicable in the place of habitual employment. It seems clear that the worker must indeed benefit from the more favourable provisions. In the same way, the worker benefits from the eventually more generous provisions of the law governing the employment contract (whether the law of the place of habitual employment or a chosen law which is more favourable to the worker).

[159] Art. 6.

despite the improved protection of workers which results from the Directive (those who work habitually in countries which provide lesser social protection benefit, at least for the period of posting, from the same advantages enjoyed by their local counterparts) the Directive pursues a goal which is far more economic than social.[160] By guaranteeing that the posted worker benefits from the content of the law of the place of posting, it seeks to level the playing field as among firms emplying a work-force within the Community, and is only indirectly concerned with levels of social protection as such.[161] This analysis is confirmed by the treatment reserved to work-ers from third countries. Indeed, the Directive defines its scope so as to include only those postings which involve two Member States, that is, situations in which a worker is transferred temporarily from one Member State to another (Article 1-1). Thus if the employer is established in a third State, the Directive is inapplicable and Article 6(2)(a) of the Rome Convention remains relevant; the *conflit mobile* disap-pears once more and the employment relationship escapes the sway of local manda-tory rules.[162] However, in such a case, given that the playing field has been levelled to a high standard as among Member States by the effect of the Directive itself, the inapplicability of mandatory protective provisions of the law of the place of post-ing when temporary labour is imported from outside the Community is likely to recreate new distortions in competition by creating an obvious incentive for Community contractors to do business with firms in third countries where lower wages are normal. This is why the Directive provides that firms established in a third country may not enjoy a more favourable treatment than their Community counterparts—which means that the provisions of the law of the place of posting, particularly as far as minimum wages are concerned, may once again be applied.[163]

A Functional Approach By re-establishing the balance upset by competitive distortions of the playing field as between Community firms, the conflict of law rule applicable in cases of the posting of workers undoubtedly asserts a corrective action over the risks of legislative competition. Adjusting the connecting factor of Article 6(2) of the Rome Convention so that the law of the new, temporary, place of performance applies, is a way of giving effect to the 'effects' test, insofar as it allows the host State to react against the externalization of costs of lower social protection on the part of the State from which the worker is posted, usually the place of establishment of the employer. In this respect, the *Arblade* and *Mazzoleni*

---

[160] See Moreau, *supra* note 147, at 890.

[161] On the instrumentalizing of labour law by competition policy, see A. Lyon-Caen, 'Droit social et droit de la concurrence', in *Mélanges Jean Savatier* (1992), 331.

[162] The internationally mandatory rules of the place of posting could then apply under Art. 7 of the Rome Convention.

[163] The principle according to which firms from third States must not receive more favourable treat-ment than Community firms is set out in Art. 1(4) of the Directive. It raises the very difficult question of the applicability of Community law to firms from third States: see S. Franck, *L' applicabilité spatiale du droit communautaire*, thesis (2004).

cases handed down by the Court of Justice before the provisions of the Directive were implemented in the relevant domestic laws, show that, in fact, a similar result could be obtained under Article 7 of the Rome Convention through a calibrated application (that is, subject to the proportionality test and in the absence of a double burden) of the internationally mandatory provisions of the law of the place of posting in the field of social protection.[164] Be that as it may, as long as the more protective provisions of the law of the place of posting are applicable, Community-wide competition between firms will no longer be triggered by different levels of wages and must find more constructive channels, based on quality rather than cost. On a methodological level, it is interesting to note that the adjustment brought about in the solution of the conflict of laws by the Directive, began with the idea that it was necessary to ensure the mandatory application of the provisions of the law of the host country, which, as the *Arblade/Mazzoleni* cases again demonstrate, generally claimed to apply as a matter of course. This of course goes directly against the country of origin principle. It also goes to show that the new regulatory conflict rules which seek to allocate jurisdiction in order to deal with cross-border externalities tend to emerge inductively from the shared social and economic regulatory goals of the relevant national laws,[165] rather than deductively, from pre-existing conceptual categories. In the same way, by introducing the law of the place of temporary posting, the Directive is in no way inspired by any of the theories of the *conflit mobile*, but considers the economic consequences of allowing the applicable law to change. No doubt these methodological changes are the sign that the private law paradigm, strongly embedded in contemporary conflicts theory, at least in its Continental version, is gradually giving ground to a functional approach, as the conflict of laws asserts a specifically regulatory role.

The Limits of the Competitive Distortion Argument In such a context, the reference in the recitals of the Directive to the elimination of competitive distortions throughout the Community[166] is perfectly comprehensible. It means that the conflict rule is designed to manage cross-border externalities linked to disparities between levels of social protection, the choice of connecting factor adjusting to this end so as to regulate regulatory competition. However, a similar reference has been used, less convincingly, in other contexts. Thus, the provisions of the 1986 Agency

---

[164] The same proportionality test seems likely to remain after the Directive has been implemented because, while the new connecting factor leads to the application of the law of the (temporary) host State, it cannot of course cover a violation of the fundamental freedoms (see on this point, the Opinion of Alber AG and Pataut, note [2001] *RCDIP* 504. Thus, a global assessment of the equivalence of the protection provided for the worker on the question of minimum wages, required by the ECJ in its *Mazzoleni* ruling (see *supra*, note 34) in the name of proportionality, still appears necessary.

[165] This observation confirms Andreas Bucher's analysis of the transformations affecting the conflict of laws through the changes affecting private law itself: see Bucher, 'L'ordre public et le but social des lois en droit international privé', 239 *RCADI* (1993) 9.

[166] Recital 5 mentions loyal competition within the Community.

Directive[167] have been given immediate, internationally mandatory, effect in relationships involving third States, whenever the situation presents a close connection with the Community.[168] The *Ingmar* case[169] invokes such a justification—for the first time in a judicial definition of the scope of Community law vis-à-vis third States[170]—explaining that the protection ensured individual agents by this Directive aims to guarantee freedom of establishment and undistorted competition through-out the internal market (point 24). An agent acting in England for a California firm must therefore enjoy the protection provided by Community law, which thereby prevails over the less protective provisions of the law chosen by the parties to govern their contract, in this instance, the law of California. The Court of Justice showed concern, in the name of the legal order of the Community, that a firm established in a third country, whose agent acts within the Community, should not be able to escape the protection provided by Community law through the mere operation of a choice of law clause. The specific function of the relevant provisions commands that they apply whenever the situation is closely related to the Community (point 25). However, it is difficult to see exactly how competition is distorted within the Community, threatening the coherence of the internal market, by the operation of party choice. While the Advocate General referred essentially to the extraterritorial scope of competition law, the Court itself concentrated, rather, on the risk of social dumping on the part of firms from third countries, linked to the fact that Community law had been harmonized so as to provide a higher protection for agents. Apart from the fact that this justification would mean that practically all harmonized fields of Community law would become internationally mandatory, indiscriminately,[171] the real issue is whether independent commercial agents repre-sent a social category which calls for special protection in respect of the conflict of laws as such. This is a controversial issue to which the Court devotes a sole, some-what laconic, paragraph.[172] It may be concluded that arguments grounded on com-petitive distortions, which call for a corrective action on the part of the conflict rule, must be used prudently. Indeed, there is no point in reducing the scope of party autonomy if there is no real risk that it will provide an incentive for a destructive race to the bottom, whether as between Member States themselves, or as between the Community and third States. On the other hand, just such a legitimate and

---

[167] Directive 86/653/EC coordinating the laws of the Member States in the field of commercial agency, OJ 1986 L382/117.

[168] On the complex relationship between applicability and imperativeness of secondary Community law, see Franck, *supra* note 163.

[169] See Case C-381/98, *Ingmar* [2000] ECR I-9305.

[170] See Idot, 'Case Note' [2001] *RCDIP* 116.

[171] *Ibid.*, at 117.

[172] *Ibid.*, at point 21. A few days later, the French Cour de cassation handed down a decision to the contrary (Cass. com. 28 Nov. 2000 [2001] D. Aff 305, note by Chevrier). On the debate on this point in Belgian law, see Nuyts, *supra* note 41; on the state of the law on this point in the United States and for an economic analysis of the various possibilities, see O'Hara, 'Opting Out of Regulation: A Public Choice Analysis of Contractual Choice of Law', 53 *Vand L Rev* (2000) 1551.

subtle illustration of corrective action on the part of the conflict rule can be found in the field of cross-border pollution.

II. Environmental protection

Designing the Conflict Rule A second illustration of the new regulatory model of the conflict rule can be found in the field of damages caused by cross-border pollution. Under the proposed Rome II Regulation on the law applicable to extra-contractual obligations,[173] the law governing the tort is, in general, the law of the place where the harm occurs.[174] In the area of environmental torts, however, the plaintiff may choose between the law of the place of the harm and that of the polluting activity which gave rise to the damage.[175] The recitals make it clear that this choice is designed to neutralize two sorts of opportunisitic behaviour on the part of firms which might be tempted to take advantage of disparities in standards of environmental protection among the different Member States in order to escape or reduce liability. On its own, a place-of-activity rule might encourage firms to set up factories in States with low protection, and could in turn provide legislators with an incentive to lower standards in order to attract firms, in a classic race-to-the-bottom type of situation. On the other hand, a place-of-harm rule might result in industries being set up in a higher protection country if natural conditions such as down-winds or rivers flowing across State boundaries meant that the effects of the pollution were in fact felt elsewhere.[176] The American experience of designing conditions for healthy regulatory competition in the field of environmental protection is instructive on this point.[177] However, although there has been much reflection on the respective merits of regulatory competition and centralized federal legislation in this field, little thought has been given to the alternative possibility of using a conflict rule both to heighten the general level of protection (since the claimant will always choose the more protective rule) and to maintain a level playing-field (since firms will not be able to exploit discrepancies in the levels of protection in order to escape liability), as the Rome II Regulation has now done.[178] Again, additional explanation may be necessary.

The Problem of Negative Spill-overs The real impact of regulatory competition in the field of environmental protection, and particularly the question whether it is

---

[173] Draft of 22 July 2003, COM(2003)427 final.

[174] *Ibid.*, Art. 3(1).

[175] *Ibid.*, Art. 7.

[176] *Ibid.*, recitals under Art. 7.

[177] See, e.g., Esty, 'Revitalizing Environmental Federalism', 95 *Mich L Rev* (1996) 570; Revesz, 'Federalism and Regulation: Extrapolating from the Analysis of Environmental Regulation in the United States' [2000] *J Int'l Econ L* 219.

[178] It is regrettable that the proposed Regulation does not extend this analysis to other fields: see Symeonides, 'Tort Conflicts and Rome II: A View from Across', in *Festschrift für Erik Jayme* (2004), 935.

likely to lead to a systematic lowering of standards in order to reduce the costs of manufacturing, thereby attracting investment, is the subject of considerable debate.[179] It is often feared that the pressures of regulatory competition, which may have the effect of sending industry from high- to low-protection States, can cause the global level of regulation to drop sub-optimally in respect of all the various interests which would otherwise come into play.[180] On the other hand, whether on a global level or in a federal or Community context, it is obviously out of the question to challenge State policy choices as such; a laxer standard of environmental protection may signify that the national economy is pursuing other priorities, such as attracting investment with a view to ensuring a high level of employment. Policy choices only become questionable, and competition distorted, when the benefits reaped by local firms through cost reduction are obtained artificially, at the price of exporting costs to neighbouring communities, which then have to suffer negative spill-overs.[181] This is the case, for instance, when a State uses lax environmental standards to attract industries, whereas the polluting effects are felt in neighbouring States (down-river or down-wind) with higher standards, whose own firms have to assume higher costs of environmental protection. The perversity of situations such as this, particularly visible on a global level, is exacerbated when firms established in high protection states delocalize their activities to States with laxer standards, while the resources generated by these activities—which represent precisely the incentive to lower standards—also escape the local community.[182] Mobile capital pushes standards to the bottom, the better to reap the profits of regulatory diversity.

The Economics of Victim Choice Very often ignored in this debate,[183] the conflict of laws offers a means of regulating cross-border externalization of costs and thus, if not of totally preventing the risk of a race to laxity under the pressure of competition, at least of modifying the incentives which attract mobile firms to countries which offer an undue competitive advantage. Indeed, in cases of

---

[179] For an overview, see Revesz, 'Rehabilitating Interstate Competition: Rethinking the "Race-to-the-Bottom" Rationale for Federal Environmental Regulation', 67 *NYU L Rev* (1992) 1210.

[180] It is no mystery that the parameter of what is globally optimal is hard to find. Here, this risk of a suboptimal level of regulation would seem to be effective where firms have homogeneous preferences in favour of the most lax regulation.

[181] Obviously, when regulatory competition leads to lowering standards to the detriment of fundamental rights, policy choices also become highly questionable, and respect for legal diversity should then give way to the definition of minimum protective standards.

[182] A similar source of imbalance can be found on a global level in cases of liability for catastrophic damage linked to delocalized industrial activities. On the degradation of the environment as a tragedy of the global commons, see *infra* 'Conclusion'.

[183] The solution generally proposed consists of measures of international cooperation with a view to substantive harmonization. However, mutual recognition is sometimes proposed as an alternative, in order to inject a dose of regulatory competition perceived as salutary nevertheless: see Revesz, *supra* note 179, and 'Federalism and Regulation: Extrapolating from the Analysis of Environmental Regulation in

cross-border pollution, the risk of seeing a State lower its environmental standards for the benefit of firms established within its territory, when the pollution occurs in another State, exists to the extent that the law applicable to the liability incurred for environmental harm is the law of the place of the conduct which gave rise to the harm. However, if, on the contrary, the law of the place of the harm were applicable, the danger would be that polluting industries established in high protection countries might set up near the border so that toxic waste or smoke travels to the neighbouring State, triggering the operation of a more lax standard of liability. An interesting response to this double problem appears in the proposed Rome II Regulation, in its Article 7, dealing with cases of cross-border pollution.[184] The governing law is, at the choice of the victim, either the law of the place where the harm occurred or that of the conduct from which it arose. The recitals explain that this solution is designed to make operators established in States with lower standards take account of the higher standards in other States, reducing their incentive either to direct the effects of their activities towards States with laxer legislations, or to delocalize their activities to such States. In fact, in either case, the point is to avoid one national community from reaping the sole profits from an economic activity of which it does not bear, correlatively, the burdens. From an internal market perspective, the playing field is levelled between firms across the Community, since the conflict rule makes it impossible to play upon the differences in levels of protection to obtain an artificial, and thus unfair, competitive advantage.

Potential Benefits in Other Fields It is regrettable that a similar approach was not retained in other circumstances where an identical risk of cost externalization is present.[185] In cases of multi-contact torts, Article 13 of the proposed Regulation allows for the conduct rules in force at the place of the tortious activity to be taken into account, independently of the law otherwise governing the tort, which will usually be the law of the place of the harm under the general presumption of Article 3. The recitals present this possibility as aiming for the same effect as its antecedent, Article 9 of the 1973 Hague Convention on the law applicable to product liability. In other words, it is designed to allow defendants to prevail themselves of the more favourable standards of conduct of the place where they acted and on which they had aligned their activity.[186] But, as Symeon Symeonides rightly points out, this

---

the United States' [2000] *J Int'l Econ L* 219; Paul, 'Competitive and Non-Competitive Regulatory Markets: The Regulation of Packaging Waste in the EU', in J. McCahery, W. Bratton, S. Picciotto, and C. Scott, *International Regulatory Competition and Coordination* (1996).

[184] Of course, the vocation of the proposed Rome II Regulation is universal, in the sense that it applies wherever the tort occurs, but the incidence of objectives which are specific to the Community is clear. On the ambiguity of the text in this respect, see de Vareilles-Sommières, 'La responsabilité civile dans la proposition de règlement communautaire sur la loi applicable aux obligations non contractuelles ("Rome II")', in Fuchs, Muir Watt, and Pataut, *supra* note 34.

[185] See in this sense Symeonides, *supra* note 178, 935.

[186] See the recitals under Art. 13.

systematic favour for the defendant in cases of cross-border tort is not always legitimate.[187] Taking the place of conduct's *conduct* rules into account under Article 13 could also be very useful in instances where the defendant's conduct gives rise to liability under that law, even though no liability is incurred under the law of the place the damage is experienced. When the harm occurs as a result of an act which is tortious under the law of the place it was done, this means that the state of conduct has an interest in regulating that activity, even if the consequences happen to unfold outside its own territory—and all the more so if they are channelled there deliberately. On the other hand, the laxer law of the place of the harm has no real interest in shielding the defendant from liability in such a case, since its policy of protecting or encouraging certain activities or types of conduct can hardly concern those which take place elsewhere. In other words, in terms of governmental interest analysis, this is a classic false conflict, in which it hardly seems legitimate to allow the defendant to escape liability just because its effects take place in a state with laxer standards.[188] The reciprocal nature of the conflict rule in Article 7 in cases of environmental pollution would certainly be equally justified in other cases of complex torts, such as those implicating the violation of privacy.

Conclusion However perfectible the solutions proposed by the Community legislator may be, they demonstrate, on the one hand, that the social and economic interests involved go far beyond those of the sole parties to the litigation, and that, despite an important and perhaps paradoxical injection of party autonomy,[189] these interests are of a nature to modify the content and structure of the rules of the conflict of laws.[190] Because of the importance given to maintaining an undistorted playing-field between Community firms, the regulatory function of the conflict of laws evidenced in these developments appears at present to be linked to the existence of a complex political structure, which combines decentralized decision-making with an integrated market. Moreover, the presence of a central legislative authority favours the emergence of uniform supra-national conflict rules devised to channel cost externalization—a result which would obviously be more difficult to obtain through a local law-maker. As Jurgen Basedow puts it, the Community acts here as a neutral arbitrator of the conflict of laws between Member States.[191] Nevertheless, there is no reason why the regulatory function with which the conflict of laws appears to

---

[187] See Symeonides, *supra* note 178, at para. 4.4.

[188] See *ibid.* The writer emphasizes that the formulation of bilateral or reciprocal rules may well conform to a functional analysis, if the chosen connecting factors remain significant whatever the content of the applicable laws. This is the case with the conflict rules in Art. 7 of the proposed Regulation.

[189] Inspired by the Dutch and German models, Art. 10 of the proposed Regulation authorizes the choice of the applicable law once the dispute has arisen, except in the field of intellectual property, where such a possibility would be 'inappropriate'. The function of party autonomy in this context calls for further elucidation.

[190] The consequences of this transformation on the procedural status of foreign law would be worth exploring further.

[191] *Trav. Comité fr dr int pr*, June 2004, publication awaited.

be invested progressively in this context, should not serve as a starting point for thinking about improving the state of affairs on a global level. The 'tragedy of the global commons' lies precisely in the fact that, in the absence of a central source of discipline on State opportunism, the international legal order is rife with regulatory unilateralism and disregard for the effects of legislation felt elsewhere.[192] However, the rules of Community law which give effect to the idea that economic due process should be respected and cost externalization avoided are in no way indissociable from their economic context. It is high time to explore the potential of the new regulatory function of the conflict of laws in a worldwide environment. Is this not the very meaning of 'global federalism'?[193]

---

[192] The expression 'tragedy of the commons' was coined by Garrett Hardin in 'The Tragedy of the Commons', *Science*, 13 Dec. 1986, see J.L. Coleman (ed.), *Readings in the Philosophy of Law* (1999), 551–6. The adjective 'global' has been added in the field of environmental protection: see Clancy, 'The Tragedy of the Global Commons', 5 *Ind J Global Legal Stud* (1998) 601.

[193] The expression is used by Fox, 'Global Markets, National Law and the Regulation of Business— a View from the Top', in M. Likoksy (ed.), *Transnational Legal Processes, Globalization and Power Disparities* (2002).

5

Law at, to or from the Centre?
The European Court of Justice and the
Harmonization of Private Law in the
European Union[†]

ANGUS JOHNSTON* AND HANNES UNBERATH**

1. INTRODUCTION

Directives are of crucial importance for the harmonization of private law in the European Union. The use of this legislative instrument invariably entails a complex interaction between different actors at national and Community level. For, unlike Regulations, Directives do not, generally speaking, have direct effect. To have direct effect they require transposition into national law. Accordingly, Directives are addressed to the Member States and leave to the States the choice as to the form and method of achieving the end established by the Directive (Article 249(3) EC). In the normal case, the Community institutions have the choice whether to legislate by means of Directives or Regulations, although exceptions are frequent.[1] However, since (at least in theory) Directives constitute a lesser interference with the national system they should be given first priority in the light of the principle of subsidiarity.[2] In the area of substantive private law, harmonization has, in the

[†] The authors are very grateful for the invitation to contribute this piece to this collection and wish to thank Albertina Albors-Llorens, John Armour, Matthew Conaglen, Ulrike Janzen, and Stephan Lorenz for their help, support, and encouragement in the writing of this chapter. Any errors and inaccuracies remain our responsibility.

* M.A. (Oxon.), LL.M. (Leiden), B.C.L. (Oxon.), University Lecturer in Law and Fellow of Trinity Hall, University of Cambridge.

** D.Phil. (Oxon.), M.Jur. (Oxon.), Institut für Internationales Recht, Rechtsvergleichung, Ludwig-Maximilians-Universität, Munich.

[1] In the field of private law, see now the important legal basis provided by Art. 95 EC. Contrast, e.g., Arts. 44, 46(2), 94, 96, 132(1), and 137(2) EC, under all of which only Directives can be adopted.

[2] See para. 6 of Protocol No. 30 on the application of the principles of subsidiarity and proportionality, annexed to the EC Treaty (added by the Treaty of Amsterdam: OJ 1997 C 340/105).

past, occurred mainly through the means of Directives.[3] By contrast, in the area of judicial cooperation in civil matters the Regulation has been the preferred instrument.[4] It seems that the Regulation will also become the preferred instrument in the field of international private law.[5]

The main advantage of Directives cannot be underestimated. They make the legislative process flexible, and flexible from both ends.[6] They enable the Community to introduce complex legislative change where it would be difficult to devise Regulations with the specificity necessary for an instrument that has direct application in the Member States. Leaving the Member States a measure of discretion as to how to achieve the desired end ensures that the Directive's aim is embedded into the framework of national laws. 'Translating' the aim of the Directive into 'national' concepts and fleshing it out by using 'national' techniques should avoid distorting the coherence of national law while achieving the desired end in a very effective

---

[3] An overview of the *acquis communautaire* in the field of contractual and extra-contractual liability is given in Annex III to the Communication from the Commission to the Council and the European Parliament on European Contract Law, 11 July 2001, COM(2001)398 final, at 52. Without exception, the relevant legislation is in the form of Directives. The following Directives all affect contractual liability and are in one way or another 'consumer Directives': Directive 1999/44/EC of the European Parliament and of the Council of 25 May 1999 on certain aspects of the sale of consumer goods and associated guarantees (OJ 1999 L 171/12); Council Directive 93/13/EEC of 5 April 1993 on unfair terms in consumer contracts (OJ 1993 L 95/29); Council Directive 90/314/EEC of 13 June 1990 on package travel, package holidays and package tours (OJ 1990 L 158/59); Council Directive 85/577/EEC of 20 December 1985 to protect the consumer in respect of contracts negotiated away from business premises (OJ 1985 L 372/31); Directive 97/7/EC of the European Parliament and of the Council of 20 May 1997 on the protection of consumers in respect of distance contracts (OJ 1997 L 144/19); Directive 94/47/EC of the European Parliament and the Council of 26 October 1994 on the protection of purchasers in respect of certain aspects of contracts relating to the purchase of the right to use immovable properties on a timeshare basis (OJ 1994 L 280/83); Council Directive 87/102/EEC of 22 December 1986 for the approximation of the laws, regulations and administrative provisions of the Member States concerning consumer credit (OJ 1987 L 42/48) as modified by Directive 90/88 (OJ 1990 L 61/14) and Directive 98/7 (OJ 1998 L 101/ 17). See furthermore Council Directive 86/653/EEC of 18 December 1986 on the co-ordination of the laws of the Member States relating to self-employed commercial agents (OJ 1986 L 382/17); Directive 2000/31/EC of the European Parliament and of the Council of 8 June 2000 on certain legal aspects of information society services, in particular electronic commerce, in the Internal Market (OJ 2000 L 171/1); Directive 2000/35/EC of the European Parliament and of the Council of 29 June 2000 on combating late payment in commercial transactions (OJ 2000 L 200/35), Council Directive 85/374/EEC of 25 of July 1985 on the approximation of the laws, regulations and administrative provisions of the Member States concerning liability for defective products (OJ 1985 L 210/29) as modified by Directive 99/34/EC (OJ 1999 L 141/20); Directive 97/5/EC of the European Parliament and the Council of 27 January 1997 on cross-border credit transfers (OJ 1997 L 43/25). See, however, Regulation 2006/2004/EC on cooperation between national authorities responsible for the enforcement of consumer protection laws (OJ 2004 L 364/1).

[4] The most important of which is Council Regulation (EC) No 44/2001 of 22 December 2000 on jurisdiction and the recognition and enforcement of judgments in civil and commercial matters (entry into force 1 March 2002): OJ 2001 L 012/1, as amended.

[5] See, e.g., the Proposal of 22 July 2003 for a Regulation of the European Parliament and the Council on the law applicable to non-contractual obligations ('ROME II') COM(2003)427(01).

[6] See, e.g., P. Craig and G. de Búrca, *EU Law: Text, Cases, and Materials* (3rd edn, 2003), at 115.

way. In an ideal world, both European and national law would thus benefit from the flexibility of Directives. At the Community level, legislation may be passed without having to adjust its every aspect to the diverse legal systems of an ever-increasing number of Member States. At the national level, the process of implementation enables the Member State to choose legislative measures that interfere least and cohere most effectively with the system of domestic law.

It is clear from these preliminary observations that Directives are of seminal importance in the process of harmonization of private law. It should, however, also be emphasized from the outset that Directives have considerable drawbacks. Ensuring that the Member States actually implement the Directive and, furthermore, that the Directive is transposed properly and uniformly across the EU is a complex task. It is primarily due to the jurisprudence of the Court of Justice (hereinafter, 'ECJ') that Directives have, on the whole, been a succesful instrument of harmonization. The position of the ECJ is not an easy one. The Court is confronted by a choice between conflicting aims: on the one hand, ensuring the effectiveness of Directives that are not (fully) implemented; and, on the other hand, maintaining the flexibility which is necessary if Directives are not to collapse into 'concealed' Regulations.

The ECJ has employed a two-pronged strategy. First, the court developed a number of techniques aimed, directly or indirectly, at increasing the effectiveness of Directives: it ascribed to Directives limited direct effect, it required national courts to interpret their national law in the light of the Directive and it introduced Member State liability for failure to implement Directives properly. The first two techniques directly facilitate the end of the Directive, while the third provides a significant incentive for the Member State to comply with the implementation requirement (and at the same time provides some measure of compensation to individuals who would have enjoyed such rights had the Member State in question properly implemented the Directive). All three techniques utilize the private citizen's desire to benefit from the rights accorded to him in Directives and his willingness to enforce them in court proceedings, thereby becoming an important agent in enforcing Community legislation. The second strategy is provided for in the Treaty and brings the Commission into play. The Commission constantly monitors the implementation process and may bring infringement proceedings under Article 226 EC if it takes the view that a Member State has not implemented a Directive appropriately (or, indeed, at all). This provides the ECJ with an invaluable opportunity to explain with binding force how closely the Directive's text must be mirrored in the national system and thus how much discretion the Directive leaves the Member State in choosing the method and means of transposing it into national law.

In the present chapter, the two strategies will be examined in turn. The aim will be to put the rationale of Directives to a test. Needless to say, given the great number of Directives it will not be possible to even attempt a comprehensive study. Rather, illustrations have been chosen in order to reveal the typical difficulties connected with legislating through Directives and to show the role played by the ECJ in the harmonization of private law in the EC thus far.

2. LOCATING THE ANALYSIS WITHIN THE SYSTEM

Before we move to analyse the various mechanisms for securing the effectiveness of Directives in the context of EC private law, we must first briefly set out how such cases reach the national and European courts. In particular, it is helpful at this stage to note more specifically a number of ways in which the practical operation of this complex system can influence the frequency and nature of the opportunities available to the ECJ significantly to influence the interpretation and development of private law within the EU. The following discussion attempts to illustrate the various scenarios and factors that may have an effect upon the significance of the ECJ's role, looking from both the EC and national perspectives.

(1) The substantive terms of an EC Directive may set only a minimum standard (a technique commonly known as 'minimum harmonization') that must be met by Member States on implementation, while allowing them to provide greater protection in that field should they so desire (subject to compatibility with the general rules of the Treaty). This situation discloses a role for the ECJ, in that it will often be called upon to interpret the nature and extent of the harmonization laid down by the relevant EC legislation. The same is true of the assessment of the scope of any permitted derogation from the EC legislation or options provided in an EC Directive for implementation (e.g. a 'menu' of choices, deemed functionally equivalent by the legislation).[7]

(2) The nature of the EC legislative process means that certain Member States in the Council may (however rarely) find themselves outvoted on a particular measure, which they must then implement in national law even though they voted against it. One possible route for ECJ influence upon the harmonization of private law in the EU is through ruling upon challenges to the validity of such EC legislation under Article 230 EC (e.g. *Working Time*,[8] *Tobacco Advertising*,[9] etc.).

(3) The approach taken by national legislation in implementing EC legislation (typically Directives) may be of great significance in determining how much of a role the ECJ may play in practice in interpreting the relevant EC legislation:

(a) The national rules may have implemented a Directive incorrectly, either intentionally or inadvertently. While this may clearly be contrary to EC law (e.g. Articles 10 and 249 EC, etc.), it may mean that national courts cannot apply those elements of the Directive under national law as between private parties. This might not prevent references under

---

[7] See, generally, Slot, 'Harmonisation', 21 *EL Rev* (1996) 378 and Dougan, 'Minimum Harmonisation and the Internal Market', 37 *CML Rev* (2000) 853.

[8] See Case C-84/94, *UK* v *Council* (*Working Time Directive* case) [1996] ECR I-5755.

[9] See Case C-376/98, *Germany* v *Parliament and Council* ('*Tobacco Advertising*') [2000] ECR I-8419.

Article 234 EC as to the requirements of the Directive, not least due to the possibility of a damages claim under the *Francovich* case-law[10] against the defaulting Member State. However, it may deter some individuals from bringing such claims based upon EC law in the first place, thus limiting the frequency of cases that might be the subject of the application of EC law in national courts and, thus, of a reference to the ECJ under Article 234 EC.

(b) A Member State's failure properly to implement EC legislation (or, indeed, a Member State's action in breach of any of the requirements of EC law) can also be taken to the ECJ by the Commission under Article 226 EC.[11] This provides the ECJ with a further (and, in the case of the private law Directives, very significant)[12] opportunity to interpret the requirements of the relevant EC legislation and to assess whether or not the Member State in question has adequately secured its aims and objectives in national law.

(c) The institutional framework adopted for the implementation and enforcement of a Directive may lead to a paucity of litigation in national courts requiring that the interpretation of the Directive be debated.[13] While this may not necessarily detract from the effectiveness of the actual implementation and enforcement of the Directive, it may well deprive the national courts of the chance to hear such cases, with a concomitant reduction in the number of cases that might become the subject of a reference to the ECJ under Article 234 EC.

(d) Conversely, the national legislator may decide that matters would be simplified if the principles and provisions underlying the EC legislation were extended to cover a closely related field, even in matters that fall outside the scope of EC legislative competence and that are solely questions of national law (e.g. rules on the tax treatment of mergers of companies from different Member States (EC law) and of companies

---

[10] See Joined Cases C-6 and 9/90, *Francovich and Bonifaci* v *Italy* [1991] ECR I-5357. The key example concerning incorrect national implementation is Case C-392/93, *R* v *HM Treasury*, ex parte *British Telecommunications plc* [1996] ECR I-1631, while on failure to implement a Directive at all, see Joined Cases 178, 179, 188, 189 and 190/94, *Dillenkofer* v *Germany* [1996] ECR I-4845.

[11] Note that actions by other Member States against a defaulting Member State *are* possible under Art. 227 EC, although the political and diplomatic ramifications of making use of this provision have ensured that it has rarely been relied upon as an enforcement mechanism. For the only examples thus far, see Case 141/78, *France* v *UK* [1979] ECR 2923 (a fisheries dispute; France (with the Commission's support) successfully proceeded against the UK) and Case C-388/95, *Belgium* v *Spain* [2000] ECR I-3121 (concerning Spanish rules of origin for Rioja wine; the Commission did not support the action and the Court rejected Belgium's arguments).

[12] See our discussion *infra* in Section 4 for various examples in this vein.

[13] For a striking example, see the role of the OFT (and its own assiduous prosecution thereof) in the identification, scrutiny, and application of the Unfair Terms in Consumer Contracts Regulations 1999 (SI 1999, No. 2083) (hereinafter 'UTCCR'), discussed briefly *infra* in Section 4A.

within a single Member State (national law)).[14] This strategy can be successful in reducing the regulatory burden imposed by different layers of legislation (EC, national, etc.), which are often drafted in different terms. However, national courts may need to know how EC law would have been interpreted by the ECJ had it applied to the facts of a particular case, so as to ensure that divergences do not develop between the 'national' and 'EC' understanding of the same terminology in parallel but distinct contexts.[15] This can have the effect of increasing the range and frequency of cases in which the ECJ is called upon to interpret EC law under Article 234 EC.

(e) A similar phenomenon to that detailed under (3)(d) can be observed in Member States that have an equality clause laid down in their national constitution:[16] here, the interpretation of the EC law point is relevant even to wholly internal, national fact situations, because the national court needs to ensure that the treatment of its own nationals is not less favourable than the treatment that would be accorded to a national of another Member State as a result of the application of EC law (e.g. on free movement (see *TK-Heimdienst*[17]) or competition (see *Bronner*[18]) grounds).

(4) National rules that relate to the procedure by which EC law rights may be enforced or to the remedies that may be available for the enforcement of EC law rights may restrict the extent to which such EC law rights may, in practice, be relied upon by private parties. Assessing whether the national rules used to enforce EC law rights are equivalent (i.e. non-discriminatory)

---

[14] See Directive 90/434/EEC (OJ 1990 L 225/1), which was at issue in Case C-28/95, *Leur-Bloem* v *Inspecteur der Belastingdienst/Ondernemingen Amsterdam 2* [1997] ECR I-4161.

[15] See, e.g., Joined Cases C-297/88 and 197/89, *Dzodzi* v *Belgium* [1990] ECR I-3763 and Case C-28/95, *Leur-Bloem, supra* note 14, and s. 60 of the UK's Competition Act 1998. Also, *cf.* Case C-346/93, *Kleinwort Benson Ltd* v *City of Glasgow District Council* [1995] ECR I-615 (where the ECJ refused to accept that the reference was admissible because national law expressly reserved the possibility of diverging from the Brussels Convention on jurisdiction and the enforcement of judgments and because national courts were not required to treat the ECJ's interpretation as binding upon them: see the note by Bishop in 20 *EL Rev* (1995) 495).

[16] See Spaventa's case note on Case C-254/98, *Schutzverband gegen unlauteren Wettbewerb* v *TK-Heimdienst Sas GmbH* [2000] ECR I-151 in 37 *CML Rev* (2000) 1265.

[17] See Case C-254/98, *supra* note 16.

[18] See Case C-7/97, *Oscar Bronner GmbH & Co. KG* v *Mediaprint Zeitungs- unde Zeitschriftenverlag GmbH & Co KG* [1998] ECR I-7791. The case concerned the application of Austrian competition law and is probably better classified under (3)(d) on its facts. However, it also serves to illustrate the systemic point made here. Bronner had applied to be given access to Mediaprint's distribution system but Mediaprint refused to agree to this. Had Bronner been a German plaintiff then EC competition law would have applied. Had those rules required that such access be given to Bronner, then in such circumstances, even if Austrian competition law had not been in the same terms as the EC rules, the application of a constitutional equality clause in Austria would have required that similar treatment be accorded to Austrian plaintiffs in the same situation as Bronner.

to those available for national law rights is a further important avenue by which private law harmonization has been developed by the ECJ under Article 234 EC rulings, while the assessment of the adequacy and effectiveness of such national rules has been another. However, a similar order potential restriction may arise where the costs of litigation are very high, thus deterring private parties from going to court to enforce their EC law rights.[19] Sometimes, this may manifest itself in the use of alternative dispute resolution mechanisms (mediation, etc.), so those EC law rights may still have a significant practical impact, but this deprives the ECJ of opportunities to receive references from national courts under Article 234 EC and thus to contribute to the process of developing EC private law principles.

(5) Finally in this brief summary, the approach taken by national courts in their operation of the procedure for making references under Article 234 EC[20] for a preliminary ruling from the ECJ is a further determinant of the frequency that case-law reaches the ECJ for its interpretation of EC Directives or the EC Treaty.[21] While some have argued that the ECJ itself has begun to offer less encouragement to national courts to make such references,[22] others assert that the doctrines developed by the ECJ under Article 234 (such as *acte clair*) have had the effect of encouraging national courts to treat their duties to refer questions of EC law for a preliminary ruling with less respect than they deserve.[23] While there is clearly no overall shortage of cases reaching the ECJ via the Article 234 route,[24] national

[19] The desire to remove this obstacle, at least in cross-border disputes, was behind Council Directive 2002/8/EC of 27 January 2003 to improve access to justice in cross-border disputes by establishing minimum common rules relating to legal aid for such disputes: OJ 2003 L 026/41.

[20] On which see, generally, D. Anderson and M. Demetriou, *References to the European Court* (2nd edn, 2002), P. Lasok and T. Millett (with A. Howard), *Judicial Control in the EU: Procedures and Principles* (2004), and Craig and de Búrca, *supra* note 6, Chap. 11. On national courts and the ECJ, see the very helpful collection of national reports and comparative analyses in A.-M. Slaughter, A. Stone Sweet and J.H.H. Weiler (eds), *The European Courts & National Courts: Doctrine and Jurisprudence* (1997) (which also addresses key questions of cooperation between the ECJ and national courts in the light of the constitutional challenge that the application of EC law has posed for many Member States and their courts). For sectoral analyses, see M. Jarvis, *The Application of EC Law by National Courts: The Free Movement of Goods* (1998), and S. Sciarra (ed.), *Labour Law in the Courts: National Judges and the European Court of Justice* (2001).

[21] For analysis of the case-law trends, see Stone Sweet and Brunell, 'The European Court and the National Courts: A Statistical Analysis of Preliminary References, 1961–95', Jean Monnet Working Paper No. 14/97 (1997) (available at www.jeanmonnetprogram.org/papers/97/97-14-.html, last visited 20 January 2005). See, further, A. Stone Sweet, *The Judicial Construction of Europe* (2004), Chap. 2.

[22] See, e.g., O'Keeffe, 'Is the Spirit of Article 177 Under Attack? Preliminary References and Admissibility', 23 *EL Rev* (1998) 509.

[23] See Arnull, 'The Use and Abuse of Article 177 EEC', 52 *MLR* (1989) 622 and A. Arnull, *The European Union and its Court of Justice* (1999), 49–69, esp. at 68, note 247.

[24] See the *Annual Report of the Court of Justice* (2003), 213 ff., esp. at 215 (showing that more cases were received than completed during 2003, increasing the total number of cases pending to 974); and this number may increase still further as the national courts of the newest Member States (post-2004

courts may be discouraged from referring questions. In some cases this may be due to the time it may take to receive an answer, and in others because they take the (not always justifiable) view that the answer to the EC law point in issue is straightforward enough for them to resolve for themselves. This is another factor in assessing the extent to which the ECJ will have the opportunity to make a contribution to the development of European private law.

Before we move to discuss the impact of the case-law of the ECJ on the nature and value of Directives in more detail, it is necessary to make one more preliminary observation. For there is a more subtle 'advantage' of Directives which is independent of the issue of flexibility and which may (in the back of the mind of the legislator) operate in favour of Directives. Dressing up secondary Community legislation in 'national clothes' may, as pointed out by Canaris,[25] increase legal certainty and the acceptance of (what is in substance) Community legislation at national level. To understand his argument, it is necessary to make a brief observation as to the ways in which legislation may be questioned on grounds of constitutionality. Regulations may be challenged by a Member State for want of legal basis within the period laid down in Article 230(5) EC (two months), but the possibility to challenge Regulations incidentally in proceedings brought by private persons is not limited as to time according to Article 241 EC. According to Article 230 EC, Directives can also be challenged directly before the ECJ, and since unanimity is no longer required under Article 95 EC any Member States' doubts as to the soundness of the legal basis of a Directive may, as explained, be likely to result in proceedings before the ECJ. However, once a Directive has been transposed into national law the validity of the relevant rules then follows exclusively from national sources. Hence, any doubt as to the appropriate legal basis at Community level no longer threatens legal certainty. The validity of the Directive may still be considered incidentally in proceedings under Article 234 EC. But the national law that implements it remains binding, whatever the outcome of the preliminary ruling.

However, doubts as to constitutionality of Community legislation cannot justify a blanket avoidance of the use of EC Regulations and a preference for Directives. The insecurity that follows from doubts as to the legal basis is a well-known phenomenon in all systems in which courts have the power to strike down legislation. There is no reason to accept the price to be paid for Directives simply in order to reduce this risk. After all, in many Member States the relevant national legislation may also be void for a variety of reasons. 'Dressing up' Community legislation may therefore have only the 'psychological' advantage that it is not easily recognizable as

enlargement) encounter practical problems and queries concerning the application of the *acquis communautaire* (often rapidly introduced and naturally as yet largely untested) in their own legal systems.

[25] *Cf.* Canaris, 'Aspekte der europäischen Rechtsangleichung mit Hilfe von Richtlinien', in C. Canaris and A. Zaccaria (eds), *Die Umsetzung von zivilrechtlichen Richtlinien der Europäischen Gemeinschaft in Italien und Deutschland* (2002), 128, at 134 ff.

such. However, if this were actually needed to increase the acceptance of Community law, this would show little confidence in the virtues of European law. Moreover, the national clothing may well conceal the need to interpret the respective provision as part of European law and thus increase the danger that each Member State creates its own blend of Community legislation by interpreting it from the perspective of its own familiar concepts. Needles to say, this danger exists also in relation to Regulations, but the European 'identity' of this type of legislation cannot be in doubt.[26]

In what follows, we will endeavour to examine a number of these issues. We will use the vehicle of Directives and how EC law has striven to make them effective in national legal systems to analyse the role of the ECJ, both generally and in its interaction with national courts and legislatures. In so doing, we will examine some of the case-law on some of the EC's 'private law Directives'[27] to assess how effectively these strategies for enforcing Directives have operated and will draw some tentative conclusions for their future use and interpretation by the ECJ in this field. It is to this analysis that we now turn.

3. MISSING IMPLEMENTATION—DOES IT MATTER?

If a Member State fails to transpose a Directive into national law (whether at all or only in part) within the time limit set in the Directive, the Commission may object to this failure in infringement proceedings under Article 226 EC. However, the ECJ was not satisfied with this state of affairs as the only mechanism for the enforcement of EC law in such cases. It took the position that other measures were needed in order to increase the effectiveness of Directives as far as possible. The Court developed three techniques which all aim to secure the effective application of Directives (at least in some respects), even if the Member State has failed correctly to transpose them into national law. This process started in the 1970s, when the Court ascribed limited direct effect to Directives; it continued in the 1980s, with the introduction of the more subtle interpretation requirement, and came to a provisional end in the 1990s, when Member State liability was established for failure to implement Directives. The first two of these techniques ensure that the end of the Directive is achieved despite the missing implementation, while the third technique accepts that the end of the Directive cannot be achieved directly but instead entitles any potential beneficiary under the Directive to monetary compensation for his lost 'expectation', at the expense of the defaulting Member State. The case-law is fairly

---

[26] Indeed, the ECJ has made it clear that Member States are not permitted to 're-enact' EC Regulations in the form of national laws, since this would be to disguise the character of Regulations as Community instruments and would undermine their direct applicability, as provided for by the EC Treaty itself in (what is now) Art. 249: see Case 34/73, *Variola* v *Amministrazione delle Finanze* [1973] ECR 981.

[27] See *supra* note 3.

well developed and (except for a few issues at the fringes) seems to have settled most major issues. In what follows, we will analyse the two techniques designed to achieve the end of the Directive in spite of missing implementation. For reasons of space we cannot discuss State liability here, which in any event is a more indirect method of increasing the effectiveness of Directives.[28]

A. Direct Effect

The most straightforward way of ensuring that the result aimed at by Directives is achieved, even if they have not been implemented correctly, is by holding them to be directly effective. This is also the most drastic measure, both from a national and an EC law perspective. At the EC level, there is a danger that this development would blur the difference between Directives and Regulations beyond recognition. The ECJ was well aware of this point from the very beginning and has cautiously avoided the trap, which nevertheless was set in front of the ECJ again and again by some of the Advocates General.[29] Direct effect would taint the very essence of Directives and all the advantages flowing from Directives would also be destroyed. If Directives had direct effect, why should the Member State bother to transpose them? Yet it is the limited discretion of the Member State as to the means of how to achieve the end in the Directive that makes them attractive as a legislative measure both at the Community level as also the national level.

---

[28] The issue of Member State liability for breaches of EC law is discussed elsewhere in this volume by van Gerven and Albors-Llorens. On this topic, see the seminal judgment in Joined Cases C-46 and 48/93, *Brasserie du Pêcheur SA* v *Germany* and *The Queen* v *Secretary of State for Transport, ex parte Factortame Ltd and others (Factortame (No. 3))* [1996] ECR I-1029 (noted by Oliver, 34 *CML Rev* (1997) 635). For discussion and development, see T. Heukels and A. McDonnell, *The Action for Damages in Community Law* (1997); Convery, 'State Liability in the United Kingdom after *Brasserie du Pêcheur*', 34 *CML Rev* (1997) 603; Craig and de Búrca, *supra* note 6, at 257–73; Dougan, 'The *Francovich* Right to Reparation: Reshaping the Contours of Community Remedial Competence', 6 *EPL* (2000) 103; and Tridimas, 'Liability for Breach of Community Law: Growing Up and Mellowing Down', 38 *CML Rev* (2001) 301; see also Papier in *Münchener Kommentar* (4th edn, 2003), v, § 839 BGB, paras. 98–103 with references; Gundel, 'Gemeinschaftsrechtliche Haftungsvorgaben für judikatives Unrecht' [2004] *EWS* 8. Of particular relevance for the topic of our argument are Joined Cases 178, 179, 188, 189, and 190/94, *Dillenkofer* v *Germany* [1996] ECR I-4845, which concerned Directive 90/314/EEC on package travel, package holidays, and package tours: failure to take any implementing measures is *per se* a sufficiently serious breach of EC law, where no other national law covers the matter (which illustrates the strong incentive given to Member States to take prompt and effective implementing action); and Case C-261/95, *Palmisani* v *Istituto Nazionale della Previdenza Sociale* [1997] ECR I-4025, focusing upon whether national time limits rendered the national remedy for Member State liability a sufficiently effective one (which time limits were upheld) and upon whether or not the national rules applied in assessing the applicable time limits in EC law cases were equivalent to those applied in comparable national proceedings. This latter point illustrates the role of the ECJ in giving guidance on what counts as 'equivalent' in such cases, which can have quite some impact upon national private law.

[29] E.g. Lenz AG: see his Opinion in Case C-91/92, *Paola Faccini Dori* v *Recreb Srl* [1994] ECR I-3325, paras. 43–73. See, also, Pescatore, 'Direct Effect: An "Infant Disease" of Community Law?', 8 *EL Rev* (1983) 155.

I. Vertical relationships

However, if the direct effect of Directives was limited this could surely do no harm, while also significantly increasing the reach of Directives? The only question was to identify a workable control factor for distinguishing between cases in which direct effect could be ascribed and those in which this was not possible. This was quickly found in the distinction between vertical and horizontal direct effect. The Member State that failed to transpose the Directive on time ought not to be allowed to rely upon national laws that contravened the end of the Directive.[30] Private persons can thus rely upon the Directive as against the State provided that the general criteria for direct effect are met. For a provision to have direct effect, it is necessary that its subject matter is unconditional and sufficiently precise.[31] If this is the case, it may be relied upon before the national courts by individuals against the State where the latter has failed to implement the Directive in domestic law by the end of the period prescribed or where it has failed to implement the Directive correctly. The argument seems to be that the State should not be allowed to 'benefit' from its 'unlawful' failure to transpose the Directive. As always the ECJ does not differentiate between the different emanations of a State, thus enabling it to adopt a wide definition of the State, and thereby securing effectiveness for Directives in a greater range of situations.[32]

II. Horizontal relationships

In proceedings exclusively between private parties, by contrast, a Directive cannot of itself impose obligations upon an individual and cannot therefore be relied upon as such against an individual; even a clear, precise and unconditional provision of a Directive seeking to confer rights or impose obligations on individuals cannot of itself apply in such proceedings. This was confirmed recently by the Grand Chamber of the ECJ in *Pfeiffer and others* v *Deutsches Rotes Kreuz*.[33] In this case, references for preliminary rulings were made in various sets of proceedings between employees and former employees of a regional branch of the *Deutsches Rotes Kreuz* (German Red Cross). The employees were emergency workers and sought to rely *inter alia* on Article 6(2) of Council Directive 93/104/EC of 23 November 1993 concerning certain aspects of the organization of working time.[34] This provision requires the Member States to take the measures necessary to ensure that the average working time for each 7-day period, including overtime, does not exceed 48 hours.[35] German

[30] E.g. Case 148/78, *Pubblico Ministero* v *Ratti* [1979] ECR 1629.

[31] See Case 26/62, *Van Gend en Loos* v *Nederlandse Administratie der Belastingen* [1963] ECR 1.

[32] E.g. Case 152/84, *Marshall* v *Southampton and S.W. Hampshire Area Health Authority (Teaching) (Marshall I)* [1986] ECR 723.

[33] Joined Cases C-397 to C-403/01, judgment of 5 October 2004, not yet reported, paras. 108–109. See, for further discussion of this case the text at *infra* note 102.

[34] OJ 1993 L 307/18.

[35] Joined Cases C-397 to C-403/01, *supra* note 33, para. 90. This includes on-call time, where the worker is required to be physically present at a place specified by his employer (para. 93), as had already

legislation, however, allowed for working time beyond the 48-hour limit and was not compatible with Directive 93/104/EC in that respect. However, since the proceedings were held to be exclusively between private parties Article 6(2) could not be ascribed direct effect even though it was sufficiently clear and unconditional.[36]

III. Evaluation

This settled jurisprudence of the ECJ denying direct effect in horizontal relationships is to be applauded. It is of first importance that Directives do not have direct effect if they lack proper national implementation. Implementation carries with it all of the advantages associated with Directives and only by insisting upon national implementation are Member States given enough scope to secure the goals of Directives within the national legal system. After all, this practical accommodation of these goals in the national legal order is a major justification for legislating through Directives.

The exception provided for in vertical relationships between private parties, on the one hand, and the State, on the other, (arguably unnecessarily) blurs the line between Regulations and Directives. The result is uncertainty at the fringes: for example, unpredictability as to the precise scope of the notion of an 'emanation of the State' for the purposes of the vertical direct effect case-law[37] creates serious concerns for various entities *vis-à-vis* their responsibilities of compliance with relevant Directives.[38] Such uncertainty might be expected to generate a wealth of references to the ECJ under Article 234 EC, as national courts are faced with arguments as to whether a particular defendant amounts to an organ of the State for the purposes of vertical direct effect. While there has been a fair range of case-law on the question, the guidance from the ECJ has not clarified the position greatly, which has no doubt acted as an encouragement to national courts to apply the relatively loose criteria for themselves.[39] This approach may deprive the ECJ of some opportunities to rule upon various substantive aspects of the Directives at issue in the national

been clarified in another case with major implications for the health sector: see Case C-151/02, *Landeshauptstadt Kiel* v *Jaeger* [2003] ECR I-8389, para. 103.

[36] Joined Cases C-397 to C-403/01, *supra* note 33, para. 109.

[37] See, e.g., the decision in Case C-188/89, *Foster* v *British Gas plc* [1990] ECR I-3313 and its application by the UK courts ([1991] 2 AC 306; [1991] 2 CMLR 217), and the subsequent UK case-law such as *Doughty* v *Rolls Royce plc* ([1992] IRLR 126; [1992] 1 CMLR 1045), *Griffin* v *S.W. Water Services Ltd* ([1995] IRLR 15) and *National Union of Teachers* v *Governing Body of St Mary's Church of England (Aided) Junior School* ([1997] ICR 334).

[38] And this uncertainty is exacerbated by the challenge to the very rationale of the vertical direct effect case-law (i.e. not allowing the *State* to benefit from its failure to implement the Directive) that is made by employing this broad notion of the State: if the defendant entity had no responsibility for such implementation, it is difficult to apply this rationale in a number of cases—see, also, Case 103/88, *Fratelli Costanzo SpA* v *Commune di Milano* [1989] ECR 1839, where the Municipality of Milan was held to count as an organ of the State for these purposes.

[39] See, e.g., Case C-343/98, *Collino & Chiappero* v *Telecom Italia SpA* [2000] ECR I-6659, esp. para. 24.

litigation, but if national courts do follow the wide interpretation of the notion of the State in such cases[40] then it may secure a more frequent and effective application of the Directives themselves in the national legal order. At a time when the resources of the European judicature to answer such questions are becoming increasingly stretched,[41] this balancing act will become ever more delicate for the ECJ.

The delicacy of this balance is nicely illustrated by the case-law stemming from *CIA Security* v *Signalson and Securitel*,[42] where the Court held that the obligation to notify to the Commission draft technical regulations as required by Directive 83/189/EEC,[43] the purpose of which is to allow the Commission to assess whether the national legislation creates a barrier to trade, was capable of being relied upon before national courts. As a result, national technical regulations that had not been notified suffered from a procedural defect and could not be applied as against individuals.[44] While in one sense this conclusion concerned the vertical relationship between a Member State's enforcement authorities and an individual company,[45] it clearly had an important impact upon the relations between private individuals,[46] as was made abundantly clear in the *Unilever Italia* case.[47] Thus even private parties may rely against other private parties upon the Member State's failure to notify a technical regulation. In the ECJ's view, this scenario does not amount to 'horizontal direct effect' in the strict sense, since the Directive's notification requirement does not itself seek to provide substantive terms by which the private parties' relations are to be regulated. Whether or not the current national law survives the test, it will still be *national* law that regulates the relations between the parties (e.g. in *Unilever Italia*, the relevant provisions of Italian contract law).[48] Even accepting this analysis,[49] however, the practical outcome is questionable: private parties cannot be

[40] A good UK example being the *NUT* v *St Mary's School* case, *supra* note 37.

[41] See, e.g., Johnston, 'Judicial Reform and the Treaty of Nice', 38 *CML Rev* (2000) 499 and A.A. Dashwood and A.C. Johnston (eds), *The Future of the Judicial System of the European Union* (2001).

[42] Case C-194/94, *CIA Security SA* v *Signalson SA and Securitel SPRL* [1996] ECR I-2201. For general discussion of these 'incidental horizontal effect' cases, see Dougan, 'The "Disguised" Vertical Direct Effect of Directives?', [2000] *CLJ* 586.

[43] OJ 1983 L 109/8.

[44] Case C-194/94, *supra* note 42, para. 48. See, however, Case C-226/97, *Criminal proceedings against Lemmens* [1998] ECR I-3711, para. 36: the use by the public authorities of a product manufactured according to a non-notified Regulation is not unlawful.

[45] See, also, Case C-13/96, *Bic Benelux SA* v *Belgium* [1997] ECR I-1753.

[46] In *CIA Security* itself, *supra* note 42, the plaintiff was suing the defendant companies for trade libel due to their claims about the non-conformity of CIA Security's products with the relevant Belgian legislation on security systems. Meanwhile the defendants counterclaimed that CIA Security had not respected the current Belgian law on the subject: CIA Security's response was that that current Belgian law had not been notified under the Directive and thus could not be applied to its products.

[47] Case C-443/98, *Unilever Italia SpA* v *Central Food SpA* [2000] ECR I-7535 (noted by Weatherill, 26 *EL Rev* (2001) 177 and 117 *LQR* (2001) 213, and Dougan [2001] *CLJ* 253).

[48] See paras. 50 and 51 of the *Unilever Italia* case, *supra* note 47, for this explanation by the ECJ.

[49] Which many find highly unpersuasive: see, e.g., the Opinions of Jacobs AG in both Case C-443/98, *Unilever Italia*, *supra* note 47, and Case C-159/00, *Sapod Audic* v *Eco-Emballages SA* [2002]

held responsible for the Member State's failure to notify and yet they suffer the consequences of having relied upon what seemed valid national law in planning their conduct. It also creates commercial uncertainty, for private parties now need to inquire whether in the process of passing a particular regulation at national level the notification obligation has been complied with in order to be able to ascertain whether to comply with the otherwise perfectly valid national law.[50]

It is thus unsurprising that in *Sapod Audic* v *Eco-Emballages*[51] the ECJ conceded that it was for the national court to determine the consequences that result from the inapplicability of that national provision as regards the nullity or unenforce-ability of a contract, subject only to the proviso that the applicable rules of national law are not less favourable than those governing similar domestic actions and are not framed in such a way as to render impossible in practice the exercise of rights conferred by Community law.[52] The Court regards the 'Notification Directive' 83/189/EEC (and its consolidating successor Directive 98/34/EC),[53] and the means of preventive control established by it, as an essential tool in protecting freedom of movement of goods.[54] The sanction of nullity is at least theoretically a powerful incentive to comply with the notification requirement. In any event, it is more effec-tive than the alternative method of enforcement by infringement procedure for each and every technical regulation at national level. This result-oriented stance of the ECJ, however, is difficult to square with the nature of Directives[55] and creates

ECR I-5031 (discussed in the subsequent text) and the clear and helpful discussion in Dougan's case note on the latter case, 40 *CML Rev* (2003) 193, at 204–10, and the references cited therein.

[50] For further criticism of this line of cases, see Schepel, 'The Enforcement of EC Law in Contractual Relations: Case Studies in How Not to "Constitutionalize" Private Law', 9 *ERPL* (2004) 661, at 672, and, for an approving view, see Gundel [2001] *EuZW* 143. Note that, in response to these case-law developments on the effect of these notification requirements, the Commission has set up a website—the Technical Regulations Information System (TRIS)—to provide information to businesses on the notification procedure and individual cases thereunder (see COM(2003)200 final, 43–4 and http://europa.eu.int/commm/enterprise/tris).

[51] Case C-159/00, [2002] ECR I-5031 (noted by Dougan, *supra* note 49). The factual scenario of this case provides even greater difficulty for the position taken by the Court on direct effect in *Unilever Italia, supra* note 47: here, the result required not only that the national rules could not be applied as between the two private parties, but also that any terms of the parties' contract that effectively corres-ponded to the terms of the now inapplicable national law. This suggests a significant role for the ECJ in shaping certain aspects of national private law in such cases, which threatens commercial certainty still further.

[52] Case C-159/00, *supra* note 51, paras. 52–53.

[53] OJ 1998 L 204/37, as amended by Directive 98/48/EC (OJ 1998 L 217/18), concerning trans-parency of regulations on information society services.

[54] See, e.g., the Commission reports on Directives 98/34/EC (COM(2003)200 final, Part II) and 98/48/EC (COM(2003)69 final). See also Weatherill's earlier analysis, 'Compulsory Notification of Draft Technical Regulations: the Contribution of Directive 83/189 to the Management of the Internal Market', 16 *YEL* (1996) 129.

[55] See, e.g., Dougan, *supra* note 49, at 204–10 for discussion of how faint the dividing line is between, on the one hand, the impact of the direct effect of the notification requirement and, on the other, traditional horizontal direct effect (if, indeed, such a distinction exists at all).

commercial uncertainty or, at the very least, imposes substantial extra burdens upon private parties to check the status of such national technical regulations before relying upon them to guide their commercial behaviour.[56] Ascribing the 'Information Directive' 83/189/EEC direct effect in proceedings between private parties is an anomaly that ought not to be generalized, as the Court itself has emphasized.

B. Interpretation

I. Origins: the von Colson *line of cases*

The posible direct effect of Directives if relied upon by private parties as against the Member State is of limited value in relation to the great number of Directives concerning private law relationships, which normally involve proceedings exclusively between private parties.[57] Council Directive of 9 February 1976 on the implementation of the principle of equal treatment for men and women as regards access to employment, vocational training and promotion, and working conditions (76/207/EEC)[58] provided the Court with an opportunity to develop a new instrument to improve the effectiveness of Directives.

In the cases of *von Colson and Kamann*[59] and *Harz*,[60] the Court for the first time indicated that the obligation arising from a Directive to achieve the result envisaged by the Directive, and the Member State's duty under Article 10 EC to take all appropriate measures to ensure the fulfilment of that obligation, are both binding on all the authorities of Member States, including the courts. In applying the national law, the ECJ concluded,[61] the national courts are required to interpret their national law in the light of the wording and the purpose of the Directive in order to achieve the result envisaged by the Directive. Ironically, in one of the cases at hand (*von Colson*) ascribing direct effect to the Directive would have been possible in principle, since the employer (who refused to engage the plaintiffs as social workers in a prison for male prisoners for reasons relating to their sex) was the *Land Nordrhein-Westfalen*.[62] The reason that the court was compelled to fashion an alternative device was that the Directive did not include a sufficiently precise obligation in relation to the

---

[56] See the TRIS website (*supra* note 50): it may help to remove some of the uncertainty and reduce some of this compliance burden on private parties, but such checks must still be made assiduously.

[57] See the references to the relevant Directives *supra* in note 3.

[58] OJ 1976 L 39/40.

[59] Case 14/83, *Von Colson and Kamann* v *Land Nordrhein-Westfalen* [1984] ECR 1891, para. 26.

[60] Of the same date, see Case 79/83, *Harz* v *Deutsche Tradax GmbH* [1984] ECR 1921, para. 26.

[61] Case 14/83, *supra* note 59, para. 26; Case 79/83, *supra* note 60, para. 26.

[62] See Case 152/84, *supra* note 32. In the *Harz* case (Case 79/83, *supra* note 60), the employer who had discriminated against the female applicant was a private party (although see Case 43/75, *Defrenne* v *SABENA* (*Defrenne II*) [1976] ECR 455 (on the horizontal direct effect of what is now Art. 141 EC on equal pay for equal work) and Case C-177/88, *Dekker* v *Stichting Vormingscentrum voor Jong Volwassenen* [1990] ECR I-3941 (concerning the impact of Art, 6 of Directive 76/207/EC, *supra* note 58—the role of this provision is discussed further in our subsequent text).

sanctions for discrimination that could be relied upon by individuals in order to obtain specific compensation.[63]

Article 6 of Directive 76/207/EC required Member States to introduce such measures as are necessary to enable all persons who consider themselves wronged by discrimination to pursue their claims by judicial process. The Member States are given discretion as to the sanctions that can be imposed, subject to the qualification that the adopted measures must be sufficiently effective to achieve the objective of the Directive. It followed that, if compensation were made available, such compensation needed to be 'effective'. In the ECJ's view, this meant that it ought to have a deterrent effect and be adequate in relation to the damage sustained; in particular it was not sufficient merely to provide for the reimbursement of any expenses incurred in connection with the application.[64] The Court stressed that the national court should take this into account in interpreting the relevant provisions of German law aimed to give effect to the Directive. However, the Court also explicitly stated that the national court was required to bring national law into conformity with the result envisaged by the Directive, provided that 'it is given discretion to do so under national law'.[65] Furthermore, the Court clarified that it was for the national court alone to interpret national law.[66]

A few years later, the *Bundesarbeitsgericht* duly acknowledged the interpretation given to Directive 76/207/EEC by the ECJ but, in the light of the wording of the relevant provision of national law and the intention of the legislator as apparent from the preparatory works, the national court felt unable to bring the relevant national provision in force at the time (§ 611a of the German Civil Code (BGB)) into conformity with the result envisaged by the Directive.[67] However, the court did not stop short at this point, but emphasized that the obligation to interpret national law in conformity with the Directive extended beyond the particular measures adopted to implement the Directives. The court held that discrimination in relation to the sex of the plaintiff constituted a sufficiently serious infringement of the general right to one's personality to justify an award of monetary compensation irrespective of a pecuniary loss of the plaintiff.[68] The court upheld the award of one month's salary as being sufficient to give effect to Article 6 of Directive 76/207/EEC.

---

[63] Case 14/83, *supra* note 59, para. 27.

[64] *Ibid.*, para. 28; *cf.* Case 79/83, *supra* note 60, para. 28.

[65] Case 14/83, *supra* note 59, para. 28; *cf.* Case 79/83, *supra* note 60, para. 28.

[66] Case 14/83, *supra* note 59, para. 25; Case 79/83, *supra* note 60, para. 25 (which, as a matter of the ECJ's jurisdiction under Art. 234 EC, must surely be correct, although this line can become rather blurred at times: see, e.g., Case C-28/95, *supra* note 14, concerning the situation where national law refers to EC rules to govern situations that are not themselves within the scope of the relevant EC provisions (often known as '*renvoi*')).

[67] BAG [1990] NJW 65, 66. The relevant provision in force at the time of the decision provided only for compensation in damages measured by the reliance interest, and in view of the court could not be extended to cover more than expenses incurred in connection with the application.

[68] *Ibid.*, at 66. See, on the origins of the right to one's personality, B.S. Markesinis and H. Unberath, *The German Law of Torts* (4th edn, 2002), at 74 ff.

The legislator reacted by adjusting the relevant provision (§ 611a BGB) so that compensation was no longer limited to the reliance interest.

Yet the right to compensation required that fault could be imputed to the employer, and fault was likewise necessary to bring oneself within the delictual protection of the right to one's personality (derived from § 823(1) BGB). When the same question was brought before the ECJ in *Dekker* (a reference for a preliminary ruling from the *Hoge Raad der Nederlanden*), the Court once again conceded that the Member States had discretion as to the sanctions for which it made provision.[69] However, the Court immediately added that the practical effect of the principles established by the Directive would be weakened considerably if the employer's liability for infringement of the principle of equal treatment were made subject to proof of fault attributable to him and also to there being no ground of exemption recognized by the applicable national law.[70] The *Bundesarbeitsgericht* in a first response to this jurisprudence held that it did not see any possibility of applying the relevant German law in a way that conformed to the result of the *Dekker* case.[71] In a preliminary ruling initiated by the *Arbeitsgericht Hamburg* at roughly the same time as this ruling of the *Bundesarbeitsgericht*, the ECJ confirmed in *Draehmpaehl* that the fault requirement of German law was contrary to Directive 76/207/EEC.[72]

The German provisions at the time were also contrary to the result envisaged by the Directive in another respect. They stipulated a ceiling for recovery of three months' salary. This was held not to comply with the requirement of providing for an effective sanction for the breach of the obligations flowing from the Directive.[73] First of all, the Court stressed that the Member State, in choosing the appropriate solution for guaranteeing that the objective of the Directive is attained, must ensure that infringements of Community law are penalized under conditions which are analogous to those applicable to infringements of domestic law of a similar nature and importance.[74] Since such a ceiling was not a general limit to monetary compensation in German law, the sanctions in the context of Community law were less effective than in domestic law. However, the ECJ indicated that, under certain

---

[69] Case C-177/88, *supra* note 62.

[70] *Ibid.*, para. 24.

[71] BAG [1996] NJW 2529, 2533 (compensation was denied accordingly).

[72] Case C-180/95, *Nils Draehmpaehl* v *Urania Immobilienservice OHG* [1997] ECR I-2195, para. 19 (noted by Ward at 23 *EL Rev* (1998) 65).

[73] A conclusion already presaged by Case C-271/91, *Marshall* v *Southampton and South-West Hampshire Area Health Authority (Teaching) (Marshall II)* [1993] ECR I-4367, para. 32. For an analysis of the ECJ's remedies case-law from a national labour law perspective, see Kilpatrick, 'Turning Remedies Around: A Sectoral Analysis of the Court of Justice', Chap. 5 in G. de Búrca and J.H.H. Weiler (eds), *The European Court of Justice* (2001), 143 ff.

[74] Case C-180/95, *supra* note 72, para. 29: an application of the principle of 'equivalence' or 'non-discrimination' developed in the Court's case-law on the scrutiny of national procedural and remedial rules for the enforcement of EC law rights (see, e.g., Craig and de Búrca, *supra* note 6, at 230–57).

conditions, the Member State could introduce a ceiling for recovery. This would be the case where the employer could prove that, because the applicant who was eventually engaged had superior qualifications, the unsuccessful applicant would not have obtained the vacant position, even if there had been no discrimination in the selection process.[75] As a result the legislator was once again forced to reconsider and adjust § 611a BGB.[76] In its present form, § 611a BGB no longer requires fault, but instead limits the maximum amount recoverable to three months' salary under the same conditions as those indicated in the aforementioned *Draehmpaehl* case, namely provided that the unsuccessful candidate would in any event not have been engaged.

This group of cases is extremely interesting for the interplay that it reveals between Directives, the case-law of the ECJ and the role of the national courts.

First, the *von Colson* case is noteworthy as the starting point for the requirement that national law is to be interpreted by the national courts as far as possible in order to achieve the result envisaged by the Directive. Indeed, one might have expected this principle of interpretation to have been developed somewhat earlier by the ECJ, given that its basic form is far less intrusive upon national law than direct effect, when viewed from a national constitutional perspective. In that sense, it is a path of 'constitutional least resistance' for the national court in giving effect to EC law. Many national legal systems already applied a similar rule of interpretation to treaties under general international law, making the assumption that (in the absence of express intentions to the contrary) the legislature intended to conform with the country's international obligations.[77]

Secondly, in *von Colson* and *Draehmpaehl* the Court clarified the principle that national law must provide effective remedies in order to protect the rights granted under Community legislation. This latter aspect of the jurisprudence of the ECJ considerably narrowed down the discretion granted to the Member States in respect of sanctions. The aim of the Directive—that persons who consider themselves wronged by discrimination are able to pursue their claims effectively by judicial process—has been given a remarkably strict and detailed interpretation by the ECJ. The flexibility, for which the Directive on its face initially seemed to provide, was stifled by the ECJ in the interest of ensuring that the aim of the Directive (i.e. that employers were effectively deterred from discriminating on the basis of sex) was achieved, and achieved as fully and effectively as possible. It is to be expected that the same (rigid) attitude on the part of the ECJ will prevail in respect of the imminent implementation of the new anti-discrimination Directives 2000/43/EC (on racial equality) and 2000/78/EC (establishing a general framework for equal treatment in

---

[75] Case C-180/95, *supra* note 72, para. 37.

[76] Law of 29 June 1998 BGBl. I, 1694.

[77] See, e.g., *Salomon* v *Commissioners of Customs & Excise* [1967] 2 QB 116 and *Garland* v *British Rail Engineering Ltd* [1983] 2 AC 751 (esp. at 771, *per* Lord Diplock), itself a case concerning the application and interpretation of EEC law in the UK courts).

employment and occupation),[78] and Directive 2002/73/EC[79] (amending Directive 76/207/EEC).[80]

The third conclusion to be drawn concerns the relationship between, on the one hand, the approach of the ECJ towards fleshing out the obligations flowing from Directives and, on the other, the interpretation requirement. At first, following the case of *von Colson*, the German courts were able to adjust national law by the means of interpretation, despite the fact that the wording of the relevant national legislation diverged from that of the Directive. Yet over time it became increasingly difficult to rely upon this approach. Each time the ECJ subsequently tightened the requirements, the legislator had to intervene and pass new legislation. This last point provides a good illustration of a particular 'weakness' of the interpretative method, which deserves to be explored in more detail.

II. The narrow limits of interpretation

In the cases of *von Colson* and *Harz*, the ECJ stressed that the obligation upon Member States (flowing from Article 249(3) EC) to transpose a Directive was also binding upon national courts in applying national law. However, while the Court sometimes disregards the internal rules of organization of a Member State,[81] in respect of the requirement of interpretation, the Court took account of the separation of powers in the Member State. The ECJ did not require the national court to do something that it was not entitled to do or which it did not have jurisdiction to do, namely to use methods of interpretation which were not recognized in that particular Member State. The Court thus held that interpretation in conformity with the Directive was required if the national court was given 'discretion to do so' under

---

[78] OJ 2000 L 180/22 and L 303/16. See, further, the Proposal for a Council Directive implementing the principle of equal treatment between women and men in the access to and supply of goods and services, 5 November 2003, COM(2003)657 final.

[79] OJ 2002 L 269/15.

[80] See the draft proposal for an Anti-Discrimination Act by the German Government of 16 December 2004, Bundestag-Drucksache 15/4583. In the UK, consultation on detailed regulations to implement Directive 2002/73/EC, *supra* note 79, is set to begin 'in spring 2005, with a view to regulations coming into force on 1 October 2005' (the deadline for implementation) (this timetable is according to the website of the UK Government's Women & Equality Unit: www.womenandequality unit.gov.uk/legislation/ – last visited 20 January 2005). The UK has implemented the Race Equality Directive in the Race Relations Act 1976 (Amendment) Regulations 2003 (SI 2003, No. 1626) and see, further, the Race Relations (Amendment) Act 2000. For implementation of Directive 2000/78/EC in the UK, see the Employment Equality (Religion or Belief) Regulations 2003 (SI 2003, No. 1660) and the Employment Equality (Sexual Orientation) Regulations 2003 (SI 2003, No. 1661). According to the website of the DTI, consultation will take place on the age discrimination aspects in the summer of 2005, with a view to bringing legislation into force on 1 October 2006 (see www.dti.gov.uk/er/ equality/statement.htm – last visited 20 January 2005).

[81] See, in particular, Case C-302/97, *Konle* v *Austria* [1999] ECR I-3099 and Case C-424/97, *Haim* v *Kassenzahnärztliche Vereinigung Nordrhein (Haim II)* [2000] ECR I-5123 (discussed by Anagnostaras, 'The Allocation of Responsibility in State Liability Actions for Breach of Community Law', 26 *EL Rev* (2001) 139).

national law.[82] Equally importantly, the Court was careful not to interfere with the interpretation of national law, which it regarded as the exclusive task of the national court.[83] This means that the reach of the interpretative method depends upon the limits of interpretation as they are laid down in each of the 25 Member States. If such discretion is accorded to a national court, then it is required by Article 249(3) EC to apply the relevant national law in conformity with the Directive. In other words, the discretion must be used in the interest of securing the effective application of Community law.

It is not the place here to explain in detail the approach to interpretation adopted in the different Member States.[84] It suffices to mention guidelines that seem to be followed by the German courts and the courts in the United Kingdom. In Germany the courts have on the whole consistently refused to 'rectify' national law in the light of a Directive if the wording of the respective provision of national law was unequivocal and was backed by a clearly expressed intention of the legislator apparent from the preparatory works.[85] The more specific and precise the provisions of national law, the more difficult it will be to use the interpretive method to secure a result that conforms to the wording and purpose of the relevant Directive. The implementation of Directive 76/207/EEC (discussed in Section 3.B.I, above) shows as much. The national courts felt unable to overcome the wording of the relevant provision on compensation, which was both specific and unambiguous in limiting damages as to the conditions of recovery (fault) and also the amount recoverable (reliance interest, later an upper limit of three months' salary). The second point that should be mentioned concerns the only more specific guideline that the ECJ has given to the national courts. Ever since *von Colson*, the ECJ has stressed that the interpretative method required the national court to consider national law as a whole, in order to assess to what extent it may be applied so as not to produce a result contrary to that sought by the Directive, yet the Court was particularly forceful if national legislation was passed in order to implement the Directive in question.[86] In the Court's view 'every national court must presume that the State had the intention of fulfilling entirely the obligations arising from the Directive

---

[82] Case 14/83, *supra* note 59, para. 28; Case 79/83, *supra* note 60, para. 28.

[83] Case 14/83, *supra* note 59, para. 25; Case 79/83, *supra* note 60, para. 25; indeed, to have held otherwise would have exceeded the Court's jurisdiction under Art. 234 EC.

[84] For an overview, see S. Vogenauer, *Die Auslegung von Gesetzen in England und auf dem Kontinent* (2001) and see also S. Prechal, *Directives in European Community Law: A Study of Directives and their Enforcement in National Courts* (1995), 195–245 (see, now, the revised 2nd edn, 2005).

[85] See also (in addition to the already cited decisions of the *Bundesarbeitsgericht*, *supra* notes 67 and 71), e.g. BGH, 19 Oct. 2004, XI ZR 337/03, sub II.3 (not yet reported); BGH [2004] NJW 154, 155; BAG [2003] NZA 742, at 747–50. For an overview, see Canaris, 'Die richtlinienkonforme Auslegung und Rechtsfortbildung im System der juristischen Methodenlehre' in H. Koziol and P. Rummel (eds), *Im Dienste der Gerechtigkeit: Festschrift für Franz Bydlinski* (2002), 47; M. Franzen, *Privatrechtsangeleichung durch die Europäische Gemeinschaft* (1999), 291–404.

[86] Case 14/83, *supra* note 59, para. 26; e.g. Joined Cases C-397 to C-403/01, *supra* note 33, para. 115.

concerned'.[87] That was *a fortiori* the case when domestic provisions were specifically enacted for the purpose of transposing a Directive.[88] Some have concluded that this presumption entitled the national courts to 'correct' the wording of the national law, whatever the circumstances of any national legislation implementing a Directive, assuming that this was also in the interest of the national legislator.[89] This is clearly *not* how German courts have understood the jurisprudence of the ECJ. Once again, the group of cases on Directive 76/207/EEC is an example in point. While it is certainly easier to apply a provision in the light of a Directive if the national legislator did not consciously deviate from the Directive than if the legislator deliberately refused to give effect to a certain result flowing from that Directive, the German courts will not easily set the wording of a provision aside and are most likely not to do so if the objectively assessed purpose of a provision does not conform to the result of the Directive.

The case-law in the United Kingdom would seem to reflect a similar understanding of the requirements of EC law in this regard.[90] Thus, the courts have been prepared to adopt more purposive and result-oriented methods of interpretation where the national implementing rules contain a gap or an ambiguity that would jeopardize the attainment of a Directive's objectives.[91] At the other extreme, the courts have refused to 'discover' room for interpretive ambiguity in national legislation where none could be said to exist. Lord Templeman's judgment in *Duke* v *GEC Reliance Ltd*[92] provided a strong and early affirmation of this point. This case concerned the deliberate retention by the UK government of discriminatory retirement ages for men and women under the Sex Discrimination Act 1975 and the question whether that legislation could be read so as to give effect to the equal treatment on that point as required under Directive 76/207/EEC, which his Lordship

[87] Case C-334/92, *Wagner Miret* v *Fondo de Garantía Salarial* [1993] ECR I-6911, para. 20. This more or less reflects the position reached by the UK courts in their approach to EC law: see, e.g., *Garland* v *BREL, supra* note 77, and *Thoburn* v *Sunderland County Council* [2002] 3 WLR 247; [2002] 1 CMLR 50 (noted by Marshall, 118 *LQR* (2002) 493, Campbell and Young [2002] *PL* 399 and Boyron, 27 *EL Rev* (2002) 771).

[88] Joined Cases C-397 to C-403/01, *supra* note 33, para. 112.

[89] E.g. Grundmann, 'Richtlinienkonforme Auslegung im Bereich des Privatrechts', [1996] *ZEuP* 399, at 418.

[90] See, e.g., Craig, 'Indirect Effect of Directives in the Application of National Legislation', Chap. 3 in M. Andenas and F.G. Jacobs (eds), *European Community Law in the English Courts* (1998), 37 ff. and, more generally, C. Boch, *EC Law in the UK* (2000).

[91] The case of *Litster* v *Forth Dry Dock Engineering Ltd* [1989] 1 AC 546 (concerning Directive 77/187/EEC, OJ 1977 L 61/26, on the protection of employees on the transfer of undertakings and the UK's Transfer of Undertakings (Protection of Employment) Regulations 1981 (SI 1981, No. 1794)) is a good example of the clarifying and gap-filling function that such interpretation can provide where implementing rules have failed to cover all eventualities. (See now Directive 98/50/EC, OJ 1998 L 201/88, as amended by Directive 2001/23/EC, OJ 2001 L 82/16.) See also *Pickstone* v *Freemans plc* [1989] 1 AC 66.

[92] [1988] AC 618, at 635–42, esp. 639–41. See also *Finnegan* v *Clowney Youth Training Programme Ltd.* [1990] 2 AC 407.

held that it could not (refusing to re-write national law so as to give effect to an improperly implemented Directive, precisely because that would in essence have led to direct effect). Given that the defendant employer was a private party, direct effect was also unavailable, so the plaintiff was left without redress. However, the possibility that a claimant may be left without any remedy at all can encourage the UK courts to be rather more flexible in applying requirements as to interpretation to achieve a particular result, even where the legislation in question was not specifically introduced to implement the relevant Directive.[93] With the advent of Member State liability, some of this pressure to use the tool of interpretation rather more strongly has been released, although it could still be argued that even a stretched interpretation is a more palatable and less controversial alternative for a court to entertain (leading to the direct grant of rights for the claimant as against another private party) than to be forced to declare the State liable in damages to the claimant (particularly where this result is so alien to the UK system, in terms of holding the legislator liable for exercising its legislative power where that power has traditionally been viewed as an absolute one that cannot be challenged by the courts).[94] Thus far, however, it must be conceded that the incidence of this phenomenon of (perhaps over-)stretched interpretation has been more frequent under the UK's Human Rights Act 1998, which willingness aligns with the absence of any satisfactory remedy in national courts for a breach of the 1998 Act by primary legislation.[95]

It follows that the interpretative method is a useful tool for achieving conformity with the result of Directives in individual cases, yet its success depends upon a number of factors that are, from the perspective of Community law, entirely accidental. The ECJ cannot do more than instruct the national court as to the meaning of Community law: it is then the national court's task to determine whether the national law can actually be applied in conformity with the Directive. Since the discretion of national courts to apply statutory or case-law may vary from Member State to Member State, the interpretative method is a relatively weak and vulnerable device for increasing the effectiveness of Directives across the Community.

It should thus be unsurprising that attempts were made to strip the *von Colson* jurisprudence of its 'national' corset. These attempts to tighten the requirements of interpretation were boosted by some passages in the much-discussed *Marleasing*

---

[93] An example may well be the case of *Webb* v *EMO Air Cargo (No. 2)* [1993] 1 WLR 49; [1993] 1 CMLR 259: see *infra* note 108.

[94] See, e.g., Craig, 'Parliamentary Sovereignty in the United Kingdom after *Factortame*', 11 *YBEL* (1991) 221, his UK country report in Slaughter, Stone Sweet and Weiler (eds), *supra* note 20, and his *Public Law and Democracy in the United Kingdom and the United States of America* (1990).

[95] Which includes Orders in Council issued under the Royal Prerogative and all secondary legislation where to impugn its validity would itself amount to a challenge to the validity of its parent statute (ss. 3 and 21(1) of the Human Rights Act 1998). See, e.g., *R* v *A (No. 2)* [2001] 2 WLR 1546 and, generally, Edwards, 'Reading Down Legislation under the Human Rights Act', 20 *Legal Sudies* (2000) 353.

case.[96] Here, the Court first repeated the *von Colson* rule that the national court was called upon to interpret national law 'as far as possible' in the light of the Directive,[97] but then added that this requirement 'precluded' the interpretation of provisions of national law in a manner contravening the Directive.[98] Subsequently this was understood by some to mean that the ECJ 'acknowledged that the non-transposed Directive, irrespective of the "vertical" or "horizontal" nature of the relationship, has the effect of "precluding" incompatible domestic provisions'.[99] Without a fuller explanation of the context of this statement, it is our view that this strong construction of the *Marleasing* judgment was erroneous. The key question raised in *Marleasing* was whether or not the general contract law rules of the Spanish Civil Code should be interpreted so as also to apply to a contract setting up a company (in the absence of specific implementation by Spain into national law of the First Company Law Directive (68/151/EEC)[100]). So long as it remained open to the Spanish court to maintain that *either* interpretation was possible under national law, the ECJ's statement—that Article 11 of the Directive 'precluded' an interpretation of Spanish law that included the general contract law grounds for nullity of a contract—merely explained which interpretive option the national court was obliged to choose if it was to ensure conformity with the Directive.

That this interpretation of the case-law is preferable is implicit in many subsequent judgments.[101] It has been recently confirmed in the aforementioned *Pfeiffer* case: when the national court 'applies domestic law, and in particular legislative provisions specifically adopted for the purpose of implementing the requirements of a Directive, the national court is bound to interpret national law, *so far as possible*, in the light of the wording and the purpose of the Directive concerned in order to achieve the result sought by the Directive'.[102] Ironically, more than one year before the ECJ handed down its judgment in the *Pfeiffer* case, in a carefully reasoned

---

[96] Case C-106/89 *Marleasing SA* v *La Comercial Internacional de Alimentación SA* [1990] ECR I-4135. See, e.g., de Búrca, 'Giving Effect to European Community Directives', (1992) 55 *MLR* 215 and contrast Maltby, '*Marleasing*: What is All the Fuss About?', (1993) 109 *LQR* 301.

[97] Case C-106/89 (note 96, above), para. 8.

[98] *Ibid.*, para. 9.

[99] Opinion of Saggio AG in Joined Cases C-240 to C-244/98, *Océano Grupo Editorial SA* v *Roció Murciano Quintero* [2000] ECR I-4941, para. 31, note 18.

[100] OJ Spec Ed 1968 (I) 41.

[101] Including the judgment in the *Océano Grupo* case: Joined Cases C-240 to C-244/98, *supra* note 99, paras. 30–32. For further discussion, see Craig, 'Directives: Direct Effect, Indirect Effect and the Construction of National Legislation', 22 *EL Rev* (1997) 519 and Craig and de Búrca, *supra* note 6, 213–20.

[102] Joined Cases C-397 to C-403/01, *supra* note 33, para. 113 (emphasis added). See, also, the text at *supra* note 33, for the ECJ's refusal in this case to accord the Directive horizontal direct effect. Note, however, that this reading of the decision does not appear to be uncontroversial: Riesenhuber and Domröse, 'Richtlinienkonforme Rechtsfindung und nationale Methodenlehre', [2005] *RIW* 47, at 51, derive from para. 116 of the judgment that the national courts are required to adopt an interpretation *contra legem*. However, even in that particular passage the Court only required the 'application of interpretative methods recognised by national law'. Contrast the Opinion of Colomer AG in Joined Cases

decision the *Bundesarbeitsgericht* had already clarified that the relevant provisions of national law could not be interpreted so as to comply with Article 6(2) of Directive 93/104/EC.[103] The reason for this somewhat unfortunate lack of coordination between the different courts lies in the fact that in the *Pfeiffer* case the reference was made by a labour court of first instance (the *Arbeitsgericht Lörrach*) before the *Bundesarbeitsgericht* issued its aforementioned decision. Furthermore, the latter national court of last instance did not consider it necessary to await clarification of the issue before it by the ECJ.[104] The practical result of this lack of coordination is that, in spite of the high profile of the *Pfeiffer* case at EC level (Grand Chamber), it is unlikely that the actual decision of the ECJ will make a difference as to the outcome of the proceedings before the national courts in which the references were made in the *Pfeiffer* case. The limited value of the interpretative method and the need for legislative action in transposing Directives into national law is once more illustrated.[105]

The ECJ was justified in its refusal to give in to the temptation to disregard the boundaries of interpretation on the national level. For had it done so, the conclusion drawn by Advocate General Saggio[106] would have been inevitable: if the national courts were bound to interpret national law in such a way as to give effect to the result pursued by the Directive regardless of whether they had discretion to do so under national law, the Directive would have acquired all-encompassing direct effect. Again, the difference between Regulations and Directives would have been diminished and all the advantages flowing from the flexibility associated with the

C-397 to C-403/01, *supra* note 33, para. 58, where he had suggested that if 'it is impossible to provide an interpretation which conforms to the Directive concerned, the national court must ensure the full effectiveness of Community law by setting aside on its own authority, where appropriate, any conflicting provisions of national law'.

[103] BAG [2003] NZA 742. The case involved facts very similar to those in the *Pfeiffer* case and draws the (with hindsight) correct conclusions as to the consequences of the *Simap* case: Case C-303/98, *Sindicato de Médicos de Asistencia Pública (Simap)* v *Conselleria de Sanidad y Consumo de la Generalidad Valenciana* [2000] ECR I-7963) for emergency workers employed by the *Deutsches Rotes Kreuz*.

[104] BAG [2003] NZA 742, at 747.

[105] In the meantime, as a reaction to Case C-151/02, *Jaeger* [2003] ECR I-838 the German legislator has amended the relevant provisions of national law: Law of 24 December 2003 [2003] I BGBl. 3002. On the controversial question whether or not the amended provisions are fully compatible with Community law, see (e.g.) Schliemann, 'Allzeit bereit—Bereitschaftsdienst zwischen Europarecht, Arbeitszeitgesetz und Tarifvertrag', [2004] *NZA* 513. In the UK, see the Working Time Regulations 1998 (SI 1998, No. 1833) amended by the Working Time (Amendment) Regulations 2002 (SI 2002, No. 3128) and by the Working Time (Amendment) Regulations 2003 (SI 2003, No. 1684) (implementing Directive 2000/34/EC, OJ 2000 L 195/41, which removed the exclusion of doctors in training from the scope of the Directive). In *R v Attorney General for Northern Ireland* ex parte *Burns* [1999] IRLR 315, an employee claimed damages from the UK for its failure promptly to implement the Directive. The national court held that the UK had indeed committed a sufficiently serious breach of EC law, but that the plaintiff had failed to show that this had caused her any loss on the facts. See, generally, C. Barnard, *EC Employment Law* (2000), at 402–20 and H. Collins, K. Ewing, and A. McColgan, *Labour Law: Text and Materials* (2002), at 371–413.

[106] *Supra* note 99.

need to transpose Directives into national law would likewise have vanished.[107] For the same reason, therefore, as that for the denial of horizontal direct effect to Directives, it is wise that the ECJ has consistently adhered to the *von Colson* jurisprudence, the key feature of which is that the interpretative method works only 'so far as possible' under national law.

Nevertheless, we must finally note that national courts have been known to change their minds as to the extent of the 'interpretability' of national law so as to conform to the requirements of a Directive, once the ECJ has ruled upon the correct interpretation of that Directive after an Article 234 EC reference. The litigation in the *Webb* v *EMO Air Cargo Ltd* saga in the UK may be said to illustrate this possibility.[108] While, strictly, this practice suggests that national courts do not always properly respect the boundary between permissible interpretation and allowing direct effect via the 'back door', the practice does reflect an understandable desire to provide a remedy in the individual case. Even so, given the availability of a damages claim against a defaulting Member State in such a situation, one could forgive the defendants in these cases for feeling somewhat aggrieved at such behaviour by the national courts. Ultimately, however, this practice is one more example of how the ECJ's interpretation of the provisions of Directives can be leveraged further into national (private) law than a strict application of the ECJ's own jurisprudence on direct effect and interpretation might suggest.

III. Consumers and the ECJ: the Heininger saga

This section concludes with a discussion of another line of cases of recent vintage, which also illustrate the complex triangular relationship between the ECJ, the national courts and the national legislator that arises in the process of implementing and applying Directives. Due to constraints of space, this discussion must be limited to the main points. In Germany, schemes whereby average earners took out a loan and invested it in immovable property had become popular in the late 1980s and early 1990s. As a matter of fact, however, the demand for commercial sites and residential premises had been overestimated and many investments did not generate any profit, but on the contrary turned out to be financially unsound. The promised tax benefits likewise did not benefit average earners to any large extent, as their tax burden was relatively small in any case. The cases became known under

---

[107] As, e.g., the *Bundesarbeitsgericht* also pointed out in [2003] NZA 742, at 750.

[108] See the judgment of the Court of Appeal at [1992] 2 All ER 43; [1992] 1 CMLR 793 and the first judgment of the House of Lords at [1993] 1 WLR 49; [1993] 1 CMLR 259 (see esp. para. 10 of Lord Keith's judgment in the CMLR report, where no discrimination under the terms of the Sex Discrimination Act 1975 was found). The final ruling of the House of Lords on the case's return from Luxembourg ([1995] 1 WLR 1454; [1996] 2 CMLR 990) saw Lord Keith attempting to fit the ECJ's reply into the scheme of the UK legislation (see paras 10 and 11), in a way which seemed to run counter to the interpretation of UK law that he had originally adopted prior to making the reference to the ECJ. The saga is noted by Deards, 2 *EPL* (1996) 71 and Boch, 33 *CML Rev* (1996) 547, and see Craig, *supra* note 101, at 530–3. See, also, BGH [2002] NJW 1881, discussed *infra* note 120.

the name of *Schrottimmobilien* ('waste property').[109] Large numbers of consumers sought to set aside the contracts that had committed them to these investments. Community law was relied upon in some of these proceedings, which is why the genesis of these cases is interesting for our purposes.

Council Directive 85/577/EEC of 20 December 1985 to protect the consumer in respect of contracts negotiated away from business premises seemed, with its right of cancellation, to provide a way of getting out of these now bitterly regretted contracts.[110] The acquisition of land or residential property is excluded from the scope of that Directive according to Article 3(2)(a). Credit agreements intended for the purpose of acquiring or retaining property rights in land or in an existing or projected building, however, were not explicitly excluded from the scope of the Directive.[111] In some cases, the credit arrangement had been concluded on the doorstep of the consumer, so the issue arose whether or not the Doorstep Selling Directive could be relied on.

At the level of national law there were two obstacles to be surmounted. First of all, credit arrangements in which credit is subject to the giving of security by way of a charge on immovable property, and is granted on usual terms for the inter-mediate financing of the same, were excluded from the scope of application of the *Verbraucherkreditgesetz* (Consumer Credit Act) in force at the time.[112] This meant that consumers could not avail themselves of the right of cancellation contained therein. The specific German statute then in force and intended to implement the Doorstep Selling Directive (the *Haustürwiderrufsgesetz*) provided for a right of can-cellation but excluded all credit agreements from its scope of application. The com-bined effect of these rules was that consumers could not set aside the credit agreement nor the acquisition of immovable property. The second obstacle was that the consumer's right of cancellation under the Consumer Credit Act in any event lapsed one year after the consumer's declaration of his intention to conclude the credit agreement. Two questions were thus referred by the *Bundesgerichtshof* to the ECJ, namely whether the Doorstep Selling Directive covered agreements for the

---

[109] See, for a discussion of these cases and their background, Bungeroth, 'Die Rückabwicklung nach dem HWiG widerrufener Immobiliarkredite', [2004] *WM* 1505. He estimated that around 300,000 consumers have fallen into financial difficulties as a result of taking part in such doubtful investment schemes.

[110] OJ 1985 L 372/31 (the Doorstep Selling Directive).

[111] They are so excluded by Art. 2 of Council Directive 87/102/EEC of 22 December 1986 for the approximation of the laws, regulations and administrative provisions of the Member States con-cerning consumer credit (OJ 1987 L 42/48) as amended by Council Directive 90/88/EEC of 22 February 1990 (OJ 1990 L 61/14, the Consumer Credit Directive). In the UK, see reg. 3(2)(a) of the Consumer Protection (Cancellation of Contracts Concluded away from Business Premises) Regulations 1987 (SI 1987, No. 2117), which excludes 'any contract–(i) for the sale or other disposition of land, or for a lease or land mortgage; (ii) to finance the purchase of land; (iii) for a bridging loan in connection with the purchase of land . . .'.

[112] The relevant legislation is reproduced in Case C-481/99, *Heininger v Bayerische Hypo- und Vereinsbank AG* [2001] ECR I-9945.

grant of credit secured on immovable property and whether the time limit for the exercise of the right of cancellation contained in the provisions of national law was compatible with that Directive.[113]

In the resulting preliminary ruling, the ECJ interpreted the relevant Directives in what appeared to be the most consumer-friendly manner, namely affirming the applicability of the Doorstep Selling Directive to credit agreements secured by a charge on land and stating that the Directive precluded national legislation imposing a time limit such as that provided for under German law.[114] The reason for excluding such credit agreements at national level from the scope of application of the Doorstep Selling Directive was—in the view of the German court—that they were intimately linked to the purchase of an interest in land, which was, as explained, in fact excluded from the scope of application of the Directive.[115] The Court, however, dismissed this argument and stated that the fact that the credit agreement was secured by a charge on immovable property did not render it any less necessary to protect the consumer.[116] As to the time limit, the German court suggested that the Member States were given discretion as to the sanctions for failing to notify the consumer of his right of cancellation. Article 5 of the Doorstep Selling Directive merely required the Member States to ensure that their national legislation laid down 'appropriate consumer protection measures' in cases where the information was not supplied. The ECJ once more referred to the need to protect the consumer and concluded that even a time limit of one year as to the exercise of the right of cancellation could not be justified. The argument from legal certainty raised in defence of the time limit did not persuade the Court, since in its view the trader could avoid any such uncertainty by complying with the requirement to provide the relevant information to the consumer.[117] The decision of the ECJ in this case can be criticized for two main reasons.

First of all, the Court did not pay any significant attention to the arguments raised concerning the discretion of the Member States in implementing Directives.[118] Even where on its face the Directive did not require anything more specific than the adoption of 'appropriate measures', the ECJ seemed to be prepared to strike down every provision which did not appear unilaterally to protect the

[113] BGH [2000] NJW 521.

[114] Case C-481/99, *above* note 112, paras. 40 and 48.

[115] This would also seem to accord with the rationale behind the UK's implementation of the Directive in reg. 3(2)(a) of the 1987 Regulations, *supra* note 111.

[116] Case C-481/99, *supra* note 112, para. 34. This is a conclusion redolent of the approach adopted by the ECJ concerning national time limits and the proper implementation of Directives in its judgment in Case C-208/90, *Emmott* v *Minister for Social Welfare and Attorney General* [1991] ECR I-4269 (see paras. 19–23: the Member State can avoid such an uncertainty by ensuring that the Directive is implemented correctly).

[117] *Ibid.*, para. 47.

[118] See, e.g., *ibid.*, paras. 43 ff.: the ECJ seems simply to assume that the exercise of the right to cancel the contract (as laid down in Art. 5(1) of the Directive) is unlimited in time, since the Directive itself provides for no express limitation of that right.

consumer but instead sought to strike a balance between the competing interests of the parties to the contract.[119] The judgment in *Heininger* necessitated considerable adjustments at the national level: first, an attempt was made to create conformity through interpretation, but eventually the legislator stepped in. After the case returned to it from Luxembourg, the *Bundesgerichtshof* somewhat surprisingly concluded that it was possible to interpret the provisions of national law so as to achieve the result of the reading given to the Doorstep Selling Directive by the ECJ and to grant the consumer a right of cancellation of the credit agreement.[120] This change of position[121] was justified by reference to a number of lower court decisions and academic writings, which had previously argued in favour of this particular interpretation. One could not say, the court stated, that these opinions were all blatantly wrong, so their very existence 'showed' that there was discretion as to how to construe national law. The court even went so far as to extend this Community-inspired interpretation of the provisions of national law beyond the scope of application of the Directive,[122] which provides a particularly vivid example of the possibility of spill-over effects from the interpretation of EC law adopted by the ECJ and required to be applied by the national courts. The *Bundesgerichtshof* refrained, however, from expressing an opinion as to whether the lack of conformity with Community law of the time limit could be remedied by interpretation.[123] The details are now of only historic interest, for in the end the legislator intervened and adjusted the relevant provisions of German law.[124] What is interesting, however, is the enormous amount of ink that was spilled in German literature and the great number of cases concerned with the question whether or not German law could be interpreted in conformity with the Directive.[125] All these efforts became moot once the legislator adapted the relevant statutory provisions to ensure that German law was in conformity with the *Heininger* judgment.

Secondly, in spite of its extreme interpretation of the Doorstep Selling Directive, the ECJ's judgment in *Heininger* did not in the end achieve the effective protection of the consumer, in any event not by the means of Community law.[126] The reason

---

[119] See Franzen, '"*Heininger*" und die Folgen: ein Lehrstück zum Gemeinschaftsprivatrecht' [2003] *JZ* 321, at 325.

[120] BGH [2002] NJW 1881, at 1883; contrast the opinion of the court expressed in the reference itself: [2000] NJW 521.

[121] Which in the end was to no avail for the applicants, since it was subsequently found that the other conditions of application were not met (the contract was not negotiated or concluded in a doorstep-selling situation): OLG Munich, [2002] BKR 912.

[122] BGH [2002] NJW 1881, at 1884.

[123] BGH [2002] NJW 1881, at 1884.

[124] Law of 23 July 2002 [2002] I BGBl. 2850. According to s. 495 BGB, the consumer has a general right of cancellation in relation to consumer credit contracts. The right of cancellation arising out of doorstep-selling practices is a subsidiary right according to s. 312a BGB. Finally, if the consumer has not been notified of his right of cancellation, then the time limit for the exercise of the right does not commence according to s. 355(3) sentence 3 BGB: in other words, it never lapses.

[125] See the rich references in BGH [2002] NJW 1881.

[126] See Franzen, [2003] *JZ* 321, at 332.

is that setting the credit agreement aside only results in an obligation owed by the consumer to return the loan. A consumer who has difficulties in meeting the obligation to pay interest, however, will rarely be able to pay back the loan itself. In other words, getting out of the credit agreement does not protect the consumer in economic terms. This is hardly surprising, for in this line of 'waste property' cases the terms of the credit agreement were not substantively unfair. The problem was with the contract for the acquisition of immovable property itself, which invariably was a bad deal for the consumer. Hence, only if the right of cancellation also affected the purchase of land could the consumer truly benefit from the cancellation. If these contracts were treated as a single unit and the consumer could transfer back the land and *thereby* also discharge his or her obligations under the credit agreement, the risk of the investment could be transferred back to the provider of the loan. However, the Eleventh Senate (which is in charge of these matters at the *Bundesgerichtshof*) did not adopt this consumer-friendly approach.[127] This did not escape criticism. The argument was voiced that, once again, this jurisprudence was not in conformity with Community law, especially the Doorstep Selling Directive. References for preliminary rulings were made accordingly and their outcome in Luxembourg is to be awaited with interest.[128]

The difficulty with this argument is obvious. Article 3(2)(a) of the Doorstep Selling Directive excludes from its scope of application the contract of sale of land or other immovables. In addition, according to Article 7 of the Directive, it is national laws that are to govern the legal effects of the cancellation. Given this clear wording of the Directive, it is not surprising that Advocate General Léger in his opinion in *Schulte* v *Deutsche Bausparkasse Badenia AG*[129] came to the conclusion that Community law did not require that the right of cancellation extended to the contract of sale of immovable property. This was a matter exclusively to be determined by reference to national law.[130] It should be noted that in the meantime the German legislator has clarified the circumstances in which a credit agreement and

---

[127] As a result, the right of cancellation is limited to the credit agreement—the two transactions are not to be treated as a unit: e.g. BGH [2002] NJW 1881, at 1884 and [2002] BKR 579, at 580 (both decisions of the Eleventh Senate), approving note by Rohe, [2002] *BKR* 577. The issue is controversial: contrast, e.g., Deutsch 'Verbraucherschutz gegen den BGH' [2003] *NJW* 2881; BGH [2004] NJW 2731; [2004] NJW 2736 (Second Senate, both decisions concerned the related context of real estate investment funds).

[128] LG Bochum [2003] BKR 706 (lodged as Case C-350/03, *Schulte* v *Bausparkasse Badenia AG*, OJ 2003 C 264/18) and OLG Bremen [2004] NJW 2238 (lodged as Case C-229/04, *Crailsheimer Volksbank* v *Conrads and others*, OJ 2004 C 201/9; see now the Opinion of Léger AG of 2 June 2005).

[129] Opinion of Léger AG in Case C-350/03, *supra* note 128, para. 114 (28 September 2004, not yet reported—text available from the Court's website (http://curia.eu.int/en/content/juris/index_form.htm); not yet decided by the ECJ). The very admissibility of the reference by the *Landgericht* Bochum was also strongly doubted by the AG in his Opinion: see paras. 38–48 (the failure to determine whether or not the contract in question was actually concluded in a 'doorstep-selling situation' meant that the questions asked could be no more than 'hypothetical'—see esp. para. 41 and the cases cited in note 18 thereto).

[130] Opinion of Léger AG in Case C-350/03, *supra* note 128, para. 94.

a contract for the acquisition of immovable property are to be treated as 'connected contracts'. According to § 358(3) sentence 3 BGB, this will be the case if the provider of credit facilitates the acquisition (beyond simply providing the credit) by closely cooperating with the provider of the immovable property. Whether the Court will follow the reasoning of the Advocate General in *Schulte*—provided that the reference is held to be admissible under Article 234 EC—remains to be seen. Yet one wonders whether, in the light of these remarks, it was really necessary to narrow the discretion of the Member States in implementing the Doorstep Selling Directive so significantly in the *Heininger* decision. In the final analysis, the Doorstep Selling Directive was simply not meant to deal with the sort of situation that arose in the *Heininger* litigation.[131]

4. POLICING IMPLEMENTATION

In the previous section we inquired whether or not the missing implementation of Directives matters. It matters because the ECJ has consistently refused to ascribe fully-fledged direct effect to Directives; instead, under certain conditions national courts are required to bring national law into conformity with the Directive, namely either by reason of the direct effect of the Directive in vertical relationships or by the Directive-friendly interpretation of national law. Missing implementation also matters because Member States may become liable in damages to private parties who have incurred loss as a result of the failure to transpose the Directive into national law. In this section, we examine the one mechanism for policing implementation that was explicitly provided for in the Treaty itself, namely infringement proceedings under Article 226 EC. In the previous section we showed how the ECJ skilfully created incentives for private parties to rely upon Directives before national courts and thus turned them into agents for the enforcement of Community law, but infringement proceedings bring the Commission into play. The Commission comprehensively monitors the implementation process in the Member States and makes frequent use of the mechanism provided for in Article 226 EC.

One may doubt whether it is useful to differentiate between the different devices that allow the ECJ to express its (binding) views as to the meaning of provisions of Directives. After all, as is clear from the examples given in the previous section, preliminary rulings proceedings regularly result in an (abstract) evaluation of national law. This usually takes the form of a statement that the Directive 'precludes' (or does not preclude) a certain rule of national law. Whether the prohibited rule is contained in a statute supposedly implementing the Directive or stems from other sources of national law is immaterial.[132] In any event, the Member States are given

---

[131] *Cf.* Bungeroth, [2004] *WM* 1505, at 1511.

[132] See, e.g., Case C-106/89, *Marleasing, supra* note 96, paras. 7 and 8. Of course, as discussed in the previous section, the precise *consequences* in national law of such an interpretation of EC law by the

a clear indication whether or not their attempts at transposing the Directive have been successful. Also, in respect of the interpretation of the Directive itself, it does not make a difference as to how the case reached the ECJ.[133] Still, there is a significant if subtle difference between the two sets of proceedings: this concerns the approach adopted towards national law.

In proceedings involving private parties who in one way or another can derive a benefit from a Directive, the ECJ, after clarifying that a certain rule of national law is not compatible with the Directive, requires the national courts to do everything possible in applying national law to achieve the result envisaged by the Directive in the individual case. And, as we have seen in the examples so far, national courts have at times gone out of their way to stretch national law so as to achieve a result that conforms to the Directive. State liability, likewise, is a measure of last resort. Hence, if Directives are to be given effect in an individual case, national law is to be interpreted and applied so far as possible in conformity with the Directive. As we will shortly see, this does not seem to be the approach adopted in infringement proceedings when analysing national law. Here, national law is often given the most Directive-hostile interpretation and in case of doubt the ECJ will find national law to have failed properly to implement the Directive.[134] Whether or not the measures implementing the Directive could in the individual case be applied in such a way as to achieve the result pursued by the Directive often does not 'win' the case for the Member State. The measures that transpose the Directive must, as we will see, be unequivocal and clear in giving effect to the Directive. This is a new and considerable source for further diminishing the flexibility of legislating through Directives.

Furthermore, it is evident that the requirements as to implementation developed in infringement proceedings can sometimes undermine the usefulness of the techniques described in the previous section. Those techniques may assist in providing a remedy in the individual case, but they do not ensure the general and overall 'correctness' of the implementation of the Directive in national law. As a result, the pressure for further 'corrective' national legislative measures does not wither away, and this pressure can be increased if the Commission applies to the ECJ to impose fines upon a Member State in persistent default in taking measures to implement a

---

ECJ will vary depending upon the relevant EC law doctrine at issue (interpretation shapes national law where it is open to different possible meanings, direct effect basically replaces the inconsistent national law on that point, etc.).

[133] Although it should perhaps be noted that the context of the reference and the observed consequences of previous ECJ judgments under Art. 234 EC can lead to a change of approach by the ECJ in subsequent cases (see Joined Cases C-267 and 268/91, *Criminal proceedings against Keck and Mithouard* [1993] ECR I-6097, esp. paras. 14–16).

[134] While acknowledging that 'it should be borne in mind that, according to the case-law of the Court, the scope of national laws, rules or administrative provisions must be assessed in the light of the interpretation given to them by national courts . . .': Case C-372/99, *Commission v Italy* [2002] ECR I-819, para. 20.

judgment under Article 226 EC.[135] This suggests that the ECJ views the techniques developed to secure the effectiveness of Directives in national law more as 'coping strategies' than long-term solutions to the problems of clear implementation.

A. The Unfair Terms in Consumer Contracts Directive

Council Directive 93/13/EEC of 5 April 1993 on unfair terms in consumer contracts[136] provides a useful starting point for substantiating the claims made by way of introduction. Article 5 of that Directive provides an interesting parallel between the interpretation of national law and the interpretation of contracts between private parties. The second sentence of Article 5 requires that in case of doubt the interpretation most favourable to the consumer ought to prevail (also known as interpretation *contra proferentem*). This means that the courts are in individual cases obliged to assess the term *in concreto* and construe it in a way that is favourable to the consumer. Article 7 of the Directive, however, also provides for a procedure by which the unfairness of terms can be assessed *in abstracto* with a view to the use of the terms in future contracts between dealers and consumers. Consumer organizations are thereby given the power to apply to a competent authority and obtain a review of the fairness of the terms to which they object (Article 7(2)). If the *contra proferentem* rule were also applied in this context it would operate to the detriment of the consumer, for it would favour upholding terms which, if not construed in a particularly consumer-friendly manner, would be unfair. It is natural, therefore, that Article 5 sentence 3 of the Directive excludes the application of the *contra proferentem* rule in proceedings brought pursuant to Article 7(2). In such proceedings, the term is to be given an objective interpretation. If we return to the interpretation of national law for a moment, the same phenomenon can be observed. As to the interpretation of such provisions *in concreto* in preliminary rulings, in case of doubt, the most Directive-friendly interpretation prevails. In infringement proceedings, national law is assessed *in abstracto* and in case of doubt the incompatibility between national law and Directive is established. The strict approach of the ECJ in infringement proceedings can, somewhat ironically, be illustrated by looking at cases that were concerned with Article 5 of the Unfair Terms Directive.[137]

In *Commission* v *Kingdom of the Netherlands*,[138] the applicant maintained that the respondent had failed correctly to transpose Articles 4(2) and 5 of the Unfair Terms Directive into national law. The Netherlands Government argued that the pre-existing

---

[135] See Art. 228 EC (discussed in its previous incarnation as Art. 171 EC by Bonnie, 'Commission Discretion under Art. 171(2) EC', 23 *EL Rev* (1998) 537) and Case C-387/97, *Commission* v *Greece* [2000] ECR I-5047.

[136] OJ 1993 L 95/29.

[137] Implemented in Germany by s. 305c(2) BGB and the *Unterlassungsklagengesetz*; in the UK, see now the Unfair Terms in Consumer Contracts Regulations 1999 (SI 1999, No. 2083).

[138] Case C-144/99, [2001] ECR I-3541.

provisions of its national law fully complied with the Directive and that therefore no further action was required.[139] This claim was backed up by references to decisions of the national courts.[140] Furthermore, the Netherlands Government contended that the Member States were entirely free to choose the form and methods necessary to transpose a Directive into national law.[141] The ECJ, however, did not follow this reasoning.

The Court conceded (as it had in fact held on a previous occasion) that legislative action on part of the Member State was not 'necessarily' required in order to implement a Directive.[142] However, it then heavily qualified this discretion of the Member States to choose the methods of implementing a Directive. It was essential, the Court stressed, that national law 'guaranteed' that national authorities will 'effectively' apply the Directive 'in full' and that individuals are made 'fully' aware of their rights and may rely upon them before the national courts.[143] The condition for securing 'full implementation' that the national law was *transparent* was particularly important, the Court was at pains to emphasize, where the Directive in question was also intended to grant rights to nationals of other Member States.[144] This is the case with the Unfair Terms Directive, as indeed with all of the other 'consumer directives'. Advocate General Tizzano's opinion brought out in more drastic terms the standard applied in infringement proceedings: the framework implementing the Directive in question 'must be designed in such a way as to remove all doubt or ambiguity' as regards the content of the relevant national legislation and its compliance with the Directive.[145]

The 'burden of proof' to establish full compliance is on the Member State, as is also clear from the judgment itself, where the Court stated that the Kingdom of the Netherlands was 'unable to show' that its legislation complied with the Directive.[146] Advocate General Tizzano even went so far as to derive from the very existence of a difference of opinion between the Commission and the Member State that the implementation was not free from ambiguity.[147] As to the merits of the case, he had particular doubts as to whether the national legislation ensured that, in proceedings brought according to Article 7(2) of the Directive, the *contra proferentem* rule of interpretation was not applied (as required by Article 5 sentence 3, as explained above).[148]

---

[139] See, for early commentary and criticism, Hondius, 'Non-implementation of the Directive on Unfair Contract Terms: the Dutch Case', 2 *ERPL* (1997) 193.

[140] For details, see the Opinion of Tizzano AG in Case C-144/99, *supra* note 138, paras. 10–13.

[141] Case C-144/99, *supra* note 138, para. 16.

[142] *Ibid.*, para. 17.

[143] *Ibid.*, para. 17. *Cf.* Case C-236/95, *Commission v Greece* [1996] ECR I-4459, para. 13.

[144] Case C-144/99, *supra* note 138, para. 18.

[145] Opinion, Case C-144/99, *supra* note 138, para. 15.

[146] Case C-144/99, *supra* note 138, para. 19.

[147] Opinion, Case C-144/99, *supra* note 138, para. 20.

[148] *Ibid.*, para. 30.

Especially noteworthy in our context is the defence of last resort of the Member State in this case. The Netherlands had suggested that in any event the national legislation could be interpreted in such a way as to ensure conformity with the Directive. The Court refuted this argument and its reasoning deserves to be quoted in full:

... even where the settled case-law of a Member State interprets the provisions of national law in a manner deemed to satisfy the requirements of a directive, that cannot achieve the clarity and precision needed to meet the requirement of legal certainty. That, moreover, is particularly true in the field of consumer protection.[149]

In the same vein, Advocate General Tizzano, in a passage referred to by the Court with approval, stated that the principle of interpretation could certainly not serve 'as an excuse' for failure to transpose or for inadequate transposition.[150]

The case is interesting because it clarified and confirmed three general principles of Community law as shaped by the case-law of a pro-active ECJ. First, while legislative action transposing a Directive into national law is not required *per se*, the pre-existing legislation of that Member State must leave no room for doubt as to its conformity with the relevant Directive. Secondly, it is for the Member State to prove that the Directive is fully effective in its national legal system. Thirdly, the requirement as to transparency of the implementation precludes the Member State from relying to any significant extent upon the willingness of its national court to apply the national law in a way that is consistent with the Directive. In the view of the ECJ, this does not constitute a full and adequate implementation of the Directive in question. The combined effect of these principles is considerably to diminish the discretion of the Member State in choosing the appropriate measure of implementation. Pre-existing legislation will only suffice if it exactly mirrors the Directive and, at least in the case of consumer Directives, the consumers are made fully aware of their rights, as accorded to them by the Directive, by the wording of the relevant provision of national law. The ECJ made perfectly clear in this case that the interpretative method may be applied in proceedings involving private parties, but it may not serve as a substitute for legislative action since it is likely to fail the transparency test.

The strict test of compliance illustrated by the previous case in relation to a claim that pre-existing national law was in conformity with the Directive applies with equal force to any legislation passed in order to transpose a Directive into national law. This is exemplified by the case of *Commission* v *Kingdom of Spain*,[151] where the Commission contended that Spain had failed to give full effect to Articles 5 and 6(2) of the Unfair Terms Directive.

As to the first plea, the Commission adopted the view that the national legislature had not stated expressly that the rule of interpretation favourable to the consumer

---

[149] Opinion, Case C-144/99, *supra* note 138, judgment para. 21.

[150] *Ibid.*, Opinion, para. 35.

[151] Case C-70/03, judgment of 9 September 2004, not yet reported.

did not apply in the case of collective actions (by 'persons or organizations, having a legitimate interest under national law in protecting consumers, ... before the courts or before competent administrative bodies for a decision as to whether contractual terms drawn up for general use are unfair') referred to in Article 7(2) of the Directive, and therefore, Article 5 sentence 3 was not properly transposed.[152] Spain maintained that the rule of interpretation *contra proferentem* did not apply in relation to proceedings within the meaning of Article 7(2).[153] Since this was in its view self-evident, expressly to repeat the exact wording of Article 5 sentence 3 of the Directive in national law would have served no practical purpose. Advocate General Geelhoed conceded that there were no specific hints that the rule of interpretation favourable to the consumer was applied in Spanish law in proceedings within the meaning of Article 7(2) and that therefore it could not be stated with certainty that Spain had failed to give full effect to Article 5 sentence 3 of the Directive.[154] Yet, he added, there was the 'legal possibility' that the *contra proferentem* rule of interpretation would be applied in such proceedings.[155] The resulting ruling of the Court demonstrated the heavy burden placed upon the Member State when it does not simply transpose the text of a Directive *en bloc*. For the Court simply stated that Spain had not succeeded in establishing that the result of the Directive *would* be achieved in the national legal system, since it could not point to any provision or decision in support of its position.[156] One might have thought that it was for the Commission, which initiated the proceedings, to identify a failure to transpose the Directive. As we have also seen, however, in the *Commission v Netherlands* case discussed previously, the burden of proof in this respect rests with the Member State. The task of defending the national implementing measure is exceedingly difficult if the national legislator has not transposed the Directive word for word. Even the most remote and most abstract possibility that the national law might be interpreted in a way that does not give full effect to the Directive seems to suffice to trigger the intervention of the Court. These remarks apply with equal force in relation to the second plea of the Commission, to which we must now turn.

Spain had exercised its discretion in implementing Article 6(2) of the Unfair Terms Directive by giving that vague and open-textured provision a more specific meaning. In the Directive it is stated that Member States shall take the 'necessary measures' to ensure that the consumer does not lose the protection granted by this Directive by virtue of the choice of the law of a non-EU Member State as the law applicable to the contract if the latter has a 'close connection' with the territory of the Member States. Spain had transposed this provision, yet (among other real or alleged failures to give full effect to the Directive) instead of simply referring to a 'close connection', Spanish law more specifically required that the declaration of

---

[152] *Ibid.*, para. 12.
[153] As to the argument of Spain, see the Opinion of Geelhoed AG, *supra* note 151, para. 6.
[154] *Ibid.*, para. 18.
[155] *Ibid.*
[156] Case C-70/03, *supra* note 151, paras. 18–19.

consent was given on Spanish territory and the party agreeing to be bound by the contract was habitually resident there.[157] Advocate General Geelhoed correctly stated that this approach to fleshing out the requirement of close connection was narrower than that of the abstract definition in the Directive.[158] As a result, the scope of protection of the Directive was prejudiced.[159] The Court adopted the same narrow view. The Member State was precluded from circumscribing what was—as the Court admitted—the 'vague' term of a 'close connection' by predetermined criteria such as residence and the conclusion of the contract.[160] The strict compliance test apparent here leaves the Member State virtually no discretion as to how to implement Article 6(2) of the Unfair Terms Directive. Spain would only have escaped the verdict of infringing Community law if it had actually used the term 'close connection' or words to that effect in transposing the Directive. This is regrettable, for neither the Advocate General nor the Court were able to point to any more specific circumstances in which the Spanish solution would generate an unsatisfactory result. In other words, the merits of the Spanish attempt at giving the provision a more concrete meaning were not even seriously considered.[161] Again the remote, abstract possibility that the interest of the consumer might be prejudiced sufficed to declare the national legislation to be incompatible with the Directive.

Before leaving the discussion of the Unfair Terms Directive, it is worth taking a brief detour to examine a significant aspect of the UK's implementation of this piece of legislation, namely the significant role played by the Office of Fair Trading in monitoring terms in consumer contracts and enforcing the Unfair Terms in Consumer Contracts Regulations 1999.[162] In this area, the Office of Fair Trading and its Unfair Contract Terms Unit[163] have had a far greater impact in practical terms than the

---

[157] Reproduced in *ibid.*, para. 25.

[158] *Ibid.*, Opinion, para. 27.

[159] *Ibid.*, para. 28.

[160] *Ibid.*, para. 33.

[161] Perhaps the best compromise, respecting the terms of the ECJ's judgment, would be for Spain to include the phrase 'close connection' as the overarching concept, but then to supplement it by using the criteria of consent having been given on Spanish territory and habitual Spanish residence as indicative of a sufficiently close connection. See, e.g., the implementation in Germany in Art. 29a EGBGB, which also indicates a further potential deviation of the Spanish provision. Under the Directive, a close connection to any of the Member States suffices, whereas the Spanish provision required a close connection to Spain. This difference, however, was not especially noted in the proceedings. In the UK, reg. 9 of the UTCCR 1999 basically reproduces the wording of Art. 6(2) of the Directive and thus avoids this potential inconsistency with the Directive.

[162] SI 1999, No. 2083. Note that other regulators, including trading standards officials and the utility regulators, are also charged with the function of considering whether complaints about the fairness of terms should be upheld: see Sched. 1 for a list of the relevant 'qualifying bodies' for these purposes. For fuller comparative discussion of the issue of standard terms and their regulation in German and English law generally, see B.S. Markesinis, H. Unberath, and A.C. Johnston, *The German Law of Contract* (forthcoming, 2006), Chap. 3, section 5, and the references cited therein.

[163] See regs. 10–15 UTCCR 1999 and the following internet address for further details: www. oft.gov.uk/Business/Legal+Powers/Unfair+Terms+in+Consumer+Contracts/default.htm (last visited

private enforcement of the Regulations in the courts.[164] Thus far, the UK courts have seen fewer than ten cases where the application of the Regulations has been required, whereas the OFT has issued detailed guidance on the area[165] and regular and voluminous bulletins on its activities in this field.[166] These bulletins include discussion of individual cases, contracts and terms referred to it and, in many cases, a discussion of the measures taken to ensure that such cases comply with the Regulations. The OFT was given this role after the view was taken that the overall benefits to be gained simply from relying upon private individuals to enforce the Regulations would neither be as great nor as efficient as charging a public body with a supervisory and enforcement function.[167] While it may be the case that some other systemic factors (such as high litigation costs or the absence of widespread litigation insurance) may also account for the relative paucity of cases on the Regulations in the UK, it seems clear that the important role played by the OFT is a (and perhaps *the*) major explanation for the lack of national case-law on the subject. This illustrates with some force how the particular choices taken by Member States in implementing EC Directives[168] may themselves have a significant impact upon the role that can be played by the ECJ in developing EC private law.

B. The Consumer Sales Directive

Directive 1999/44/EC of the European Parliament and of the Council of 25 May 1999 on certain aspects of the sale of consumer goods and associated guarantees[169] represents one of the most ambitious attempts at Community level of harmonization of private law so far. It covers the right to demand subsequent performance if

21 January 2005). For some early discussion, see, e.g., Bright, 'Winning the Battle Against Unfair Terms', 20 *Legal Studies* (2000) 331.

[164] For recent discussion of the major issues that have arisen in the courts thus far, see Ervine, 'The Unfair Terms in Consumer Contracts Regulations in the Courts', 2004 *SLT* 127.

[165] *Unfair Contract Terms Guidance* (OFT 311, Feb. 2001).

[166] These bulletins are all available on-line, by accessing the OFT's publications page (available at www.oft.gov.uk/News/Publications/Leaflet+Ordering.htm, last visited 21 January 2005). The most recent edition (*Unfair Contract Terms Bulletins 27 and 28* (OFT 743, September 2004)) covers cases from January to June 2004 and runs to some 147 pages.

[167] Indeed, the argument runs that consumers would largely remain unaware of harsh and/or non-negotiated terms in such (often standard-form) contracts and would instead seek out the lowest prices, leading to a vicious circle of harsher terms imposed by business to ensure ever lower prices. See Goldberg, 'Institutional Change and the Quasi-Invisible Hand', 17 *J L & Econ* (1974) 461 (reprinted in V.P. Goldberg (ed.), *Readings in the Economics of Contract Law* (1989), 169–73), Trebilcock, 'An Economic Approach to the Doctrine of Unconscionability', in B.J. Reiter and J. Swan (eds), *Studies in Contract Law* (1980), 379, at 390–421 and Law Commission (CP No. 166) and Scottish Law Commission (CP No. 119), *Unfair Terms in Contracts: A Joint Consultation Paper* (2002), 7–10. Most recently, see Ogus, 'What Legal Scholars Can Learn From Law and Economics', 79 *Chicago-Kent L Rev* (2004) 383, at 390–1.

[168] Compare, e.g., the approach originally taken by Italy in implementing Art. 7 of the Unfair Terms Directive (*supra* note 3): Case C-372/99, *Commission v Italy* [2002] ECR I-819.

[169] OJ 1999 L 171/12.

non-conforming goods are delivered, the right to termination and the right to price reduction. It does not concern issues related to the passing of mercantile risk and the right to recover damages. The Directive has been transposed in quite different ways in the various Member States.[170] For reasons of space only certain aspects of the implementation in Germany[171] and England[172] can be examined in this chapter. If, in the course of future infringement proceedings, the same rigorous test of compliance is applied as we have discussed above in relation to the Unfair Terms Directive, both the English and the German measures aiming to give effect to the Directive will not survive unchanged for long. It suffices here to give an example from each of the two jurisdictions.

The Directive has been used as a model for the recent German reform of the contract of sale. Unlike the transposition in England, the structural elements of the system of remedies envisaged by the Directive have been implanted into the very heart of the German law of obligations.[173] The reason for this so-called 'grand solution' (*große Lösung*) was that it has the advantage of reducing the number of overlapping regimes of rules. As a result, the impact of the Consumer Sales Directive extends beyond the areas to which it itself claims to apply and has a 'spill-over' effect upon other (cognate and related) parts of national (private) law: this provides an excellent illustration of one aspect of the possible spill-overs from EC law into national private law (as discussed in Section 2, above). For instance, the right to terminate the contract (§ 323 BGB, an essential aspect of the rights granted to the consumer in Article 3 of the Directive) is defined in the general part of the law of obligations, which applies to all contracts. § 323 I BGB, however, requires that the buyer must (even after breach has been established) set a period of time within which performance must be rendered before the contract may be terminated. The Directive does not require as much as this: it suffices that the buyer has requested that the seller cure the defect or deliver substitute goods and that a reasonable time has passed (Article 3(3)). Construing German law in the sense envisaged by the Directive is not possible, for the Second Commission on the reform of the BGB expressly rejected the removal of the requirement to set a period of time for performance.[174] Applying the fall-back provision of § 323(2) nr. 3 BGB might provide

---

[170] See for an overview e.g. Mansel, 'Kaufrechtsreform in Europa und die Dogmatik des deutschen Leistungsstörungsrechts', 204 *AcP* (2004) 396 (Austria, Greece, Finland, Italy, Spain, UK).

[171] See, for more detailed discussion of whether the German implementation is in conformity with the Directive and whether conformity can be achieved by the interpretative method, Unberath, 'Die richtlinienkonforme Auslegung am Beispiel der Kaufrechtsrichtlinie' [2005] *ZEuP* 5.

[172] On the implementation in England, see R. Bradgate and C. Twigg-Flesner, *Blackstone's Guide to Consumer Sales and Associated Guarantees* (2003); Reynolds, 'Specific Performance—a Regular Remedy for Consumers', 119 *LQR* (2003) 541; Arnold and Unberath, 'Die Umsetzung der Richtlinie über den Verbrauchsgüterkauf in England' [2004] *ZEuP* 366 (comparative).

[173] For treatment of the truly comprehensive reform of the German law of obligations, see Markesinis, Unberath and Johnston, *supra* note 162, Chap. 9, and for a comparative discussion of the contract of sale, see *ibid.*, Chap. 10, Section 2.

[174] See Unberath, *supra* note 171, 5, at 29 with references.

a solution in consumer sale situations,[175] but this device is in any event not sufficient implementation, as it is not a fully *transparent* regulation of the rights of the consumer. Furthermore, it would distort the uniform application of the German Civil Code depending upon whether or not the individual case fell within the scope of application of the Directive. It is not to be expected that the ECJ would tolerate such an obvious deviation from the wording of the Directive, were the matter to be raised before it. It must be stressed again: even if in individual cases the national court would dispense with the requirement that a period for performance must be set by the consumer, the legislation would not withstand infringement proceedings under Article 226 EC because the consumer is not fully and unambiguously made aware of his or her rights.

In England, the Consumer Sales Directive was transposed in a much less sweeping fashion by inserting special provisions for consumer sales into the Sale of Goods Act 1979 and the Supply of Goods and Services Act 1982, while also slightly altering pre-existing provisions of these Acts.[176] Article 3(3) of the Directive was implemented correctly by the 2002 Regulations (see s. 48B(2) of the Sale of Goods Act 1979). The main challenge for English law lay elsewhere and was of a more fundamental nature. The newly added s. 48B of the Sale of Goods Act 1979 for the first time entitles the buyer to demand enforced performance in English law as a matter of right (rather than merely at the court's discretion). This comes close to a revolution in the remedies for breach of contract. It is probably for this reason, and due to the inertia of traditional reasoning, that in s. 48E it is provided that the court (in ordering specific performance or in giving effect to a remedy to which the buyer had not resorted) may make such orders either 'unconditionally or on such terms and conditions as to damages, payment of the price and otherwise as it thinks just'. The provision runs contrary to the aim of the Directive to grant the consumer clear and unconditional rights.[177] English courts may well recognize the need to exercise the discretion accorded to them under this provision in conformity with the Directive. However, again it is unlikely that the ECJ will accept this sign of good will. Rather, it seems likely that the Court will point to the possibility, even if it is a remote one, that the rights of consumers may not be fully effective in English law and as a consequence will regard the respective provision as being contrary to the wording and purpose of the Consumer Sales Directive.

5. CONCLUSION

The upshot of this brief survey is that the ECJ has significantly increased the effectiveness of Directives as a legislative instrument. The Court has pursued a

---

[175] The issue is controversial. In this sense, e.g., see *ibid.*, at 31; Lorenz, in *Münchener Kommentar* (4th edn, 2004), iii, Vor § 474 BGB, para. 19.

[176] Sale and Supply of Goods to Consumers Regulations 2002 (SI 2002, No. 3045).

[177] See, further, Arnold and Unberath, *supra* note 172, at 377 and 382.

two-pronged strategy. On the one hand, in individual cases it has required the national courts to apply their own law as far as conceivably possible in the light of the wording and purpose of the relevant Directive. On the other hand, if an abstract review of compliance with the Directive is called for, the Court has considerably tightened the requirements as to correct and full implementation. The examples discussed above indicate that it is difficult for the Member State to convince the Court that it has given full effect to the Directive in question, if the implementing measures do not transpose the Directive word for word. The 'carbon copy' method is thus clearly the safest way to implement Directives.[178] One cannot deny that in such cases the Court is faced with a difficult task: making sure that Directives are fully complied with while also maintaining flexibility for Member States in accommodating the aims of Directives within the national legal system. However, diminishing the discretion of Member States in this drastic fashion undermines the very essence of Directives, the very reason why they exist as a means of legislation, namely flexibility.

We would not go as far as to suggest that Directives should not 'survive' in this field.[179] It must be stressed once again that Directives can be a useful Community legislative instrument where the subject matter is complex and the differences between the legal systems of the Member States are considerable. Yet, in our view the Court has gone too far in its endeavour to give Directives *effet utile* and at times unnecessarily interfered with the exercise of the discretion accorded to Member States by Directives. The imminent need to police the implementation of the Consumer Sales Directive will undoubtedly provide a series of test cases for the future approach of the ECJ. It is to be hoped that a more flexible attitude will prevail than in relation to the implementation of other consumer Directives.[180] It must be remembered that Directives come at a price. It is the price, as the present chapter has tried to show, of considerably complicating the legislative process by requiring action at different levels and in different Member States (as well as adding another layer of complexity to the task faced by national courts in interpreting and applying the law in the case at hand). If the flexibility of Directives is not achieved in practice then these drawbacks may well outweigh the advantages. Regulations might then prove to be the better instrument of harmonization.[181] This would not only

---

[178] And may explain the UK's penchant for this approach via numerous statutory instruments, although this does create difficulties of overlapping measures protecting substantially similar interests (e.g. the Unfair Contract Terms Act 1977 and the Unfair Terms in Consumer Contracts Regulations 1999: see Law Commission and Scottish Law Commission, *supra* note 167).

[179] See the thought-provoking article by Weir, 'Difficulties in Transposing Directives' [2004] *ZEuP* 595.

[180] See, further, the ECJ's case-law on the implementation of the Product Liability Directive (85/374/EEC, OJ 1985 L 210/29), such as Case C-52/00, *Commission* v *France* [2002] ECR I-3827 and Case C-154/00, *Commission* v *Greece* [2002] ECR I-3879, discussed in Weir, [2004] *ZEuP*, at 601 ff.

[181] In this sense, see also Kieninger, 'Koordination, Angleichung und Vereinheitlichung des Europäischen Vertragsrechts' [2004] *Schweizerische Zeitschrift für internationales und europäisches Recht*

free up legislative resources at the national level but also allow the Community institutions to focus upon bringing the meaning of its legislation into the open, rather than having to chase after any deviation (real or apparent) between the different levels of legislation. Both sets of resources, needless to say, are in short supply.

Considering the merits and demerits of the different categories of legislative instruments at Community level is all the more important in the light of the current wholesale revision of the *acquis communautaire* in the field of private law and the ambitious plans for further harmonization. In the year 2001, the European Commission launched a process of consultation about the way in which 'problems resulting from divergences between national contract laws' should be dealt with at the European level.[182] In the subsequent 'Action Plan' for 'a more coherent European contract law',[183] the Commission identified three areas in which measures were called for: first, to increase the coherence of the EC *acquis* in the area of contract law; secondly, to promote the elaboration of EU-wide general contract terms; and, thirdly, to examine further whether problems in the European contract law field may require non-sector-specific solutions, such as an optional instrument. Central to this (by all accounts ambitious) project of harmonization of contract law is the Common Frame of Reference (CFR), which will contain definitions of legal terms, fundamental principles and model rules of contract law. Its purposes are manifold.[184] It suffices here to mention the two functions that have an immediate impact upon secondary legislation. The CFR will provide a 'toolbox' for the Commission itself when presenting proposals for future legal instruments in the area of contract law and in reforming the existing legislation. In the view of the Commission, national legislators should use the CFR when transposing EC Directives in the area of contract law into national legislation and should also draw on the CFR when enacting legislation in areas of contract law that are not regulated at Community level. A great number of the harmonization measures affecting contract law are what one could call 'consumer protection laws'. It comes as little surprise, therefore, that an integral part of the sweeping revision process envisaged in the 'Action Plan'[185] is to make an assessment of the effectiveness and quality of measures that aim to protect the consumer.[186] It is suggested that the revision ought to include an inquiry into

---

483, at 506. *Cf.* Tröger, 'Zum Systemdenken im europäischen Schuldvertragsrecht' [2003] *ZEuP* 525, at 536–8, for further criticism as to the usefulness of Directives.

[182] Communication from the Commission to the Council and the European Parliament on European Contract Law, 11 July 2001, COM(2001)398 final, at 7.

[183] Communication from the Commission to the European Parliament and the Council, 12 Feb. 2003, COM (2003)68 final.

[184] See Communication from the Commission to the Council and the European Parliament, 'European Contract Law and the Revision of the *Acquis*: The Way Forward', 11 October 2004, COM(2004)651 final, at 2–4.

[185] *Ibid.*, at 3–4; COM(2003)68 final, *supra* note 183, at 19.

[186] See the (lengthy) list of relevant 'consumer' Directives in *supra* note 3. See, also, the comparative discussion of some of these Directives and their national implementation from the perspectives of German and English law in Markesinis, Unberath, and Johnston, *supra* note 162.

whether the present regime of Directives remains faithful to the idea of flexibility. If this is not the case, it might be better to bring about the intended reform by means of Regulations. Whatever the developments in legislative technique, the importance of the impact made by the ECJ upon the interpretation and application of EC private law principles in the Member States will continue to be a growing and fruitful field for further study and research. At the same time, this chapter has tried to show that the legislative techniques used, both at EC and national level, have a significant impact upon the nature of the ECJ's contribution to this process, both to date and for the future.

6

A Coordinated Approach to Regulation and Civil Liability in European Law: Rethinking Institutional Complementarities

FABRIZIO CAFAGGI*

1. CIVIL LIABILITY, REGULATION AND THE TRANSFORMATIONS OF THE REGULATORY STATE

Civil liability is a much older regulatory device than administrative regulation. The emergence of a regulatory State is a relatively new phenomenon.[1] Within regulatory States different modes of regulation and administrative tools have developed, including the extensive use of private law.[2]

---

* I would like to thank Federica Casarosa and Marinella Baschiera for research assistance and the students of the Academy Summer School of 2004 for useful discussions in the classroom where I first presented these ideas.

[1] See on the subject J. Jordana and D. Levi Faur (eds), *The Politics of Regulation: Institution and Regulatory Reforms for the Age of Governance* (2004), at 145 ff.; P. Rosanvallon, *Le modèle politique français* (2004); the essays in 'La Regulation, Nouveaux modes? Nouveaux territories?', 109 *Revue française d'administration publique* (2004); F. Roche (ed.), *Règles et pouvoirs dans les systèmes de régulation* (2004) and *Régulations économiques: legitimité et efficacité* (2004); Glaeser and Schleifer, 'The Rise of the Regulatory State' [2003] *J Economic Literature* 401; Taggart, 'The Nature and the Functions of the State', in P. Cane and M. Tushnet (eds), *The Oxford Handbook of Legal Studies* (2003), at 101; Majone, 'The Regulatory State and its Legitimacy Problems', 22 *West European Politics* (1999) 1; A. Dixit, *The Making of Economic Policy—A Transaction-cost Politics Perspective* (1997); Majone, 'From the Positive to the Regulatory State. Cases and Consequences of Changes in the Mode of Governance', 17 *J Public Policy* (1997) 139.

[2] In relation to the USA, see Stewart, 'The Reformation of American Administrative Law', 88 *Harvard LR* (1975) 1667 and 'Administrative Law in the Twenty-first Century', 78 *NYU LR* (2003) 437 ff. In the latter article Stewart points out the two concurring functions of administrative law: negative and affirmative. The negative function serves 'to prevent unlawful or arbitrary administrative exercise of coercive power against private persons'. As to the affirmative tasks Stewart states: 'through new procedural requirements and approaches to judicial review, it ensures that regulatory agencies exercise their policy making discretion in a manner that is reasoned and responsive to the wide range of social and economic interests affected by their decisions, including both the beneficiaries of regulatory programs

The relationship between civil liability and regulation as devices for risk assessment and risk management has been extensively explored.[3] But new developments in both strategies suggest the need to reconsider their interaction in the light of the European framework of legal integration. Historically there have been different modes of interaction between civil liability and administrative regulation.[4] In the last part of the nineteenth century and the first part of the twentieth, the emergence of regulation, and in particular that of welfare regulation, was primarily due to significant limits of compensation. These shortcomings were associated with the

and those subject to regulatory controls and decisions'. In relation to the Italian system see Cassese, 'Tendenze e problemi del diritto amministrativo' [2004] *Rivista Trimestrale Diritto Pubblico* 901. As far as the French system is concerned see P.-L. Frier, *Précis de droit administrative* (2001), in particular at 280–4. Frier, describing the ways in which administrative powers are exerted, highlights the specificities belonging to different types of administrative intervention by means of '*actes de droit privé* '. Accordingly, public entities ('*les personnes publiques*') may operate outside their strict *puissance publique*, either in the framework of so defined '*gestion privée*' or in the framework of their *puissance privée*. Frier holds that '*depuis une vingtaine d'années, une nombre de plus en plus important des décisions prises en cette matière sont administratives, car elles experiment la puissance publique, qu'elles en réglementent l'usage general, ou qu'elles soient détachables de sa gestion même. Si les actes relatifs à l'organisation des services publics industriel et commerciaux, sont toujours de nature administratives, ceux, individuals, de gestion son de droit privé, même si leur auteur est une personne publique*'. The implied criteria used to draw such distinctions are those set out in extensive case-law. The analysis of contractual phenomena in relation to public administration is carried out at 323–38. See also R. Chapus, *Droit Adminitratif Général* (2000); L. Venezia and Y. Gaudemet, *Traité de droit administrative* (1994). In relation to the English system see P. Craig, *Administrative Law* (5th edn, 2003).

  [3] Among the vast and ever growing literature, see G. Calabresi, *The Costs of Accidents* (1970); J. Stapleton, *Disease and the Compensation Debate* (1986); D. Sugarman, *Doing Away with Personal Injury Law* (1989); P. Schuck (ed.), *Tort Law and the Public Interest: Competition, Innovation, and Consumer Welfare* (1991); Stapleton, 'Tort, Insurance and Ideology', 60 *MLR* (1995), 820; P. Atiyah, *The Damages Lottery* (1997); Cane, *The Anatomy of Tort Law* (1997); Cane, *Atiyah's Accidents: Compensation and the Law* (1999); M. Franklin and R. Rabin, *Tort Law and Alternatives* (7th edn, 2001); C. Harlow, *State Liability, Tort and Beyond* (2004).

  [4] The relationship varies quite significantly according to the function of administrative law and of civil liability in each legal system. For example the development of administrative law, and in particular of judicial review, in the USA was a response to the weaknesses of tort law as a control mechanism of agencies created to regulate industrial accidents. See S. Stewart, *Administrative Law in the Twenty-first Century*, *supra* note 2, at 439. In the US system Stewart enucleates five different approaches which characterized different stages in the development of administrative action in the USA; Stewart also notes that at present the last four paradigms are still used and that they can be seen as complementary: '[t]he tort and adjudicatory-hearing models will continue to be used to redress unlawful administrative impositions on specific persons. Analytic management of regulation and interest representation will continue to be used to structure and review agencies' exercise of discretionary lawmaking powers. The latter two systems operate in parallel and largely independently', at 444. A different development is that in continental Europe where administrative law developed as a device to express State authority over citizens. On this development see Cassese, *supra* note 2, where he also notes that under the current circumstances of globalization we are facing a 'gradual convergence' of national administrative law systems: phenomena of convergence are mainly seen in a common set of institutions concerning independent agencies, regulation, privatizations, individual access, and participation in administrative proceedings and judicial review of administrative action.

internal structure of civil liability and the weaknesses of other branches of private law, especially contract and labour law.[5] Worker compensation regimes for industrial accidents are only one example of an emerging body of legislation stimulated by the combined weaknesses of civil liability and labour law. While the causes of the development of administrative regulation are multiple, it is quite clear that in that context (the limits of) civil liability triggered welfare regulation.[6]

More recent cases in the area of mass torts have offered other examples of regulatory intervention caused by the inability of civil liability to provide for victims' adequate compensation.[7] In some contexts the main problem was related to the

[5] See for different accounts focusing on the USA, M. Horwitz, *The Transformation of American Law, 1870–1960. The Crisis of Legal Orthodoxy* (1992); C. Friedman, *Law in America, A Short History* (2004), at 125 ff.; Glaeser and Schleifer, *supra* note 3; Jordana *et al.*, *supra* note 1. For the English model see Craig, *supra* note 2; C. Parker, C. Scott, N. Lacey, and J. Braithwaite, *Regulating Law* (2004); Cane (1997), *supra* note 3. For the French model see M. Fabre Magnan, *Les obligations* (2004), at 635 ff.; G.Viney, *La responsabilité civile* (1995).

[6] On the complementarity of social security to tort law in general, see B.S. Markesinis, *The German Law of Obligations, vol. II, The Law of Torts: A Comparative Introduction* (1997), at 895, and Zweigert and Kötz, *Introduction to Comparative Law* (1998), at 463. See also on the topic Howarth, 'Three Forms of Responsibility: On the Relationship between Tort Law and the Welfare State', 60 *Cambridge LJ* (2001) 553. In Nordic countries, welfare e.g. through the setting up of governmental insurance schemes, was seen as a more efficient compensatory device than compensation through liability regimes, because it was seen as providing equal compensation for all injured parties and reallocating risk more evenly than in the case of civil liability. The welfare regulation approach was an acknowledged choice, however, now diminishing in importance. About Nordic welfare state and liability see T. Wilhelmsson and H. Samuli (eds), *From Dissonance to Sense: Welfare State Expectations, Privatisation and Private Law* (1999). On the relationship between tort regulation and social security see W. van Gerven, J. Lever, and P. Larouche, *Tort Law* (2000), at 18–32. As regards the Italian system, see also C. Salvi, *La responsabilità civile* (1998); see also P.G. Monateri, 'La responsabilità civile, Torino', in *Trattato di diritto civile diretto da R. Sacco*, (1998); Alpa, G., 'La responsabilità civile', in *Trattato di diritto civile, Milano*, 1999. As regards the German system, see B.S. Markesinis and U. Unberath *The German Law of Torts. A Comparative Treatise* (4th edn, 2002), at 724–30.

[7] Asbestos and tobacco constitute interesting case studies. See Sugarman, 'Precise Justice and Rough Justice: Scientific Causation in Civil Litigation as Compared with Administrative Compensation Plans and Mass Tort Settlements', in G. Comandè and G. Ponzanelli, *Scienza e diritto nel prisma del diritto comparato* (2004). For the English system I refer to the well-known case of *Fairchild* v *Glenhaven Funeral Services Ltd* [2002] UKHL 22, [2002] 3 WLR 89. See Weir, 'Making it More Likely v. Making it Happen', 61 *CLJ* (2002) 519. As far as the Italian system is concerned two different approaches have been put forward in literature. Civil liability has been perceived as a device performing mainly deterrent and regulatory functions by Ponzanelli, 'Mass Tort nel diritto italiano', [1994] *Responsabilità civile* 173. *Contra* the opinion that burdens of stricter liability could be imposed as pure regulatory devices: see Cafaggi, 'Immunità per i produttori di sigarette: barriere culturali e pregiudizi di una giurisprudenza debole', in [1997] *Danno e Responsabilità* 750, comment on a judgment of the Lower Court of Rome, 4 April 1997, now reversed in 2005 by the Court of Appeal of Rome, which has recognized the right to recovery of the relatives of a smoker who died of lung cancer. Asbestos mass tort cases have deeply influenced tobacco litigation. On the tobacco litigation in the USA and its implications for the goals of the tort system see Rabin, 'The Third Wave of Tobacco Litigation', in R. Rabin and S. Sugarman (eds), *Regulating Tobacco* (2001), at 176–206. As highlighted by Rabin, the first step of the new trend in tobacco litigation is marked by the well-known case *Castano* v *American Tobacco Co.*, 160 FRD 544, revised 84

requirements of civil liability (in particular to the difficulty of proving causal link or to the limited range of available remedies) that undermined the chance of receiving compensation.[8] In other cases the potentially unequal compensation within a relatively homogeneous group of victims, due to the particular features of adjudication, has suggested the adoption of regulatory schemes.[9] These areas extend from asbestos to tobacco, from vaccines to infected blood, from adulterated or poisoned food to drugs.

It should be noted that these 'administrative' alternatives have mainly emerged in relation to the compensatory functions. The boundaries of and the interaction between civil liability and regulation in relation to deterrence are much more subtle.

A somewhat different phenomenon has arisen more recently with de-regulation and the reduction of the resources and operations of the welfare state.[10] In many areas de-regulation, which occurred in the 1980s, has imposed greater burdens on civil liability from both a deterrence and a compensation perspective. The response in different legal systems has not been homogeneous, but the expansion of strict liability, that of available remedies, primarily economic losses, and the increased level of compensation for personal injury can be interpreted as a consequence of the new

F 3d 734 (5th Cir. 1996). Concerning regulatory functions performed by tobacco litigation and arguing for the need for complementing torts devices with control strategies, Rabin observes that '[a]t no time, however, have litigation-associated costs operated as a rational scheme, from a regulatory perspective, in affecting the demand for the product'; at 200. For a detailed comparative assessment of the asbestos mass tort cases in the US and Europe from an economic standpoint, see White, 'Asbestos and the Future of Mass Torts', NBER Working paper note 10308 (2004), especially at 12. White illustrates continuous shifts in the balance between regulatory measures and civil liability rules facing asbestos litigation. See also J. Weinstein, *Individual Justice in Mass Tort Litigation: the Effect of Class Actions, Consolidations, and Other Multiparty Devices* (1995); and C. Scott and J. Black, *Cranston's Consumer and the Law* (2000), at 122.

    [8] See in the American system Franklin and Rabin, *supra* note 3, at 785 ff. In the English system see S. Deakin, A. Johnston, and B.S. Markesinis, *Markesinis and Deakin's Tort Law* (6th edn, 2003). In the French system see Fabre Magnan, *supra* note 5, at 637, and previously J. Viney, *Vers la construction d'un droit européen de la responsabilité civile: les apports possibles du droit français* (1986). In the Italian system see G. Comandé, *Risarcimento del danno alla persona e alternative istituzionali: studio di diritto comparato* (1999).

    [9] Typically this has occurred in motor accident compensation. In the French system an example is provided by the structure of the Loi Badinter, van Gerven *et al.*, supra note 6, at 587; J. Viney and M. Jourdain, *Traité de droit civil—Les conditions de la responsabilité* (1995), at 1089 ff., Fabre Magnan, *supra* note 5, at 800 ff. The application of a similar regulatory pattern was made in Italy in the case of personal injuries derived from compulsory vaccination: see G. Ponzanelli, *La responsabilità civile: profili di diritto comparato* (1992). Yet, for schizophrenic regulatory responses to related problems arising in the field of personal injuries and the National Health system, see a recent judgment released by the Italian Constitutional Court in the case of a person who contracted HIV by being exposed to the virus as a consequence of blood transfusion: Corte Costituzionale, 22 June 2000, note 226, annotated in [2001] I *Foro Italiano* 5. For a broader and more recent comparative view, see also Sugarman, 'Precise Justice and Rough Justice: Scientific Causation in Civil Litigation as Compared with Administrative Compensation Plans and Mass Tort Settlements', in Comandè and Ponzanelli, *supra* note 7.

    [10] See Harlow, *supra* note 3; C. Allcock *et al.*, *Social Policy* (2000); D. Fraser *The Evolution of the British Welfare State* (3rd edn, 2003).

regulatory functions, perhaps unintentionally attributed to civil liability by States' legal systems.[11]

It should be emphasized, however, that in many cases de-regulation has translated into a change of regulatory techniques rather than the abandonment of regulation altogether.[12] The relevant question is related to the impact of these regulatory changes on the structure and the performance of civil liability. For example, how has the shift from command and control to responsive or market-based regulation affected standards of conduct or remedies in civil liability?

In relation to economic losses the role of civil liability has expanded to correct market failures (particularly asymmetric information in financial markets and professional malpractice).[13] In relation to personal injuries, civil liability has provided responses both to market failures, particularly externalities, and to the reduction of welfare measures due to the fiscal crisis of the welfare state that began in the early 1970s.

The current legal and institutional landscape is characterized by the coexistence of civil liability and administrative regulation in many fields in order to perform both deterrent and compensatory functions: from financial markets to privacy; from product safety to environmental protection; from professional malpractice to road traffic accidents. Modes of interaction within these fields illustrate the relative functional complementarity between administrative regulation and civil liability. In the first case the limits of civil liability did not ensure sufficient protection to workers and victims of road traffic accidents, thence stimulating the creation of regulatory schemes, primarily aimed at compensation. In the second case de-regulation has decreased the level of protection and forced civil liability to expand its boundaries to protect old and new victims. Civil liability and administrative regulations have often operated as complements, one covering the weaknesses of the other.

2. THE RELATIONSHIP BETWEEN REGULATION AND CIVIL LIABILITY IN THE FRAMEWORK OF EUROPEAN INTEGRATION

In this chapter I will concentrate on European product safety and, to a lesser extent, on European environmental protection to examine their interaction and its conse-

---

[11] The expansion of regulatory functions of civil liability concern both deterrence and regulation.

[12] See, e.g., Picciotto, 'Introduction: Reconceptualizing Regulation in the Era of Globalization', 29 *J L and Society*, '*New Directions in Regulatory Theory*', *Special Issue* (2002) 1.

[13] For a comparative analysis see M. Bussani and E. Palmer, *Pure Economic Loss in Europe* (2003), and 'The Frontier between Contractual and Tortious Liability in Europe: Insights from the Case of Compensation for Pure Economic Loss', in A.S. Hartkamp and I.M. Hesselink (eds), *Towards a European Civil Code* (2004), at 697 ff. On this issue, see earlier P. Cane, *Tort Law and Economic Interests* (1991). Cane distinguishes among four different types of economic losses that may occur in relation to interference with or invasion of economic interests: reduction of the value of existing assets; interruption of a stream of income; failure to realize or obtain some increase in one's asset; and, finally, accretion of the defendant's assets. See also Cane, 'Contract, Tort and Economic Loss', in M. Furmston (ed.), *The Law of Tort* (1986).

quences on the institutional design. My thesis is that civil liability and regulation are functional complements and not necessarily functional equivalents. In fact they often reflect different approaches to individual and collective responsibilities associated with the harmful consequences of unlawful conduct. I shall test this hypothesis in the light of recent regulatory changes which have occurred at European level.

The changes taking place in the area of regulation of product safety and environmental protection have been rather significant. They are related to both actors and techniques. The presence of private regulators setting technical standards has always been an important feature of product safety regulation.[14] The emergence of self-regulation and private regulators in the area of environmental law is, however, relatively new.

Together with private bodies devoted to technical standardization, a plethora of other private actors today populate the regulatory space, giving rise to different forms of regulation: from self-regulation, to delegated regulation, to co-regulation.[15] These changes require the term 'regulation' to be given a broader meaning, to encompass private and public regulation and different forms of co-regulation.[16] The new role of private regulators in the fields of products and environmental liability, however, poses new challenges and questions in relation to several different areas, but primarily for civil liability regimes and remedies.[17]

---

[14] Developments concerning the role of private regulators are discussed by Ladeur, who examines desirable forms of cooperation between private and public actors in the decision-making processes. See Ladeur, 'The Introduction of the Precautionary Principle into EU Law: a Pyrrhic Victory for Environmental and Public Health Law? Decision making under Conditions of Complexity in Multi-level Political Systems', 40 *CML Rev* (2003) 1462. For a detailed recognition of normative background and implementation of private governance in relation to standard-setting focusing on product safety, see H. Schepel, *The Constitution of Private Governance. Product Standards in the Regulation of Integrating Markets*, PhD Thesis, EUI, Florence, 2003. A detailed analysis of standard-setting activities performed either by private actors, or by institutional actors, is carried out in M. Egan, *Constructing a European Market* (2001) and E. Vos, *Institutional Frameworks of Community Health and Safety Regulation. Committees, Agencies and Private Bodies* (1999).

[15] Examples of legislative delegation of standard-setting powers are frequent. See Annex II ('The Model Directive'), Council resolution on a new approach to technical harmonization and standards, OJ 1985 L 136/1. For a wider-ranging perspective on the issue see Cafaggi, 'Le rôle des acteurs privés dans le processus de régulation: participation, autorégulation et régulation privée', in *La Régulation, Nouveaux modes? Nouveaux territoires?*, 109 *Revue française d'administration publique* (2004) 23. See G. Majone, 'Strategy and Structure the Political Economy of Agency Independence and Accountability', paper presented at OECD Meeting, London, 10–11 January 2005 (available at www.oecd.org).

[16] Black has re-defined regulation as a sustained and focused attempt to alter the behaviour of a subject according to identified purposes with the intention of producing a broadly identified outcome or outcomes. This process may involve functions of standard-setting, information-gathering, and behaviour modification: Black, 'Regulatory Conversations', 29 *J L and Society* (2002) 163, at 170. See also Scott, 'Regulation in the Age of Governance: The Rise of the Post Regulatory State', in J. Jordana *et al.*, *supra* note 1, at 145–74.

[17] Some of the challenges to contract law have been examined elsewhere. See Cafaggi, 'Gouvernance et responsabilité des régulateurs privés', [2005] *Revue Internationale de Droit Economique* 323; and *Self-regulation and European Contract Law* (forthcoming).

The relationship between civil liability and regulation cannot be analysed without reconsidering the profound internal changes that have taken place in each area.

Internal changes in regulatory techniques have been significant, moving from command and control to cooperative or incentive-based regulation.[18] Less visible but equally important modifications have also affected the evolution of civil liability.[19] The models of regulation have been modified at national and European level, although often not at the same pace. Parallel, although not necessarily symmetrical, changes have occurred on the other side of the Atlantic.[20]

Legislative style has also changed: EU institutions have moved from very detailed towards principle-based legislation. The new approach to standardization is only the epiphenomenon of a more diffuse change.[21] The use of responsive and market-based regulation in the field of environmental liability has increased significantly.[22] The

---

[18] See Stewart, 'The Importance of Law and Economics for European Environmental Law' [2002] *Yearbook of European Environmental Law* 1, at 9 ff. Stewart underlines changes in relation to both the USA and Europe. He points out that moves away from command and control have been quite relevant in the USA, while European systems have evolved into 'negotiated command and control'. For a relatively different conclusion in relation to environmental law see Betlem, 'Environmental Liability and Private Enforcement of Community Law', in Hartkamp *et al.*, *supra* note 13, at 677 ff: 'it is nevertheless true that environmental law is and is likely to remain clearly dominated by regulatory command and control regimes with tort or delict as most junior partner'.

[19] 'Internal' simply means that they have occurred in civil liability and regulation, but it does not imply that these changes have not been stimulated by the interaction of the two. Examples may be provided by the causation principle in civil liability.

[20] Stewart, *Administrative Law*, *supra* note 2, at 448. According to Stewart, '[t]he answer lies in the adoption of new regulatory methods and instruments to ease the problems created by over-reliance on centralized command and control methods. Two such new methods are emerging in regulatory practice. They are government-stakeholder network structures and economic incentive systems'. Moreover he states that: '[r]ather than attempting to dictate unilaterally the conduct of the regulated, regulatory agencies have developed a number of strategies to enlist a variety of governmental and nongovernmental actors, including business firms and non-profit organizations, in the formulation and implementation of regulatory policy. Here are some examples: agency-supervised regulatory negotiation among representatives from industry, public interest, and state and local government to reach consensus on new agency regulations outside the formal administrative law rulemaking processes; cooperative arrangements involving governmental and non governmental entities in delivering families service or administering Medicare; and negotiation, in the draconian shadow of the Endangered Species Act, of regional habitat conservation plans by federal natural resource management agencies, private landowners, developers and state and local governments. In these examples, federal agencies are active, often dominant partners in the process and the result is a quasi contractual working relationship among the participants to solve regulatory problems on a coordinated basis. Rather than centralized mass-production, this methodology embraces a post-industrial strategy for producing regulation. Its watchwords are flexibility, innovation, benchmarking, transparency and performance measures, and mutual learning by doing. In the European Union this approach is being widely used under the title of the Common method of coordination'.

[21] See Council Directive 98/34/EC laying down a procedure for the provision of information in the field of technical standards and regulations, OJ 1998 L 204/37.

[22] For the European experience see M. Faure (ed.), *Deterrence, Insurability, and Compensation in Environmental Liability* (2003), at 37 ff., 39 ff.; Betlem, 'Environmental Liability and Private Enforcement of Community Law', in Hartkamp *et al.*, *supra* note 13, at 677 ff. For the US experience see R. Revesz,

promotion of environmental agreements has been an important example of 'regulated' self-regulation.[23]

These changes have been determined, among other factors, by: (1) the need to increase compliance while reducing the costs of monitoring; and (2) the need to foster innovation while regulating product safety and environmental protection.[24] Clearly, while these strategies can be contextually analysed as responses to failures of command and control, they are based on very different premises and they can combine with civil liability in radically different ways.[25]

Civil liability has also changed. We have witnessed different phenomena such as the following.

(1) The increasing expansion of strict liability in areas where fault used to be the principle. Product liability and environmental protection provide good examples.[26]

Environmental Law and Policy (2nd edn, 2000); Stewart, 'A New Generation of Environmental Regulation', 29 *Capital University LR* (2001) 21. In general see N. Cunningham and P. Grabonsky, *Smart Regulation: Designing Environmental Policy* (1998).

[23] See Communication from the Commission to the Council and European Parliament on Environmental Agreements, COM(96)561, 27 November 1996. Voluntary and environmental agreements are widely used throughout Europe, especially in the Netherlands, Germany, Great Britain, and Denmark. There are also agreements at a Community level. The Netherlands, where in the majority of cases environmental targets are met through (legally binding) environmental agreements, appear to have the most mature system. In Europe voluntary and environmental agreements are used mainly in the area of waste management and for reduction of greenhouse gases.

[24] Standard-setting, both in product safety and environmental protection, should not be conceived as an obstacle to innovation but, if adequately designed, as a vehicle to promote innovation. This is the core criticism of command and control regulation that generally can at best ensure the adoption of existing technologies and does not provide incentives to innovate. See, in the American context, Stewart, *supra* note 18, at 11. See also Revesz, *supra* note 22. In the European context see Spindler, 'Market Process, Standardisation, and Tort Law', 4 *ELJ* (1998) 316; Monti, 'Enviromental risk: a comparative law and economics approach to liability and insurance', [2001] *European Review of Private Law* 51; Faure, *supra* note 22.

[25] For a short, yet very effective, comparison of network regulatory strategy and economic incentives strategies see Stewart, *supra* note 2, at 451–2.

[26] A clear example of such a trend is provided by the well-known English case, *A and others* v *National Blood Authority* [2001] 3 All ER 289, especially at paras. 50, 74–7. Reference is to be made also to the French system, where even if from a purely normative viewpoint plaintiffs are required to give evidence of the defendants' fault, such a requirement has been progressively emptied of its content. Furthermore, this development of the French system took place long before the implementation of the Product Liability Directive, thus proving the 'internal' nature of the described change. See J.-S. Borghetti, *La responsabilité du fait des produits. Étude de droit comparé* (2004), at 208 ff. and 518 ff. and reference to relevant case-law there contained. For a description in terms of policy of the alternative between strict liability and fault see respectively the White Paper on Environmental Liability (COM(2000)66 final), and the Green Paper on Product Liability (COM(1999)396 final). The White Paper states '[s]trict liability means that fault of the actor need not be established, only the fact that the act (or the omission) caused the damage. At first sight, fault-based liability may seem more economically efficient than strict liability, since incentives towards abatement costs do not exceed the benefits from reduced emissions. However, recent national and international environmental liability regimes tend to be based on the

(2) The erosion by civil liability of areas covered primarily by disciplinary mechanisms, such as professional malpractice, illustrates phenomena of 'publicization' of functions and relationships that used to belong to private spheres; what previously had been an internal disciplinary matter for the profession has today become the object of judicial scrutiny.

(3) Finally the (potential) shift from tortious to contractual liability by reason of the use of self-regulation is an important change.[27]

The justifications for imposing liability have changed accordingly. The boundaries between individual and collective responsibilities do not overlap with those of civil liability and regulation. Civil liability can no longer be considered the domain of individual responsibility, while regulation remains more strongly correlated with collective responsibility.

An inquiry into the modes of interaction between regulation and civil liability therefore becomes very relevant to evaluating the effectiveness of the European strategy in the fields of product safety and environmental protection. To the extent that regulation has increasingly provided new standards for examining the conduct of potential injurers, the corresponding modifications in civil liability have proved significant for the definition of standards in negligence and strict liability. But the influence of regulation in the field of civil liability is and can be profound, judging from recent developments in the content and structure of remedies in relation to violations of environmental and product standards.

3. LIABILITY AND REGULATION IN PRODUCT SAFETY AND ENVIRONMENTAL PROTECTION: FUNCTIONAL COMPLEMENTS OR ALTERNATIVES?

Risk control associated with product safety and environmental protection is generally managed by considering the regulatory and liability approaches separately. Each strategy can be based on regulation, encompassing private and administrative types and different forms of co-regulation, and on liability, generally extra-contractual. Sometimes, however, contractual liability is employed as a result of the development of self-regulation.[28]

principle of strict liability, because of the assumption that environmental objectives are better reached that way'. See for the product context Reimann, 'Product Liability in Global Context: the Hollow Victory of the European Model' [2003] *ERPL* 132.

[27] See on this issue F. Cafaggi, *Contractualizing Standard Setting in Civil Liability?* (unpublished manuscript).

[28] Contractual liability operates when potential injurers have undertaken obligations to act or not to act within the framework of a code of conduct. These obligations are often directed towards third parties although they are not necessarily enforceable by them. An example of this trend may be seen in *Lloyds TSB General Insurance Holdings Ltd and others* v *Lloyds Bank Group Insurance Company Ltd; Abbey National plc* v *Lee and others* [2001] EWCA Civ 1643, [2002] 1 All ER (Comm) 42, [2002] Lloyd's

What is the relationship between regulation and civil liability at European and national level for controlling and managing these risks? To what extent is there complementarity between them? Or do civil liability and regulation operate as alternatives? In the area of product safety the differences are quite significant. The liability regime tends to be all-inclusive.[29] After 1999 agricultural products were integrated into the liability system. On the other hand, the regulatory regime defined by the General Product Safety Directive (hereinafter GPS Directive)[30] is under-inclusive. The scope of the GPS Directive is residual.[31] It applies only to products not regulated by other Directives, and in this case it provides only for matters not included in the specific Directives.[32] Drugs, cars, and toys constitute other relevant areas of sector regulation. Food is perhaps the most prominent case. Within this area, EC

Rep IR 11. In particular, as regards the last judgment, Longmore LJ at para. 56 states: 'I agree that the appeal should be dismissed. The liability of the claimants arises from the fact that their representatives failed to give "Best Advice" pursuant to the Lautro code. As my Lord explains, that is a personal not a vicarious liability; it is also a liability that does not depend on negligence or any breach of duty of care. Once it is established that "Best Advice" has not been given, liability is automatic. The failure to give "Best Advice" was a breach of the provisions of the Financial Services Act 1986 or the Lautro rules and constitutes the relevant act or omission for the purposes of (a) the definition of that term contained in para 2 of the endorsement to section 3 of the policy and (b) the deductible clause in condition 2 of the same section.' The case in point also dealt with the problem of enforceability of such obligations by third parties, applying in point the aggregate clause doctrine.

[29] See Council Directive 85/374/EEC of 25 July 1985 on the approximation of the laws, regulations and administrative provisions of the Member States concerning liability for defective products, OJ 1985 L 210/29 (hereinafter the PL Directive), Art. 1, and Directive 1999/34/EC of the European Parliament and of the Council of 10 May 1999 amending Council Directive 85/374/EEC on the approximation of the laws, regulations and administrative provisions of the Member States concerning liability for defective products, OJ 1999 L 141/20.

[30] Directive 2001/95/EC of The European Parliament and of the Council of December 2001 on general product safety (hereinafter the GPS Directive), OJ 2001 L 11/04. See S. Weatherill, *EU Consumer Law and Policy* (2nd edn, 2005), 204 ff.; C. Hodges, *European Regulation of Consumer Product Safety* (2005), 27 ff.

[31] See recitals 11, 12, and 13 of the GPS Directive, *supra* note 30:

(11) In the absence of more specific provisions within the framework of community legislation covering safety of the products concerned all the provisions of this directive should apply in order to ensure consumer health and safety.

(12) If specific Community legislation sets out safety requirements covering only certain risks or categories of risks, with regard to the products concerned the obligations of economic operators in respect of these risks are those determined by the provisions of the specific legislation, while the general safety requirement of this Directive should apply only to the other risk.

(13) The provisions of this directive relating to the other obligations of producers and distributors, the obligations and powers of Member States, the exchanges of information and rapid intervention situations and dissemination of information and confidentiality apply in the case of products covered by specific rules of Community law, if those rules do not already contain such obligations.

[32] See Art. 1(2) of the GPS Directive, *supra* note 30. On the relationship between the GPS Directive and sector directives see also Guidance Document on the Relationship between the GPSD and Certain Sector Directives (available at http://europa.eu.int/comm/consumers/cons_safe/prod_safe/ DGSP/revisedDGSP-en.htm).

Regulation 178/2002 has established a different regulatory regime for food safety from that in the GPS Directive.[33] Until 2002 both Directives could be considered as setting minimum harmonization standards; however after the ECJ's much-criticized judgments of 2002 the liability Directive 374/85[34] (hereinafter the PL Directive) should be considered as a total harmonization, while the GPS Directive continues to provide a minimum standard.[35] Treaty provisions concerning consumer protection also play an important role. In particular Article 153 EC defines the goal of high level of consumer protection (Article 153(1)) and imposes that consumer protection shall be taken into account in defining and implementing other Community policy and activities (Article 153(2)).

In the area of environmental protection the principles are defined by treaty provisions, and in particular the precautionary principle, the principle of prevention, the principle that environmental damage should be rectified at source, and the polluter pays principle (Article 174 EC).[36] However, an important principle that plays a much greater role in environmental liability is its horizontal effect on other European policies, among which is product safety (Article 6 EC). The Environmental Liability Directive has represented a further shift from civil liability to regulation.[37]

In the area of product safety, coordination between the two strategies is absent or, at best, implicit.[38] No explicit signs of complementarity can be seen in the Directives. The only stated clear principle of coordination in the field of product safety is that the regulatory Directives (in particular EC Directive 01/95) cannot be interpreted as decreasing the level of consumer protection ensured by the PL Directive.[39]

---

[33] Art. 21 of Regulation 178/2002/CE of the European Parliament and of the Council of 28 January 2002 laying down the general principles and requirements of food law, establishing the European Food Safety Authority and laying down procedures in matters of food safety states: '[t]he provisions of this Chapter shall be without prejudice to Council Directive 85/374/EEC of 25 July 1985 on the approximation of the laws, regulations and administrative provisions of the Member States concerning liability for defective products'.

[34] PL Directive, *supra* note 29, at 51.

[35] An account of discontinuities in food regulation at European level is provided by Chalmers, 'Food for Thought: Reconciling European Risks and Traditional Ways of Life', 66 *MLR* (2003) 532. For an interesting account of recent developments of the ECJ's case-law on food safety see Dabrowska, 'GM Foods, Risk Precaution and the Internal Market: Did Both Sides Win the Day in the Recent Judgement of the European Court of Justice?', 5 *German LJ* (2004) 151.

[36] See Kramer, 'Thirty Years of EC Environmental Law: Perspectives and Prospectives' [2002] *Yearbook of European Environmental Law* 155, at 162 ff.; Faure (ed.), *supra* note 22.

[37] See Betlem, *supra* note 18, at 677 ff., but with reference to the common position.

[38] Not only does coordination seem to be very weak but choices concerning liability and the regulatory strategies seem to diverge quite significantly. This however does not seem to be the result of a specific institutional design but more the outcome of different institutional approaches within both the Commission and each Member State.

[39] See Art. 17 of the GPS Directive, *supra* note 30: '[t]his Directive shall be without prejudice to the application of Directive 85/374/EEC'. See also Art. 18(3) in relation to criminal liability: '[a]ny decision taken by virtue of this directive and involving restrictions on the placing of a product on the market requiring its withdrawal or its recall shall be without prejudice to assessment of the liability of the party concerned in the light of the national criminal law applying in the case in question'.

A functional analysis, aimed at identifying current and potential complementarities between the two strategies (i.e regulation and liability), implies that they can be read as functional complements. Such complementarity, however, does not imply functional coincidence. The rationales that justify civil liability, in particular the justifications for holding injurers responsible for product-related injuries, are often different from those employed to hold those regulated responsible. For example, in the case of civil liability the importance of human agency is highly relevant, and this has a bearing on causation. Causation does not play such a significant role in economic regulation, while in welfare it may not play any role at all.[40]

Starting from the general assumption that two main goals of civil liability are deterrence and compensation, functional complementarity can be tested by asking whether regulation on product safety and environmental protection can also promote deterrence and compensation. While it is well established that the function of regulation in this field is primarily to achieve deterrence, in the last 20 years there has been a proliferation of administrative schemes for regulating compensation for product- and environment-related injury by means of the setting up of either *ad hoc* or general purpose funds.[41] The conventional view that associates administrative regulation with deterrence and civil liability with compensation is, therefore, at least debatable.

Several combinations can occur in theory:

(1) Both administrative regulation and civil liability use tools to deter and compensate, but in different ways. For example, regulation preserves minimum standards of both deterrence and compensation, while civil liability operates to increase the levels of deterrence and compensation when certain conditions occur.

(2) The deterrence and compensation functions are allocated to administrative regulation and civil liability respectively or, vice versa, administrative regulation can primarily serve compensation while civil liability, perhaps in association with criminal liability, promotes deterrence. Thus, within this strategy we can further differentiate between two types of combination:

   (a) Deterrence is mainly the province of regulation, while civil liability intervenes to compensate once violations have occurred and harms materialized.

   (b) Compensation is ensured by administrative schemes, generally no-fault-based insurance schemes, leaving deterrence to civil liability or even to criminal law.

We can therefore conclude that deterrence and compensation can in theory be pursued either through an integrated strategy (by combining civil liability and regulation) or by separating the two (regulation—deterrence, civil liability—compensation, or

---

[40] For a general analysis of causation link see van Gerven *et al.*, *supra* note 9, at 427, and Markesinis, *supra* note 6, at 103; on the functional selection of the person to be charged of the damages, see Atiyah, *supra* note 8, at 480; and W.V.H. Rogers, *Winfield and Jolowicz on Tort* (1998), at 34.

[41] See Harlow, *supra* note 3, at 46.

the opposite, regulation—compensation, civil liability—deterrence) and allocating a specific function to each domain within a coordinated framework.

To consider regulation and civil liability as functional complements may imply the recognition of a 'regulatory' function for civil liability.[42] But is it feasible and desirable? The answer to this question should not be purely normative, but grounded in the specific features of civil liability systems. There may be some civil liability systems that emphasize their regulatory functions and others that do not. An important role in identifying the nature and level of regulatory functions played by civil liability is related to the institutional framework, and in particular to the function of the judiciary and its effectiveness.[43] If the possibility that civil liability may play a regulatory function is accepted, the theoretical question should then move to the different ways in which regulation and civil liability can regulate. As a matter of positive law there are differences in the regulatory functions of civil liability systems, yet, at a certain level of generality, it is possible to contend that every liability system has some regulatory function. Unfortunately no final choices have been made at the European level concerning either the regulatory function of civil liability in the field of product safety and environmental protection or which strategy should be used for which goals and how they should be combined.[44]

---

[42] The debate concerning the regulatory functions of private law in general and specifically on civil liability is in place. Different streams of scholarship advocate such a function. Typically this is the approach of law and economics: see Calabresi, *supra* note 3; Shavell, 'Liability for Harm versus Regulation of Safety', 13 *J Legal Studies* (1984) 357, 'A Model of the Optimal Use of Liability and Safety Regulation' [1984] *Rand J Econ* 271 ff., and *Economic Analysis of Accident Law* (1987); W.M. Landes and R. Posner, *The Economic Structure of Tort Law* (1987); Ackerman, 'Tort Law in the Regulatory State', in Schuck, *supra* note 3, at 80 ff.; Faure, *supra* note 22; S. Shavell, *Foundations of Economic Analysis of Law* (2004). This approach has also been endorsed by the socio-legal studies movement: see H. Collins, *Contract Law* (2004). Critiques of this approach are made by some tort scholars. See, e.g. Stapleton, 'Regulating Torts', in C. Parker *et al.*, *supra* note 5, at 122 ff. For contributions concerning the relationship between tort and environmental regulation see Abraham, 'The Relation between Civil Liability and Environmental Regulation: An Analytical Overview', 41 *Washburn LJ* (2002) 379; Cane, 'Tort Law as Regulation', 31 *Common Law World Review* (2002) 305 and 'Using Tort Law to Enforce Environmental Regulation?', 41 *Washburn LJ* (2002) 427; Hylton, 'When Should We Prefer Tort Law to Environmental Regulation?', 41 *Washburn LJ* (2002) 515.

[43] The same rules of negligence or strict liability may or may not play a regulatory function due to the role of the judiciary in the specific legal system.

[44] See Green Paper of 14 May 1993 on Remedying Environmental Damage, COM(93)47, at 11, para. 2, and Commission Green Paper of 28 July 1999: Liability for defective products, COM(1999)396 final, at para. 3.2. The explanation of this bias is based on the different sources (the general directorates respectively in charge) that have produced the two Directives, although this justification is certainly part of the story, but it cannot be conclusive. See on the institutional questions Howell, 'Product Liability. A History of Harmonisation', in Hartkamp *et al.*, *supra* note 13, at 645. The analysis that followed the Communication of the Commission concerning Europeanization of contract law has shown that inconsistencies may occur even among Directives that are prepared by the same directorates. The question of coordination certainly has an institutional dimension that can be solved by ensuring duties to coordinate the text with Directives already in place concerning related subjects, but it relates to substantive questions that should be carefully scrutinized.

Important evolutions, however, have recently been occurring. Integration between health and consumer policies should soon become a reality and a corresponding institutional framework accordingly defined.[45]

Furthermore there are important signs that an integrated approach between product and service safety and also between product safety and environmental protection is needed.[46] Less strong is the emphasis on coordination between regulation and liability in the field of product safety.[47] In more general terms, a coordinated functional approach is advocated for consumer protection.[48] Such an approach should be endorsed not only in law-making but also in adjudication.[49]

It is important to note that the choice is constrained not only by internal factors concerning competences and general principles relating to the internal market, but also by 'external' sources such as international Conventions.[50]

The task of this chapter is twofold:

(a) to show how the evolution of the regulatory system poses new challenges both to the civil liability system and to its interaction with regulation;

---

[45] See Communication from the Commission to the European Parliament, the Council, The European Economic and Social Committee and the Committee of Regions, 'Healthier, Safer, More Confident Citizens: a Health and Consumer Protection Strategy. Proposal for a Decision of the European Parliament and of the Council Establishing a Programme of Community Action in the Field of Health and Consumer Protection 2007–2013', Brussels, 6 April 2005, COM(2005)115 final. The Commission states clearly: '[t]his Communication and the attached programme proposal bring together Public Health and Consumer Protection policies and programmes under one framework to make EU Policy work better for citizens'. Such a task implies a new implementation device: '[t]o implement the Joint Health and Consumer Programme, the Commission will be assisted by one single executive agency, which will consist of an extended version of the existing Public Health Programme's executive agency encompassing the "Consumer Institute"'.

[46] See Temmink, 'From Danish Bottles to Danish Bees: The Dynamics of Free Movement of Goods and Environmental Protection—A Case Law Analysis', 1 *Yearbook of European Environmental Law* (2000) 61.

[47] For the product/service safety question, see Communication on the safety of service, Doc. 10506/03 CONSOM 66 MI 143 (2003) and Council Resolution of 1 December 2003 on safety of services for consumers, OJ 2003 C 299/01. For integration between product safety and environmental protection see the Communication from the Commission to the Council and the European Parliament, Integrated Product Policy (IPP), COM(2003)302 final, 18 June 2003, in particular at para. 2: 'product expertise is increasingly concentrated in the hands of those who are responsible for their design. It is very difficult for regulators, let alone the general public, to have any realistic idea of what technical changes are achievable. For this reason any product policy needs to ensure that producers and designers become more responsible for ensuring that their products fulfil agreed criteria on health, safety and the environment'.

[48] See Green Paper on Consumer Protection, COM(2001)531 final, 2 Oct. 2001.

[49] See van Gerven, 'The ECJ Case-law as a Means of Unification of Private Law?', in Hartkamp *et al.*, *supra* note 13, at 117, who advocates a less textual and more teleological interpretation by the ECJ: 'ECJ case law would surely be more effective from a viewpoint of coherent and uniform application, if the Court were to take the habit of dealing with consumer law litigation from a more comprehensive viewpoint, that is viewing any specific directive within the broader context of consumer legislation as a whole'.

[50] E.g., in the environmental protection field the choice or the combination between tort and regulation is also affected by international conventions, e.g. the Aarhus Convention.

(b) to emphasize the importance of a new coordinated approach of liability and regulation to deter and to compensate for product- and environment-related injuries.

Following the (stereo)typical description of the regulatory process I will analyse in turn standard-setting, monitoring, and enforcement to show the current lack of a coordinated approach and the need to pursue one. The analysis will concern only specific aspects, emphasizing issues related to complementarity in the light of new rules introduced by European legislation. The chapter is primarily positive. I sketch out an agenda for normative suggestions in the conclusions.

It is important to emphasize that the different combinations of civil liability and regulation may be affected by the multi-level regulatory system in which they operate. For example, as is clear from the ECJ's *Munoz* case, standard-setting may occur at the European level and follow a specific 'regulatory' approach, while enforcement of the rule may occur at national level through the use of civil liability systems.[51] In national legal systems breach of Community regulations would be sanctioned under general civil liability law. Some differences exist in the ability to recover, particularly in England, where breach of statutory law is still interpreted relatively narrowly.[52]

4. FRAMING THE QUESTIONS: COMPLEMENTARITY OF STANDARD-SETTING IN CIVIL LIABILITY AND REGULATION? WHAT ARE THE INSTITUTIONAL CONSEQUENCES?

Standard-setting is the institutional activity through which levels (quantitative aspect) and types (qualitative aspect) of conduct of those causing injury and their victims are determined. It affects the level of protection afforded to potential victims, and influences the potential level of competition on safety that firms may engage in. The modes of standard-setting and instruments employed may be relevant for determining effects on competition between firms. While the relationship between competition and regulation has been widely explored, the possibility that standard-setting in civil liability may have pro- or anti-competitive effects has not been adequately considered. Although they are not the focus of this chapter, the effects on the competitive structure of the market caused by the choice between civil liability and regulation will be emphasized.

First I will focus on the relationship between technical and legal standard-setting, and then outline different methods of standard-setting in regulation and civil liability,

---

[51] Case C-253/00, *Antonio Munoz y Cia, Superior Fruiticola SA* v *Frumar Ltd, Redbridge Produce Marketing Ltd* [2002] ECR I-7289, note by Biondi, 40 *CML Rev* (2003) 1241.

[52] On the impact of *Munoz* see Betlem, *supra* note 18, at 692 ff. For a comparative analysis of breach of statutory duty see Deakin *et al.*, *supra* note 8, at 358–73. See also Von Bar, *The Common European Law of Torts* (2000). See also D. Fairgrieve, *State Liability in Tort. A Comparative Law Study* (2003), at 36–41.

discussing the current modes of interaction and suggesting improvements in some areas. In the areas of product safety and environmental protection, in particular, the distinction between technical and normative standards is very relevant to the following questions.

(a) Who should produce the standards?[53]
(b) How should the standards be generated?[54]

This distinction has had relevant consequences on the processes of harmonization of European product safety.[55] While the processes of Europeanization and

---

[53] See the GPS Directive's recitals (*supra* note 30):

(14) In order to facilitate the effective and consistent application of the general safety requirement of this Directive, it is important to establish European voluntary standards covering certain products and risks in such a way that a product which conforms to a national standard transposing a European standard is to be presumed to be in compliance with the said requirement.

(15) With regard to the aims of this Directive, European standards should be established by European standardisation bodies, under mandates set by the Commission assisted by appropriate Committees. In order to ensure that products in compliance with the standards fulfil the general safety requirement, the Commission assisted by a committee composed of representatives of the Member States, should fix the requirements that the standards must meet. These requirements should be included in the mandates to the standardisation bodies.

(16) In the absence of specific regulations and when the European standards established under mandates set by the Commission are not available or recourse is not made to such standards, the safety of products should be assessed taking into account in particular national standards transposing any other relevant European or international standards, Commission recommendations or national standards, international standards, codes of good practice, the state of the art and the safety which consumers may reasonably expect. In this context, the Commission's recommendations may facilitate the consistent and effective application of this Directive pending the introduction of European standards or as regards the risks and/or products for which such standards are deemed not to be possible or appropriate

and Art. 3(4): '[c]onformity of a product with the criteria designed to ensure the general safety requirement, in particular the provisions mentioned in paragraphs 2 or 3, shall not bar the competent authorities of the Member States from taking appropriate measures to impose restrictions on its being placed on the market or to require its withdrawal from the market or recall where there is evidence that, despite such conformity, it is dangerous'.

[54] See *supra* note 20.

[55] While, e.g., normative standards at national level can be considered barriers to trade and scrutinized under Art. 28 EU, technical standards, due to their voluntary nature, have been considered outside the domain of free movement and within that of competition. See H. Schepel and J. Falke, *Legal Aspects of Standardisation in the Member States of the EC and EFTA*, Comparative Report (2000), I, at 55. A case in point is the ECJ's judgment in Case C-23/99, *Commission of the European Communities* v *French Republic* [2000] ECR I-7653. In particular, in Mischo AG's Opinion, the compatibility of technical standards requirements for products to enter a Member State's territory is analysed according to the principle of proportionality which is part of the Court's case-law on Arts. 30 (now Art. 28) and 36 (now Art. 30) EC. See Case C-23/99, also at 132. In Case C-166/03, *Commission of the European Communities* v *French Republic* [2004] not yet published, for instance, France was reckoned to have infringed the duty to fulfil its obligations under Art. 28 in establishing guaranteed standards for precious metals. The Court found that these standards were not justified either on grounds of consumer protection, or on those of fairness of trade, but, on the contrary, they were likely to produce the undesirable effect of quantitative

internationalization of technical standards are consolidated, normative standards are still mainly defined by national institutions (regulators and judges) in accordance with European legislation.[56] A second important phenomenon is related to the pursuit of an integrated strategy to protect safety and environment through technical standards. The approach advocated for technical standards is less significant for normative standards.[57]

restrictions on free movement of goods. See at paras 17–21: '[i]t is common ground that the terms to be used to indicate the proportion of the precious metal content of articles and the method by which it should be indicated are, as Community law currently stands, not harmonised. It is also common ground that Article 522a of the CGI is applicable without distinction to French products and to products imported from other Member States. Furthermore, the provision of the CGI in question is admittedly intended to ensure fair trading and consumer protection. However, the contested legislation imposes, in respect of articles of the two lower levels of purity marketed at the retail stage to individuals, a redundant double designation, since it requires the use not only of the fineness of the article, which gives objective information on its level of purity, but also the term "gold alloy" which gives much less precise information on the same subject. It follows that the system requiring a double description laid down by Article 522a of the CGI is *not proportional to the aim of ensuring fair trade and consumer protection, and that that aim can be achieved by measures less restrictive to intra-Community trade.* Consequently, it must be held that, by reserving the term "gold" for articles of a fineness of 750 parts per thousand, whilst those of a fineness of 375 or 585 parts per thousand are termed "gold alloy", the French Republic has failed to fulfil its obligations under Article 28 EC' (emphasis added). A similar approach is taken by the Court in a homogeneous group of cases: see, among others, Case C-358/01, *Commission* v *Kingdom of Spain*, 6 November 2003, not yet reported. Codes of conduct may be regarded as potential obstacles to free movement of goods and freedom to provide services, although the assessment of the two should also take into account the possibility of praying in aid the exemption in ex Art. 36 EC, especially if applied to the provision of services. See Vos, *supra* note 14, at 251 ff.; M. Egan, *Constructing a European Market* (2001). See also C. Joerges, K.H. Ladeur, and E. Vos, *Integrating Scientific Expertise into Regulatory Decision-making. National Traditions and European Innovations* (1997); C. Joerges, H. Schepel, and E. Vos, 'The Law's Problems with the Involvement of Nongovernmental Actors in Europe's Legislative Process: The Case of Standardization under the "New Approach"', EUI Working Paper Law 99/9 (1999).

   [56] See General Guidelines for the Cooperation between CEN, CENELEC and ETSI and the European Commission and the European Trade Association, OJ 2003 C 91/04, at 7: '[s]tandardisation activities in Europe have moved substantially from the national level to the European and international level. The role of the national standards organisations has, in consequence, taken a new dimension in the context of European and international standardisation. The national standards bodies will however, continue to play an important role in international and European standardisation. They contribute on a national level to consensus, in many cases provide support to the technical work as a permanent link between market players in particular SMEs, consumers and environmentalists, and provide access to, and advice on, both international and European standards. The official adoption through public enquiry and formal vote on European standards is carried out by national standards bodies'.

   [57] See Communication of the Commission on Integrated Product Policy, *supra*, note 47, and Communication of the Commission on the Integration of Environmental Aspects into Standardisation, COM(2004)130 final, 25 February 2004: '[i]n its communication on Integrated product policy, the Commission pointed out that standards have a high potential to support sustainable development, comprising economic, social and environmental aspects. It also listed standards as one of the tools whose improvements could help in establishing the framework for the continuous environmental improvement of products throughout their whole life cycle. Standardisers are now encouraged to give greater consideration to environment. Accordingly in its recent Communication on the integration of environmental

There is often an unfortunate overlap in the distinction between technical and normative standards and that between public and private bodies.[58] Such overlap may negatively affect the ability to achieve an effective coordination strategy between regulation and civil liability. The former distinction refers to the nature of the rules, and the latter to the body that generates the standards. Private bodies produce technical standards, but can also produce normative standards. They can generate normative standards by laying down codes of conduct which are binding 'regulatory contracts'. Public bodies, on the other hand, can use non-binding devices (soft law) together with binding rules to regulate behaviour.[59] Public bodies can also set technical and behavioural standards. Therefore, to maintain the difference between technical and normative standards, one should not associate the distinction between binding and non-binding standards with that between public and private bodies.[60] Consequently, for the purpose of the application of rules on free movement of goods (Article 28 EU) and competition law (Article 81 EU in particular), the driving criterion should be the binding nature of the rules, and not the public or private nature of the standard-setter.[61] However, the public or private nature of the regulatory body may have some impact on the breadth of the group of those people to whom the standards should apply.

aspects into standardisation, the Commission has, as key message, strongly encouraged all stakeholders in standardisation to take sustainable steps aiming to integrate environmental protection into standardisation'. See also Scott and Black, *supra* note 7, at 392, in relation to the costs of using national standards: '[n]ational voluntary standards of the sort created by the BSI [British Standards Institution] create risks of fragmentation of international markets, either because regulators fail to recognise equivalent standards from other jurisdictions, or because business themselves believe that regulatory requirements downstream require them to ensure that components or process supplied by others should meet national standards'.

[58] On this point see G. Majone, *Regulating Europe* (1996), at 25. In the policy documents concerning the new approach to standardization a distinction is often drawn between technical and normative aspects in relation to the allocation of powers between public and private powers. See, e.g., Commission Report on Efficiency and Accountability in European Standardisation under the New Approach, COM(98)291 final.

[59] On the general question of the role of soft law in European law see L. Senden, *Soft Law in European Community Law* (2004).

[60] However, even voluntary standards can become indirectly binding. For example, in the case of European technical standards, while they are held to be voluntary, Member States have an obligation to comply with them. They have to recognize that products manufactured in compliance with standards defined by European standardization bodies are in conformity with essential requirements. See Case C-112/97, *Commission* v *Italy* [1999] ECR I-182; Case C-100/00, *Commission* v *Italy* [2001] ECR I-2785; Case C-103/01, *Commission* v *Germany*, judgment of 22 May 2003. See also Vos, *supra* note 14, at 268 ff.

[61] In relation to Art. 81 and its application to self-regulatory agreements see the *Guidelines on the Applicability of Article 81 of the EC Treaty to the Horizontal Cooperation Agreements*, OJ 2001 C 3/02, that consider standardization and define the standardization agreements: '162 Agreements to set standards may be either concluded between private undertakings or set under the aegis of public bodies entrusted with the operation of services of economic interest, such as the standard bodies recognised under Directive 98/34/EC. The involvement of such bodies is subject to the obligations of Member states regarding the preservation of competition in the Community'.

Technical standards produced by private bodies strongly influence the effectiveness of regulation and of civil liability.[62] It is unclear recently whether European institutions have been favouring the substitution of legal standards by technical standards associated with a higher level of accountability of standardization bodies.[63] These changes may have important repercussions in the design of institutional complementarities between regulation and civil liability, as will be described later. Instead of conceiving the two as alternatives and shifting from normative to technical standardization, a more integrated approach to the production of technical and normative standards should be favoured.[64] The current institutional framework can be improved by promoting stakeholders' participation in technical standard-setting and revising the European co-regulatory model of technical standardization in the fields of both product safety and environmental protection.[65] But the idea of regulatory compliance also needs to be revised in the light of the new relationship between technical and legal standards.

When we focus specifically on regulation of product safety, we see that significant differences still exist between the technical and normative approaches. The harmonizing role of technical standards in product safety has been much greater than in product liability.[66] European and international technical product standardization has

---

[62] See Spindler, *supra* note 24, at 316.

[63] See, e.g., Communication from the Commission to the European Parliament and the Council on the Role of European Standardisation in the Framework of European Policies and Legislation, COM(2004)674 final, 18 October 2004, and Council Conclusions, 21 December 2004.

[64] See Council Conclusions, 17 December 2004, Annex to the Presidency Conclusions 13830/04 ENT 140 +ADD 1 on the Communication on Standardisation, *supra* note 57:

'[r]ecommendations for further actions:

   a) A more extensive use of European Standardisation in European policies and legislation
     1 invites the Commission and the Member States to make a wider use of European [i.e CEN, Cenelec, ETSI] and international standards in their policies; particular attention should be paid to the role of standards in simplification of existing EU legislation, in order to meet the needs of stakeholders, including SMEs;
     2 recognises that further progress can be made in new areas of legislation in making wider use of general references to voluntary standards, taking into account European policies on governance and better regulation;
     3 invites the member states to apprise decision-maker of the advantages of European standardisation in support of Community legislation and policies'.

[65] See the Council Conclusions on the Communication on Standardisation, *supra* note 57:

   b) Improving the efficiency, coherence, visibility of European standardisation and its institutional framework
     1 notes that adequate participation in standardisation of all parties concerned [social partners, NGOs, environmental interest groups, consumers, SMEs authorities, etc.] is not sufficiently implemented at present within all member states, European standardisation should be recognised as a strategic tool for competitiveness and for the uniform application of technical legislation in the internal market. The commitment of everybody should be reactivated in this respect.

[66] See *supra* text and notes 54–7.

contributed to technical harmonization at supranational level which, in turn, has played a role in promoting and effectively achieving legal standardization.[67] In terms of actors contributing to the definition of standards the role of regulators, both public and private, often operating in a coordinated fashion, has been significant.

Technical and scientific knowledge affects normative standards even when it is not incorporated in technical standards. In the area of product liability and safety the definitions of defectiveness and safety are correlated to the state of the scientific knowledge and technology. Where the development risk defence has been introduced the legal regime more closely resembles negligence than strict liability.[68] References to

---

[67] See for instance Vos, *supra* note 14, at 252–9, 268–81. Describing the institutional framework and the activity of standard-setting performed by regulatory bodies in the European panorama, Vos establishes a clear connection between them and market regulation in the light of the EU treaties' goals. For a paradigmatic example of the foregoing, see the Communication on Standardisation, *supra* note 57:

4.3 European standardisation and the challenge of globalisation

– The Commission will continue to promote international standards drawn up by the international
  standardisation bodies [ISO, IEC, ITU] and to support their transposition in the EU.
When international standards are developed and transposed into European standards in support of European policies, European standardisation organizations must ensure that these standards are consistent with the objectives of EU policies.

[68] See PL Directive 374/85, *supra* note 29, Art. 7(e) and the GPS Directive, *supra* note 30, Art. 3(3)(e). The ECJ has interpreted Art. 7(e) of the PL Directive stating that 'the clause providing for the defence in question does not contemplate the state of knowledge of which the producer in question actually or subjectively was or could have been apprised, but the objective state of scientific and technical knowledge of which the producer is presumed to have been informed. However, it is implicit in the wording of Article 7(e) that the relevant scientific and technical knowledge must have been accessible at the time when the product in question was put into circulation. It follows that, in order to have a defence under Article 7(e) of the Directive, the producer of a defective product must prove that the objective state of scientific and technical knowledge, including the most advanced level of such knowledge, at the time when the product in question was put into circulation was not such as to enable the existence of the defect to be discovered. Further, in order for the relevant scientific and technical knowledge to be successfully pleaded as against the producer, that knowledge must have been accessible at the time when the product in question was put into circulation. On this last point, Article 7(e) of the Directive, contrary to what the Commission seems to consider, raises difficulties of interpretation which, in the event of litigation, the national courts will have to resolve, having recourse, if necessary, to Article 177 of the EC Treaty'. See Case C-300/95, *Commission* v *UK* [1997] ECR I-2649. See also, for a critical evaluation of the relationship between the definition of defective product and development risk defence, Stapleton, 'Products Liability in the United Kingdom: The Myths of Reform', 34 *Tex Int'l LJ* (1999) 50 at 53, where the author explains that 'to the extent that a producer is sued for in-house design defects and in-house failure to warn defects (potentially the most explosive categories), the more reasonable interpretation of the ambiguous words of the Directive means that he will in practice virtually always escape liability if he has used all reasonable care. This result is a product of the interaction between the Directive's concept of defect and the only reasonable interpretation of its development risk defence. In other words, in my view, in jurisdictions that have implemented the Directive with the development risk defence the only workable and reasonable interpretation of it is, in relation to in-house design and in-house warning defects, that the Directive in practice does not impose strict liability on producers.'

technical and scientific knowledge concerning standard-setting for defectiveness and safety imply that producers, and to some extent distributors, should decide taking into account available knowledge and technology. Of course, when science and technology have not (yet) been translated into standards or consensus, compliance becomes more difficult to evaluate because knowledge is diffuse and sometimes conflicting.[69]

Legal standards are differently defined in the areas of civil liability and regulation. These differences are not only institutional, concerning the different roles of legislators, regulators, and judges, but also functional.[70] Although civil liability and regulation can both promote, and do in fact promote, deterrence and compensation, there is a tendency to associate deterrence with regulation and compensation with civil liability. This tendency emerges, for example, quite strikingly in relation to the evaluation of human lives and environment for purposes of compensation and deterrence.[71] Such evaluation is very important, not only for compensation purposes but also for standard-setting. It should be noted that divergences in regulation and civil liability are not always justified by the supposedly different goals pursued by each strategy.

Differences in standard-setting emerge not only between civil liability and regulation but also within each field. In continental legal systems the standard of fault in civil liability is generally legislatively defined (due care, diligence) and the role of

---

[69] For the debate on product liability and the role of scientific knowledge see *Restatement of the Law Third, Torts: Products Liability*, s. 402A) and American Law Institute, *Restatement Third on the Law of Torts: Liability for Physical Harm*, Proposed final draft, N1 (2005), in particular in relation to burden of proof in causation, at 477 ff. Specifically on the risk development defence see Borghetti, *supra* note 26, at 59–62 and reference to the vast case-law there contained. The role of scientific knowledge in relation to product liability regimes also concerns possible defects which may depend on the projectual phase of the product rather than on the actual manufacturing activity: for the German system see again *ibid.*, at 125–7. If para. 823 BGB provides a principle of negligence liability for project defects, different solutions may be reached when there are European, national, or international provisions establishing safety standards (at 127). The problem is at the very core of the risk development defence. See *A and Others* v *National Blood Authority*, *supra* note 26.

[70] From a comparative perspective the institutional differences are also related to civil liability systems. The clearest example is the different function of judges in civil and common law countries and within each legal family. In civil law jurisdictions civil liability standards are generally defined by the legislator and specified by judges in the case-law. In common law jurisdictions the general definitions used to be provided by judges; the development of statutory law has increased, in particular in the field of product safety, bringing about the allocation of power between legislature and judiciary which is similar to that generally taking place in civil law jurisdictions. However, important differences still exist between common and civil law and within these legal families. See Zweigert and Kotz, *supra* note 6; Von Bar, *supra* note 52, at 237; van Gerven, *supra* note 9, at 674; B. Koch and H. Koziol (eds), *Unification of Civil Liability, Strict Liability* (2002), at 106; Rials, *Le juge administrative français et la technique du standard. Essai sur le traitement juridictionnel de l'idée de normalité* (1980), at note 93. These distinctions are, however, relative, as the analysis concerning convergence of legal systems shows.

[71] On different regulatory techniques for determining the value of life for regulatory purposes see Revesz and Stavins, 'Environmental Law and Policy', NYU Public Law Research Paper 82 (available at http://ssrn.com/abstract=552043).

judges is to verify whether or not a breach has occurred.[72] But the power of judges to specify the standard of due care is significant, given the width of the codified definition. Clearly, in common law jurisdictions when there are no relevant statutes judges define the standards while juries, when they operate, verify the existence of a breach.[73]

The level of expected harm is a relevant variable for determining the level of precautions to be taken to avoid negligence.[74] Not only is human life valued differently when considered in the fields of civil liability and regulation, but variations may occur even within civil liability. For example, the value of life defined to set the precautionary level owed by potential injurers often differs from the value attributed to life when an injury has occurred and has to be compensated.[75]

---

[72] See Zweigert and Kotz, *supra* note 6; Von Bar, *supra* note 52, at 249, where the author states that 'the (few) specially codified standard of care, and the (abundant) "nominate torts" of judge-made common law are regularly complemented by a further autonomous *Normgenerator*: the general duty of care': van Gerven *et al.*, *supra* note 9, at 54 ff.

[73] For a comparative analysis of negligence standards in European legal systems see Von Bar, *supra* note 52; Deakin *et al.*, *supra* note 8, at 167–84; van Gerven *et al.*, *supra* note 9, at 280 ff.

[74] This correlation is explicitly acknowledged in the US law and, perhaps less explicitly, in the UK. See for the US *Restatement Second of Torts* and *Restatement Third on the Law of Torts*, *supra* note 69, section 3 Negligence: '[a] person acts negligently if the person does not exercise reasonable care under all the circumstances. Primary factors to consider in ascertaining whether the person's conduct lacks reasonable care are the foreseeable likelihood that the person's conduct will result in the harm, the foreseeable severity of harm that may ensue, and the burden of precaution to eliminate or reduce the risk of harm': at 34. In the UK see Stapleton, *supra* note 68, at 53. In particular the author states that '[a]lthough liability in negligence includes carelessness by those who carry, store or resell the dangerous good, it is more commonly a route used to target the carelessness of manufacturers, especially with regard to manufacturing errors. In the case of manufacturing errors, carelessness is effectively presumed by U.K. judges. It follows that, since a manufacturer cannot in practice defend such a manufacturing defect claim by proof that he used reasonable care, this judicial attitude created and continues to maintain a covert area of strict liability masquerading as negligence liability'. See also Scott and Black, *supra* note 7, at 189, where the authors recognize that '[w]ith the exception of the basic principle of the [Consumer Protection] Act 1987, . . . , it is widely assumed that the key elements of liability—the concept of defectiveness, principle of causation, and scope of harm for which recovery is permitted—are virtually identical under the legislation as under common law negligence'. In civil law jurisdictions the express evaluation of expected harm is not generally acknowledged but it is implicitly considered. For the French system see Viney, *Traité de droit civil. Introduction à la responsabilité* (1998), at 65. For the Italian system see Cafaggi, *Profili di relazionalità della colpa* (1996). In comparative perspective see B.S. Markesinis (ed.), *The Gradual Convergence. Foreign Ideas, Foreign Influences and English Law on the Eve of the 21st Century* (1994), at 72; Von Bar, *supra* note 52, at 20; Zweigert and Kotz, *supra* note 6, at 599 and 615 ff.

[75] See Weir, *supra* note 7, at 7. See also Ladeur, *supra* note 14, at 15. See also Franklin and Rabin, *supra* note 3, at 605, commenting on *General Motors Corporation* v *Sanchez*, SC Texas (1999), 997 SW 2d 584. In particular in the judgment the court states: 'We believe that a duty to discover defects, and to take precaution in constant anticipation that a product might have a defect, will defeat the purpose of strict liability. Thus, we hold that a consumer has no duty to discover or to guard against a product defect, but a consumer's conduct other than the mere failure to discover or guard against a product defect is subject to comparative responsibility [negligence]. Public policy favours reasonable conduct by consumers regardless of whether a product is defective. A consumer is not relieved of the responsibility to act reasonably nor may a consumer fail to take reasonable precautions regardless of a known or unknown product defect'.

In strict liability regimes, based on defect, the procedure for standard-setting is relatively similar to 'due care' in negligence. In the area of product safety and environmental law, standards are often specified by the regulatory activity of different regulators. With the intervention of European law, product liability has also become predominantly statutory in common law countries.[76] In this area, too, the differences between civil and common law countries are less relevant than they used to be.[77] Frequently, however, judges consider liability even if injurers have complied with regulation. If within negligence compliance with regulations does not rule out liability, the same is (or should be) *a fortiori* the case in strict product liability.[78] In an absolute liability regime no standards are set, as the injurer is liable for the injuries if a causal link can be proved, but regardless of the level of precaution taken.

In the field of product liability a higher level of harmonization has been achieved.[79] While the differences between civil and common law jurisdictions are becoming less and less significant as far as the methodologies of standard-setting in civil liability are concerned, the distinctions, internal to each legal family may, however, be considerable and increasing.[80] This is in part due to the Europeanization of Member States' private law systems. European harmonization may recombine national legal

---

[76] See J. Stapleton, *Products Liability* (1994), at 11; Howell, 'Product Liability A History of Harmonization', in Hartkamp *et al.*, *supra* note 13, at 645; S. Whittaker, *Liability for Products—English Law, French Law and European Harmonisation* (2005). See also Reimann, *supra* note 26: '[j]urisdictions joining the product liability bandwagon have uniformly cast their special regimes in statutory form rather than relying on judicial decisions, restatements, or the like. This is no wonder in countries belonging to the civil law orbit, e.g., in continental Europe, Latin America, most Asian nations, and Quebec. But it is also true in several common law jurisdictions, namely United Kingdom, Ireland, and Australia. As a result, the field now has a legislative centrepiece in the vast majority of legal systems recognising it has a special subject. In fact, the only country where product liability is clearly established as a field with its own rules and principles (such as strict liability), but still remains a matter of case law, is the United States'.

[77] Von Bar, 'Liability for Information and Opinions Causing Pure Economic Loss to Third Parties: a Comparison of English and German Case Law', in Markesinis, *supra* note 74, at 98; see also on product liability in England J. G. Fleming, *The Law of Torts* (1998), Chap. 23; in Germany Markesinis, *supra* note 40, at 91–102; in France and Germany Zweigert and Kötz, *supra* note 6, at 676; in Europe Von Bar, *supra* note 52, at 418–24.

[78] See for a statement the French Civil Code implementing the PL Directive, *supra* note 29, in Arts. 1386-1 to 1386-18. On this issue see Fabre Magnan, *supra* note 5, at 830 ff. For the Italian system see Cafaggi, 'La responsabilità del produttore', in N. Lipari (ed.), *Trattato di diritto privato europeo* (2003).

[79] For a thorough analysis of comparative product liability see Reimann, *supra* note 26; Howells, 'The Relationship between Product Liability and Product Safety. Understanding a Necessary Element in European Product Liability through a Comparison with the US Position', 39 *Washburn LJ* (2000) 305.

[80] On the convergence of European systems of civil liability see Deakin *et al.*, *supra* note 8, at 536. The relationship between European law and national legal systems in the area of tort law has been explored by van Gerven, 'The Emergence of a Common European Law in the Area of Tort Law: the EU Contribution, in Tort Liability of Public Authorities in a Comparative Perspective', in D. Fairgrieve, M. Andenas, and J. Bell (eds), *The British Institute of International and Comparative Law* (2002), at 125, and previously, 'Bridging the Unbridgeable: Community and National Tort Laws after *Francovich and Brasserie*' [1996] *ICLQ* 520. On the impact of European law on civil liability national legal systems see also Von Bar, *supra* note 52.

systems in different ways from those existing before the formation of a European legal system.[81]

The institutional differences between strict liability and negligence, in particular the role of judges, increase when a law and economics approach is endorsed. This is probably due to the fact that such an approach has developed in the Anglo-American setting.[82] In negligence the standard is set by judges or by the legislator. In strict liability the injurer will define its own conduct and be held responsible for the injuries which have occurred, regardless of the level of care adopted by the injurer.[83]

5. COMPLEMENTARITY OF STANDARD-SETTING IN EUROPEAN PRODUCT CIVIL LIABILITY AND PRODUCT SAFETY

A taxonomy of factors contributing to the definition of standards in the field of product liability and safety at the European level is very complex. It is useful to start the analysis by underlining the differences between the definition of 'defect' in the PL Directive, 85/374, and that of 'safe product' in the amended GPS Directive. The PL Directive, when defining defect and the expectations of consumers, refers to regulation only briefly in relation to causes of exclusion of liability.[84] It is clear,

---

[81] For the relationship between European legislation and judicial intervention and the national systems of private law see van Gerven *et al.*, *supra* note 6, at 101, note 4, and *id.*, 'Comparative Law in a Texture of Communitarisation of National Laws and Europeanisation of Community Law', in D. O'Keefe (ed.), *European Union Law, Liber Amicorum in Honour of Lord Slynn of Hadley* (2000), at 43 ff. Van Gerven distinguishes between the bright and dark sides of harmonization and qualifies the latter as the disruptive effect of harmonization on national legal systems. See Schulze, 'European Private Law and Existing EC Law', 13 *ERPL* (2005) 3; Muller Graf, 'EC Directives as a Means of Private Law Unification', in Hartkamp *et al.*, *supra* note 13, at 77. See further R. Schulze, H. Schulte-Nolke, and J. Jones (eds), *A Casebook on European Consumer Law* (2002); Von Bar, *supra* note 52.

[82] See Shavell, *supra* note 42; *id.*, *Economic Analysis of Accident Law* (1987); R. Cooter and T. Ulen, *Introduction to Law and Economics* (3rd edn, 2000); A. Ogus, *Regulation, Economics and the Law* (2001); Landes and Posner, *supra* note 42.

[83] See Shavell, *supra* note 42; see also *id.*, 'Uncertainty over Causation and the Determination of Civil Liability', [1985] *JLE* 587. Shavell argued that there is an economic justification for limiting the liability of the injurer to the damage that he has actually caused. Damages should, therefore, be allocated across potential tortfeasors in proportion to the probability that they caused the harmful event. Shavell argued that a proportional liability rule had particular appeal on grounds of efficiency 'where the chance of uncertainty over causation is significant', and pointed to health-related and environmental risks as examples of where this may be the case

[84] See Art. 7 of PL Directive, *supra* note 29,: '[t]he producer shall not be liable as a result of this Directive if he proves . . . d) that the defect is due to compliance of the product with mandatory regulations issued by the public authorities', and Art. 13: '[t]his Directive shall not affect any rights which an injured person may have according to the rules of the law of contractual or non-contractual liability or a special liability system existing at the moment when this Directive is notified'. For a comparative analysis of product liability regimes in national systems see Borghetti, *supra* note 26. See also Howells, 'Product Liability—A History of Harmonisation', in Hartkamp, *et al.*, *supra* note 13, at 645 ff. A wider set of comparative data is presented by Reinmann, 'Liability for Defective Products at the

however, that judges cannot decide whether a product is defective without taking into account regulation(s) concerning product safety.[85] In the GPS Directive the definition of product safety is the combination of several concurring legal sources.[86] The European Commission has issued two decisions on notification procedures, clarifying the criteria that national authorities should use to evaluate the dangerous nature of a product, according to the principles defined in the Directive.[87]

Beginning of the Twenty First Century: Emergence of a Worldwide Standard?', 55 *AMJCL* (2003) 751: in particular on the causation principle at 772–4. In Reinmann's perspective two paradigms of legal regimes emerged from the comparative analysis: an American approach and a European approach. As far as the former is concern, the plaintiff bears the burden of proof, which may be made even harder by courts according to specific requirements to be met in the individual case; the doctrine applied is that of *res ipsa loquitur*. Conversely the European approach is characterized by a twofold regime assigning the burden of proof. Pursuant to Art. 4 of the Directive, the plaintiff needs to establish the causal link between the alleged defect and the harm. Art. 7 provides for legitimate causes of exemption from liability which might be used as defences by defendants. An example of the practical functioning of the European regime may be provided by a recent judgment released in Spain by the *Tribunal Supremo* (N.151/2003), 21 February 2003, reported at [2005] 2 *ERPL* 171, in comparison with late developments of other Member States' systems. The issue at stake in the case is the inversion of the burden of proof due to the combination of the normative definition of product defect and safety standards requirements that the product itself has to meet according to the Spanish Products Liability Act 22/1994. The manufacturer must therefore bring evidence that the product meets safety requirements that allows it to avoid the application of s. 3 of the Act, implementing Arts. 2 and 6(1) of the Directive. As far as the Dutch system is concerned, even before the implementation of the Directive there had been a well-known leading case establishing that the producer might be held liable for the damage caused by a defective product when the latter did not offer the consumer the degree of safety to be reasonably expected (Hoge Raad, 24 December 1993 [1994] NJ 214, *Leebeek-Vrumona BV*). Italian case law presents similar features: see Jacometti, *Italian case note, ibid.*, at 178–94. The national literature is also unanimous in acknowledging scarcity of case-law: see Tribunale di Monza, 20 July 1993 [1993] C (Contratti) 359, note by Carnevali [1994] I FI (Foro italiano) 252, note by Ponzanelli; Tribunale di Milano, 13 April 1995 [1996] DR 381, note by Ponzanelli; Tribunale di Roma, 11 May 1998 [1998] DR 1147, note by Ponzanelli [1998] I FI 3661, note by Palmieri; Tribunale di Milano, 31 January 2003 [2003] DR 634, note by Bitetto; [2003] RCP 1151, note by Della Bella; and, lastly, Tribunale di Vercelli, 7 April 2003 [2003] DR 1001, note by Ponzanelli. It is to be added that Italy has recently implemented the GPS Directive, *supra* note 30, by means of Legislative Decree note 172/2004. Obviously at the moment there is no case-law in which the producer-defendant has used the argument of regulation compliance as a defence or as a means to reverse the (reversed) burden of proof in product liability cases. Hence it is not yet possible to assess its effects on civil liability cases.

[85] It is important to use the plural (regulations) not only because a product can be a complex one but also because there can be concurring regulations.

[86] See Art. 3 of the GPS Directive, *supra* note 30, and in particular para. 3. See Weathenll, *supra* note 30, at 199 ff. and Hodges, *supra* note 30, at 224 ff.

[87] See Commission Decision 2004/418/CE, 29 April 2004, OJ 2004 L 151/00, laying down guidelines for the management of the Community Rapid Information system (RAPEX) and for notifications presented in accordance with Art. 11 of the GPS Directive, *supra* note 30, and Commission Decision 2004/905/EC, OJ 2004l L 381/63, laying down guidelines for the notification of dangerous consumer products to the competent authorities of the Member States by producers and distributors, in accordance with Art. 5(3) of Directive 2001/95/EC of the European Parliament and of the Council; *Guidance Document on the Relationship between the GPSD and Certain Sector Directives* (available at http://europa.eu.int/comm/consumers/cons_safe/prod_safe/DGSP/revisedDGSP-en.htm).

I shall consider in turn: (1) the definition of standards for producers and distributors; (2) the definition of standards for consumers; (3) the role of technical standards; and (4) the *ex ante/ex post* distinction in relation to time evaluation of defectiveness and safety.

(1) While the level of risk is at the core of the definition of safety in the GPS Directive, it plays no explicit relevant role in the definition of defect in the PL Directive.[88] In health and product safety regulation standards are broadly defined by a legislative act (Article 2 of the GPS Directive) and specified by regulators. In the two Commission Decisions the relevant elements that producers and distributors should consider in notifying the

---

[88] Compare Art. 6 of the PL Directive, *supra* note 29, and Art. 2(b) of the GPS Directive, *supra* note 30. If the risk-utility test were adopted to define defect, then risk would also play a strategic role in the liability system.

See Commission Decision 2004/418, *supra* note 87, para. 3(2): '[t]he level of risk could depend on a number of factors such as for example the type and vulnerability of the user and the extent to which the producer had taken precautions to guard against the hazard and warn the user. It is considered that these factors should also be taken into account in determining the level of risk that is regarded as dangerous and requires producers to notify the competent authorities'. See Reinmann, 'Liability for Defective Products at the Beginning of the Twenty-first Century: Emergence of a Worldwide Standard?', 51 *Am J Comp L* (2003) 767, where the author emphasizes that '[i]f the definition of a "product" is perhaps the easiest problem among the conditions of liability, the determination of what constitutes a "defect" is probably the most difficult. Three factors complicate the matter: the panoply of formulated definitions, the competition between two basic tests, and the existence of three defect types suggesting different treatment. First, there is a considerable diversity of definitions in the various product liability regimes. Some of these definitions are not very helpful to begin with because they are terribly imprecise or outright tautological. In addition, several systems eschew the notion of a "defect" altogether but rather ask whether the product was "dangerous", had a "safety deficiency" or created an (undue) "risk". [. . .] Second, most systems ultimately tend to rely on one of two tests. The first of these tests looks to justified consumer expectations: roughly speaking, a product is defective if it is more dangerous than the average consumer has reason to anticipate. This test prevails in the majority of jurisdictions. It rules supreme in Europe where it is codified in art. 6 (2) of the EC Directive and consequently applies in all EU member states as well as in most other European countries [. . .]. The other major approach is the risk-utility analysis. It renders a product defective if its risks outweigh its utility. To put it more colloquially: there is a defect if the product is more dangerous than absolutely necessary in light of its purpose. This test tends to dominate in the United States. There, it lies at the heart of the Third Restatement and looks like the trend of the future. [. . .] Third, there are three basic types of defects which may call for different treatment: manufacturing defects, design defects, and insufficient warnings (sometimes called instruction defects). While these categories are almost generally recognized in theory by scholars and often even by courts, legal systems differ as to their recognition on the level of black letter law. The majority of specialized product liability regimes do not distinguish between them. Thus the EC-Directive applies the same rules to all defect types, as do the many statutes modeled after it in jurisdictions inside and outside of Europe. [. . .] A minority of countries apply different approaches to the various categories. Such differentiation is pervasive in the United States where liability for manufacturing defects tends to be considerably stricter than in design and warning cases, but the distinction is apparently also persistent (in spite of the EC Directive) in Italian law and built into the Russian Consumer Protection Act.'

dangerous nature of a product are listed.[89] A definition of serious risk, recalling that of the GPS Directive, is further specified therein.[90] It is important to note that the probability and severity of the potential injury (or injuries) are factored into the evaluation of the dangerous nature of the product in accordance with the American model of liability. In the Decisions specific procedures for assessing the probability and severity of the risk are provided.[91] These methodologies could easily be employed by the judiciary to define defectiveness even within a strict liability regime.[92] The transplant of legal models concerning risk assessment could operate within liability, within regulation, and between the two.

(2) Standard-setting also concerns the conduct of consumers. Consideration of consumers' conduct in preventing or reducing hazards has had different relevance in the liability and regulatory systems. While the role of consumer expectation as an objective standard is crucial in the PL Directive, in the GPS Directive it only contributes to defining the conformity of the product to the general safety requirement.[93] Furthermore, while in the PL Directive consumer conduct is relevant for the application of comparative negligence and assumption of risk criteria, consumers' conduct is not really considered in relation to the GPS Directive except for the definition of

---

[89] In Annex I to Commission Decision 2004/418, *supra* note 87, a risk-utility test is provided at 68: '[i]n determining whether a product is dangerous under the terms of GPSD several issues should be analysed: the utility of the product, the nature of the risk, the population group exposed, previous experience with similar products, etc. A safe product must have no risk or only present the minimum risk compatible with the product's use and needed in order to ensure useful operation of the product . . . Producers and distributors should analyse the information collected and decide whether a particular hazardous situation should be notified to the authorities taking into account:

- The gravity of the outcome of an hazard depending on the severity and the probability of the possible health and safety damage. Combining the severity and probability gives an assessment of the gravity of the risk . . .
- The severity of health/safety damage for a given hazard should be that for which there is a reasonable evidence that the health and safety damage attributable to the product could occur under foreseeable use. This could be the worst case from health and safety damage that have occurred with similar products.
- The probability of health and safety damage for a normal user who has an exposure corresponding to the intended or the expected use of the defective product has also to be considered as well as the probability of the product being or becoming effective.'

[90] See Commission Decision 2004/418, *supra* note 87, at 92 ff.

[91] See Commission Decision 2004/905, *supra* note 87, at 74–5.

[92] It should be emphasized that these decisions were issued in relation to notification procedures, and therefore the comparison with the PL Directive, *supra* note 29, should be limited. Having specified that, one can conclude that the GPS Directive as interpreted by the European Commission defines a regulatory model whose standards are very similar to negligence as it is generally defined in common law jurisdictions. This constitutes an additional difference from the Liability Directive that on the contrary should be interpreted as introducing a strict liability regime.

[93] See Art. 6 of the PL Directive, *supra* note 29, and Art. 3(3)(f) of the GPS Directive, *supra* note 30.

serious risk.[94] While the structure of the liability system has been predominantly relational, that of the regulatory regime has been primarily unilateral.[95] The two Commission Decisions seem to shed new light on the possibility of considering consumer conduct and not just consumer expectations in the regulatory regime in order to determine standards of conduct, moving from unilateral to relational in the regulatory field also. In this case regulation follows the logic underlying the evolution of the liability regime.[96]

(3) The role of technical standards is different in the PL and the GPS Directives. While in the GPS Directive the definition of safety is pre-dominantly based on technical standards, in the PL Directive technical standards play a relatively small explicit role for the definition of defect.[97] In the PL Directive references to the state of scientific and technical knowledge are made in relation to the exclusion of liability, but they do constitute, at least explicitly, an element of the definition of defect.[98] On the contrary, in the GPS Directive the conformity of safety to technical standards is very important. Article 3(2) of the GPS Directive distinguishes between

[94] See Art. 8 of the PL Directive, *supra* note 29, which explicitly mentions fault of the injured person and the national legislation implementing this provision. In point, see also Reinmann, *supra* note 88.

[95] In the PL Directive, *supra* note 29, both standards for manufacturers' and consumers' conduct are defined. In the regulatory Directive, the standard-setting function predominantly concerns manufacturers' conduct, while consumers' conduct is considered only in relation to what manufacturers have to do.

[96] See Commission Decision 2004/418, *supra* note 87, at 92 and 93, and Commission Decision 2004/905, *supra* note 87, at 74: '[t]he potential of an hazard to materialise as an actual negative effect on health/safety will depend on the degree to which the consumer is exposed to it when using the product as intended or as it could reasonably be expected during its lifetime. In addition the exposure to certain hazards may in some case involve more than one person at a time. Finally when determining the level of risk presented by a product by combining the severity of the hazard with the exposure consideration should be given also to the ability of the exposed consumer to prevent or to react to the hazardous situation. This will depend on the hazard, the warnings given and the vulnerability of the consumer who may be exposed to it'. For a broader perspective on relational regulation see Cafaggi, *supra* note 17, at 623.

[97] The procedure to define technical standard is defined by Art. 4 of the GPS Directive, *supra* note 30: '[f]or the purposes of this Directive, the European standards referred to in the second subparagraph of Art. 3(2) shall be drawn up as follows:

(a) the requirements intended to ensure that products which conform to these standards satisfy the general safety requirement shall be determined in accordance with the procedure laid down in Art. 15(2);

(b) on the basis of those requirements, the Commission shall, in accordance with directive 98/34 of the European Parliament and of the Council of June 22 1998 laying down a procedure for the provision of information in the field of technical standards and regulations and of the rules on information society services call on the European standardisation bodies to draw up standards which satisfy these requirements;

(c) on the basis of those mandates, the European standardisation bodies shall adopt the standards in accordance with the principles contained in the general guidelines for cooperation between the Commission and those bodies'.

[98] See Art. 7(e) of the PL Directive, *supra* note 29.

conformity to specific rules of national law, in which case the product *is deemed* to be safe, and conformity with voluntary national standards transposing European standards, in which case the product *shall be presumed* to be safe. Conformity to general safety requirement is evaluated according to different, concurring elements among which voluntary standards and codes of good practice are expressly mentioned.[99]

The adoption of European technical standards is clearly promoted by the GPS Directive in order to achieve a higher level of harmonization.[100] The definition of these standards is at least partially delegated to standardization bodies, but manufacturers can adopt their own standards regardless of those set by such bodies in accordance with the criteria defined by Article 3(3) of the GPS Directive.[101] Such adoption, however, would shift the burden of proof associated with the presumption of safety, grounded on conformity with voluntary national standards.

(4) In relation to the traditional distinction that refers to civil liability as an *ex post* and to regulation as an *ex ante* technique it should be pointed out that, while conformity implies the presumption of safety, subsequent controls can take place if the monitoring system, defined by the GPS Directive, reveals the existence of risks for consumer health and safety.[102] These controls can trigger remedial action by producers and distributors. But competent authorities can also require the adoption of specific measures before the product is circulated or can forbid circulation altogether.[103]

---

[99] See Art. 3(4) of the GPS Directive, *supra* note 30.

[100] See *ibid.*, rec. 26: 'It is necessary, for the purpose of ensuring a consistent, high level of consumer health and safety protection and preserving the unity of the internal market, that the Commission be informed of any measure restricting the placing on the market of a product or requiring its withdrawal or recall from the market. Such measures should be taken in compliance with the provisions of the Treaty, and in particular Arts. 28, 29 and 30 thereof'.

[101] *Ibid.*, Art. 3(3) states: '[i]n circumstances other than those referred to in paragraph 2 the conformity of a product to the general safety requirement shall be assessed by taking into account the following elements in particular, when they exist:

  (a) voluntary national standards transposing relevant European standards other than those referred to in paragraph 2;
  (b) the standards drawn up in the Member State in which the product is marketed;
  (c) Commission recommendations setting guidelines on product safety assessment;
  (d) product safety codes of good practice in force in the sector concerned;
  (e) the state of the art and technology;
  (f) reasonable consumer expectations concerning safety'.

[102] For the *ex ante/ex post* distinction see the analysis by Shavell, *supra* note 42.

[103] Art. 8 of the GPS Directive, *supra* note 30, allows competent authorities to impose conditions prior to the marketing of a product, to require that a product be marketed with warnings concerning any risks. See in particular Art. 8(b)(ii) and (c). Art. 8(e) concerns banning: 'for any dangerous product [competent authorities can] ban its marketing and introduce the accompanying measures required to ensure the ban is complied with'. See also Commission Decision 2004/418, *supra* note 87, at 90 ff. For a detailed examination see Hodges, *supra* note 30 at 129 ff.

The GPS Directive defines a system of monitoring and control of product safety that operates *ex post* when the product is on the market or is about to be circulated in the market. It is a regulatory device that reacts to unsafe products placed in the markets.

There are critical aspects in both Directives as to standard-setting concerning product defectiveness and safety.[104] Two problems in particular emerge:

(a) Given the existing legislative framework, which mechanisms are in place between the GPS and PL Directives to coordinate the standard-setting process?

(b) Is there an implicit functional differentiation of the two systems that justifies the current differences?

The coordination between techniques for defining standards in product liability and safety by the two Directives is unsatisfactory. While an approach based on institutional complementarity might justify different considerations of the role of technical standards in regulation and liability, it is certainly a mistake to neglect their role in the field of liability. There is no reason to justify such a disproportion concerning the importance of technical standards. While their importance in the regulatory field can be recognized, more relevance should be attributed to them in the liability system.[105] The role of technical standards, however, should be linked to innovation and promote the pro-competitive scope of civil liability, replacing the norm that prevents judges from evaluating liability in the light of existing safer products in the market.[106] While this evidence should not be conclusive, it could contribute to the assessment of defectiveness by considering what is available for consumers in the marketplace of goods or ideas.

But what is the implicit allocation of tasks concerning risk management and control of product safety at the European level? A significant difference between the two Directives concerns the relevance of time in evaluating defectiveness or safety. While the PL Directive fixes the point at which the product is put into circulation as the time at which defectiveness should be evaluated, the GPS Directive imposes an evaluation of safety encompassing the use of a product by consumers.[107] This

---

[104] See on the subject Howells, *supra* note 84, at 645 ff., 652 ff.

[105] One implicit reason for the relatively light weight of technical standards in the field of liability may be related to the fact that standardization bodies are mainly driven by industries. Technical standards end up playing an important function through expert evidence in trials. Instead of neglecting the importance of technical standards for liability purposes a more representative structure of private standardizing bodies should be favoured. If sufficient guarantees of participation were given in technical standard-setting functions they could play a more relevant role in the liability system. On the relationship between governance of private regulators and liability, see Cafaggi, *supra* note 15.

[106] See Art. 7 of the PL Directive, *supra* note 29.

[107] For the interpretation of *ibid.*, Art. 7(a) see Case C-203/99, *Henning Veedfald* v *Arhus Amtskommune* [2001] ECR I-03569. The ECJ held that 'Art. 7(a) of Council directive 85/375/EEC of 25 July on the approximation of the laws, regulations and administrative provisions of the member States

distinction forces a critical rethinking of the *ex ante* versus *ex post* perspective as applied to the relationship between civil liability and regulation.

In the product liability field the time at which the product is circulated defines quite clearly the domain of civil liability. The development risk defence contributes to the determination of a time limit for the evaluation of defectiveness.[108] Regulation of consumer safety for risks whose existence becomes known after the goods' circulation is (implicitly) attributed to the GPS Directive, in which an important set of duties, enforceable through criminal sanctions, is defined to monitor product safety, even when the products are circulating in the market. Translated into costs, the manufacturer will bear civil liability-associated costs within a limited period, while the manufacturer will bear regulatory-associated costs and criminal liability costs for the whole life of the product.[109]

In relation to the circulation of the product this distinction does not resemble the traditional *ex ante* versus *ex post* distinction. On the contrary, the current approach at the European level suggests that, while the PL Directive uses an *ex ante* system of evaluation, the regulatory approach in the GPS Directive uses predominantly an *ex post* perspective.[110] While conformity to general safety requirements

concerning liability for defective products is to be interpreted as meaning that a defective product is put into circulation when it is used during the provision of a specific medical service, consisting in preparing a human organ for transplantation, and the damage caused to organ results from that preparatory treatment'.

[108] See Case C-300/95, *Commission* v *United Kingdom* [1997] ECR I-2649, where the Court states that the 'state of scientific and technical knowledge did not merely include: the practices and safety standards in use in the industrial sector in which the producer is operating, but [extends to] the state of scientific and technical knowledge, including the most advanced level of such knowledge, at the time when the product in question was put into circulation'. For an analysis of the case, see Stapleton, *supra* note 74, at 58. See Case C-52/00, *Commission* v *France* [2002] ECR I-3827, at para. 47: '[i]n regard to the arguments based on Article 15 of the Directive it should be noted that whilst that provision enables the Member States to remove the exemption from the liability provided for in article 7 (e) thereof it does not authorise them to alter the conditions under which that exemption is applied. Nor does article 15 authorise them to cancel or amend the rules governing derogations provided for in article 7 (d). That interpretation is not negated by the Directive 92/59, which does not concern the producer's liability for products he puts into circulation'. See also for the French legislation J. Calais-Aulois and F. Steinmetz, *Droit de la consommation, Précis, droit privé* (6th edn, 2004), at 332: 'Nous regrettons que le législateur français de 1998 ait cru bon d'exonérer le producteur du risqué de développement. Nous pensons que l'exonération est contestable dans son principe même. L'argument d'équité nous parait plus fort que les arguments d'ordre économique. Ces derniers peuvent d'ailleurs se retourner si on visage le long terme: les produits se vendent d'autant plus facilement qu'ils sont réputé plus surs ; et ils sont réputé plus sur s'ils sont fabriqués dans un pays qui n'hésite pas à mettre une lourde responsabilité sur la tête de producteurs. [. . .] La jurisprudence française a d'ailleurs la possibilité de rendre le producteur responsable du risque de développment: nous savons que le systeme nouveau, issu de la directive, laisse subsister d'autres systemes de responsabilité [. . .] Nous souhaitons que cette jurisprudence soit maintenue'.

[109] One can add liability costs that may be incurred under national systems in conjunction with criminal violations.

[110] It should be clear that here *ex ante* and *ex post* refer to the evaluation of defectiveness and not to the time of enforcement. From an enforcement perspective the PL Directive, *supra* note 29, remains an *ex post* device.

can be presumed at the time of circulation, controls on safety may occur when the product is used, to verify the existence of product-related risks.[111]

The institutional design, defined by the two Directives, should be integrated by adding the component of national civil liability systems.[112] National general civil liability systems, in particular negligence, may 'back up' regulatory duties established by the GPS Directive. The ability to use national civil liability systems as a complement to the GPS Directive depends on the different legal systems, in particular the relationship between civil liability and criminal liability.

As regards deterrence, the GPS and PL Directives concur in defining the legal regime before the product is circulated, while after the product is circulated the main risk management device becomes regulation through the GPS devices. As regards compensatory function, consumers can claim compensation for harms caused by defects existing before the product was circulated under the PL Directive, while they can use ordinary national civil liability, associated with the violation of one of the duties defined by the GPS Directive, where the danger becomes clear after the product has been circulated.[113]

The current differences between the two Directives in relation to standard-setting and the risk management strategies they aim to achieve are hardly justifiable under an institutional complementarity approach. There are no good reasons for ruling out the use of the European product liability regime after the product is circulated, especially if an important set of duties may arise in relation to new knowledge concerning the existence of product-related risks. This is not simply a question of harmonization.[114] In the framework of institutional complementarity it is a regulatory

---

[111] See Arts 3 and 8 of the GPS Directive, *supra* note 30, and the analysis below. In particular Art. 8(1)(a) states: '1. For the purposes of this directive, and in particular of Article 6 thereof the competent authorities of the member states shall be entitled to take, inter alia, the measures in (a) and in (b) to (f) where appropriate:

   (a) for any product:
      (i) to organise, even after its being placed on the market as being safe, appropriate checks on its safety properties, on an adequate scale, up to the final stage of use or consumption;
     (ii) to require all necessary information from the parties concerned;
    (iii) to take samples of products and subject them to checks.'

[112] The forms of integration will vary whether the Directives are seen as establishing minimum or total harmonization. In both cases integration is possible but it operates in different ways.

[113] I have criticized the use of civil liability to complement regulatory techniques in the light of the complementarity approach, claiming that the use of regulatory strategies should be, at least in some cases, independent of the use of civil liability in cases of violation. This conclusion does not imply that civil liability cannot reinforce deterrence for certain 'regulatory duties' but the two strategies, if complementary, should generally be independently enforced. The burden of monitoring and enforcing regulatory duties should be placed on the regulator, not on the judicial system. See Cafaggi, *supra* notes 15 and 17, and previously Cafaggi, 'La nozione di difetto ed il ruolo dell'informazione. Per l'adozione di un modello dinamico-relazionale di difetto in una prospettiva di riforma' [1995] *Rivista Critica del Diritto Privato* 447.

[114] One could in fact argue that compensation for product-related harms is taken care of by national legal systems of civil liability that ensure compensation when duties established by the GPS Directive, *supra* note 30, are breached. From this perspective the problem could be framed as one of

matter.[115] The reasons for limiting liability should be given within a regulatory framework and not (or at least not only) within a harmonization one.

The proper differentiation between regulation and liability should characterize the different nature of the duties imposed on manufacturers, distributors, and consumers, but most importantly the different instruments used for enforcing the duties of manufacturers and other parties along the production and distribution chain. So, as we shall see, while the regulatory domain should govern the procedures for recall and withdrawal, too complex to be defined by a judge, liability can be used to enforce duties concerning cases of unsafe and defective products related to specific classes of consumers or individual consumers when the defectiveness emerged after the product was circulated.

The main purpose of this illustration has been to show the interdependence between standard-setting in civil liability and regulation, the insufficient coordination between the two at European level, and the desirability of a coordinated approach.

6. THE COMPLEMENTARITY IN MONITORING COMPLIANCE AND THE USE OF CIVIL LIABILITY AS A TOOL FOR ENSURING COOPERATION AMONG PUBLIC AND PRIVATE ACTORS—THE CASE OF PRODUCT SAFETY

Monitoring compliance with legal standards differentiates the civil liability strategy from administrative regulation quite significantly. In the civil liability system monitoring is essentially achieved by the parties, and in particular by the potential victims, although potential injurers may have strong incentives to (self-)monitor as well.[116] Monitoring has to translate into action when there is evidence that unsafe products are in circulation. It may refer to products that were already defective when introduced into the market, or to products that were correctly deemed safe when produced but have become defective as a result of new scientific or technological evidence. There are two main categories of action:

(a) duties to inform; and
(b) duties to act.

---

harmonization, since the conditions under which these duties can be enforced depend on national systems, while for harms related to defects existing before the product is circulated the conditions of liability are harmonized by the PL Directive, *supra* note 29. Whether or not choosing a different strategy that harmonizes liability systems by considering the whole life cycle is an open question. But the main problem is that there is no reason for having a liability system independent of regulation before the product is circulated and dependent on regulation afterwards. The complementarity between the two should be functional, not temporal.

115 For the distinction between harmonization and regulatory questions see *infra* text and notes 160 ff.

116 These incentives are based on deterrence and reputational factors, i.e. the amount of damages they would have to pay and the loss they would suffer if one of their products were defective.

I shall consider here the duty to inform and later, within the section devoted to remedies, the duties to act. Duties to inform are mainly directed to competent authorities and to consumers. I shall first address the duties to inform competent authorities and then the duty to inform consumers, to the extent that this can be considered to be part of the monitoring system. To leave the task of monitoring product safety compliance with standards to potential injurers and victims would be highly inappropriate.[117] Many products require sophisticated techniques for effective monitoring and high costs that individual manufacturers may not be able to afford, let alone consumers. For this reason, monitoring has always been the task of regulators that have performed directly or, more rarely, indirectly by delegating this function to other bodies.[118] In the regulatory domain monitoring used to be done by the regulator, at least in traditional models of command and control. With the evolution of new models of regulation, peer monitoring has been associated with hierarchical monitoring, and more cooperative relationships between regulators, the regulated, and third parties have taken place.[119] In the field of product safety, monitoring the safety of products during their lifetime has always been shared between public authorities and producers.[120] Producers and their distribution chain have

---

[117] On the relationship between product safety and market surveillance see the papers published at the conference on European Market Surveillance Programming, organized by DG SANCO, Brussels, 10–11 March 2005.

[118] For the UK regime see Scott and Black, *supra* note 7, at 401, '[r]esponsibilities for monitoring and enforcement of product safety and food safety rules are split between the minister, local authority trading standards departments and (in respect to food safety) local authority environmental health departments. . . . The European Commission has exercised a co-ordinating role in respect of product safety since the establishment of the system for rapid exchange of information (RAPEX) in 1984 [Council Decision 84/133 EEC]. Under this regime member States have a duty to inform the Commission of measures taken to address dangerous products, and the Commission then informs the other Member States'.

[119] See I. Ayres and J. Braithwaite, *Responsive Regulation* (1992); Ogus, *supra* note 82; Cunningham and Grabonsky, *supra* note 22; R. Baldwin and M. Cave, *Understanding Regulation. Theory, Strategy and Practice* (1999); R. Baldwin, C. Scott, and C. Hood (eds.), *A Reader in Regulation* (1998); C. Scott, *Regulation: a Reader* (2003).

[120] See Art. 5(3) and (4) of Directive 01/95, *supra* note 30: '[w]here producers and distributors know or ought to know, on the basis of information in their possession and as professionals, that a product that they have placed on the market poses risks to the consumer that are incompatible with the general safety requirements, they shall immediately inform the competent authorities of the member states thereof and under the conditions laid down as in Annex I, giving details, in particular of action taken to prevent risk to the consumer' and '[p]roducers and distributors shall, within the limits of their respective activities, cooperate with the competent authorities, at the request of the latter, on action taken to avoid the risks posed by products which they supply or have supplied. The procedures for such cooperation, including procedures for dialogue with the producers and distributors concerned on issues related to product safety shall be established by competent authorities'. See Commission Decision 2004/905/EC, *supra* note 87, at point 2.2: '[t]he purpose of the notification is to enable the competent authorities to monitor whether the companies have taken appropriate measures to address the risks posed by a product already placed on the market and to order or take additional measures if necessary to prevent the risks. The notification also allows the competent authorities to assess whether they should check other similar products on the market. Therefore competent authorities must receive adequate information to enable them to assess whether an economic operator has taken adequate measures with regard to a dangerous product. In this

always been key players, given the incentive of potential damage to their reputations. But the roles of individual consumers and consumers' associations has increased. The GPS Directive endorses a collaborative model of monitoring, extending to distributors' duties to monitor and to inform manufacturers and competent authorities about risks.[121] Even beyond these duties, self-monitoring by producers and distributors constitutes a very important part of the regulatory chain that allocates the burdens and responsibilities between the public authorities, self-regulatory bodies, and individual operators.[122]

Distributors are generally closer to the products, since they have a relatively stable relationship with consumers. Distributors are more easily able to obtain information from consumers and have therefore been considered a key component in the monitoring chain for product safety.[123] The monitoring system envisaged by the GPS Directive is aimed at triggering controls and actions by national competent authorities. The monitoring system of the PL Directive is aimed at achieving compensation for violations that have occurred and harms that have materialized.

If producers or distributors violate duties to monitor, this will be punished by imposing administrative or criminal sanctions.[124] Legal systems vary in permitting corresponding action in civil liability to compensate consumers for violations of duties to monitor.

Systems that deny the possibility to sue in civil liability basically define a rigid complementarity; violations of regulatory duties are sanctioned only by administrative and criminal liability.

Systems that allow actions for civil liability for violations of duties concerning standard-setting, monitoring, and enforcement define a flexible complementarity in which civil liability may be used to reinforce the regulatory model and to protect the interests of third parties, who are generally not directly involved in the regulatory processes.

7. COMPLEMENTARITY IN REMEDIES—COREGULATION, REMEDIES, AND THE EXAMPLE OF THE ENVIRONMENTAL LIABILITY DIRECTIVE

The Environmental Liability Directive, 2004/35 (hereinafter, the EL Directive) is a good illustration of the new regulatory schemes and their potential influences on

respect it should be noted that GSPD entitles the competent authorities to request additional information if they feel unable to assess whether a company has taken adequate measures with regard to a dangerous product'. For notification concerning safety of food products see Regulation 178/2002 of the European Parliament and the Council, OJ 2002 L 031/1, as amended by Regulation 1642/2003, OJ L 245/4.

[121] See Art. 5(2) of GPS Directive, *supra* note 30.

[122] See the GPS Directive, *supra* note 30, in particular, the duties of producers and distributors defined by Art. 5(1).

[123] See Art. 5(2) of Directive 01/95, *supra* note 30.

[124] See, e.g., Art. 11 of Italian decreto legislativo 172/2004 implementing the GPS Directive, *supra* note 30.

the relationship between regulation and civil liability.[125] Despite its title the Directive is basically aimed at defining the relationship between the regulatory authority (the competent authority), the polluters, and private parties, mainly, but not just, non-governmental organizations, that may be affected by environmental damage.[126] The EL Directive in the drafting process shifted from a liability to a regulatory perspective, thus attracting numerous criticisms.[127]

The competent authority, or the set of competent authorities, has to be defined by Member States.[128] It is quite clear, however, that they are administrative and not judicial authorities.[129]

These authorities have a duty to identify the polluter, to assess damages, and to determine what remedial measures should be taken.[130] They have monitoring and enforcement functions. Unlike in typical regulatory Directives focusing on standard-setting, here the focus is on remedies and the procedures by which they have to be identified and implemented. It clearly emerges from the Directive that the type of environmental damage considered requires a set of remedies involving multiple parties and a complex procedure. This is certainly a specific feature that cannot be generalized to the entire field of civil liability, but it is (or can become) typical of mass torts.

The main scope of the EL Directive is the identification of remedies and associated procedures relating to the likelihood of the occurrence of environmental damage or

---

[125] Directive 2004/35/CE of the European Parliament and of the Council of 21 April 2004 on environmental liability with regard to the prevention and remedying of environmental damage, OJ 2004 L 143/56.

[126] While polluters are considered injurers and mainly responsible for remedies, non-governmental organizations and other private parties do not have a right to compensation (Art. 3(3)) but they 'shall be entitled to submit to the competent authority any observations relating to instances of environmental damage or an imminent threat of such damage of which they are aware and shall be entitled to request the competent authority to take action' (Art. 12(1)).

[127] In relation to the draft proposal see the criticisms of Betlem, *supra* note 18, at 679 concerning in particular conflict with the Aarhus Convention which requires a private action to be available to non-public bodies to ensure compliance with environmental law by other non-public bodies.

[128] The GPS Directive, *supra* note 30, Art. 6(2) states: 'Member States shall establish or nominate authorities competent to monitor the compliance of products with the general safety requirements and arrange for such authorities to have and use the necessary powers to take the appropriate measures incumbent upon them under this Directive'.

[129] See *ibid.*, Art. 11, but especially Art. 13, in which the review procedures are regulated. From the wording of that Article it is quite evident that competent authorities cannot be national judges. Art. 13(1) states: 'the persons referred to in Article 12(1) shall have access to a court or other independent and impartial public body competent to review the procedural and substantive legality of the decisions, acts or failure to act of the competent authority under this directive'. Other arguments in favour of the administrative nature of the authority are based on the procedure defined by Art. 7 concerning remedial measures.

[130] See Art. 11(2): '[t]he duty to establish which operator has caused the damage or the imminent threat of damage, to assess the significance of the damage and to determine which remedial measures should be taken with reference to Annex II shall rest on the competent authority. To that effect, the competent authority shall be entitled to require the relevant operator to carry out his own assessment and to supply any information and data necessary'.

to harms already materialized. Measures designed to combat environmental damage are distinguished by being preventive and remedial.[131] The polluter is required to take preventive action when there is an imminent threat of environmental damage even if it has not yet occurred. When damage has occurred the polluter is obliged to take remedial action. In both cases the competent authority may require the operator to take the necessary preventive and remedial measures and/or give instructions to the operator to act to prevent or reduce the environmental harm. While a specific provision determines modalities of remedial measures, no specific provisions are identified for deciding on preventive action.

The procedure on remedial measures states that the polluter has to identify such measures in accordance with Annex II, and then submit them for approval to a competent authority (Article 7(1)).[132] The competent authority will decide in cooperation with the operator (Article 7(2)) and invite affected persons, natural or legal, to submit their observations and take them into account (Article 7(4)). Such procedure illustrates a cooperative method of defining the appropriate remedies for environmental harm that allows the party—who is likely to be best informed about the conditions of the polluted site and the methods of repair—to define a suitable plan, but it gives the competent authority the final word and responsibility for avoiding self-interested solutions.

The changes with respect to command and control are relatively radical, since the definition of which remedies should be adopted is the outcome of a cooperative procedure. But the differences when compared with judicial procedure are relevant as well. Under the Directive it is the injurer who makes the proposal, while in a typical judicial setting it is the victim who identifies the remedies.

While there is no analogous procedure for preventive measures (Article 5), it is clear that for the definition of these measures, too, some type of cooperative procedure should take place. The wording of Article 5 of the EL Directive permits the choice of different approaches, ranging from a more hierarchical one to a more cooperative one.

---

[131] See Arts. 5 and 6 of the EL Directive, *supra* note 125.

[132] Annex II is devoted to different remedies that can be undertaken: '[r]emediation of damage to water or protected species or natural habitats.

Remedying of environmental damage, in relation to water or protected species or natural habitats, is achieved through the restoration of the environment to its baseline condition by way of primary, complementary and compensation remediation, where

    (a) Primary remediation is any remedial measure which returns the damaged natural resources and/or impaired services to, or towards, baseline condition

    (b) "Complementary" remediation is any remedial measure which returns the damaged natural resources and/or services to compensate for the fact that primary remediation does not result in fully restoring the damaged natural resources and/or service

    (c) "Compensatory" remediation is any remedial measure taken to compensate for interim losses of natural resources and/or services that occur from the date of damage occurring until primary remediation has achieved its full effect'.

If this Directive is to be interpreted as a 'regulatory Directive', what can its impact be on national environmental civil liability systems from the perspective analysed in this chapter? What will happen to those cases brought before a court in which recovery is sought? It is unclear whether the Directive pre-empts judicial solutions. There are no explicit provisions and therefore it is unlikely that Member States, when implementing it, will opt for a single strategy based on administrative procedures, precluding the judicial one. By the same token, however, once preventive and remedial actions are approved by the competent authority and implemented, a judge should not be able to order different measures in a civil liability action. The role of the judiciary will be limited to judicial review procedures concerning those decisions defined in Article 13.

Here regulatory compliance should exclude liability. However damages not considered by the Directive, such as personal injuries, harm to property, and economic losses would still be recoverable.[133] In these cases judges can certainly operate in different ways to ensure reparation. Potential conflicts can arise (more probably in relation to harm to property and personal injuries rather than in connection with economic losses) between the remedies or preventive actions approved by competent authorities and potential remedies available in legal action.

Beyond the question of the priority to be given to regulatory institutions in relation to environmental damage, the main lesson provided by the Directive in the perspective of this chapter comes from the relationship between injurer and regulator (who is also the person entitled to seek recovery) *vis-à-vis* that typically established in judicial proceedings concerning environmental civil liability. The above-described procedures move towards a higher level of involvement of the parties, in particular the injurer, although the final word, substantiated by the conferral of the power to approve, is still given to the competent authority. The recognition of the superior knowledge of the injurer and its ability to operate promptly in its own self-interest to protect the site from further damages has perhaps been a relevant consideration for establishing the cooperative procedure in the new environmental liability Directive. While it is clear that the legal regime of environmental harm could not be mechanically transplanted into the general civil liability system, the institutional mechanism defined by the Directive can provide useful insights.

First, in relation to environmental harm, the level of complexity of the accident may suggest the use of different procedures, but also affects the choice between a regulatory and a liability strategy. Often this choice can only practically be made *ex post*, when the consequences of the unlawful conduct are clear. However, in a coordinated framework a procedure for choosing between regulation and liability should be defined *ex ante*. When the level of complexity of the environmental harm allows a combination of liability and regulation, reform of the civil procedure system

---

[133] See rec. 14 of the EL Directive, *supra* note 125.

would be useful to allow for the appointment of masters to monitor the reparation process in the civil liability context. Judges may not be the best parties to follow these procedures and the available resources suggest the use of special independent appointees. More generally, the considerable impact on communities of harm to the environment suggests that stakeholders' participation should be improved in the civil liability system. Functional complementarity does not imply equivalence, and therefore forms of participation and monitoring activities may and should still vary according to the different strategies, regulation and liability.

8. THE COMPLEMENTARITY OF REMEDIES IN CIVIL LIABILITY AND ADMINISTRATIVE REGULATION—THE CASE OF PRODUCT SAFETY AND PRODUCT LIABILITY

The field of European product safety gives another good illustration of a system of institutional complementarities between liability, administrative regulation, and self-regulation in relation to remedies. The PL Directive provides compensation for injuries suffered in relation to the marketing of defective products. Limitations on compensation are, however, strict, since harm to the product itself and economic losses are not recoverable under the Directive. Thus, the decision whether such damages are recoverable is left to the discretion of individual Member States. From the perspective of remedies, the main feature missing from the PL Directive is a provision concerning injunctive relief. Not only is compensation conditional upon the traditional requirement that harm has to materialize, but no complementary judicial measures such as product recall or withdrawal have been indicated in the PL Directive. In theory, the silence on product recall can be interpreted as an implicit reference to national legal systems, at least for those that had already recognized recall. In fact, in many systems judicial orders concerning product recalls were already available under the civil liability of negligence or equivalent fault principles.[134] But still the Directive is incomplete and has only partially harmonized the area of remedies.

---

[134] Forms of product recall existed in specific areas (drugs, etc.) and were administered by sector authorities. After the ECJ judgments of 2002 it is unclear whether judges could resort to remedies different from those available under the Directive. The suggested solution is that they can order a recall under national tort law only if there is fault, while they could not in the absence of fault be given complete harmonization. See Case 52/00, *Commission* v *France*, *supra* note 108, at para. 22: '[t]he reference in Article 13 of the Directive to the rights which an injured person may rely on under the rules of then law of contractual and non contractual liability must be interpreted as meaning that the system of rules put in place by the Directive which in Article 4 enables the victim to seek compensation where he proves damage, the defect in the product and the causal link between the defect and the damage, does not preclude the application of other systems of contractual or non contractual liability based on other grounds such as fault or warranty in respect of latent defects'.

An open question concerns the application of Directive 98/27 on injunctions for the protection of consumer interests.[135] Legal systems differ as to its applicability to product liability and safety.[136] Also important for defining available remedies is the coordination with Directive 2005/29 on unfair commercial practices, where injunctions against unfair practices are regulated. The focus in this section is on complementarity with the GPS Directive.[137]

The initial General Safety Directive (Council Directive 92/59/EEC of 29 June 1992) filled the gap to some extent by introducing a relatively clear measure of product recall. The new GPS Directive takes an important step forward: it clarifies the distinction between product recall and product withdrawal (Article 2) and it briefly regulates the procedures of product withdrawal and product recall (Article 8(f)(i) and (ii)).[138] Under the amended GPS Directive product 'recall' means any measure aimed at achieving the return of a dangerous product that has already been marketed.[139] Product withdrawal is any measure aimed at preventing the distribution, display, or offer of a product.[140] Product recalls and withdrawals can take place in at least two different ways:

(1) as independent and voluntary actions of producers; or
(2) as implementation of orders coming from competent authorities.

---

[135] Directive 98/27 EC of the European Parliament and of the Council of 19 May 1998 on injunctions for the protection of consumers' interests, OJ 1998 L 166/51.

[136] See for the French system Calais-Aulois and Steinmetz, *supra* note 108, at 600 ff.

[137] See Art. 11(2) of Directive 2005/29 on unfair commercial practices, of 11 May 2005, OJ 2005 L 149/22. 'Under the legal provisions referred to in para. (1), Member States shall confer upon the courts or administrative authorities powers enabling them, in cases where they deem such measures to be necessary taking into account all the interests involved and in particular the public interest: (a) to order the cessation of or to institute appropriate legal proceedings for an order for the cessation of unfair commercial practices; or (b) if the unfair commercial practice has not yet been carried out but is imminent, to order the prohibition of the practice, or to institute appropriate legal proceedings for an order for the prohibition of the practice, even without proof of actual loss or damage or of intention or negligence on the part of the trader.'

[138] See Art. 8(1)(f) of the GPS Directive, *supra* note 30: '[f]or the purpose of this Directive, and in particular of Article 6 thereof, the competent authorities of the Member States shall be entitled to take, inter alia, the measures in (a) and (b) to (f) below, where appropriate:

(f) for any dangerous product already on the market:
   (i) to order or to organise its actual and immediate withdrawal and alert consumers to the risks it presents
   (ii) to order or coordinate or, if appropriate to organise together with producers and distributors its recall from consumers and its destruction in suitable conditions'.

[139] See *ibid.*, Art. 2(g): ' "recall" shall mean any measure at achieving the return of a dangerous product that has already been supplied or made available to consumers by the producer or distributor'.

[140] See *ibid.*, Art. 2(h): ' "withdrawal" shall mean any measure aimed at preventing the distribution, display and offer of a product dangerous to the consumer'. The wording of the procedures in Art. 8 is not entirely consistent with this distinction because withdrawal and recall both seem to refer to products already on the market.

Producers who are or become aware of the dangerous nature of a product should recall or withdraw it.[141] Lack of prompt action can trigger liability through not having taken appropriate measures.[142] Evidence shows that producers are generally effective at recalling products from the market when there is a serious risk to consumers.[143]

When action is not taken by producers it can be prompted or ordered by competent authorities.[144] The effective conditions under which the choice between product withdrawal and recall has to take place are not spelled out in the Directive.

In national legislations implementing the Directives, the conditions are spelled out in a little more detail, but significant discretion is still left to the decision-makers.[145] Both the decisions to recall and withdraw are taken by one or more coordinated, administrative authorities, but within a framework that promotes cooperation with manufacturers and distributors.[146] The relevance of consumers' cooperation also emerges both for the discovery of defects and for the effectiveness of the recall.[147] While it may appear at first sight an example of command and control, in practice it has often translated into cooperative regulation.

Two interesting features of the remedial structure associated with defective or dangerous products should be analysed. The first relates to the current structure of complementarity, implicitly defined by the two Directives (PL 85/374 and GPS 01/95). The second is associated with the relatively 'cooperative' nature of the process through which the relevant actors, and particularly the competent authorities, reach decisions concerning which control and which remedies should be used.

---

[141] See Art. 5(1)(b) of Directive 2001/95, *supra* note 30: '[w]ithin the limits of their respective activities producers shall adopt measures commensurate with the characteristics of the products which they supply, enabling them to:

(a) . . .

(b) choose to take appropriate action including, if necessary to avoid these risks, withdrawal from the market, adequately and effectively warning consumers or recall from consumers'.

[142] Such liability is based on national civil liability systems and not on the PL Directive, *supra* note 29.

[143] For the UK see Department of Trade and Industry, Consumer Affairs Directorate, *Transposing the Revised General Product Safety Directive* (2001).

[144] See Art. 8 of the GPS Directive, *supra* note 30.

[145] Formally the competent authorities; *de facto* it is often a consensual decision by administrative authorities and producers.

[146] See Commission Decision 2004/418, *supra* note 87: '[o]ther measures and actions that authorities can adopt or take and should notify are:

– agreements with producers and distributors to take actions necessary to avoid risks posed by products;

– agreements with producers and distributors to organise jointly the withdrawal, the recall of products from consumers and their destruction or any other relevant action;

– agreements with producers and distributors to coordinate the recall of a product from consumers and its destruction'.

[147] See Art. 8 of the GPS Directive, *supra* note 30, and the section concerning monitoring compliance, above. See, e.g., Art. 6(7) of the Italian decreto legislativo 172, 21 May 2004, implementing the Directive.

The remedial structure, defined by the two Directives together, seems clearly to distinguish between: (1) compensation, based on the liability system articulated in the PL Directive; and (2) deterrence, implemented through 'regulatory' devices, and in particular the GPS Directive. The fact that withdrawal and recall are administered not by the judiciary but by administrative authorities means that such authorities have been considered institutionally better equipped to evaluate the desirability of these measures and the means of implementation.

The relevance of the principle of proportionality for the decision-making process undertaken by an authority is well spelled out.[148]

As mentioned, this conclusion does not imply that each Member State's legal system could not permit judges to order a manufacturer to recall a defective product or to withdraw it and subject its marketing to specific safety conditions. No specific limitations on exercising this option have been introduced by the Directives, and national civil liability systems often give this option.[149]

What are the possible reasons for giving administrative authorities the power to recall a product or to withdraw it from the market at the European level? Two sets of reasons can be identified: the first is institutional, and the second is substantive, but connected with the institutional framework. On the institutional side the traditional argument against a judicial product recall is time: it has to be simultaneously a prompt and also a very thoughtful decision. Often, at least in many legal systems, judges may lack sufficient time to decide promptly, especially when the features of the product are such that harm is at least potentially very high. On the other hand, the nature of judicial intervention is such that it is the result of a dispute whose features are generally associated with a relatively small number of litigants when compared with those that can be negatively/positively affected by the decision.

In this context it may be difficult to admit evidence that takes into account the needs and positions of consumers other than those involved in the litigation. This analysis would be particularly useful in relation to a product where the preferred level of safety may differ for various classes of consumers.[150] Not to mention the situation in which other considerations, concerning for example environmental protection, may need to be taken into account. There is some evidence, although not yet conclusive, that these conditions are better associated with administrative authorities than with the judiciary. Such a complex and multi-layered analysis would be better

---

[148] See Art. 8(2) of GPS Directive, *supra* note 30: '[w]hen the competent authorities of the member states take measures such as those provided for in paragraph 1, in particular those referred to in (d) to (f) they shall act in accordance with the treaty and in particular Articles 28 and 30 thereof in such a way as to implement measures in a manner proportional to seriousness of the risk and taking due account of the precautionary principle. In this context they shall encourage and promote voluntary action by producers and distributors in accordance with obligations incumbent on them under the Directive and in particular Chapter III thereof, including where applicable by the development of codes of good practice'.

[149] But see *supra* text and notes 106–7, 134 on the potential implications of ECJ case-law.

[150] See again the GPS Directive, *supra* note 30.

taking place in a setting in which the regulator is or should be adequately equipped to evaluate the opportunity to adopt different remedies concerning how the product is to be introduced onto the market, and also, where necessary, recalling it.

A second set of reasons is substantive. While the solution of a final recall is certainly available, the possibility of a partial or temporary recall is more attractive, aimed at reintroducing the product to the market once the problem is solved. It is important that there is a monitoring system in place to administer these solutions. Judges could monitor only with great difficulty, assuming they had the power and resources to do so. Moreover, since often the products to be recalled are sold in the whole of the European market, a cooperative system among regulatory authorities is required. Such a system is developing among administrative authorities, while it is not yet available among the national judiciaries.

For these reasons, while the choice on liability initially made by the Directive seemed inappropriate because it severely limited the available set of remedies, it appears more acceptable if it is framed in a context of institutional complementarity. Seen in the light of the GPS Directive, the lack of injunctive relief appears less problematic.

The functional allocation between regulation and liability suggests that remedies concerning large numbers of dangerous defectively designed products should take place under the GPS Directive, while more specific and relatively diffused defects should be remedied under the PL Directive. The key feature is related to a design defect and the way in which the two systems interact. It can be inferred that while the regulatory Directive ought to apply as soon as the danger becomes known, the PL Directive can apply only when harms materialize. But if, for whatever reason, the administrative authority has not intervened and a judge finds a product to have been defectively designed, should the competent authority intervene, at least to verify whether the defectively designed product should be recalled? A coordination mechanism should require administrative authorities to examine the matter.

Analogous problems may occur in the field of failure to warn, especially if judges not only order pecuniary sanctions but impose informational requirements on producers and distributors.

Coordination mechanisms between judicially defined duties to warn and regulatory information requirements are strategically very relevant, both at the standard-setting and the remedial level to ensure that a consistent overall regulatory strategy is applied.

9. CIVIL LIABILITY TO ENSURE EFFECTIVE REGULATION? THE LIABILITY OF REGULATORS IN THE FIELD OF PRODUCT SAFETY AND ENVIRONMENTAL PROTECTION

The shift towards regulation or the increasing importance of product safety regulation poses problems associated with its effectiveness in all domains: standard-setting, monitoring, and enforcement. The effectiveness of regulation as a risk management system for product safety is partly dependent upon regulators' liability. Civil liability of regulators may contribute to realizing a diffuse control mechanism for dealing with omission or defective regulation. The civil liability system here is not a complement of regulation, but it constitutes an integral part of the regulatory system affecting its efficacy and accountability. Changes in actors and techniques influence the articulation of the regulators' liability system. But who are the regulators in the field of product safety?

The identity of product safety and environmental regulators and the modes of regulation have changed in the past 20 years, especially since the adoption of the new approach.[151] The importance of private standardization bodies has increased. Their role has changed in particular with the Normalization Directive of 1998,[152] and their relevance has been recognized even more by the GPS Directive. Within this pattern a growing importance is attributed to European standardizing bodies.[153] Other private actors populate the regulatory scene in the areas of product safety and environmental protection.[154] Consumers' associations play an increasing regulatory role in relation to both safety and environmental protection. Trade associations have also increased their influence. Furthermore, it is important to underline that private regulators are called to play a strategic role, not only in standard-setting but also in relation to monitoring and enforcement.[155] The role of private actors in the regulatory chain has also been recognized. It has already been mentioned that, both

---

[151] See Scott and Black, *supra* note 7, at 390: '[the] highly detailed vertical measures of regulation from the EC have, since the 1980s, been gradually displaced by so-called "new approach" or "framework" directives. These legislative instruments set out minimum requirements while leaving the filling in of much of the detailed to voluntary standards and "soft law" '. See also Calais-Aulois and Steinmetz, *supra* note 108, at 301, '[l]es premières directives verticales contenaient des règles techniques extrêmement précises. Devant l'ampleur de la tâche, une "nouvelle approche" fut entreprise en 1984: les directives se bornent à poser pour chaque produit, les exigences fondamentales; elle n'ont pas à entrer dans le détailles de spécification techniques: celle-ci relèvent des normes élaborées par les organismes de normalisation. Il existe une vingtaine des directives "nouvelle approche", concernant des produits très variés'.

[152] See Vos, *supra* note 14; Schepel and Falke, *supra* note 55.

[153] See Communication on Standardisation, *supra* note 57.

[154] See Scott and Black, *supra* note 7, at 383, where the authors state that '[c]ontemporary product safety regimes (both within the UK and in other jurisdictions) often generate a hierarchy of norms, within which the presence of detailed statutory standards take precedence but if there are no such statutory standards then private or industry standards govern the products. Only when there are no detailed standards of any kind can enforcement officers and courts fall back on general product safety standards which, because they are necessarily open-textured, give wide discretion in their interpretation. In practice the detailed content of general safety standards is often filled in by private standards set by standardisation institutions or industry groups. It is argued that the presence of the capacity of government to set statutory standards encourages industry to develop effective self-regulation, obviating the need for statutory approach'.

[155] Consider in the UK, e.g., where, on the basis of the Enterprise Act, Part 8 (Stop Now Orders), the Consumers' Association is given the right to use Stop Now Orders to clamp down on traders who harm the collective interests of consumers. The French legal system has similar enforcement devices for designated consumer associations.

in monitoring and enforcement, producers and distributors in the field of product safety and polluters in the area of environmental liability can play a key role in gathering information about risks and managing safety-related risks.[156] The new regulatory roles played by private actors combine well with the new responsibilities of public regulators in relation, for example, to product recall and withdrawal.[157] How has this growing importance of private regulators translated into a change in the liability regime of regulators?

We should distinguish between liability of public and private regulators. While the liability of public authorities is relatively well defined, even though not homogeneous across all the Member States, the liability of private regulators that combine with public regulators in setting standards, monitoring compliance, or enforcing the rules is relatively less clear.[158] It is unclear whether the liability regime applicable to these bodies is analogous to that of public regulators or whether it remains that of private organizations with some adjustments due to the nature of the activity in question (regulation in the public interest). Current private law instruments do not offer satisfactory responses and a new framework is needed.[159]

10. A COORDINATED APPROACH TO CIVIL LIABILITY AND REGULATION FOR SAFE PRODUCTS AT THE EUROPEAN LEVEL? WHAT ARE THE IMPLICATIONS FOR HARMONIZATION STRATEGIES?

The interaction of civil liability and regulation in a European perspective should be related to the strategies of European harmonization The issue should be framed in the context of the broader question of the relationship between consumer protection, health and safety protection, and market integration.[160]

Before addressing the theme of future strategies of harmonization in the area of product safety and environmental protection in the light of the institutional complementarity approach, it is useful to address the preliminary question of the relationship

---

[156] See *supra* text to notes 14 ff.

[157] See *supra* text to notes 14 ff.

[158] On this topic see Cafaggi, *supra* note 17.

[159] For this conclusion see *ibid.*

[160] See Weatherill, 'Consumer Policy', in P. Craig and G. de Búrca, *The Evolution of EU Law* (1999), at 702 ff.; *id. supra* note 30; and *id.*, 'Why Object to the Harmonization of Private Law by the EC?' [2004] *ERPL* 633, at 635: 'harmonization at EC level was required. So the strict constitutional purpose of harmonization was originally rule-making designed to make an integrated market, but its effect was to allocate to the Community level (albeit typically not exclusively) the competence to decide on the substance of the rules in question'. The ECJ has defined the relationship between consumer protection and market integration in recent cases. See Case C-52/00, *Commission v France, supra* note 108, at para. 15.

between harmonization, market integration, and regulation.[161] This relationship can take different forms:

(1) harmonization without regulation;
(2) regulation without harmonization; and
(3) combined yet not necessarily symmetric levels of harmonization and regulation.

Harmonization without regulation can take place when there is de-regulation through pure negative integration. Regulation without (hierarchical) harmonization can take place in the regulatory competition context.[162] Such competition can, for example, use international private law as a regulatory device.[163] In this discussion, the focus will be on the combination between harmonization and regulation, since the field has been both partially harmonized and partially regulated.

The harmonization strategies in the field of product safety have proceeded separately and, as was analysed earlier, coordination has often been purely negative, i.e. the more recent Directives provide that rights protected by previous Directives should not be affected. Both Directives in the field of product safety were enacted to define minimum standards that Member States could increase in their national standards.[164] As mentioned, recent interventions of the ECJ in the field of product liability pose more serious questions concerning the level of harmonization, shifting from a minimum harmonization perspective to total harmonization.[165] The landscape has therefore

---

[161] For a more detailed analysis see Cafaggi, *supra* note 17.

[162] See *ex multis*, D. Esty and D. Géradin (eds), *Regulatory Competition and Economic Integration* (2001); W. Bratton *et al.* (eds), *International Regulatory Competition and Coordination* (1996).

[163] See, e.g., Muir Watt, 'Experiences from Europe: Legal Diversity and the Internal Market', 39 *Texas Int'l LJ* (Spring 2004) 429; *ead.*, 'The Challenges of Market Integration for European Conflicts Theory', in Hartkamp *et al.*, *supra* note 13, at 191 ff.; Way, 'Transnational Liftoff and Judicial Touchdown: The Regulatory Function of Private International Law in an Era of Globalisation', 40 *Columbia J Transnat'l L* (2002) 209.

[164] See Art. 3(4) of the GPS Directive, *supra* note 30, and Art. 13 of the PL Directive, *supra* note 29. Art. 3(4) states: '[c]onformity of a product with the criteria designed to the ensure general safety requirement, in particular the provisions mentioned in paragraphs 2 or 3, shall not bar the competent authorities of the Member states from taking appropriate measures to impose restrictions on its being placed on the market or to require its withdrawal from the market or recall where there is evidence that, despite such conformity, it is dangerous'. Art. 13 states: '[t]his Directive shall not affect any rights which an injured person may have according to the rules of the law of contractual or non-contractual liability or special liability system existing at the moment when this directive is notified'. In general for the competence system on consumer protection see Weatherill, *supra* note 160, at 641: '[t]he consumer protection title limits the EC to measures that supplement State action, pursuant to article 153(3)(b). Arts. 176, 137 and 153 EC Treaty, governing competences to legislate in the fields of environmental protection, social policy and consumer protection respectively, stipulate that national measures that are stricter than the agreed Community standards are permitted. So common EC Rules are of a minimum nature'. See also *id.*, 'Competence Creep and Competence Control', 23 *YEEL* (2004) 1.

[165] See Case C-52/00, *Commission v France, supra* note 108, at paras. 20, 21, 22, 23, and 24; Case C-183/00, *Maria Victoria Gonzales Sanchez v Medicina Asturiana SA* [2002] ECR I-03901; Case C-154/00, *Commission v Hellenic Republic* [2002] ECR I-03879. These judgments have been strongly

changed: while product liability is 'fully' harmonized in so far as the questions touched by the PL Directive are the object of harmonization, product safety continues to be harmonized only as far as minimum standards are concerned.[166]

An additional difference between liability and regulation should be considered. While administrative regulation concerning product safety and environmental standards is subject to mutual recognition, but for few exceptions, the liability system is generally not.[167] It should be clarified that mutual recognition has not worked homogeneously across different modes of regulation. Much more problematic has been mutual recognition for privately defined technical standards. The new forms of regulation, incorporating privately set technical standards, therefore pose a serious challenge to the strategy of mutual recognition. Thus in the regulatory domain a serious problem concerning negative integration is related to the different regimes of administrative and private regulation in relation to freedom of goods. While the first are scrutinized under Article 28 EC, the second are only considered under the umbrella of competition law (Article 81 EC).[168] This distinction implies, for example, that technical standards produced by public regulators are evaluated under Article 28, while those produced by private bodies are evaluated under Article 81. This conclusion poses even greater problems once it is applied to self-regulation and

criticized because they do not correctly interpret Art. 13 of Directive 374/85, *supra* note 29. On the role of these cases see van Gerven, *supra* note 9, at 112. For a critique see Howells, *supra* note 84, at 645; Cafaggi, *supra* note 27; Joerges, 'On the Legitimacy of Europeanisation of Private Law: Considerations on Justi(ce)-fication (*justum facere*) for the EU Multi-level System', in Hartkamp *et al.*, *supra* note 13, at 178.

[166] See Case C-52/00, *Commission* v *France*, *supra* note 108, at paras. 20, 21, 22, 23, and 24. See also Calais-Auloy and Steinmetz, *supra* note 108, at 329.

[167] For the use of mutual recognition as the harmonizing technique in the field of product safety standards see recs. 29 and 30 of the GPS Directive, *supra* note 30:

(29)   It is primarily for the member states in compliance with Articles 28, 29 and 30 thereof to take appropriate measures with regard to dangerous products located within their territory.

(30)   However, if the member States differ as regards the approach to dealing with the risk posed by certain products, such differences could entail unacceptable disparities in consumer protection and constitute a barrier to intra-community trade.

Note, however, that Art. 3(3)(b) of the Directive mentions among the elements upon which conformity to the general safety requirement should be assessed the standards drawn up in the Member State in which the product is marketed. This criterion suggests that when the place of manufacturing and place of marketing are different, both should be taken into account.

[168] See Calais-Aulois and Steinmetz, supra note 108, at 300, 'Nous savons que l'article 28 du Traité CE (ancien article 30) interdit, entre Etats Membres de l'Union Européenne, les restrictions quantitatives à l'importation "ainsi que toutes mesures d'effet équivalent". Si elle était appliqué telle quelle, l'interdiction serai dangereuse pour la santé et la sécurité des consommateurs, puisqu'elle empêcherait chaque Etat membre des prendre des règles de sécurité plus rigoureuses que celles des autres Etats membres et qu'elle conduirait ainsi à une alignement des législation par les bas. Ils ont admis, dans l'article 30 (ancien article 36), des dérogations à l'article 28, notamment pour des raisons des "protection de la santé et de la vie des personnes et des animaux". La protection de la santé est considéré comme plus importante que la libre circulation des marchandises. Il en résulte que les règles nationales concernant la sécurité des produits peuvent valablement entraver le commerce intra-communautaire'.

private regulation in the fields of product safety and environmental protection.[169] Privately defined standards whose production has been delegated to private bodies or has been recognized *ex post* by public authorities fall into a grey area.[170]

The main problems for a fully integrated approach to liability and regulation are related to civil liability. In this field mutual recognition is not yet applied except in a few exceptions. Standards defined by courts are therefore purely domestic, unless a Directive harmonizes them. To the extent that the PL Directive operates, stand-ard harmonization occurs at European level, while, for those aspects left to Member States, the degree of heterogeneity is higher. Perhaps lack of debate is due to lack of recognition of the regulatory function of civil liability. In this context judicially defined standards are not mutually recognized.[171] They circulate more as 'case-law'

---

[169] See Temmink, *supra* note 46, at 61 ff.

[170] When there is state or public intervention the ECJ has been willing to allow scrutiny under Art. 28. See Schepel, *supra* note 15.

[171] See however Directive 98/27, *supra* note 135, on injunctions for the protection of consumer inter-ests in relation to standing. Recital (11) and Art. 4. of Recital (11) states that: '[w]hereas for the purpose of intra-community infringements the principle of mutual recognition should apply to these bodies and/or organisations whereas the member states should, at the request of their national entities, communicate to the Commission the name and the purpose of their national entities which are qualified to bring an action in their own country according to the provisions of this directive'. Art. 4(1) states that: '[i]ntra-community infringements Each member-state shall take the measures necessary to ensure that, in the event of an infringement originating in that Member State, any qualified entity from another member state where the interests protected by that qualified entity are affected by the infringements, may seize the court or admin-istrative authority referred to in Article 2 on the presentation of the list provided for in paragraph 3. The Courts or administrative authorities shall accept this list as proof of the legal capacity of the qualified entity without prejudice to their right to examine whether the purpose of the qualified entity justifies its taking action in a specific case'. See also Regulation (EC) No 2006/2004 of the European Parliament and of the Council of 27 October 2004 on cooperation between national authorities responsible for the enforcement of the consumer protection law (Regulation on consumer protection cooperation), OJ 2004 L 364/01. At Art. 9(2) on coordination of market surveillance and enforcement activities, it states: '[w]hen competent authorities become aware that an intra-Community infringement harms the interests of consumers in more than two Member States, the competent authorities concerned shall coordinate their enforcement actions and requests for mutual assistance via the single liaison office. In particular they shall seek to conduct simul-taneous investigations and enforcement measures'; while at Art. 16(1) on enforcement coordination, it states: '1. To the extent necessary to achieve the objectives of this Regulation, Member States shall inform each other and the Commission of their activities of Community interest in areas such as:

  (a) the training of their consumer protection enforcement officials, including language training and the organisation of training seminars;
  (b) the collection and classification of consumer complaints;
  (c) the development of sector-specific networks of competent officials;
  (d) the development of information and communication tools;
  (e) the development of standards, methodologies and guidelines for consumer protection enforce-ment officials;
  (f) the exchange of their officials.

Member States may, in cooperation with the Commission, carry out common activities in the areas referred to in (a) to (f). The Member States shall, in cooperation with the Commission, develop a common framework for the classification of consumer complaints'.

through comparative law references employed by the judiciary both at national and European level.[172]

How should mutual recognition or some type of functional equivalent operate, if at all possible, in the context of a coordinated strategy between regulation and liability? If one recognizes the regulatory function of civil liability, the standards set by judges in relation to defectiveness could be considered as a source of interpretation by the courts of other legal systems in which the product is circulated.[173] Lack of mutual recognition or alternative solutions coordinating regulatory and liability standards pose a serious risk of diverging judicial opinions concerning product standards, even if they operate within the framework of the PL Directive.[174] Certainly the ECJ can reduce these problems, but only to a limited extent.

The more general question concerning governance of normative differences stemming from minimal harmonization of product safety and environmental protection cannot be avoided. In particular a crucial issue is that of different modes and degrees of enforcement.[175]

[172] It should be mentioned that a strategic role can be played by the common principles of tort law elaborated by the ECJ in relation to liability for breach of Community law while applying Art. 288(2). The rule-finding exercise of the ECJ develops a peculiar multi-level rule-finding system. See for example Joined Cases *Brasserie du Pêcheur and Factortame* [1996] ECR I-1029, and AG Tesauro's Opinion ECR I-1066 where compensation and the duty to mitigate damage by the victim were clearly identified; in particular see paras 80–87. On these matters van Gerven, 'Taking Art. 215(2) EC Treaty seriously', in J. Beatson and T. Tridimas (eds), *New Directions in European Public Law* (1998), 36 ff., Lenaerts, 'Interlocking Legal Orders in the European Union and Comparative Law', 52 *ICLQ* (2003) at 873. For a critical view of the role of the ECJ see Weatherill, *supra* note 160, at 637: '[t]he Court's view is commonly that once a legal concept is embedded within a harmonization directive it cannot be allowed to depend for its meaning on local preference or tradition. In order to make real the harmonized nature of the regime it must be endowed with an autonomous European meaning'. See *Fairchild (suing on her own behalf) etc.* v *Glenhaven Funeral Services Ltd and others etc.* [2002] UKHL 22.

[173] Currently such a system could be implemented by referring to the duty of sincere cooperation in Art. 10 EC as applied to courts. I am indebted to Bruno de Witte for this suggestion. Several practical problems should however be tackled if this option were to be used: Which judgments should be considered? Only those of Supreme Courts? What if precedents are not entirely consistent?

[174] According to Calais-Aulois and Steinmetz, *supra* note 108, at. 602, a system of mutual recognition has been introduced by Directive 98/27.

[175] See Husu-Kallio, *Welcome Address Conference on European Market Surveillance Programming*, Brussels, 10 March 2005 (available at http://europa.eu.int/comm/consumer): '[w]hile a comprehensive and largely harmonised framework of consumer product rules and standards exists, the approaches, means, instruments and practices for market surveillance and enforcement are in general very diverse. The differences are at least partly rooted in the different internal institutional and administrative systems of the member states and are an unavoidable part of our diversity. Traditionally enforcement has been considered a matter covered by subsidiarity considerations. This has led to a variety of methods and internal organisations of national authorities. We have to take this fact into account in looking for ways to achieve the optimal enforcement of product legislation that we are aiming for'. See Communication from the Commission to the European Parliament, the Council, the Economic and Social Committee and the Committee of the Regions Consumer policy strategy 2002–2006, COM(2002)208 final. The European Commission has welcomed private initiatives on monitoring and enforcement. For example, it has published private initiatives on its official website: Mouvement des Entreprises de France (MEDEF), Initiating

If the optimal approach is multi-level regulation, in particular to define minimum standards at European level and to allow Member States to increase the level of protection, the crucial question is how to govern excessive divergences that could undermine harmonization without resorting to complete harmonization. Reference to the ECJ to ensure coherent interpretation of the Directive may not be the most effective instrument. A governance mechanism that monitors standards implementation to which both regulators and judges contribute would be highly desirable. The legal basis for this can be found in Article 153(3.b) EC. Coordination mechanisms in both the fields of product safety and environmental protection are already in place for administrative authorities.[176] In the short term, the most plausible institutional strategy is to empower them with a stronger coordination function.[177] In the long run, a more sophisticated mechanism should be devised to monitor standard-setting and compliance, to ensure that divergences are compatible with the harmonization strategy and will not become barriers to trade, impermissible under Article 28 EC.

11. CONCLUDING REMARKS

The influence of regulation, both administrative and private, on European civil liability has been a relatively neglected topic. Similarly the influence of civil liability

a Code Of Conduct for European Governance, 2001. Specific proposals concerning mutual recognition of judgments relating to consumer law in relation to injunctions have been made. See Calais-Aulois and Steinmetz, *supra* note 108, at 602: '[d]ans l'état actuel du droit, il faut appliquer le règlement communautaire du 22 décembre 2000, qui prévoit une procédure d'exequatur peu compatible avec la nécessaire rapidité de la cessation. Pourquoi ne pas admettre, en cas d'infraction à une directive, que le jugement de cessation rendu dans un Etat membre soit de plein droit exécutoire dans les autres Etats membres ?. . . . La réforme, certes, est ambitieuse; elle supposerait une réforme du règlement du décembre 2000'.

The risks of mutual recognition have also been highlighted and compared with alternative solutions based on uniform rules of conflict of laws. See in this volume H. Muir Watt, 'Integration and Diversity: The Conflict of Laws as a Regulatory Tool', at Chap. 4.

[176] See Art. 10 of the GPS Directive, *supra* note 30: '1. The Commission shall promote and take part in the operation of a European network of authorities of the Member States competent for product safety, in particular in the form of administrative cooperation.

2. This network operation shall develop in a coordinated manner with the other existing community procedures, particularly RAPEX. Its objective shall be in particular to facilitate:

(a) the exchange of information on risk assessment, dangerous products, test methods and result, scientific developments as well as other aspects for relevant control activities;
(b) the establishment and execution of joint surveillance and testing projects;
(c) the exchange and expertise and best practices and cooperation in training activities;
(d) improved cooperation at Community level with regard to the tracing, withdrawal or recall of dangerous products'.

[177] Coordination of administrative authorities takes place both within the RAPEX system and the European Safety Network in the field of product safety and according to sectoral legislation with the Recreational Craft Administrative Cooperation Group, Market Surveillance in the Machinery sector, among other examples.

on regulation is generally not deeply analysed. Often the regulatory space is defined without considering the actual and potential role of civil liability.

Changes in the regulatory environment do not allow the juxtaposition of regulation as a centralized rigid system of risk management and civil liability as a highly decentralized, bottom-up regulatory system. New regulatory techniques, especially incentive-based, have introduced a high level of decentralization which has dramatically reduced monitoring and compliance costs while, to a lesser extent, increasing coordination costs.[178]

This chapter has raised two questions on the positive dimension:

(1) Whether there is any explicit or implicit coordination between regulation and civil liability in the field of European environmental protection and product safety; and
(2) What each 'strategy' could learn from the other.

On the normative dimension this essay has focused on whether higher coordination is desirable and what 'institutional' consequences such coordination may bring about in terms of liability of regulators and harmonization strategies.

The analysis has shown that (1) on a positive level there is reciprocal influence of the two techniques, and (2) on a normative level a higher degree of coordination is desirable at European and national level in the field of environmental protection and product safety. Such coordination presupposes an effective system of liability for regulators and more coherent harmonization strategies. Such strategies should not focus solely on legislative harmonization, but rather they should consider multi-level rule-finding techniques such as those developed by the ECJ in the area of extracontractual liability of European and national institutions. The importance of rule-finding is strategic, and that methodology should also be expanded to regulatory law.

As to the mutual learning aspect, recent developments of regulatory techniques, incorporated into the European legislative framework, can provide powerful insights for the civil liability system. While the complexity of regulatory analysis, favoured by the frequent use of regulatory impact assessment, cannot be entirely mimicked in the civil liability area, the adoption of impact evaluation for the most important judicial decisions should be promoted both at European and at national level. Awareness and transparency of the efficiency and distribution effects of civil liability judgments through impact evaluation assessment could also improve the proposed coordinated strategy.

While economic reasons, mainly associated with the costs of administrative regulation and some of the transformation of the regulatory State, have recently overburdened civil liability with functions related to risk assessment and risk management, the more useful perspective is to conceive of civil liability and regulation as functional complements rather than functional equivalents in relation to both deterrence and compensation.

---

[178] See in relation to the environment for the USA, Stewart, *supra* note 4, at 9.

What are the main differences between regulation and civil liability within a coordinated strategy?

While regulation, especially the type based on cost-benefit analysis, is grounded on risk assessment that permits the differentiation of risks and the weighing of them in relation to the decision on whether and how to regulate, civil liability tends to be over-inclusive once it is in place. In civil liability internal partitioning concerning risk management has occurred over the centuries in relation to different risks (for example, liability for the acts of wild animals versus liability for dangerous activities), between negligence and strict liability and within each regime. Within civil liability, however, environmental and product-related risks are still considered relatively homogeneous in comparison to the level of specification and differentiation recently employed in the regulatory field. Such highly tailored regulation has made possible the introduction of different forms of incentive-based regulations but also the consolidation of a 'negotiated' system of command and control.[179]

When the level of risk differentiation is very high, civil liability may perform better. The strong decentralized decision-making system of civil liability permits highly specific and relatively idiosyncratic factors to be taken into account.

Regulation still performs better for highly homogeneous risks and when they are coupled with relatively homogeneous harms. On the contrary, when homogeneity of risks and harms is low, civil liability can be a better device.

Regulation is preferable to civil liability when the cost-benefit analysis encompasses several risk–risk and benefit–benefit analyses, i.e when, within the same regulation or in different regulations, trade-offs among risks and among benefits have to be made. Civil liability is relatively ill-suited to such trade-offs, and the selection of litigants may affect the ability of the judge to evaluate the external risks and benefits of the decision concerning product defectiveness and consequent remedies.

In the area of monitoring compliance, clearly civil liability may be insufficient. Furthermore, to leave the parties to bear the costs, especially when they are potential victims, may have unwelcome distributional consequences. The Directives on product safety have introduced a coordinated system of monitoring using regulation, and criminal and civil liability.

Regulatory monitoring systems that impose specific duties on parties to organize network monitoring may satisfactorily complement the existing incentives for potential injurers and victims both to detect unknown risks and to monitor known hazards.

In the domain of enforcement a strategy that distinguishes *ex ante* from *ex post* remedies has become obsolete. The preventive nature of civil liability suggests the coupling of compensatory remedies with injunctions. The difference should not be based primarily on the nature of the remedy but (1) on the conditions to which they are subject, (2) on the institutions that administer them, and (3) on the effects, general or specific, they produce.

---

[179] See for a comparative analysis Stewart, *supra* note 4, at 9 ff.

The level of coordination between regulation and civil liability is insufficient, both at European and national levels. Changes in the regulatory environment have already caused and will in future bring about important modifications of the liability system. Two main points have to be addressed for a coherent European institutional design:

(1) the choice between different approaches to regulation and liability: i.e the alternatives of sector-specificity or general effect; and

(2) the different harmonizing strategies: i.e. minimum versus complete harmonization.

Regulation of product safety is mainly based on specific products; and the GPS Directive is residual. The PL Directive includes all products. It remains to be demonstrated that there are good reasons for having different approaches, one specific and the other general. But even if there were good reasons for having fragmented regulatory Directives and a unified liability system the problem of coordination mechanisms remains, and is perhaps even more relevant. The same liability system has to be complemented by different regulatory strategies for drugs, food, toys, cars, etc.

Currently the degree of harmonization is different. From the multi-level regulation perspective such differences impose different balances between the European and the national levels for regulation and for liability. The current state is criticizable for this asymmetry. Such asymmetry again poses serious problems for vertical coordination even beyond functional complementarity.

European legislative intervention to integrate the different strategies is needed both in the field of product safety and in that of environmental protection. The means and the goals of the coordination should be on the agenda of future scholarship and policy-making.

7

Consumer Law, Competition Law and the Europeanization of Private Law

ALBERTINA ALBORS-LLORENS*

INTRODUCTION

The aim of this chapter is to relate two fields of Community competence—consumer law and competition law—to the growing process of Europeanization of private law, a topic which has been the subject of an intense academic debate over the past few years. From the outset we can appreciate a contrast in the perceived contributions of these two areas towards a harmonized system of private law. While secondary legislation and case-law in the field of consumer protection have been generally accepted as playing an important role in that process, comparatively less attention has been devoted to the contribution effected by competition law. This chapter has three main themes. First, it will consider the role of these two areas in the Europeanization of private law. Secondly, it will argue that through legislation and interpretation by the Community judicature, competition law has had a silent, but nevertheless effective, role in that process. Finally it will examine the increasing overlap and mutual influence between consumer law and competition law in the EC and their prospects as joint contributors to the gradual convergence of the European systems of private law.

1. CONSUMER LAW

A. The Development of Consumer Law in the EC[1]

The original version of the EC Treaty did not provide for a specific legal basis for action of the EC institutions in matters of consumer protection. There were only

---

* Lecturer in Law, University of Cambridge and Fellow, Girton College, Cambridge. I am extremely grateful to Joanne Scott for her very helpful comments on an earlier draft.
[1] For a comprehensive coverage of this topic see S. Weatherill, *EC Consumer Law and Policy* (1997) at 1–35; and G. Howells and T. Wilhelmsson, *EC Consumer Law* (1997) at 6–25.

four references to the interests of consumers. Two of these were made in the context of the objectives and organization of the Common Agricultural Policy[2] and the other two in the context of the competition provisions in the Treaty.[3] The latter provide a telling indication of the close links between competition law and consumer law, an issue that will be explored later in this chapter.[4] It was not until the signature of the Treaty of European Union in 1992 that a specific legal basis for action in the field of consumer protection was inserted into the Treaty.[5] However, legislation with an impact on consumer issues began to develop long before Maastricht,[6] mostly through the enactment of EC Directives based on Articles 94 EC (ex Article 100) and 95 EC (ex Article 100a).[7] These provisions allow the Council to adopt harmonizing legislation in the context of the establishment and functioning of the internal market. Directives adopted on the basis of these provisions constitute the bulk of consumer legislation in the Community. As Weatherill pointed out, harmonization legislation has acted as an 'indirect consumer policy'[8] and as an 'indirect form of regulatory activity'[9] because although these Directives were enacted with the prime purpose of contributing to market integration, they all had a clear effect on consumer issues. These Directives range from those on the protection of the economic and legal interests of consumers[10] to those impinging

---

[2] See Art. 33(1)(e) EC (ex Art. 39(1)(e)) which lists as one of the objectives of the CAP 'to ensure that supplies reach consumers at reasonable prices' and Art. 34(2) EC (ex Art. 40(2)), which enshrines the principle of non-discrimination in this field by stating that 'the common organisation shall be limited to the pursuit of the objectives set out in Article 33 and shall exclude any discrimination between producers or consumers within the Community'.

[3] See Art. 81(3) EC (ex Art. 85(3)), which provides that one of the conditions for an agreement, decision or concerted practice that falls within the prohibition in Art. 81(1) EC to benefit from an exemption is that it should allow 'consumers a fair share of the resulting benefit'. Furthermore, Art. 82 EC (ex Art. 86) lists as an abusive practice the limitation of 'production, markets or technical development to the prejudice of consumers' by a dominant company.

[4] See *infra* Section 2.C.

[5] See Art. 153 EC (ex Art. 129a).

[6] 'Soft law' had an important role in the field of consumer protection from the early 1970s (see Weatherill, *supra* note 1, at 9–12) and has continued to do so after Maastricht (*ibid.* at 28–30). For recent Commission initiatives see 'Consumer Policy Strategy 2000–2006' (COM (2002) 208 final).

[7] Art. 95 EC (ex Art. 100a) was introduced by the Single European Act and provides for the adoption of harmonization measures by qualified majority voting, while Art. 94 EC (ex Art. 100) provides for the adoption of measures by unanimity.

[8] See Weatherill, *supra* note 1, at 6.

[9] See S. Weatherill and P. Beaumont, *EU Law* (3rd edn, 1999), at 1037.

[10] See, e.g., Directive 85/577/EEC to protect the consumer in respect of contracts negotiated away from business premises (OJ 1985 L 372/31); Directive 87/102/EEC on consumer credit (OJ 1986 L 42/48); Directive 90/314 on package travel, holidays and package tours (OJ 1990 L 158/59); Directive 93/13 on unfair terms in consumer contracts (OJ 1993 L 95/29); Directive 94/47 on the protection of purchasers in respect of certain aspects of contracts relating to the purchase of the right to use immovable properties on a timeshare basis (OJ 1994 L 280/83); Directive 97/7/EC on the protection of consumers in respect of distance contracts (OJ 1997 L 144/19); Directive 98/27 on injunctions for the protection of consumers' interests (OJ 1998 L 166/51); Directive 1999/44 on certain aspects of the sale of consumer

on consumer health and safety[11] and on consumer information.[12] In recent years, however, the European Court of Justice has increasingly referred to *both* market integration *and* consumer protection as combined objectives of these Directives.[13]

Among recent developments, the Commission's proposal for a framework Directive destined to harmonize the relationship between unfair competition and consumer protection, which has very recently become the Unfair Commercial Practices Directive,[14] deserves special mention.[15]

The European Parliament and the Council have also used Article 95 EC as a legal basis to adopt Regulations with an impact on consumer protection, although on a much lesser scale than as a basis for Directives. The recent Regulations on genetically modified organisms are an example of this kind of unifying legislation.[16]

B. The Debate on the Europeanization of Private Law

The expression 'Europeanization' is understood in this context as the building of a new *ius Commune* in Europe through the intervention of EC law and the work of the EC institutions, and in particular, of the European Court of Justice (ECJ).

---

goods and associated guarantees (OJ 1999 L 171/2); Directive 2000/31 on legal aspects of information society services, in particular electronic commerce in the Internal Market (OJ 2000 L 178/1).

[11] See, e.g., Directive 76/769 on the restrictions on the marketing and use of certain dangerous substances (OJ 1976 L 262/201); Directive 85/374 on liability for defective products (OJ 1985 L 210/29); Directive 88/378 on the safety of toys (OJ 1988 L 187/1); Directive 93/15 on the placing on the market and supervision of explosives for civil uses (OJ 1993 L 121/20); Directive 98/53 on the sampling methods and forms of analysis for the official control of the levels for certain contaminants in foodstuffs (OJ 1998 L 201/93).

[12] See, e.g., Directive 84/450 on misleading advertising (OJ 1984 L 250/17, as amended by Directive 97/55, OJ 1997 L 290/18); Directive 2000/13 on labelling, presentation and advertising of foodstuffs (OJ 2000 L 109/29); Directive 2001/37 on the manufacture, presentation and sale of tobacco products (OJ 2001 L 194/26).

[13] See, e.g., Cases C-178, C-179, C-188, C-189, and C-190/94 *Dillenkofer* [1996] ECR I-4845, para. 39, where the Court, interpreting Directive 90/314, held that '. . . the recitals in the preamble to the Directive repeatedly refer to the purpose of protecting consumers. [T]he fact that the Directive is intended to assure other objectives cannot preclude its provisions from also having the aim of protecting consumers . . .'. See also the Opinion of Tizziano AG in Case C-168/00, *Leitner* [2002] ECR I-2631, at para. 3.

[14] This proposal (COM(2003)356 final) was presented by the Commission in June 2003 and represented a follow-up to the Green Paper on EU Consumer Protection (COM(2001)531 final). The final text of the Directive was approved on 11 May 2005 (OJ 2005 L 149/22).

[15] Other proposals include the proposal for a new Directive on consumer credit (COM(2002)443 final) and for a new Directive on injunctions for the protection of consumers' interests (COM(2003)241 final). If approved, these will replace the existing Directives in those fields (see *supra* note 10).

[16] See Regulation 1829/2003 (OJ 2003 L 268/1) on genetically modified food and feed; Regulation 1830/2003 (OJ 2003 L 268/24) on the traceability and labelling of genetically modified organisms and the traceability of food and feed products produced from genetically modified organisms; and Regulation 65/2004 (OJ 2004 L 10/5) establishing a system for the development and assignment of unique identifiers for genetically modified organisms.

The debate as to whether a comprehensive and systematic process of Europeanization is desirable has intensified in recent years.[17]

On the one hand, there are those who think that this specific goal is to be endorsed and acted upon. They advocate a unified system of private law, either through codification[18] or through the combined action of legislation, permeation of general principles developed by the ECJ and by the national courts, and comparative study of the solutions adopted by the national legal systems.[19] Codifiers, in particular, argue that there is much to be gained from a convergence of national systems in private law matters. Their arguments are chiefly economic. They argue, for example, that while a unification of contract law is not mandated by the Treaty in order to achieve the objectives of the internal market, it would undeniably ease the uncertainty which is currently associated with transnational contracts and would fortify and encourage commercial exchange in the Community.[20] More cautious[21]—but still sympathetic—viewers of this process include Zimmermann,[22] who emphasizes that contract law and company law 'are more than mere appendages to the free movement of goods, persons, services and capital'.[23] He observes that the basis for the development of a unified system of European private law would be the 'emergence of "an organically progressive" legal science, which would have to transcend national boundaries and disciplinary divides and which would revitalise a common tradition.'[24]

---

[17] See M. van Hoecke and F. Ost (eds), *The Harmonisation of European Private Law* (2000). For an excellent analysis of the wider phenomenon of globalization without state intervention see G. Teubner (ed.), *Global Law without a State* (1997).

[18] For arguments in favour of a European codification of contract law, see Lando, 'Optional or Mandatory Europeanization of Contract Law', 3 *ERPL* (1995) 59; Basedow, 'A Common Contract Law for the European Market', 33 *CML Rev* (1996) 1169. More nuanced approaches to codification would include non-legislative initiatives (Riedl, 'The Work of the Lando Commission from an Alternative Viewpoint', 8 *ERPL* (2000) 71) or the adoption of a European contract code with 'open-textured rules' (Chamboredon, 'The Debate on a European Civil Code: for an "Open Texture" ', in Hoecke and Ost (eds), *supra* note 17, at 63).

[19] See van Gerven, 'The Case Law of the European Court of Justice and National Courts as a Contribution to the Europeanization of Private Law', 3 *ERPL* (1995) 367, at 376–8; van Gerven, 'ECJ Case-law as a Means of Unification of Private Law?', 5 *ERPL* (1997) 293. See also Larouche, '*Ius Commune* Casebooks for the Common Law of Europe: Presentation, Progress and Rationale', 8 *ERLP* (2000) 101.

[20] See Basedow, *supra* note 18, at 1181–7.

[21] Concerns have been voiced because, while a gradual harmonization of private law seems to be taking place at a substantive level, co-ordination of national procedural standards seems to be lacking. See Schwartze, 'Enforcement of Private Law: the Missing Link in the Process of European Harmonisation', 8 *ERPL* (2000) 135, at 135–46.

[22] 'Savigny's Legacy, Legal History, Comparative Law and the Emergence of a European Legal Science', 112 *LQR* (1996) 576.

[23] *Ibid.*, at 583.

[24] *Ibid.*, at 605. Lando has classified his own approach to the unification of European Private Law as that of a 'codifier' in contrast to Zimmermann's approach, which is that of a 'cultivator'. See Lando, 'European Contract Law after 2000', 35 *CML Rev* (2000) 821, at 827.

On the other hand, there are those who reject this project of integration, mainly on the grounds of the profound differences between the legal systems of the Member States and between their approaches to legal science, and what is perceived as the insurmountable civil–common law divide.[25]

Despite these different perspectives on unification, it remains a fact that a degree of piecemeal Europeanization has occurred in the field of private law and that consumer protection law has been an important instrument in this process. The most cursory examination of the main texts on European private law yields the observation that many of the measures falling in that category deal with consumer protection.[26] Hence the importance that academic writers have ascribed to consumer Directives as contributors to the Europeanization of private law, and in particular of contract law.[27]

C. THE CONTRIBUTION OF THE CONSUMER PROTECTION DIRECTIVES TO THE EUROPEANIZATION OF PRIVATE LAW

As explained earlier, EC Directives with an impact on consumer issues were initially adopted with the chief purpose of promoting market integration. This supranational objective was to be achieved largely through the dismantling of barriers put in place by national authorities and not through the unification of the systems of private law in Europe. Therefore, it is not surprising that the degree of harmonization in private law matters that has resulted from these Directives, while important, has been on the whole fragmented and incidental. Furthermore, several of the consumer protection Directives focus only on the specific protection of the rights of the consumers in the pre-contractual bargaining period and in the period immediately after an agreement has been concluded. This restricts their general effect even further.[28] For example, Article 4 of Directive 97/7 EC on the protection of consumers in respect of distance contracts[29] sets out the information that should be made available to the consumer prior to the conclusion of any such contract,[30] while Articles 6, 7 and 8 outline the consumer's rights in the period immediately

---

[25] See Collins, 'European Private Law and Cultural Identity of States', 3 *ERPL* (1995) 353; Legrand, 'European Legal Systems are not Converging', 45 *ICLQ* (1996) 52 and 'Against a European Civil Code', 60 *MLR* (1997) 44.

[26] Directives in other fields include ones on commercial law, company law, banking law, insurance law, labour law, intellectual property law and telecommunications.

[27] See J. Smits, *The Making of European Private Law* (2002), at 13 and Reich, 'European Consumer Law and its Relationship to Private Law' 3 *ERPL* [1995], 285.

[28] See Weatherill, 'Prospects for the Development of European Private Law through *Europeanization* in the European Court–the case of the Directive on Unfair Terms in Consumer Contracts', 3 *ERLP* (1995) 307 at 313.

[29] *Supra* note 10.

[30] This information includes the identity of the supplier, the main characteristics of the goods or services, the price of the goods including taxes, delivery costs, the minimum duration of the contract, etc. Art. 5 of the Directive gives consumers the right to receive written confirmation of that information.

following the conclusion of a contract.[31] Other consumer Directives sharing this approach include Directive 85/577, which protects consumers in respect of contracts negotiated away from business premises[32] or Directive 90/314 on package travel, package holidays and package tours.[33] These Directives influenced the harmonization of consumer contract law especially after their provisions have been interpreted by the ECJ[34] but their potential 'spill-over' effect into the general contract law of the Member States seems to have been more limited.[35]

It can be argued, however, that the potential of some of the consumer Directives in the Europeanization process is far greater. An early example is found in the decision of the European Court in *Complaint against X (Nissan)*.[36] The case arose in the context of one of the Directives on consumer information: Directive 84/450 on misleading advertising.[37] There, the Court interpreted narrowly Article 2(2) of the Directive, which defines the term 'misleading'. In that case, the owner of a French garage advertised the sale of Nissan cars by saying 'buy your new vehicle cheaper'. The advertising referred to Nissan cars that had been imported from Belgium and which were cheaper than other imported Nissan cars because they had fewer accessories than the standard models sold in France. The exclusive importer of Nissan cars into France complained that such advertising was misleading. In particular, it contended that the cars could not be said to be 'new' because they had been registered before importation and that the claim that they were cheaper was also misleading.

The Court took a proactive stance. First, it held that the claim that the cars were new could not be considered as misleading because the newness of a car is not lost on registration but rather on being first driven on a public highway. The Court then left it to the national court to decide whether the advertising concealed the fact that the cars were already registered, or whether the fact that the cars were registered would have deterred consumers from purchasing the cars.[38] Secondly, the Court

---

[31] These include the right of withdrawal (Art. 6), the obligation of the supplier to execute the order within a maximum of 30 days following that on which the consumer forwarded the order (unless the parties have agreed otherwise) (Art. 7), or the right of a consumer to request cancellation of a payment where fraudulent use has been made of the consumer's payment card (Art. 8).

[32] See *supra* note 10.

[33] See *ibid*.

[34] See, e.g., Case C-361/89, *Criminal Proceedings against Patrice di Pinto* [1991] ECR I-1189, where the Court interpreted the notion of 'consumer' in Directive 85/577 or Case C-91/92, *Faccini Dori* v *Recreb* [1994] ECR I-3325, where the Court held, *inter alia*, that Art. 5 of that same Directive (regarding the minimum period within which notice of cancellation must be given) was unconditional and sufficiently precise. In the context of the interpretation of Directive 90/314 on package travel, package holidays and package tours, see Cases C-178, C-179, C-188, C-189 and C-190/94, *Dillenkofer* (*supra* note 13) where the Court interpreted, Art. 7 of that Directive in order to apply the conditions for State liability. The Court held that Art. 7 conferred rights on individuals and that the content of those rights was sufficiently identifiable.

[35] See Klauer, 'General Clauses in European Private Law and "Stricter" National Standards; the Unfair Terms Directives', 8 *ERPL* (2000) 187.

[36] Case C-373/90, [1992] ECR I-131.

[37] See *supra* note 12.

[38] Case C-373/90, *supra* note 36, paras. 13–15.

observed that the assertion that the cars in question were cheaper would only be misleading if consumers were not made aware that the cars had fewer accessories than other Nissan cars imported into France.[39]

The importance of this ruling is plain because it showed the Court interpreting the term 'misleading', which is absolutely central to Directive 84/450. Weatherill explained that although it would seem that the interpretation of this expression would be entirely dependent on the specific facts of a case, the Court was prepared to 'give it a European shade of meaning in a specific context in which its application is called for'.[40] The Court was careful to leave to the national court the assessment of the circumstances of the case and the final application to the facts, but it nevertheless provided clear guidance on how to interpret the term misleading in the context of advertising and parallel imports.

There are two consumer Directives whose potential to influence general contract law in the Member States has already been widely acknowledged.[41] These are Directive 93/13 on unfair terms in consumer contracts (hereinafter referred to as the Unfair Terms Directive) and Directive 1999/44/EC on aspects of the sale of consumer goods and associated guarantees.[42]

D. The Unfair Terms Directive

Directive 93/13 on unfair terms presents important differences in relation to previously enacted consumer protection Directives. Principally, and as observed by Weatherill, this Directive does not limit itself to regulating the rights of a consumer immediately before and after a transaction, but takes the extra step of regulating the 'fairness' of a contract.[43] In other words, the harmonization aim in this Directive evolves from protecting 'procedural fairness' to embracing the goal of 'substantive fairness'.[44] It is this trait that endows the Directive with significant potential in the process of Europeanization of contract law.[45]

The legal basis of the Directive is Article 95 EC and hence the prime role of the Directive as an instrument to facilitate market integration and the stimulation of

---

[39] *Ibid.*, para. 16.

[40] Weatherill, *supra* note 28, at 309–11.

[41] The *European Review of Private Law* dedicated special issues in 1995 and 2000 to Directives 93/13/EEC and 1999/44/EC respectively. See, in particular, the introductions to these issues by Joerges at 3 *ERPL* (1995) 173–5 and 8 *ERPL* (2000), pp. vii–x.

[42] *Supra* note 1.

[43] *EC Consumer Law and Policy, supra* note 1 at 77. Weatherill examines criticisms of this form of regulatory technique on the ground that it could be seen as being at variance with the principle of freedom of contract. He questions, however, whether the idea of free negotiation is still a reality in consumer contracts in modern market conditions (*ibid.*).

[44] *Ibid.*, at 78.

[45] See Pinto Monteiro, 'The Impact of the Directive on Unfair Terms in Consumer Contracts on Portuguese Law', 3 *ERPL* (1995) 231, at 234; Hondius, 'The Reception of the Directive on Unfair Terms in Consumer Contracts by Member States', 3 *ERPL* (1995) 241, at 254 and Klauer, *supra* note 35, at 190.

competition is patently clear in the opening paragraphs of the Preamble.[46] The Preamble goes on to refer, however, to the other important aim of the Directive, which is the protection of the economic interests of consumers, in particular against the abuse of power by a seller or supplier.[47]

I. The provisions and structure of the Unfair Terms Directive

The Directive, like other consumer Directives, provides for a minimum level of harmonization below which national legislation cannot fall, but leaves Member States freedom to impose higher standards of consumer protection.[48] Article 1 demarcates the legislative aim of the Directive, namely the approximation of 'the laws, regulations and administrative provisions of the Member States relating to unfair terms in contracts between a seller or supplier and a consumer'. Article 2 defines the notions of 'consumer' and of 'seller or supplier' for the purposes of application of the Directive.[49]

The substantive provisions of the Directive are set out in Articles 3 and 4. In particular, Article 3(1) reads:

(1) A contractual term which has not been individually negotiated shall be regarded as unfair if, contrary to the requirement of good faith, it causes a significant imbalance in the parties' rights and obligations arising under the contract, to the detriment of the consumer.

Two important points can be extracted from the wording of Article 3(1). First, it makes it clear that the subject matter of the Directive is *standard* terms, namely those that have not been individually negotiated. Secondly, it lays down that a term will qualify as unfair if: (a) it causes an imbalance in the parties' rights and obligations arising from the contract to the detriment of the consumer; and (b) it is contrary to the requirement of good faith.

Article 3(3) refers to the Annex to the Directive, which contains an indicative and non-exhaustive list of terms that may be regarded as *unfair*. Article 4(1) complements Article 3 by stating that:

the unfairness of a contractual term shall be assessed, taking into account the nature of the goods or services for which the contract was concluded and by referring, at the time

---

[46] See paras. 1–7 of the Preamble.

[47] See paras. 8–11 of the Preamble.

[48] See Art. 8 of the Directive. See also Dougan, 'Minimum Harmonization and the Internal Market', 37 *CML Rev* (2000) 853.

[49] Thus, the Directive defines as *consumer* 'any natural person who, in contracts covered by the Directive, is acting for purposes which are outside his trade, business or profession' (Art. 2(b)), and as *seller or supplier* 'any natural or legal person who, in contracts covered by the Directive, is acting for purposes relating to his trade, business or profession, whether publicly owned or privately owned' (Art. 2(c)). The concept of *consumer* was interpreted by the Court in Joined Cases C-541 and C-542/99, *Cape v Idealservice* [2001] ECR I-9049, where the Court held that this notion referred only to natural persons and that legal persons could not be included (see paras. 12–17).

of conclusion of the contract, to all the circumstances attending the conclusion of the contract and to all the other terms of the contract or another contract of which it is dependent.

Article 4(2) provides that terms relating 'to the main subject matter of the contract' and to the adequacy of price and remuneration are excluded from an assessment of 'unfairness' under the Directive, provided that such terms are drawn up in plain and intelligible language. The limiting effect of this clause cannot be underestimated as it removes from the control of the Directive crucial elements of consumer contracts. The Preamble to the Directive gives an example by referring to insurance contracts. In that context, the terms which clearly define or circumscribe the insured risk and the insurer's liability are said to be excluded from an assessment of unfairness. Likewise, Article 4(2) suggest that the price agreed by the parties, even if set at a level clearly above what would be deemed a reasonable price, would seem to be excluded from the scope of the Directive. Howells and Wilhelmsson explain that the rationale behind this exclusion of the central terms of a contract, and particularly price-related terms—which appears in several European jurisdictions[50]—is a traditional approach to contract law based on the freedom of contract of parties that operate in an efficient market.[51]

Article 5 of the Directive encapsulates two clear ideas. First, we find a rule of transparency, as it states that terms offered to the consumer must be drafted in plain and intelligible language.[52] Secondly, we find a rule of interpretation: in case of doubt about the meaning of a term, the interpretation more favourable to the consumer should prevail.

Finally, Articles 6 and 7 deal with the obligations placed on the Member States to ensure the effective enforcement of the principles enshrined in the Directive. On the one hand, Article 6 refers to the protection of individual consumers. Article 6(1) imposes on Member States the obligation to implement a sanction that will apply to unfair terms in consumer contracts. Thus, it provides that such terms will *not be binding* on the consumer and that the contract shall continue to bind the parties upon those terms only if it is capable of continuing in existence without the unfair terms. On the other, Article 7 sets out a more general framework of protection and imposes on Member States the duty to adopt measures for the prevention of the

[50] See Hondius, *supra* note 45, at 247.

[51] See Howells and Wilhelmsson, *supra* note 1, at 94. They also rightly point out that the scope of the exclusion clause is not very precise, given that it may not always be easy to insulate those terms that refer 'to the main subject of the contract' from other minor clauses.

[52] This is the third reference in the Directive to the importance attached to transparency in the field of consumer protection. The first is implicit in Art. 3(1), which shows that only terms not individually negotiated are covered by the Directive. This has the aim of protecting consumers against terms which they did not have the opportunity to negotiate themselves. The second is found in Art. 4(2) of the Directive, according to which the exclusion clause will apply only if the terms in question have been drawn up in plain and intelligible language.

continued use of unfair terms in consumer contracts.[53] Interestingly, Article 7 of
the Directive justifies the imposition of these preventive remedies on the need to
protect the interests of consumers *and of competitors*. It is clear from the Preamble
to the Directive that competition will be stimulated and indirectly benefit from the
removal of unfair terms in consumer contracts, but Article 7 makes one explicit
reference to the interests of competitors in the operative part of a consumer
protection Directive.[54]

II. The Unfair Terms Directive and its potential in the process of Europeanization of private law

There are three aspects in the Unfair Terms Directive that have traditionally been
singled out as enjoying important potential in the process of Europeanization of
private law.[55] The first two are the references to the substantive notions of 'unfairness'
and 'good faith' found in Article 3 of the Directive. The third is the sanction
imposed by Article 6(1) of the Directive on unfair terms and relates to the enforcement of the principles set out in the Directive. As explained above, unfair terms
will not be binding on the consumer.

Article 3(1) and Article 4(1) provide, respectively, a definition of unfairness and
a set of elements used to ascertain whether a contract includes unfair terms. These
provisions can affect the process of Europeanization by being interpreted by the
European Court in response to a preliminary reference or as a result of national
courts interpreting their national law in the light of EC Directives, following the
Von Colson and *Marleasing* interpretative principle of indirect effect.[56]

This two-fold influence was vividly illustrated in *Océano Grupo Editorial* v *Rocio
Murciano Quintero*,[57] the first set of cases where the Court was called upon to interpret Directive 93/13. It concerned actions brought by two Spanish sellers of encyclopaedias against four consumers who failed to meet the payment of sums due
under contract for the purchase by instalments of the encyclopaedias. The contracts
included a term conferring jurisdiction for any disputes arising from the contract
on the courts of Barcelona, the city where the sellers had their main place of business, but where none of the buyers resided. In the absence of clear guidance from

---

[53] While Art. 7(1) sets out this duty in a general way, Art. 7(2) refers specifically to the inclusion
of provisions whereby persons or organizations with a legitimate interest may take action under national
law to question the fairness of contractual terms drawn up for general use.

[54] On the relationship between Competition and Consumer law, see *infra* Section 2.C.

[55] See Hondius, *supra* note 45, at 246–55; Tenreiro, 'The Community Directive on Unfair Terms
and National Legal Systems', 3 *ERPL* (1995) 273.

[56] See Case 14/83, *Von Colson and Kamann* v *Land Nordrhein-Westfalen* [1984] ECR 1891 and
Case C-106/89, *Marleasing* v *La Comercial* [1990] ECR I-4135.

[57] Joined Cases C-240 to C-244/98, [2000] ECR I-4941. See further Stuyck, 'Annotation on Joined
Case C-240/98 to C-244/98', 38 *CML Rev* (2001) 719.

domestic legislation in force at the time, the national court made a reference to the European Court. The national court asked whether it could determine of *its own motion*—and with the guidance provided by the Directive—whether such a contractual term was unfair when making a preliminary assessment as to whether or not the claim should be allowed to proceed.

The Court seized the opportunity to provide a first interpretation of the notion of 'unfairness' in Article 3(1) of the Directive. The Court explained that a term that conferred exclusive jurisdiction on a court in the territorial jurisdiction where the seller or supplier had its main place of business, fulfilled all the criteria to be considered as unfair. Such a term would force a consumer to submit to a court that might be situated a long distance from the consumer's domicile. The costs involved in making an appearance could act as a deterrent and cause the consumer to forgo any legal remedy, particularly in disputes involving small amounts of money.[58] By contrast, the term would be much less onerous to the seller.[59] The term clearly caused an imbalance in the parties' rights and obligations, was contrary to good faith and resulted in detriment to the consumer. Furthermore, the Court identified the term as one falling within the list of examples in the Annex to the Directive.[60] Having decided that the term in question was by nature unfair, the Court went on to hold that the national court had jurisdiction to evaluate this term of its own motion.[61]

A second important aspect of the case aired by both the Advocate General and by the Court[62] was the relationship between national law and unimplemented Directives. Directive 93/13 was not transposed into Spanish law until 1998 and the Spanish implementing legislation had not entered into force when the facts of the case took place. A 1984 Law on Consumer Protection was applicable instead. The Court confirmed the *Marleasing* interpretative principle and held that national law, whether predating or postdating a Directive should be interpreted, *insofar as possible*, in the light of the Directive. The Court then focused on the case at hand and held that this principle would require the national court to *favour* an interpretation of national law that would allow it to decline any jurisdiction granted to it by such a jurisdictional clause.

The *Océano* judgment therefore seemed to provide an indication of the vast potential of Directive 93/13 in the process of Europeanization of private law. First,

---

[58] *Supra* note 57, para. 22.

[59] *Ibid.*, para. 23.

[60] The Court classified the term as one that would have the object or effect of excluding or hindering the consumer's right to take legal action, a category referred to in the Annex to the Directive (see para. 1(q) of the Annex).

[61] The Court based its reasoning on Arts. 6 and 7 of the Directive and the idea that Member States are responsible for ensuring the enforcement of the Directive principles, and that therefore it could not be left to consumers to defend themselves against unfair contractual terms (see paras. 25–29 of the judgment).

[62] See the Opinion of Saggio AG (at paras. 27–39) and the judgment of the Court, paras. 30–32.

in a move similar to that in *Nissan*,[63] the Court interpreted unfairness in a specific context: a jurisdictional clause. Secondly, it highlighted the indirect effect that the provisions of the Directive may have in the interpretation of national law and in the relationships between private parties. The Court even went a step further by suggesting the specific interpretation that the national court should favour.

A recent judgment of the Court, however, might appear at variance with the proactive approach followed in *Océano*. In *Freiburger Kommunalbauten GmbH Baugesellschaft* v *Hofstetter*,[64] a municipal construction company sold to Mr and Mrs Hofstetter a parking space in a multi-storey car park. Under the terms of the contract, the whole price was due upon delivery of a security by the contractor and, in the event of late payment, the purchaser was liable to pay default interest. Mr and Mrs Hofstetter claimed that such a term was unfair and paid the price only after they had accepted the parking space free of defects. The construction company claimed default interest for late payment. The national court made a reference to the European Court asking whether a term that would require a purchaser to pay the total price for a building, irrespective of whether there has been any progress, upon delivery of a security by a contractor was an unfair term.

The Court stated that the concepts of 'good faith' and 'significant imbalance in the parties' rights' in Article 3 of the Directive provided only general guidance on the factors that may render a contractual term unfair. A full assessment, however, needed to be carried out by the national court taking into account the factors listed in Article 4.[65] The Court then held that while it would be competent to interpret the general criteria in Article 3, it should not rule on the application of these criteria to a *particular* term.[66] It was therefore for the national court to decide whether the contractual term at issue was unfair.

The Court, obviously aware of the difficulties of reconciling its ruling with that in *Océano*, went on to distinguish the two cases. The Court held that the assessment of the jurisdictional clause in *Océano*:

. . . was reached in relation to a term which was solely to the benefit of the seller and contained no benefit in return for the consumer. Whatever the nature of the contract, it thereby undermined the effectiveness of the legal protection of the rights which the Directive affords to the consumer. It was thus possible to hold that a term was unfair without having to consider all the circumstances in which the contract was concluded and without having to assess the advantages and disadvantages that the term would have under the national law applicable to the contract.[67]

---

[63] See *supra* note 36.
[64] Case C-237/02, Judgment of 1 April 2004, not yet reported.
[65] *Ibid.*, at paras. 19–21 of the judgment.
[66] See also the robust Opinion of Geelhoed AG at paras. 25–30.
[67] See *ibid.*, at para. 23 of the judgment.

Does the Court's ruling suggest a clarification of its previous interpretation of Article 3(1) of the Directive or simply a retreat from the approach in *Océano*? Either interpretation seems defensible.

The Court based the distinction between these two cases on the fact that the jurisdictional clause in *Océano* was unfair *per se* given that it directly undermined the effectiveness of the legal protection of the rights granted by the Directive.[68] Such a clause exclusively benefited the sellers and produced no benefit whatsoever for the consumers. It was therefore possible to infer that it caused a significant imbalance between the rights and obligations of the parties to the detriment of the consumer, without it being necessary to apply the criteria in Article 4 of the Directive.

By contrast, the contractual term in *Hofstetter* could only be fully assessed by taking into account all the circumstances attending the conclusion of the contract and the consequences of the term under national law. It was clear from the arguments of the parties that while such a clause would be *prima facie* disadvantageous for consumers, only a full examination of national law would reveal whether it really caused a significant imbalance within the meaning of Article 3(1) of Directive 93/13.[69]

The Court thus indicated that references requesting an assessment of *unfairness* concerning specific contractual terms would not be entertained unless these can be appraised without having to take into account all the circumstances of the contract.[70] This would explain the ostensibly divergent results in *Océano* and in *Hofstetter*. The upshot is that the Court will be prepared to interpret *in general* the Article 3(1) criteria—significant imbalance, good faith and detriment—but not to apply them to specific contractual clauses unless these are *per se* unfair.[71]

On the one hand, the ruling in *Hofstetter*, seems to limit the potential of the Directive as a player in the process of Europeanization of private law. Thus, it stands

---

[68] As Stuyck points out, it could well be that if a consumer does not defend himself in court, a national judge may be unable to examine the circumstances of the case (*ibid.*, at 729).

[69] The referring court was itself inclined not to view the term as unfair under German law, and there were powerful arguments advanced by the construction company and the German Government in that respect (see paras. 14 and 16 of the judgment). For example, the German Government argued that the disadvantages suffered by a consumer having to pay the full price of a building, irrespective of any progress in construction, were compensated for by the bank guarantee provided by the builder. This would cover cases of either non-performance or defective performance of the contract.

[70] A certain parallel can be found between this kind of reasoning and anti-trust analysis in the context of Art. 81(1) EC. Certain agreements by their very nature have the potential to restrict competition. Hence they are automatically caught by the Art. 81(1) EC prohibition without it being necessary to demonstrate any restrictive effects on competition. These include horizontal agreements that fix prices or vertical agreements that confer absolute territorial protection. By contrast, other agreements whose object is not clearly anti-competitive need to be evaluated by considering their effects on the relevant market. This evaluation requires extensive market analysis.

[71] In *Hofstetter*, *supra* note 64, the Court was at pains to emphasize that the list of examples of unfair contractual terms in the Annex to the Directive was merely indicative, and that 'a term appearing in the list need not *necessarily* be considered as unfair'. It followed, therefore, that even terms appearing in the list would have to be assessed in the light of the Art. 4 criteria (*ibid.*, para. 20). See also Case C-478/99, *Commission v Sweden* [2002] ECR I-4147, at para. 17 of the judgment.

in contrast with the Court's approach in *Nissan* and in *Océano* where the Court interpreted, respectively, the notions of *misleading* advertising and *unfairness* and where it unavoidably did so with a specific context in mind. On the other hand, and despite the self-restrained reasoning in *Hofstetter*, it must not be forgotten that the Court also made clear that it would continue to interpret the criteria that form part of the notion of unfairness in Article 3(1). The paucity of decisions in this area makes it difficult to draw clear conclusions at this stage, but it is to be hoped that future decisions of the Court will illustrate further the impact of a general interpretation of these criteria.

At this stage, it is pertinent to focus on one of the general criteria encapsulated in the notion of unfairness in Article 3, namely the fact that the term must be contrary to the requirement of *good faith*. How can this be assessed? The Preamble to the Directive refers to several elements that may assist in this process. These include 'the strength of the bargaining position of the parties, whether the consumer had an inducement to agree to the term and whether the goods or services were sold or supplied to the special order of the consumer'. The Preamble also goes on to state that the requirement of good faith may be satisfied by the seller 'where he deals fairly and equitably with the other party whose legitimate interests he has to take into account'. The potential of this notion is great not only in the sphere of consumer law, but in the general area of European contract law, should the notion be interpreted by the Court and then exported into national law. In his 1994 study, Collins skilfully considered various interpretative approaches to the concept of good faith, taking into account the differences between the civil and common law traditions.[72] On the basis of the guidance provided by the Preamble to the Directive, he suggested that the term 'good faith' in Article 3 could refer to social market considerations and, in particular, to the obligation of the trader or supplier to take account of the interests of the consumer. This would be a very broad construction of the expression of good faith that could certainly prove influential in other areas of private law.[73]

Unfortunately the Court has not had the opportunity to interpret this notion so far. It remains to be seen how future rulings will define the reach of this potentially wide component of the test of unfairness.

Finally, the third element in Directive 93/13, which is relevant to the debate on Europeanization, is the sanction provided in Article 6(1), which introduces a Community-wide sanction that will apply to all unfair terms in consumer contracts in the EC. Furthermore, it introduces a common rule on severance, in that it

---

[72] Collins, 'Good Faith in European Contract Law', 14 *OJLS* (1994) 229.

[73] Collins examined the potential impact that such interpretation could have on the common law. He concluded that it 'should strengthen those elements in the common law which recognise obligations arising from relations of dependence, duties to be careful and respect the other's interests during the negotiations, and requirements of co-operation during the performance of the contract' (*ibid.*, at 254). On the general concept of good faith, see M.W. Hesselink, *The New European Private Law* (2002), at 195–223.

determines that a contract will continue to bind the parties if it is capable of continuing in existence without the unfair terms. The Article 6(1) rule therefore creates, at a Community level, a clear restriction on contractual freedom for private parties, albeit limited to the sphere of consumer law.

E. The Directive on Certain Aspects of the Sale of Consumer Goods and Associated Guarantees

Despite the absence of rulings from the Court, a brief consideration of Article 2(1) of Directive 1999/44 on certain aspects of the sale of consumer goods and associated guarantees seems pertinent.[74] That provision contains a general principle, namely that the seller must deliver goods to the consumer that are *in conformity* with the contract of sale. Article 2(2) goes on to provide a list of requirements for consumer goods to be presumed to be in conformity with the contract. The idea that goods should be in conformity with the contract is a substantive notion common to the legal traditions of the Member States. However, should the European Court be prepared to interpret that expression—as it was prepared to interpret the notions of 'misleading' in *Nissan* or of 'unfairness' in *Océano*—there could be substantial potential for influence not only on consumer law but also on general contract law.

2. COMPETITION LAW

A. Competition Law and Policy in the EC

Unlike consumer law, competition has been a major area of policy since the inception of the European Community.[75] The competition provisions in the Treaty can be broadly divided into two main groups. On the one hand, Articles 81 and 82 EC focus on the activities of private undertakings. Their aims are, respectively, the control of anti-competitive practices that result from collusion between undertakings, and the control of abuses of dominant position. On the other, Article 86 EC refers to the behaviour of public undertakings and undertakings granted special rights, and Articles 87–89 contain rules on the granting of State aid. An extensive body of secondary legislation including both substantive[76] and procedural[77] measures and a wealth of Commission decisions and judgments from the Community judicature have supplemented and developed this framework.

---

[74] See *supra* note 10.

[75] See Art. 3(g) EC Treaty and Arts. 81–89 EC, all of which were present in the original version of the Treaty.

[76] See, e.g., Regulation 139/2004, the EC Merger Regulation (OJ 2004 L 24/1) or the system of block exemption regulations (see *infra* note 89).

[77] See, e.g., Regulation 1/2003 on the application of Arts. 81 and 82 EC (OJ 2004 L 1/1).

Crucially, the competition provisions have been interpreted not only to encourage economic activity so as to maximize efficiency and consumer welfare—as it would be the case in any system of free competition—but also to promote the Single Market objective of the Treaty.[78] As the Court has emphasized, the removal of barriers to the free movement of goods, persons and services imposed by Member States would be a fruitless exercise if undertakings and Member States were able to divide the territory of the Member States along national lines by means of anti-competitive practices.[79] This market integration slant has gained the Commission much criticism, particularly in areas like vertical restraints where territorial restrictions were severely treated, even though these might have been necessary to minimize economic risk or might eventually have led to an increase in trade.[80] It is difficult, however, to see how else the Commission and Court could have struck a balance between two objectives (i.e. economic benefit and market integration) which on many occasions operate as opposing forces.

B. Competition Law and the Europeanization of Private Law

With a few exceptions,[81] little attention has been paid to the role of EC competition law in the creation of a European system of private law. This seems surprising given that, unlike most of the other Single Market provisions, both Articles 81 and 82 EC refer to the activities of private parties and that infringements of these provisions often take the form of contractual clauses. One of the arguments of this chapter is that competition law has a significant role to play in the wider process of Europeanization, regardless of its perceived insularity.

There are, of course, important differences between Articles 81 and 82 EC and other areas of private law such as consumer law. First, these provisions regulate the behaviour of private undertakings but they simultaneously protect a public interest objective by preserving and promoting the competitive process. Secondly, Articles 81 and 82 EC pursue a high degree of substantive uniformity in the field of competition across the EC while internal market Directives harmonize rather than integrate consumer law.[82] Finally, consumer contracts are assessed and regulated by

---

[78] See the Commission's *IXth Report on Competition Policy* (1979), at 9–11 and the *XXIXth Report on Competition Policy* (1999), at 19. For a recent and very clear endorsement of the key role played by competition policy in the Single Market see Case C-126/97, *Eco Swiss* v *Benetton* [1999] ECR I-3055 at para. 36 of the judgment. See also Ehlermann, 'The Contribution of EC Competition Policy to the Single Market', 29 *CML Rev* (1992) 257 and Albors-Llorens, 'Competition Policy and the Shaping of the Single Market', in C. Barnard and J. Scott (eds), *The Legal Foundations of the Single Market: Unpacking the Premises* (2002), 311.

[79] See Cases 56 and 58/64, *Consten and Grundig* [1966] ECR 299 at 340.

[80] See, amongst others, Hawk, 'System Failure: Vertical Restraints and EC Competition Law', 32 *CML Rev* (1992) 973.

[81] See Caruso, 'The Missing View of the Cathedral: the Private Law Paradigm of European Legal Integration', 3 *ELJ* (1997) 3.

[82] See *supra* Section 1.A.

considering mainly the effect of contractual obligations on the parties to the contract and by placing emphasis on the protection of the consumer, who is viewed as the weaker party. By contrast, anti-competitive contractual clauses are principally examined in relation to the effects they have on third parties and on the relevant market. For example, when two undertakings agree to share the Community markets, their agreement will be considered not in terms of the effect it has on those undertakings but rather in terms of its object to distort competition with the Common Market and to divide the markets of the EC. In this respect, it can be well understood that the interpretation of terms in the Directives on consumer protection is seen as having more potential for a spill-over effect on general contract law than the competition provisions. However, an attempt will be made here to show that despite its specialist nature, competition law has significant potential in the process of convergence of the national systems of private law. This can be gleaned not only from the provisions in the Treaty and in secondary legislation, but also from the principles developed by the Community judicature.

I. Treaty provisions

Article 81(1) EC influences relationships between private parties in two main respects:

(a) with the imposition of an absolute prohibition on anti-competitive agreements, decisions and concerted practices; and

(b) by setting out a list of anti-competitive practices (price fixing, market sharing, ties-in, etc.).

These two elements clearly restrict the contractual freedom of undertakings through the Community. Article 81(2) EC, on its part, imposes a sanction of nullity on any terms that breach Article 81(1) EC. As early as 1966, the Court interpreted this as an automatic sanction.[83] We find here a clear parallel with the sanction imposed by Article 6(1) of the Unfair Terms Directive.[84] Unlike Directive 93/13, however, the Treaty did not impose a Community-wide rule on severance of offending clauses.[85]

Although Article 82 EC controls mainly unilateral anti-competitive behaviour, abusive clauses are frequently included in contracts concluded between dominant companies and their distributors or customers. Thus, by providing a list of potentially abusive practices, this provision has also had an unavoidable impact in curtailing the freedom of dominant companies to negotiate. Consider, for example, one of the practices in the list: the imposition of unfair terms on clients. In *United Brands*,[86]

---

[83] See Case 56/65, *STM* v *Maschinenbau Ulm* [1966] ECR 235.

[84] See *supra* note 10.

[85] Thus, in *Kerpen and Kerpen* the Court emphasized that the consequences of nullity for other parts of the agreement were a matter for national law (Case 319/82, [1983] ECR 4173, at para. 12 of the judgment).

[86] See Case 26/76, *United Brands* v *Commission* [1978] ECR 207.

one of the seminal cases on Article 82 EC, the Court considered whether several of the clauses imposed by United Brands on its distributors were unfair. It is clear that the Court construed the *unfairness* of these clauses in the context of an abuse of dominant position and the effect that the clauses would have in competition, but a potential for overlap into consumer contracts may be identified. For example, a consumer is viewed as the weaker party in a consumer contract, just as a small market operator is viewed as the vulnerable party when contracting with a dominant company. Likewise, in *United Brands* the issue of excessive pricing—another potentially abusive practice—was discussed. The Court took the view that abusive pricing takes place 'where a price has no reasonable relation to the economic value of the product supplied'.[87] It could well be that this kind of assessment could prove influential in other areas of private law.[88]

II. Secondary legislation

The past few years have seen the passage of some very important reforms in EC competition law, both at substantive and at procedural level. At substantive level, some of the most important changes have taken place in the context of block exemption Regulations.

 The Commission has enacted new systems of block exemption Regulations on both horizontal and vertical agreements.[89] In the field of vertical agreements, the adoption of the new *umbrella* block exemption Regulation, Regulation 2790/99, was a revolutionary step in several ways. From a competition perspective, for the first time it linked exemption to market power, allowed for the consideration of most kinds of vertical agreements within the scope of *one* legislative measure, and removed the formalism and straitjacket effect of the old system of block exemption Regulations.[90] From the point of view of private parties, it has two important

---

[87] Case 26/76, *supra* note 86, at para. 250.

[88] As seen above (see *supra* Section 1.D.I), Art. 4(2) of the Unfair Contract Terms Directive excludes the adequacy of price and remuneration from an assessment of the *unfairness* of clauses in consumer contracts, but the kind of interpretation followed in *United Brands* could have an impact in other fields. See, e.g., Art. 6 of Directive 86/653 on the harmonization of the laws of the Member States relating to self-employed commercial agents (OJ 1986 L 382/86). It provides that, in the absence of an agreement or customary practice, a self-employed agent shall be entitled to *reasonable remuneration*. Any assessment of what is a *reasonable relation between price and economic value* in a competition case might be important in this context. Other interpretations given by the Court in the field of both Arts. 81 and 82 EC, such as, e.g., on the meaning of the term undertaking (see e.g. Case C-41/90, *Höfner and Elser v Macroton* [1991] ECR I-1979, para. 21 of the judgment) may also prove important in other areas.

[89] See for vertical agreements Regulation 2790/99 (OJ 1999 L 336/21); Regulation 1420/2002 (OJ 2002 L 203/30) and Regulation 772/2004 (OJ 2004 L 123/11). For horizontal agreements, see Regulation 2658/2000 (OJ 2000 L 304/3) and Regulation 2659/2000 (OJ 2000 L 304/7).

[90] For a very comprehensive coverage of this topic and of the wider implications of the Regulation on private parties, see Whish, 'Regulation 2790/99, the Commission's New Style Block Exemption for Vertical Agreements', 37 *CML Rev* (2000) 887; V. Korah and D. O'Sullivan, *Distribution Agreements under the EC Competition Rules* (2002) and P. Taylor, *Vertical Agreements: the New Regulation in Context* (2000).

consequences. First, Articles 4 and 5 of the Regulation provide two lists of prohibited contractual clauses. In Article 4, we find typical hard-core restrictions of competition such as price fixing, territorial and customer restrictions, etc., while Article 5 refers to non-compete obligations. Secondly, the Guidelines that accompany the Regulation make it clear that while the Article 5 clauses are severable, the presence of any Article 4 clause will take the whole agreement outside the scope of the block exemption.[91] The list of prohibited clauses thus limits the choice of contracting undertakings[92] and the introduction of a common rule on severance takes another step towards integration. More so, if compared with the general sanction in Article 81(2) EC.[93]

At a procedural level, and following 40 years of a partially decentralized system of enforcement of Article 81 EC, the 1999 White Paper constituted a dramatic development.[94] The essence of the White Paper was a proposal to render Article 81(3) EC directly applicable and to abolish the system of notifications and individual exemptions.[95] This would end the Commission's monopoly in the application of Article 81(3) EC and enable national courts and national competition authorities to apply this provision, just as they had always applied Articles 81(1) and (2) and 82 EC. These important changes have now been laid in a legislative form in Regulation 1/2003, which entered into force in May 2004 and have led to a truly decentralized application of Article 81 EC.[96] At first sight, it would appear that this process of decentralization would have an effect counter to integration. However, one of the main concerns of the White Paper was to preserve a uniform interpretation of Articles 81 and 82 EC. Mechanisms have been put in place by Regulation 1/2003 to this effect, and these will act alongside the traditional mechanism of preliminary references from the national courts. These include the ability for the Commission to submit written observations to national courts applying Articles 81 and 82 EC or its right to be informed by the national competition authorities of any proceedings involving these provisions.[97] It seems, therefore, that every effort has been made to ensure that the process of decentralized enforcement

---

[91] See the Guidelines on Vertical Agreements (OJ (2000) C 291/1) at paras. 46, 57, 66, and 67.

[92] The two block exemption Regulations on horizontal agreements (see *supra* note 89) also share in the approach of Regulation 2790/99 in terms of setting out a list of prohibited clauses. The old system of block exemption regulations limited even more the contractual freedom of undertakings because private parties were given not only a set of contractual clauses which were prohibited, but also a list of the *only* clauses that were permitted. In the new system, clauses that are not expressly prohibited are, by implication, allowed.

[93] See *supra* Section 2.B.I.

[94] OJ 1999 C 132/1.

[95] See further Ehlermann, 'The Modernization of EC Antitrust Policy: a Legal and Cultural Revolution', 37 *CML Rev* (2000) 537.

[96] OJ 2003 L 1/1.

[97] See Arts. 11, 15, and 16 of Regulation 1/2003. Additionally, Art. 10 of the Regulation gives the Commission power to enact decisions of a declaratory nature, with a view to clarifying the law, particularly when new agreements or practices have not been settled in the case-law.

does not detract from a uniform interpretation of Articles 81 and 82 throughout
the EC. Other aspects of the Regulation, such as the allocation of the burden of
proof in the application of the conditions in Article 81(3) EC also suggest a measure of procedural harmonization in the field of disputes involving contracts restrictive of competition and consequently an impact on private law disputes.[98] However
the Regulation, while clearly making provision for substantive uniformity, does not
offer a harmonized system of remedies, and there are already calls for the adoption
of a Community Regulation that would create common standards in this field.[99]
Presently, case-law developments in the field of compensation claims seem already
to be pointing towards convergence.[100]

III. Case-law of the Community judicature

One of the key areas of EC law developed almost entirely by the Community
judicature is the remedies which are available before the national courts in cases of
breach of EC law. Articles 81 EC and 82 EC[101] can be enforced at national level
and a very important aspect of this enforcement is the provision of compensation
for damages resulting from a breach of these provisions.

The EC Treaty did not regulate the remedies that apply when Community rights
are enforced before the national courts and there are very few areas where legislative
harmonization of these remedies has taken place. The European Court, however,
provided a set of guiding principles in some early decisions. Thus, in *Rewe-Zentral* v
Landwirtschaftskammer für das Saarland,[102] the Court took the view that the
provision of these remedies should be left to national law, provided that the national
remedy is effective and non-discriminatory. The principles of procedural autonomy,
non-discrimination and effectiveness were then given flesh in a series of preliminary
rulings.[103] In 1991, the landmark ruling of the Court in *Francovich*[104] added a
further dimension to this process by deciding that, as a matter of EC law, Member
States could be made liable in damages in cases where they had acted in infringement
of EC law. This decision therefore created a remedy of a *Community* nature and

---

[98] See Art. 2 of Regulation 1/2003, *supra* note 96.

[99] See van Gerven, 'Substantive Remedies for the Private Enforcement of EC Antitrust Rules before
National Courts', in C.-D. Ehlermann and I. Atanasiu (eds), *European Competition Law Annual 2001* (2001),
at 81–2 and 'Harmonization of Private Law: Do We Need It?', 41 *CML Rev* (2004) 1, at 17.

[100] See *infra* Section 2.B.III.

[101] Arts. 81(1) and (2) and 82 EC were declared to have direct effect early in the case-law (see Case
127/73, *BRT* v *SABAM* [1974] ECR 51).

[102] Case 33/76, [1976] ECR 1989.

[103] Through preliminary rulings, the Court provided guidance on the compatibility of certain
national rules and principles with the principles of effectiveness and non-discrimination. See, e.g., Case
199/82, *San Giorgio* [1983] ECR 3595; Case C-213/89, *Factortame (I)* [1990] ECR I-2433;
Case C-377/89, *Cotter* [1991] ECR I-1155; Case C-271/91, *Marshall (II)* [1993] ECR I-4367; Case
C-188/95, *Fantask* [1997] ECR I-6783, etc.

[104] Joined Cases C-6 and 9/90, *Francovich* v *Italy* [1991] ECR I-5357.

a uniform set of conditions to determine State liability, even if the interpretation of these conditions was left to national law.[105]

Soon enough, a debate started as to whether a similar Community right to damages ought to apply to horizontal situations, namely to cases where private parties are held responsible for a breach of EC law and are being sued by other private parties before the national courts.[106] Given that Articles 81 and 82 EC are concerned with the activities of private undertakings, it was clear that competition cases would be a fertile testing ground for this argument. In a competition case, *Banks* v *British Coal Corporation*,[107] a compelling Opinion by Advocate General van Gerven argued the case for a Community right to damages in cases where an individual suffers loss or damage as a result of an infringement of Community law by another private party. Unfortunately, the Court was not required to deal with this issue in *Banks*, but an opportunity to revisit it arose a few years later.[108]

In *Courage* v *Crehan*,[109] a party to an anti-competitive agreement sought damages against its co-contractor. Under English law, a party to an illegal agreement is prevented from seeking damages against its co-contractor. This rule operates as a reflection of the estoppel principle. The Court of Appeal made a reference to the European Court asking whether a party to an agreement prohibited under Article 81(1) EC might be given rights against the other party, and in particular whether it could seek compensation for loss against its co-contractor. Furthermore, the Court asked whether the English rule at issue was compatible with EC law. The European Court held that Article 81 EC conferred rights on individuals even where they are party to an anti-competitive agreement and that these rights should include, in principle, the right to compensation for loss suffered as a result of that agreement.[110] It then went on to condemn the English bar, but only insofar as it was an *absolute* one and would *always* prevent a party to an illegal agreement from recovering damages from its co-contractor. Thus, the Court explained that EC law would not preclude, for example, a national court from refusing damages to a party to an anti-competitive agreement who bore significant responsibility for the illegality of the agreement.[111]

---

[105] *Ibid.,* at para. 40. See further van Gerven, 'Bridging the Unbridgeable: Community and National Tort Laws after *Francovich* and *Brasserie*', 45 *ICLQ* (1996) 507; T. Tridimas, *The General Principles of EC Law* (1999), at 321–48.

[106] See, in particular, C. Jones, *Private Enforcement of Anti-trust Law in the EU, UK and USA* (1999), at 75.

[107] Case C-128/92, [1994] ECR I-1209.

[108] In the interim period, the decision of the Court in Case C-242/95, *GT-Link A/S* v *Danske Statsbaner (DSB)* [1997] ECR I-4449, was interpreted as lending support to the views of van Gerven AG in *Banks* (see A. Jones and B. Sufrin, *EC Competition Law* (2001), at 987).

[109] Case C-453/99, [2001] ECR I-6297.

[110] *Ibid.,* at para. 26. Interestingly, the Court added a policy argument and emphasized that actions for damages between co-contractors could contribute effectively to the maintenance of healthy competition (see *ibid.*, para. 27).

[111] *Ibid.*, paras. 29–35.

Academic writers construed the judgment in *Courage* as introducing a Community right to damages in cases of breach of Articles 81 and 82 EC that would apply not only to third parties[112] but also to parties to an agreement prohibited under Article 81(1) EC.[113] The ruling certainly lends itself to this interpretation in a competition context.[114] Whether this principle is developed further[115] or extended to other areas of EC law[116] involving disputes between private parties will depend on future developments in the case-law. But, if that were the case, this would be an outstanding example of the contribution of competition case-law to the process of harmonization of contractual and non-contractual private liability in cases where a breach of EC law is involved.[117]

C. The Role of the Consumer in EC Competition Law[118]

From the outset, it is clear that consumer interests lie at the heart of competition policy, and the maximization of consumer welfare features very prominently among its goals.[119] The combined effect of promoting the competitive process and intervening to curb anti-competitive practices is understood to lead to a better allocation of resources, which in turn enhances consumer gains.

Furthermore, two express references to consumer interests are found in the wording of Articles 81 and 82 EC.[120] First, Article 81(3) EC which provides for exemptions from the prohibition in Article 81(1) EC, lists as the second condition for exemption that an agreement must allow 'consumers a fair share of the resulting benefit'. Secondly, Article 82 lists as an abusive practice the 'limitation of production, market or technical development to the prejudice of consumers' by a dominant company. The impact of these references will be examined in sequence.

---

[112] National legal systems have generally recognized a damages remedy available to victims of anti-competitive practices, though in practice there has been a very limited culture of private enforcement of Arts. 81 and 82 EC (see further Jones and Beard, 'Co-contractors, Damages and Article 81: the ECJ Finally Speaks', 23 *ECLR* (2002) 246 at 251; Komninos, 'New Prospects for Private Enforcement of EC Competition Law: *Courage* v. *Crehan* and the Community Right to Damages', 39 *CML Rev* (2002) 447 at 450; Caruso, *supra* note 81, at 18–22).

[113] See Jones and Beard, *supra* note 112, at 256 and Komninos, *supra* note 112, at 466.

[114] For a more cautious view, see Albors-Llorens, '*Courage* v. *Crehan*: Judicial Activism or Consistent Approach?', 61 *Cambridge Law Journal* (2002) 38–41.

[115] In *Courage* v *Crehan*, unlike in *Francovich*, the Court did not develop a set of conditions for liability. It therefore remains to be seen how the Court interprets the concepts such as causation and damage in the context of private relations.

[116] Areas like social policy or free movement of persons have very significant potential in this respect.

[117] See further van Gerven, *supra* note 99.

[118] See further Reich, 'Competition Law and the Consumer' in L. Gormley (ed.), *Current and Future Perspectives on EC Competition Law* (1997) and Stuyck, 'European Consumer Law after the Treaty of Amsterdam: Consumer Policy in or beyond the Internal Market', 37 *CML Rev* (2000) 367 at 399.

[119] See S. Bishop and M. Walker, *The Economics of EC Competition Law* (1999).

[120] See *supra* Section 1.A.

How have the Commission and the Court interpreted the consumer benefit clause in Article 81(3)? The conditions for exemption under Article 81(3) EC are cumulative conditions,[121] and hence the assessment of whether an agreement produces a consumer benefit will follow a successful fulfilment of the first condition, namely that it produces an *economic* or *technical* benefit. The decision of the Commission in *Re Synthetic Fibres Agreement* illustrates a typical pattern of Commission reasoning in this area.[122] It involved nine petrochemical groups from seven Member States which agreed to reduce capacity in the production of six synthetic textile fibres. The parties to the agreement decided upon this course of action in view of the difficulties experienced by the European synthetic fibres industry. An imbalance between supply and demand had been caused by a combination of weak demand and increased import penetration. The agreement fell clearly within the scope of Article 81(1) EC and the parties notified the agreement to the Commission, as necessary under the 'old' system of enforcement, with a view to securing an exemption. The Commission first found that the agreement created an economic benefit. By concentrating on making certain products and giving up production of others, the signatories to the agreement would become more specialized and specialization would lead to improved technical efficiency and to an increase in profits, thus restoring the competitiveness of each party.[123] The Commission then turned to consider whether the agreement would produce any consumer benefit. It took the view that consumers would gain from the emergence of a more competitive industry and that specialization would result in better products. Furthermore, the number of producers remaining for each product would be sufficient to ensure choice and security of supply. The Commission acknowledged that prices might rise initially, but that there were enough alternative sources of supply in Europe and elsewhere for consumers to switch to other suppliers if the parties to the agreement tried to charge excessive prices.[124]

In early days, the Commission was criticized for treating the consumer benefit clause in Article 81(3) EC as a purely formal condition that would be automatically satisfied if the agreement was found to produce an economic or technical benefit. Robust calls were made for a more thorough investigation on consumer gains.[125] In recent years, however, the Commission has paid heed to this advice and there are now several examples of decisions where a much more analytical approach to the determination of a benefit to consumer interests has been taken.[126] This provides

---

[121] See Joined Cases 56 and 58/64, *supra* note 79, at 350.

[122] OJ 1984 L 207/17.

[123] *Ibid.*, at paras. 28–38 of the decision.

[124] *Ibid.*, at paras. 39–41 of the decision.

[125] See, in particular, Evans, 'European Competition Law and Consumers: the Article 85(3) Exemption', 2 *ECLR* (1981) 425.

[126] A good example is Commission Decision 92/204/EEC (building and construction industry in the Netherlands), OJ 1992 L 92/1, at paras. 120–3. See also the judgment of the Court of First Instance dealing with the challenge to the Commission decision, which is very detailed on this point (Case T-29/92, *SPO* v *Commission* [1995] ECR II-289, at paras. 286–300 of the judgment).

a telling indication of the growing association between competition policy and consumer interests.

The explicit reference to consumer interests in Article 82 EC—abuse as limitation of production, markets or technical development—has been developed in some Commission decisions.[127] Furthermore, consumer interests have also permeated other forms of abuse, such as refusals to supply. One of the key examples is perhaps the well-known *Magill* litigation.[128] Two television companies published their own weekly TV guides providing information on the programmes that would be shown on their own channels and used their copyright to prevent the publication of comprehensive TV guides. The cases were decidedly controversial, given the involvement of intellectual property rights and the apparent legitimacy of the actions of the copyright holders. The Court of First Instance first and the European Court, on appeal, took the view that such activities amounted to an abuse of dominant position.[129] The judgment of the European Court was particularly enlightening. When supporting the case for existence of abuse, the first reason given by the Court was that the refusal to provide the information prevented the emergence of a new product (i.e. comprehensive TV guides) for which there was 'potential consumer demand'. The importance given by the Court to consumer demand in this judgment was therefore crucial.[130]

Beyond the notion of abuse and despite the absence of an express allusion to consumer preferences, these are taken into consideration when applying other aspects of Article 82 EC. The most obvious example refers to the definition of the relevant product market where dominance will be assessed. Consumer preferences lie at the very heart of this determination. As early as in *Continental Can*,[131] the Court made it clear that the degree of substitution between products and services from a consumer point of view would define the breadth of the relevant product market. Put simply, if butter has special characteristics and attributes as a result of which a consumer of butter would never contemplate buying margarine

---

[127] For a good example see Commission Decision 2001/892/EEC (cross-border mail) OJ 2001 L 331/40. There, the Commission emphasized that where a dominant company limits the provision of a service to the prejudice of consumers it breaches Art. 82 EC. The case concerned the interception and delay of the delivery of incoming cross-border mail from the UK by the State-owned German postal company. In deciding the existence of abuse, the Commission took into account that dissatisfied customers would be discouraged from using postal operators in the UK for destinations in Germany due to the frequent disruptions (see paras. 170–7 of the Decision).

[128] Joined Cases C-241 and 242/91 P, *RTE and ITP* [1995] ECR I-743. See Greaves, 'The Herschel Smith Lecture 1998: Article 86 and Intellectual Property Rights', 20 *EIPR* (1998) 379 and J. Faull and A. Nikpay, *The EC Law of Competition* (1999), at 631.

[129] Case T-69/89, *RTE* v *Commission* [1991] ECR II-485 and Case T-76/89, *ITP* v *Commission* [1991] ECR II-575 and Joined Cases C-241 and C-242/91 P, [1995] ECR I-74.

[130] See *ibid.*, at para. 55. More so, when compared with the more modest proposal of the Advocate General in that case (see para. 97 of the Opinion of the AG and the commentary in Faull and Nikpay (*supra* note 128, at 631)).

[131] Case 6/72, [1973] ECR 215, at para. 32 of the judgment.

instead—even if the price of butter was raised—this would suggest that butter and margarine form separate product markets. In some decisions, the Commission and the Court have also looked at the degree of supply substitutability,[132] but they demand that inter-changeability continues to be the central criterion in terms of defining the parameters of the relevant product market and hence of a position of dominance.[133]

Finally, consumer interests are important in the field of merger control. Article 2(1) Regulation 139/2004[134] provides for a series of criteria that are used by the Commission when making a substantive assessment of whether a concentration is compatible with the Common Market. Among these, the interests of consumers feature prominently.[135] Furthermore, the Commission Guidelines on the assessment of horizontal mergers make repeated references to consumer benefits.[136]

CONCLUSION

This chapter has considered the roles that EC consumer law and competition law have played in the ongoing process of convergence of European private law. In both cases, the combined action of legislation and of the case-law of the Community judicature has been examined. The harmonization potential of consumer protection Directives and, in particular, of the Unfair Terms Directive, has already been extensively discussed by leading private lawyers. This chapter has sought to add a further dimension by arguing that competition law also might have a unifying effect on the legal parameters that apply to private relations across the Community. Furthermore, an attempt has been made to illustrate that some of the competition developments have a significant potential for spillage onto other areas of private law.

Another theme has been the exposure of an increasingly close relationship between these two areas. Most of the consumer protection Directives refer to the stimulation of competition as one of their objectives and several of them make specific references to the protection of the interests of competitors in some of their provisions.

---

[132] See Case 322/81, *Michelin* [1983] ECR 3461, at para. 41 of the judgment.

[133] See also the Commission Notice on the definition of the relevant market for the purposes of Community competition law, OJ 1997 C 372/5, at para. 7. In the field of mergers, consumer behaviour and demand side factors in general are also used to define the relevant market (see e.g. Case IV/M.430, *Procter & Gamble*, OJ 1994 L 354/32).

[134] OJ 2004 L 24/1.

[135] See Art. 2(1)(b).

[136] OJ 2004 C31/03. See, e.g., para. 8 of the Guidelines, where the Commission puts consumer interests at the very heart of merger evaluation: '[e]ffective competition brings benefits to consumers, such as low prices, high quality products, a wide selection of good and services, and innovation. Through its control of mergers, the Commission prevents mergers that would be likely to deprive consumers of these benefits by significantly increasing the market power of firms' (see also paras. 79–84 of the Guidelines).

On its part, the competition provisions in the Treaty and their interpretation by the Community judicature have reflected the importance that consumer interests and preferences have in anti-trust analysis. It is argued that this closeness could result in a mutual incidence in terms of the process of harmonization of European private law. Even though there are obvious differences between consumer contracts and those including anti-competitive terms, some of the concepts and approaches developed in one of these fields might have an impact on the other. The development of principles of non-contractual liability in private relations in a competition context, for example, could well transpose into consumer cases and thereafter onto other areas of private law. Likewise, interpretations of the notion of unfairness in Article 3 of the Unfair Terms Directive may influence the construction of certain abusive practices under Article 82 EC. After all, one of the objectives of the Unfair Terms Directive is to protect consumers against the abuse of power by a seller or supplier.[137] It may be time, therefore, to abandon a compartmentalized view of competition law and consumer law and to consider them as related operators, which can not only independently affect the process of Europeanization, but also enrich it further as a result of their reciprocal influence.

---

[137] See paras. 8–11 of the Preamble to Directive 93/13, *supra* note 10.

8

Transformation of Contract Law and Civil Justice in the New EU Member Countries: The Example of the Baltic States, Hungary and Poland*

NORBERT REICH

1. INTRODUCTION

A. Functions of European Contract Law as the Theoretical Starting Point

Instead of trying to analyse European private law under EU influence as a whole, I will limit myself to the transformation of contract law because the discussion is most advanced here, and because it is an area in which I can contribute most from my research and teaching. My concept of European contract law is a functional one and has been described elsewhere.[1] I will distinguish between three main functions of modern European contract law, namely:

- autonomy;
- regulation; and
- information.

By 'autonomy' I understand the fundamental function of any contract law in a market economy such as the one enshrined in the EC and EU Treaties, namely the making of economic transactions by subjects of private law (natural persons including consumers, business entities, the State acting in its 'dominium' function) as securely and efficiently as possible, and their effective enforcement under the *pacta sunt servanda* rule, once the conditions of a 'free meeting of minds' are met. At the

* I wish to express my thanks to my colleagues, Prof. Dr. L. Vékás, Budapest, and Doz. Dr. Ewa Baginska, Torún, to my LL.M. students, J. Petkevica and A. Svjatska, Riga, and M. Petrevicius and T. Samulevicius, Vilnius, for valuable help in preparing the national reports for this chapter. Errors and misunderstandings are of course my responsibility. The state of the law is that before the accession of the countries studied, i.e. before 1 May 2004. A prior version has been published in 23 *Penn State Int L Rev* (2005) 587.

[1] See Reich, 'The Tripartite Function of Modern Contract Law in Europe: Enablement, Regulation, Information', in F. Werro and T. Probst (eds), *Le droit privé suisse face au droit communautaire européen* (2004), at 145–72.

same time, even in a liberal economic and legal context, autonomy is not without borders; therefore, its inherent restrictions have to be made the subject of reflection, most notably by the principle of 'good faith'.

The 'regulatory function' of contract law may be the subject of doubt by many, notably liberal authors; they may fear a return to 'socialism'. I do not share this scepticism, but am convinced that this regulatory function has always been present in contract law, sometimes hidden in general clauses like those concerning 'good morals', 'public policy', and '*ordre public*', and later more openly in the deliberate protection of the weaker party in labour and consumer transactions. National[2] and European constitutional law also invades contract law, for example in the theory of the 'direct horizontal effect' of fundamental freedoms, and the non-discrimination principle.[3] Regulation may come from 'without' contract law, for example by way of restrictions on certain types of gambling contracts or lotteries,[4] but in recent times it has been introduced into contract law itself, for example by consumer law becoming part of contract law.[5] This will not be discussed in detail here, but 'consumer law' will be taken as part of the European *acquis* which has therefore greatly contributed to the transformation of contract. But consumer law may inspire a completely new orientation of traditional civil law principles.

'Information' is itself a rather vague concept, because it can already be found in traditional rules on fraud and misrepresentation as part of contract formation. These rules have been extensively studied elsewhere and will not be subject to my reflections. I am concerned with more subtle and differentiated rules on information provision by one of the parties to the (future) contract who either is in possession of this information or is required by law to provide this information, and the other party who requires this information for rational decision-making. Again, consumer law is a good example of this new principle, which departs from the classical rule of *caveat emptor*, but it is not limited to this area. Transaction cost economics may help to define the conditions and limits of this information paradigm in modern contract law.[6] I am interested not so much in looking at the highly specific and technical rules on information provision, but rather at the emergence of general principles and rules for its effective enforcement[7] without endangering the *pacta sunt servanda* principle.

---

[2] See Canaris, 'Wandlungen des Schuldvertragsrechts—Tendenzen zu seiner Materialisierung', 200 *Archiv für die civilistische Praxis* (2000) 1.

[3] See N. Reich, *Understanding EU Law—Objectives, Principles and Methods of Community Law* (2nd edn, 2005), at 17–18 referring to the case-law of the ECJ.

[4] As an example see Case C-275/92, *HM Customs and Excise Services* v *Schindler* [1994] ECR I-1039.

[5] See Rott, 'German Sales Law Two Years after Implementation of Dir. 1999/44/EC', 5 *German LJ* (2004) 237.

[6] See S. Grundmann, 'Information, Party Autonomy and Economic Agents in European Contract Law', 39 *CML Rev* (2002) 269; Kerber and Vanberg, 'Constitutional Aspects of Party Autonomy and Its Limits', in S. Grundmann *et al.* (eds), *Party Autonomy and the Role of Information in the Internal Market* (2001), at 49–79.

[7] See Wilhelmsson, 'Private Law Remedies against the Breach of Information Requirements of EC Law', in R. Schulze, M. Ebers, and H.C. Grigoleit (eds) *Informationspflichten und Vertragsschluss im Acquis communautaire* (2002), at 245–65.

B. The Enlargement Process

The enlargement process is mainly concerned with the new Member States coming from the 'former socialist' bloc. I deliberately chose the Baltic States, particularly Latvia where I lived from 2001 to 2004 and thus had convenient access to information. I also extended my research to Hungary and Poland which had enacted Civil Codes while still under the socialist regime, in 1959 and 1964 respectively, that were substantially modified but not completely abolished after the demise of socialism, though new codifications are on the agenda.[8] I will explain the differences in their contribution to modern contract law, as compared to that of the Baltic States. Again, I have had to rely on secondary sources which, however, seem to be better elaborated because these countries, in contrast to the Baltic republics which lost their independence in 1940 and again in 1944, never had to abandon their academic and professional contacts with the 'Western' world even during the darkest days of socialism.

After the 1990s, all of these countries became politically and legally linked to the European '*acquis*' by the so-called Europe Agreements (*infra* at Section 2.D), which exercised a deep influence on their contract law before accession. This will be shown by looking at the transformation (not implementation) of two important, so-called 'horizontal' European Directives, namely 93/13/EEC of 5 April 1993 on unfair terms in consumer contracts[9] and 99/44/EC of 25 May 1999 on the sale of consumer goods and associated guarantees.[10]

The enlargement process cannot, however, be understood without at least referring briefly to the prior legal system under socialist principles and its transformation under the rules of market economy. This was an autonomous legal revolution which the countries under scrutiny had undertaken before membership of the EU was ever discussed. This revolution has a truly constitutional character[11]—the abolition of socialist elements of property, of legal personality, and of restrictions of autonomy by a complex (some may say corrupt) licensing and regulation system, and its replacement by liberal principles of market economy. This cannot be studied here in great detail, but it must be remembered as a precondition to the current contract law and its tripartite function as described here.

C. 'Relative Autonomy' of Contract Law and Civil Justice

This chapter aims at a legal-theoretical analysis of the transformation process of contract law in the jurisdictions studied. Therefore, attention will be paid to the integration of these modern functions of contract law into the relevant legal systems.

---

[8] For Hungary *cf.* the paper by Vékas, 'Die Vorbereitungsarbeiten zu einem ungar. Zivilgesetzbuch', 13 *Wirtschaft und Recht in Osteuropa (WIRO)* (2001) 13.

[9] OJ 1993 L 95/29.

[10] OJ 1999 L 171/12.

[11] See A. Fogelklou and F. Sterzel (eds), *Consolidating Legal Reform in Central and Eastern Europe—An Anthology* (2003).

It may be a surprise to many observers that, despite similar political-economic principles, their implementation in the transformation process has been very different. There is clearly no 'European' model of private, or even only of contract, law, while there are indeed several models, traditions, and systems, and these vary greatly between the new Member States.

Among Marxist authors in the heyday of socialism this was known as the 'relative autonomy' of law[12] to explain why, despite the social and political revolution which had taken place in the countries studied, their legal systems still contained elements of 'traditionalism', particularly under the influence of the continental codification idea.

It can be shown that this ideological paradigm also worked the other way round: even under principles of market economy, the old socialist codes were not immediately replaced by new ones which reflected the imperatives of the transformation process. Sometimes only incremental changes were introduced into prior existing codes, but there is an inherent tendency to reshape legal reality by codification. The legal staff itself, whose older members were trained under the socialist regime, did not immediately convert to liberal ideas of market economy and government of laws (*Rechtsstaatlichkeit*).

Within this systemic transformation process, another question becomes crucial: how to integrate specific protective laws into the more general, and to some extent abstract and formal, codification principles? This is not specific to the contract law of the new Member States, but has been debated with equal passion in 'old' Member States like Germany, France, and Italy.[13] Labour law had been completely separated from general contract law and will therefore not be studied here. With regard to consumer law, the debate is still open, and we must thus study the different legal mechanisms for integrating this new, still rather unsystematic, area of law into the more general principles of contract law. This is not a merely theoretical debate. It also has great importance for the understanding and application of contract law itself: how far can 'specific private laws' (*Sonderprivatrechte*) inspire or, for its critics, undermine general contract law? Should an integrationist or a separatist approach be used? The debate has not ended, with some countries like Germany choosing an integrationist approach in its *Schuldrechtsmodernisierungs-Gesetz* (Act modernizing the German law of obligations) of 2001.[14]

The solutions found in the countries studied here are particularly relevant for the future of European contract law. Indeed, they form a wide field of legal and systematic experimentation, the results of which are slowly emerging. Can they contribute to answering the central question of 'codification' of European contract

---

[12] See N. Reich, *Sozialismus und Zivilrecht* (1972), at 33–7.

[13] References by Vékás, 'Privatrecht des Verbraucherschutzes in der EU', in L. Vékás and M. Paschke (eds), *Europäisches Recht im ungarischen Privat- und Wirtschaftsrecht* (2004), at 19–24.

[14] See Micklitz, 'The New German Sales Law: Changing Patterns in the Regulation of Product Quality', 25 *J Consumer Policy* (2002) 379; Rott, *supra* note 5; Grundmann, 'Germany and the Schuldrechtsmodernisierung 2002', 1 *European Review of Contract Law* (2005) 129 at 144–7.

law, namely either to systematize the existing *acquis* in consumer law or to favour an integrationist approach?[15]

2. CONTRACT LAW: FROM SOCIALISM TO MARKET ECONOMY

A. Overview

The Baltic countries, on the one hand, and Poland and Hungary, on the other, were forced into a socialist system of economy which obviously had a decisive influence on their respective contract law systems and principles. Owing to substantial political differences in the realization of this process, the impact on the legal system was quite different and will be mentioned below. The politico-economic specifics are, however, quite similar, even if their intensity has varied over time and place.

The socialist economy, in its conflict with market economy, is based on a completely different concept of property and the legal relations emerging from it. They will be briefly mentioned, without going into detail or repeating the century-long debate on their ideological origin and truth.

Since, according to Marxist theory, the system of private property in capitalist economies permits the extortion of the fruits of production by the owner and thus establishes a system of 'class-dominance', a socialist system which aims to overcome this process of unjust dominance and distribution of economic resources must and will at first radically modify the system of property ownership. Instead of a prevalence of private property over land and the means of production, a mechanism of socialist property must be introduced. In the Soviet model of socialism, the State becomes the main owner of property, which is allocated to economic unities (State enterprises etc.) for management only, not for full use and disposal. Alongside this State property, certain forms of collective, co-operative, or communal property are installed, the extent of which has varied greatly over time. There is no autonomous contract regime on the use and transfer of this type of socialist property. It underlies State supervision and disposal. In the interest of socialist economy, a certain transactional autonomy relating to the proceeds from running production (*Umlaufvermögen*), not to the stock of property itself, will be guaranteed to socialist entities, and in this context contract law plays a certain, yet limited, role. The *pacta sunt servanda* rule exists, but subject to the imperatives of the socialist economy, and therefore litigated before a special type of court, the so-called '*gosarbitrage*'. Contract law is not governed by the principle of autonomy, but by discretionary regulation, obligation to contract (*kontrahierungszwang*) and a rather restrictive licensing system, depending on the type of economic activity.[16]

---

[15] See the different answers in the contributions to S. Grundmann and J. Stuyck (eds), *An Academic Green Paper on European Contract Law* (2002). For a codification of European consumer law, *cf.* H. Rösler, *Europäisches Konsumentenvertragsrecht* (2004), at 250–88.

[16] Reich, *supra* note 12, at 275–303, Loeber, *Der hoheitlich gestaltete Vertrag* (1969) referring to the Soviet debate.

Whether elements of private property, mainly small businesses, were allowed to exist in parallel to socialist economic entities was subject to intense debate and conflict in the socialist economies before their own complete abolition, and there have been substantial changes in the countries studied, which will be discussed later (*infra* 2.B–2.C). Also, with regard to foreign investment different rules were imposed, always subject to State control and revocation.

Personal (in striking difference from 'private') property was allowed in all socialist countries and formed part of the civil law, but was restricted to items for personal and family use. It should not be used to create private property. Contractual relations with the latter objective were regarded as against the principle of socialist economy, and therefore void.

Parallel to this concept of property law, the law of persons systematically distinguished between those subjects who were managing State socialist property, namely socialist production and distribution entities, so-called socialist enterprises with a certain margin of discretion concerning the retention of profits for investment purposes, and other entities such as communes, branches of permitted political parties (mostly relating to the governing Communist parties and their auxiliary organizations), labour unions, recreation associations, etc. Other entities in the economic and social sphere were subject to a strict licensing system.[17] There was obviously no freedom of association, only a gradual alleviation of existing restrictions subject to the discretion of the ruling party.

In this system of socialist property and legal persons, a rather elaborate, but to some extent irrelevant, contract law system existed, playing a very limited role in legal practice. Between 'socialized entities' this was not conceptualized as an expression of 'party autonomy', but as the transmission of the will of the ruling class (the Communist party and its State and societal organs) into the economy. Limited autonomy was granted only in transactions regarding 'personal property'. Therefore, many transactions, even though quite common in socialist countries, were regarded as illegal, and therefore became part of an ever-growing black market—a phenomenon that explains to some extent the priority that is still given to criminal law over private law in legal practice, and the fundamental problems in the process of transformation to civil justice. Contract law operated more in the 'shadow of the law', instead of being a central part of the law itself as in market economies.

After the fall of socialism—a truly fundamental revolution—both the system of socialist property and that of licensing of legal entities and specific types of contracts were abolished. At the same time, a process of privatization and restoration of formerly nationalized property was initiated.[18]

---

[17] See Kordasiewicz and Wierzbowski, 'Polish Civil and Commercial Law', in A. Frankowski and B. P. Stephan (eds), *Legal Reform in Post-Communist Europe* (1995), at 163, 184–8.

[18] A typology of privatization is given by Brunner, 'Privatisierung in Osteuropa', 45 *Osteuroparecht* (1999) 2.

B. The 'Baltic Revolution'

The formerly independent Baltic states came under Soviet dominance in 1940, and then again in 1944 after the retreat of the German occupation forces. For these formerly independent countries, this implied a 'double revolution':

- A *political revolution*, since they became part of the Soviet Union as Soviet Republics, which implied loss, not only of sovereignty, but also of independent legislative functions. In civil law matters, this led to a separation of the Union competence to lay down 'fundamentals' of civil law, from that of the republics, to implement them in separate codes.[19]
- An *economic and social revolution*, which consisted in taking over the above-mentioned principles concerning ownership, legal personality, and restricted autonomy.

It is obvious that this double revolution brought to a halt the already quite advanced codification work taking place in the three republics:[20]

- Latvia had enacted its Civil Code in 1937. This came into force in 1939 and could not survive the Soviet take-over. It was immediately replaced by the RSFSR Code of 1924 in 1940.
- The Estonian codification was almost completed before the Soviet take-over, but the draft Code of 1939 was never formally enacted. It did not play any further role.[21]
- The Lithuanian codification work proved to be particularly difficult and protracted because of the several civil law systems which existed in this country, namely German law in the Klaipeda (Memel) region, Polish law (modelled on the *Code Napoléon*) in Wilna (Vilnius), (pre-revolutionary) Russian law in Kaunas, and Baltic law in Palanga. The merging of these different systems was not successful before the war.[22] A draft Code was prepared in 1940 but lost after Soviet occupation.[23]

After the Baltic Revolution in 1990–1991, which re-established the three formerly independent republics as sovereign States,[24] it was obvious that the law stemming from Soviet times had to be abolished and replaced by new civil legislation. However,

[19] Reich, *supra* note 12, at 311–26.

[20] See Loeber, 'Kontinuität im Zivilrecht nach Wiederherstellung staatlicher Unabhängigkeit', in J. Basedow *et al.* (eds), *Aufbruch nach Europa—75 Jahre Max Planck Institut für Privatrecht* (2001), at 943–54.

[21] *Ibid.*, at 948.

[22] *Ibid.*, at 951.

[23] Schulze, 'Das litautische Zivilrecht—Enwicklung, IPR und allgemeiner Teil', *Wichtige Gesetze des Ostens (WGO)* (2001), 331 at 332.

[24] See A. Lieven, *The Baltic Revolution* (1994), at 194.

this process happened differently in the three Baltic States, which explains the divergence of civil jurisdictions in this region:

- Latvia decided to re-enact the Civil Code of 1937 in 1992–1993, and to amend it mostly with regard to family and inheritance law. A draft commercial code including the regulation of certain transactions was prepared but never enacted. The existing commercial law is limited to company law and to formal questions on registration and the like. A separate Consumer Rights Act was enacted in 1999. It served to enact the relevant EU consumer law Directives into Latvian law, and has been amended with the coming of new Directives, for example, in 2001, to implement the Sales Directive 99/44. This dual system will be analysed in more detail below.[25]
- Estonia decided on a step-by-step codification of its civil law, starting with the most urgent subjects in property law.[26] Finally, in 2002 a comprehensive Code of Obligations was enacted which closely followed the Swiss and Dutch models, thereby including both commercial and consumer transactions. It is based on a 'comparative approach'.[27] EU consumer Directives have been included in the Code. This monist system is important from a legal-theoretical point of view.
- Lithuania decided first to 'de-socialize' the existing (socialist) civil law and at the same time to prepare a new comprehensive codification which was enacted on 18 July 2000.[28] This came into force on 1 June 2001. Its contract law closely follows the UNIDROIT principles.[29] Its part 6 contains the general principles as well as detailed rules of contract law, including consumer contracts. A separate Consumer Protection Law of 2000 exists, but the Code provisions will take priority over special laws (Article 1.3(2)). This has led to a parallel regulation of consumer contracts, notably those determined by EC Directives, while conflicts are solved not by the *lex specialis* principle, but by the *lex superior* rule.[30]

The different contract law systems in the Baltic States enable us to look at contract regulation as an experimental field, and to draw some conclusions for the future European contract law model.

---

[25] See Broka, 'Topical Issues of Protection of Consumer Rights', in University of Latvia (ed.), *Problems of Transformation of Law in Connection with European Integration. Current Topics in Latvian Law* (2002–3), at 345–55.

[26] See Kaërdi, 'Estonia and the New Civil Law', in H. McQueen, A. Vaquer, and S. Espiau (eds), *Regional Private Laws and Codification in Europe* (2003), at 250, 253–5; Paju, 'Basic Features of Estonia Property Law' [2000] *ZEuP* 87.

[27] Kaërdi, *supra* note 26, at 257; Sein and Kull, 'Die Bedeutung des UN-Kaufrechts im estnischen Recht', [2005] *IHR* 138.

[28] See Mikelenas, 'Unification and Harmonisation of Law at the Turn of the Millennium: the Lithuanian Experience', 5 *Uniform L Rev* (2000) 243–61; Schulze, *supra* note 23, at 339–53.

[29] Mikelenas, *supra* note 28, at 252–4.

[30] See Schulze, *supra* note 23, at 340.

C. Hungary and Poland

The 'revolution' which took place under Soviet dominance in these countries was a social and economic, more than a political, revolution. It meant the take-over of the Soviet system of socialist property and legal persons, but left formal jurisdiction with the constitutional authorities of these countries and gave them at least some margin of 'relative autonomy'. The solutions and techniques used in contract law are therefore to some extent different from those used in the Soviet Union and its republics like the Baltic States before their revolution. Both countries enacted their Civil Codes, Hungary in 1959 and Poland in 1964, which show some specifics and which are still in force today, even though the underlying economic systems have been substantially changed.

I. Hungary

The Hungarian Civil Code of 1959 deviated from the Soviet model to the extent that it recognized private property rights, although to a limited extent.[31] The Code was elaborated in the reform period which was abolished by Soviet occupation in 1956, and was adopted briefly after the execution of the leader of the reform government, Imre Nagy. It allowed the acquisition of ownership rights in land and anything else that could be taken into possession. Ownership rights could be acquired by transfer, manufacture, separation, accretion, adverse possession, and inheritance. Ownership was defined in the traditional sense, but it did not include using the property in a manner that would needlessly disturb others or jeopardize another's property rights. In parallel to this limited regime of 'private' property, the Code recognized socialist property and provided that it enjoyed 'increased legal protection'. It authorized private ownership of land, in contrast to the Soviet Union, but did not stop or reverse collectivization.[32] Full privatization occurred only after 1991.[33]

The introduction of the 'New Economic Mechanism'[34] increased the need for consumer protection. The first moderate rules were included in the Civil Code in 1977 by Act IV, allowing challenge to unfair contract terms. In section 209 the concept of general contract terms was, however, not defined. This was done only in 1997.[35]

Later reform concentrated on enacting a separate Consumer Protection Act. As a forerunner, in 1984 the Act to Prohibit Unfair Business Practices was enacted. This was substantially amended by Act LXXXVI of 1990 on the prohibition of

---

[31] See Spall, 'The Development of Private Property Rights in Communist Hungary and the Theory of Path Dependent Institutional Change' [2004] *Global Jurist Topics* 1.

[32] See Vékás, *supra* note 13, at 25.

[33] See Gobert, 'Eigentumsordnung und Privatisierung in Ungarn' [1997] *WIRO* 361.

[34] See Cseres, 'The Hungarian Cocktail of Competition Law and Consumer Protection: Should it be Dissolved?', 27 *J Consumer Policy* (2004) 43, at 46.

[35] Vékás, *supra* note 13, at 27.

Unfair Market Practices.[36] Finally, in 1997 Act No. CLV on Consumer Protection was adopted, and it came into force in 1998. It implemented several EC Directives, including the one on consumer credit.[37]

Directive 93/13 was transposed as Act CXIX of 1997 and amended sections 205(3), (5), (6), 207(2), and 209–209(d) of the Civil Code (*infra* 3.B.V). The Sales Directive, 99/44 was introduced into the Civil Code by Act XXXVI of 2002 (*infra* 4.B.IV).

Hungary therefore can be said to have a *modified uniform system*, but with a clear preference for putting consumer protection Directives, as far as they relate to contract law, into the Code as general legislation, and not into the special legislation on consumer protection (with the exception of consumer credit) or other separate acts (for example, package holidays).

Hungary is working on a new Civil Code which, according to one of its proponents, will be comprehensive legislation including commercial and consumer contracts.[38]

II. Poland

Polish civil law was codified by the Civil Code of 25 April 1964 which is still in force today. Naturally, its provisions bear characteristics of the earlier political system, the most salient having been the excessively privileged position of so-called 'social property'.[39] On the other hand, its system and rules are reminiscent of traditional continental codes. Socialist economy was ruled by decrees of the Council of Ministers, which was empowered to regulate commerce between 'the units of the socialised economy' (Article 2). This was done to a great extent, but stayed completely outside civil law. Economic activities by private persons, including the founding of legal persons, were based on a system of licences.

Surprisingly, the imposition of martial law on Poland in 1981 led to a further liberalization of the economy and therefore a re-establishment of civil law relations. 'The idea began to be advanced that "socialism" did not rule out the adoption of certain elements of a market economy'.[40] State enterprises gained more autonomy, the founding of small businesses was eased, and consumer protection inserted into the Code. By the Act of 23 December 1988 the State endorsed the freedom to engage in economic activity and the replacement of the almost universal system of licensing.[41]

The political changes after the demise of the Communist regime introduced traditional elements of property into the emerging (somewhat chaotic) market

---

[36] Cseres, *supra* note 34, at 51.
[37] *Cf.* the critique by Vékás, *supra* note 13, at 9.
[38] See Vékás, *supra* note 8.
[39] See Kordasiewicz and Wierzbowski, *supra* note 17, at 165.
[40] *Ibid.*, at 166.
[41] See Gralla, 'Polen—Gesetz über die Wirtschaftstätigkeit' [1992] *WIRO* 215.

economy. The Civil Code underwent a first stage of reform on 28 July 1990.[42] The concept of property was unified as a legal category. Privatization began, but was not completely implemented. Privatization through liquidation was used more frequently than commercial privatization—a sign of the bad state of the Polish economy.[43] Foreign investment was allowed almost without restriction.

Contractual autonomy was secured by abolishing the rules that pertained to the socialized elements of the economy, for example, the influence of the bureaucracy on engaging in and shaping of contractual relations. Article 353(1) of the Civil Code restored the principle of freedom of contract, with the reservation that what was contracted could not be contrary to the law or 'the principles of social coexistence' (*infra* 3.B.VI). A clear borderline was drawn between civil law transactions of a unilateral (consumer) and bilateral (professional) character. The first were treated more rigorously against the professional and in favour of the consumer.[44] A separate consumer law emerged, even though it was limited to some particular rules concerning payment, exclusion clauses, prescription periods, modification of the amount under inflationary conditions, and *clausula rebus sic stantibus*. Here, the Council of Ministers could intervene in order, in the interests of consumers, to restore the contractual equality of the parties. This power was used in practice under the Regulation of 30 May 1995, even though it was too reminiscent of the old system of contract regulation.[45]

Later changes in consumer law, in particular those imposed by EU Directives, were included in the Civil Code. Directive 99/44 was, however, transposed into separate legislation (*infra* 4.B.V). Poland can therefore be said to have maintained a *mixed system* of contract law. There has been a debate on drafting a new codification, but no concrete proposals have been published to my knowledge.

D. The Importance of the Europe Agreements

When it became clear that the above-mentioned former socialist governments and (Soviet) republics were to become members of the EU, they concluded association agreements (the Europe Agreements) to prepare them for membership and to guarantee the adoption of the so-called '*acquis communautaire*'. The Europe Agreements with Poland and Hungary were concluded in 1993–1994,[46] and with the Baltic states in 1997–1998.[47] They contain provisions on taking over the '*acquis*', for example, in the area of financial services, consumer protection, product liability, and

---

[42] See Pazdan, 'Zur Änderung des polnischen Zivilrechts', 37 *Osteuroparecht* (1991) 13.

[43] See Gralla, *supra* note 41, at 182.

[44] *Ibid.*, at 192.

[45] See Jara, 'Polen—Verbraucherkauf' [1996] *WIRO* 258; St. Heidenhain, *Das Verbraucherschutzrecht in Polen und in der EU* (2001) at 70.

[46] For Poland, see OJ 1993 L 348/1; for Hungary, see OJ 1993 L 347/1.

[47] For Latvia, see OJ 1998 L 26/1; for Lithuania, see OJ 1998 L 51/1; for Estonia, see OJ 1998 L 68/1.

labour law. Obviously, these provisions were so vaguely drafted that they do not have direct effect, in contrast to the non-discrimination rules of the EA,[48] but put an '*obligation de moyen*' on the future Member States which was supported by the so-called PHARE programmes and monitored by the Commission in its accession progress reports. Most countries under scrutiny indeed tried to make their legislation conform as much as possible with EU law.[49] This process terminated with accession on 1 May 2004.

The following analysis will pay special attention to the integration of consumer contract law into the existing civil legislation of the countries under scrutiny. It will be placed into the general concepts of contract law which have been described as autonomy, regulation, and information. Particular attention will be paid to legal-systematic questions which, even though striving to attain the same objectives, have used surprisingly different legal techniques and means of implementation. These will be classified here as:

- the monist approach (Estonia);
- the dualist approach (Latvia);
- the parallel approach (Lithuania);
- the modified monist approach (Hungary); and
- the mixed approach (Poland).

3. AUTONOMY

A. Recognition of Autonomy in Civil Legislation of New Member States

Primary Community law presupposes the autonomy of economic actors, but does not in itself guarantee it expressly.[50] However this will not be discussed in detail here.

All Civil Codes or Laws of Obligation of the countries investigated contain a guarantee of freedom of contract, the classical one being written into Article 1415 of the Latvian Civil Code of 1937:

An impermissible or indecent action, the purpose of which is contrary to religion, laws of moral principles, or which is intended to circumvent the law, may not be the subject matter of a lawful transaction; such transaction is void.

This is a somewhat 'old-fashioned' recognition of the principle of autonomy. The main problem is of course to define the limits of the law which restricts such freedom;

---

[48] See Reich, 'The Constitutional Relevance of Citizenship and Free Movement in an Enlarged Union', 11 *European Law Journal* (2005) 675.

[49] See Bober and von Redeker, 'Polens Gesetzgebung im Zuge der EG-Rechtsangleichung—Zur polnischen Debatte über Gesetzesfehler und das Gesetzgebungsverfahren', 48 *Osteuroparecht* (2002) 83 with regard to Poland; Vékás and Paschke, *supra* note 13, with regard to Hungary.

[50] See Müller-Graff, 'Basic Freedoms—Extending Party Autonomy across Borders', in Grundmann *et al.*, *supra* note 6 at 135–50.

here the fundamental freedoms of EC law have to be taken into account but will not be discussed in this context.[51]

A more 'modern definition' can be found in section 5 of the Estonian Code on Obligations and in Article 6.158 of the Lithuanian Civil Code:

- Section 5 of the Estonian Code states: '[u]pon agreement between the parties to an obligation or contract, the parties may derogate from the provisions of this Act unless the Act expressly provides or the nature of the provision indicates that the derogation from this Act is not permitted, or unless the derogation is contrary to public order or good morals or violates the fundamental rights of a person'.
- Article 6.158(1) of the Lithuanian Civil Code states: '[t]he parties to a contract are entitled to conclude contracts freely and to engage on their own will into mutual rights and obligations, and to conclude contracts which are not foreseen by this law, provided it does not violate the law . . .'.

The Estonian formula is particularly interesting and innovative, as it limits the 'fundamental freedom of contract' to the equally 'fundamental rights of a person'.

B. Good Faith and Pre-formulated Terms in (Consumer) Contracts

This section will be concerned with defining inherent limitations in the broad autonomy principles. Under continental legal tradition, they have been spelled out by the good faith principle. This has played a role in the control of so-called standard form and other unilaterally drafted contracts. Article 3(1) of EC Directive 93/13 on unfair contract terms has for the first time recognized this principle in Community law, which has thus become part of the *acquis*. It is, however, subject to a number of limitations, the most important of these being its personal application to a consumer as 'a natural person acting outside his trade, business or profession'. It is also not applicable to individually negotiated clauses and to clauses relating to the subject matter and the price of the transaction 'insofar as these terms are in plain intelligible language' (Article 4(2)). We will examine whether a more general approach has emerged in the Codes under investigation, which EU law would allow under the minimum harmonization principle.

I. Estonia

Sections 6 and 7 of the Estonian Act on obligations recognize the principles of 'good faith' and 'reasonableness'.

Good faith, supplemented by the new principle of reasonableness (probably borrowed from common law), is regarded as a guiding principle of the law of obligations,

---

[51] See Reich, *supra* note 3, at 269–74; O. Remien, *Zwingendes Vertragsrecht und Grundfreiheiten des EG-Vertrages* (2003), at 178.

including the interpretation of contracts: see section 29(5) No. 4. The relationship between the two principles is, however, not clear and has to be shaped by judicial interpretation; no precedents seem to exist.

Standard terms are regulated by sections 35–44 of the Act. Their prominent position makes it clear that they are an inherent limitation of autonomy. The Estonian legislator thereby implemented Directive 93/13, but at the same time extended its sphere of application, thus shaping a general law of standard terms, including such traditional rules on the irrelevance of surprising terms for the contents of the contract (section 37(3)), the priority of individual agreements over standard terms (section 38), the 'battle of forms' (section 40), and the '*contra proferentem*' rule of interpretation (section 39(1)).

Specific consumer protection provisions are included in the so-called black list in section 42(3), which widened the material sphere of the 'indicative list' of Article 3(3) of Directive 93/13; a total of 37 terms have been blacklisted. Section 44 provides for a presumption of unfairness of blacklisted clauses which have been inserted 'into a contract for the purposes of economic or professional activities of the person'. In a judgment of 15 March 2005, the Tarta Court of Appeal banned jurisdiction clauses as unfair, based on the case-law of the ECJ in *Océano*.[52] Section 36(2) and (3) relates to the international application of the rules on standard terms which is not limited to consumers residing in Estonia. With regard to business entities having '... their economic or professional activities and their places of business related to the contract or the performance thereof ... in Estonia', the rules of the Act on standard terms apply even if another law is applicable to the contract. Such broad application of Estonian law is contrary to the freedom of choice rules of Article 3 of the Rome Convention of 1980.[53] It also goes beyond Directive 93/13 because it is not limited to the law of a non-member country. With EU membership, Estonia may have to amend its Code of Obligations.

II. Latvia

Latvian law has enshrined the good faith principle in Article 1 of the Civil Code of 1937, which reads laconically '[r]ights shall be exercised and duties performed in good faith'.

The place of this norm in the overall structure of the Civil Code is said to be an acknowledgement of its fundamental importance in the implementation of civil law. In court practice, however, a narrow, subjective approach is preferred. The typical cases concern '*abus de droit*'. Thus, Article 1 of the Civil Code is considered to be a legal tool that can be used, *inter alia*, to prevent the exercise of rights in conditions when the entitled person has no protected interests, for instance, when the rights are used to achieve unfair aims.[54]

---

[52] Order 2-2-146/05 (not yet published); ECJ Case C-240/98, [2000] ECR I-4491.

[53] Reich, *supra* note 1, at 270.

[54] See K. Balodis, *The Principle of Good Faith in Latvian Civil Law. Likums und Tiesibas—Law and Justice* (2003), at 2–9, esp. at. 7.

The Latvian Civil Code recognizes the ability of the parties to a contract to use standard-form contracts. This follows from the general civil law provisions allowing the parties to choose freely the form in which to draw up a contract, and not binding them (except for cases when mandatory norms apply[55]) to obey any formalities or models.[56]

In the dualist Latvian system of civil law, the Consumer Rights Protection Act of 1999 (CRP Act) has implemented Directive 93/13, but has also introduced a number of particularities which may be seen as the emergence of new principles of contract law. Article 5 established the (normative) principle of legal equality between business and consumer, while Article 6(1) prohibits the use of such terms 'as are in contradiction with the principle of legal equality of the contracting parties, this law or other regulatory enactments'. This broad principle is not limited to standard or pre-formulated terms.[57] Only Article 6(3) takes up the wording of Article 3(1) of Directive 93/13 and at the same time blacklists 12 clauses from the 'indicatory list' of the Annex. The most important has been the extension of the concept of consumer to business entities acting outside their market activities:

consumer—a natural or legal person who expresses a wish to purchase, purchase or might purchase goods or utilises a service for a purpose which is not directly related to his or her entrepreneurial activity.

This has led to Latvian courts applying the consumer protection legislation to the purchase of cleaning material by a business company because this was outside its normal activity, quite contrary to the relevant case-law of the ECJ in *Idealservice*.[58] This leads to particular problems in the field of consumer credit where section 8(3) of the CRP Act allows the 'consumer' to perform the obligation of repayment before the period specified in the contract, without compensating the bank for lost profits even in the case of mortgage loans. It is not known whether this extension of consumer law to business activities has happened merely by accident or as a result of a misunderstanding of the relevant EC Directive, or whether it can be seen as the opinion of the Latvian CRP Act. In any case, it must be interpreted restrictively so as to exclude business entities not needing legal protection from falling under the definition of 'consumer'.

In clear violation of EC law, the Act does not provide for automatic nullity of unfair terms against the consumer, but allows only that the term 'shall be declared, upon request of the consumer, null and void, but the contract shall remain effective if it may continue functioning also after exclusion of the unfair provision'. This seems to rule out an *ex officio* disregard of the term by a court of law, as in the *Océano* judgment of the ECJ.[59]

[55] E.g., Arts. 1475, 1477, 1483, 1484, and 493 Civil Code.

[56] Art. 1492 Civil Code.

[57] See the critique of similar formulations in the Hungarian law by Vékás, *supra* note 13.

[58] Decision of the Riga regional court, No. C 33168300/504/02 against ECJ Case C-541/99, *Cape snc* v *Idealservice* [2001] ECR I-9049.

[59] See Cases C-240–244/98, *Océano Grupo Editorial* v *Rocio Murciano Quintero* [2000] ECR I-4491.

III. Lithuania

Article 1.5 of the Civil Code entrenches general principles of good faith, reasonableness, and justice. Courts must follow these principles in interpreting and applying legal norms. The same rules apply to the situation in which courts have discretion. Article 6.380 provides that obligations must be exercised in good faith; Article 6.158 acknowledges that each party must act in accordance with good faith, and the parties may not exclude or limit this duty. Lithuanian courts have on repeated occasions confirmed these principles.

Article 6.185(1) of the Lithuanian Civil Code provides a definition of standard terms—those contract provisions which are prepared in advance for general and repeated use by one party and which are actually used without negotiation with the other party. This provision basically reiterates Article 2.19 of the UNIDROIT principles.[60] Article 6.185(2) provides that standard terms of a contract proposed by one party bind the other only if the latter had due opportunity to become acquainted with these standard terms. Accordingly, standard terms cannot be used against a party if he did not have a proper chance to familiarize himself with the standard terms.

Article 6.186 introduces the definition of 'surprising terms'. No term contained in standard terms which is of such a character that the other party could not reasonably have expected it to be effective. A term is not surprising if it was expressly accepted by that party when it was duly disclosed. In determining whether a term is of such a character, regard should be had to its content, language, and presentation. Again, the provision in question reiterates UNIDROIT principles.[61] Article 6.186(3) also provides that, when a contract was concluded on the basis of standard terms, the other party has the right to demand the termination or amendment of the contract where standard terms, even if they are not against the law, exclude or limit the legal liability of the party which prepared them, or violate principles of equality of the parties and the balance of their interests, or conflict with the principles of reasonableness, good faith, and fairness.

The currently effective Law on Consumer Protection and the Civil Code centralized regulation of the consumer protection issues. Those laws have been harmonized with the main EU consumer protection legislation,[62] including Directive 93/13. As regards their wording with respect to consumer protection, the Law on Consumer Protection and the Civil Code are almost identical and at present the courts apply both in parallel.

Article 6.188 of the Civil Code gives a consumer the right to ask a court to avoid the unfair terms. On the other hand, the court can declare contractual terms void *ex officio* when such terms are contrary to the imperative/mandatory rules. The Civil Code does not expressly state whether the consumer protection rules entrenched in

---

[60] For the importance of the UNIDROIT principles see Mikelenas, *supra* note 28, at 252–4.
[61] Art. 2.20 Civil Code.
[62] *Doing business in Lithuania* (available at www.infolex.lt/portal/ml/start.asp?act=dobiz).

Article 6.188 are mandatory. It is not clear whether the court is able to set aside the application of the relevant term even where the consumer has not raised the fact that it is unfair.

The Article also contains a non-exhaustive list of the terms which are regarded as unfair.[63] This list is a verbatim translation of the Annex to the Unfair Terms Directive, but transposed into a blacklist. However, the unfairness of a contractual term is determined by the court, taking into account the nature of the goods or services for which the contract was concluded and taking into account all the circumstances surrounding the conclusion of the contract, and the provision is merely a word-for-word implementation of Directive in question.

It is important that this list is not exhaustive—other contractual terms may be regarded as unfair, provided that they are contrary to the requirements of good faith and cause an imbalance in the mutually enjoyable rights and obligations between the seller, service provider, and consumer.[64]

It should be pointed out that the *contra proferentem* rule applies not only in litigation where one party is a consumer; it also applies where there is doubt about the meaning of it and which works in favour of the party which accepted it.[65]

IV. Hungary

As mentioned above, Act CXIX of 1997 amended the Civil Code to regulate general contract terms. These broad provisions are not limited to consumer contracts and therefore have a wider application than Directive 93/13, while others, particularly those regarding blacklisted clauses, are limited to consumer contracts.[66] The Hungarian legislator did not go as far as the Estonian law.

Section 209/C contains a definition of standard terms which insists that the user (which, contrary to the former law, can also be a private party) determines the contract conditions in advance, unilaterally, and for the purpose of repeated contract conclusion without the other party being able to participate. It does not, however, require the clause not to have been individually negotiated.[67] The burden of proof concerning (non-)participation in the drafting of the contract is imposed on the user, a rule restricted to consumer contracts. The insistence on 'participation' and not on 'negotiation' may be due to a misunderstanding of the relevant EC law provisions, which at that time had not been officially translated.

The concept of unfairness was defined in section 209/B(1) by reference to the concept of 'good faith' under Directive 93/13, well known in Hungarian law. In

---

[63] Art. 6.188(2) Civil Code.

[64] Art. 6.188(3) Civil Code.

[65] Art. 6.193(4) Civil Code.

[66] For the time effects of Directive 93/13 see Case C-302/04, *Ynos Kft* v *Janos Vargo* and Opinion of AG Tizzano of 22 Sept. 2004.

[67] For a critique see Vékás, *supra* note 13, at 26 f., 32–3. This is probably due to the fact that the original draft version of Directive 93/13 was taken over.

specifying the Directive, it tries to give two examples of a one-sided and unjustified imposition of rights and duties (section 209/B(2)), namely:

- if the clause deviates substantially from central provisions of contract law;
- if it is incompatible with the subject matter or provisions of the contract.

Vékás observes that this way the non-mandatory provisions of the Civil Code become mandatory.[68]

The main criticism of the Hungarian regulation is concerned with the widening of the ambit of Directive 93/13 (respectively its Hungarian implementation) to include business-to-business (B2B) contracts.[69] If, on the other hand, one starts from the assumption—which is the basis of this chapter—that the good faith principle is also rooted in B2B contracts, even though in a somewhat less intensive way, these contracts should not be excluded from the unfairness control of pre-formulated clauses. The yardstick may be a different and less intrusive one, and the confusion of the Hungarian legislator between 'normal' and 'consumer' contracts may not be a very promising and successful approach.

V. Poland

As mentioned above, the re-establishment of a market economy in Poland and the abolition of special relationships between socialist enterprises led to the recognition of the equality of all civil law subjects, and thus the rejection of the privileged position of socialist enterprises, and of contractual freedom.[70] According to Article 353.1 of the Civil Code of 1964 as amended in 1990: 'the parties are free to determine their legal relationship according to their free will, provided that its contents and objectives do not contradict the nature of the legal relation, the law and the principles of social coexistence'. The good faith principle is indirectly recognized in Article 7 of the Civil Code: 'if the law determines certain legal consequences by referring to good or bad faith, there is a presumption of good faith'.

By Act of 2 March 2000, in force since 1 July 2000, Article 384 *et seq.* of the Civil Code of 1964 were amended to modernize the existing law on standard contract clauses and to introduce specific rules of consumer protection under the impact of EC Directive 93/13 and the Europe Agreement with Poland.[71]

Article 385.3 contains a 'grey list' of 23 clauses which, in cases of doubt, are regarded as 'wrongful provisions'. The provisions of the Code mention the transparency

---

[68] See Vékás, *supra* note 13, at 28, 34.

[69] *Ibid.*, at 34–40.

[70] See Poczobut, 'Zur Reform des polnisches Zivilrechts (mit einigen rechtsvergleichenden Bemerkungen)', 7 *ZEuP* 75, at 82.

[71] Surdek/Binieda, 'Protection of Competition and Consumers', in Z. Brodecki (ed.), *Polish Business Law* (2003), at 470–3; Heidenhain, *supra* note 45, at 222 with detailed references to the Polish legislative procedure.

principle of Article 4(2) of the Directive in Article 385 §3, in conformity with ECJ case-law.[72]

The structure of the new law is somewhat complicated because general questions of the law of standard contract terms are mixed with specific rules on consumer protection, taking different concepts as starting points. There are no rules concerning 'surprising clauses'. The *contra proferentem* rule is only applied to consumer contracts, not as a general principle of the interpretation of standard forms.

4. REGULATION

A. Generalities—the Importance of Directive 99/44 for General Contract Law

The following section will be devoted to analysing the importance of Directive 99/44 for the contract law of the countries studied here. It is meant to be a consumer protection Directive, as clearly stated in paragraph 1 of its 'recitals'. It is therefore limited to consumer sales in a personal and substantive sense:

- personal, insofar as only consumers as 'natural persons acting for purposes which are not related to [their] trade, business or profession' come within its ambit of protection;
- substantive, insofar as only consumer goods as 'tangible movable goods' are covered with some exceptions, and not immovable property, rights, and obligations.

With this limitation, the provisions of the Directive and Member State law implementing it are mandatory and cannot be waived (Article 7(1)).

But the importance of the Directive goes far beyond this narrow regulatory approach with respect to consumer protection:

(1) First, it extends regulation beyond mere consumer protection, because in Article 4 it provides for a right of redress of the last seller against his or her seller, or the manufacturer, or the importer of the product in the chain of distribution. It is not clear how far this right can be contracted out of; there is no provision similar to Article 7(1) of the Directive, and paragraph 9 of the 'recitals' is rather ambiguous on this point. On the one hand, it gives the last seller a right to 'pursue remedies against the producer, the previous seller in the same chain of contracts or any other intermediary, unless he has renounced that entitlement'. At the same time, the 'principle of freedom of contract' is said to be safeguarded, and it is left to national law to determine 'against whom and how the seller may pursue such remedies', thereby implicitly stating that the seller must be able as such to pursue

---

[72] See Case C-144/99, *Commission* v *Netherlands* [2001] ECR I-3541; Heidenhain, *supra* note 45, at 250; Reich, *supra* note 3, at 280; Vékás, *supra* note 13, at 33 with regard to Hungarian law.

these remedies, and that they cannot be completely contracted out of. This ambiguity must, however, be resolved by national law. This chapter will not go into the discussion of such a highly controversial point,[73] but will simply look at the solutions adopted by the Member States under scrutiny.

(2) Secondly, the concepts used in the Directive itself, especially on conformity stemming from the United Nations Sales Convention, have a much broader sphere of application than consumer sales; they may imply a general paradigm change in sales, and even more in contract, law. It is suggested that dualist systems of contract law will have more problems with implementing the Directive than monist ones, and that countries which decide upon a new codification of contract law will be better off than those that have to merge the imperatives of the Directive into their pre-existing contract law.

(3) Thirdly, the question of remedies has been intensely debated and resolved in a rather detailed, though not complete, way. This responds to the general Community law principle of '*ubi res ibi remedium*'.[74] It does not, however, refer to compensation, but leaves this to the Member States under the minimum harmonization principle.

B. The Importance of Directive 99/44 on Contract Law within the Enlargement Process

I. Estonia

The Estonian Code of Obligations regulates sales law in its sections 208–237. It uses Directive 99/44 to modernize sales law in general, while section 237(1) provides that in consumer sales the legal remedies provided cannot be contracted out of. The same is true if:

a contract is entered into as a result of a public tender, advertising or other similar economic activities taking place in Estonia . . . with a purchaser residing in Estonia regardless of the country whose law is applied to the contract.

The buyer's remedies are set out in sections 220–225 and are nearly identical for business-to-business (B2B) and business-to-consumer (B2C) contracts. Section 228 contains a provision on redress for a seller in consumer sales, but only in cases of 'a statement by the producer, previous seller or other retailer with respect to particular characteristics of the thing'. This is somewhat narrower than Article 4, because there redress can be sought 'because of a lack of conformity resulting from an act or omission by the producer . . .'. These rules are not mandatory, but may be caught by the principles of unfair term legislation (*supra* 2.B.I).

---

[73] See N. Reich and H.-W. Micklitz, *Europäisches Verbraucherrecht* (2003), at paras. 17.19–17.22.

[74] See van Gerven, 'Of Rights, Remedies and Procedures', 38 *CML Rev* (2001) 501; Reich, *supra* note 3, at 239.

Section 230(1) contains detailed rules on warranties. The transparency requirements of the Directive are correctly implemented. In addition to Article 5 of the Directive, there are certain presumptions concerning the content of the warranty.

II. Latvia

In the dualist system of Latvia, the Civil Code of 1937 does not regulate the remedies for non-conformity in sales contracts as such, but establishes general rules on liability in so-called 'alienation contracts for consideration' (*entgeltlicher Veräußerungsvertrag*), for example, sales, barter, and pledge. The alienator has to guarantee that the 'property has no hidden defects and possesses all the good qualities which are warranted or presumed' (Article 1593). Article 1612 *et seq.* regulate in detail the duties of the alienator and the remedies of the acquirer which are, as in traditional Roman systems, limited to rescission and reduction of the price. The limitation period for the first is six months, and for the second it is one year (Articles 1633, 1634).

Under the existing Latvian law, Directive 99/44 could not simply be enacted into the Civil Code because it starts from a completely different concept. Therefore, an amendment of the CRP Act was made on 22 November 2001. This reinforced the dualist system of Latvian law.

The CRP Act lists all the criteria indicating that goods do not conform to the contract by reiterating in the negative form the criteria for goods presumed to be in conformity with the contract listed in the Sales Directive,[75] adding several other grounds, such as counterfeit goods, inappropriate packaging, etc.

The CRP Act restates the four means of redress available to the consumer precisely as defined in the Sales Directive.[76] The peculiarity of Latvian implementation is that when non-conformity is claimed within a period of six months after delivery, the consumer has the free choice of the four remedies provided for by the Sales Directive—a questionable implementation, not taking into account the detailed two-step procedure of enforcing claims which the Directive introduced after long debates in the Parliament and the Council, suggesting a complete harmonization of the hierarchy of remedies (with the exception of compensation).[77]

Six months after delivery, priority is given to repair or replacement. If these means are not available or cause considerable inconvenience to the consumer, the contract can be rescinded, but the payment made to the consumer should take natural depreciation of goods into consideration. There are no such provisions in the Sales Directive. It seems justified to take the interests of the sellers into consideration here, as Latvian law does.

---

[75] Art. 14(1) of the CRP Act, transposing Art. 2(2) of the Sales Directive.

[76] Art. 28 of the CRP Act, transposing Recital 10 to the Sales Directive, *supra* note 75.

[77] See Rott, 'Minimum Harmonisation for the Completion of the Internal Market? The Example of Consumer Sales Law', 40 *CML Rev* (2003) 107, at 129; Reich, 'Stichtag 1. Mai 2004: Eine erweiterte Union—auch ein erweitertes europäisches Zivilrecht? Zur Rolle der baltischen Privatrechtssysteme in der EU' [2004] *ZEuP* 449.

Another interesting point is that under Latvian law a guarantee is an undertaking by a seller going beyond (that is, granting more than) the protection of the CRP Act.[78] If the guarantee does not specify something more, it cannot be called a 'guarantee'. Latvian law thus gives more protection to consumers in this respect.

According to section 33 of the CRP Act, the seller is entitled to pursue remedies against the person liable in the contractual chain. It seems that no private arrangement can avoid the liability of the final seller. This right of subrogation has been included in the CRP Act to make enforcement of consumer claims effective, and therefore it is not possible to contract out. The Latvian legislator has not changed the provisions of the Civil Code even though they may be based on a different theory of liability and have shorter prescription periods than foreseen by the Directive.

Latvian implementation, although not formally integrated into the old Civil Code of 1937, will amend general civil law beyond the realm of consumer protection in three directions.

(1) The broad consumer concept (*supra* 3.B.II) means that certain B2B transactions will also be caught by the CRP Act and will take priority over the rules of the Civil Code.

(2) Questions of redress for the seller from his or her suppliers will be solved by subrogation, for example, by applying the norms of the CRP Act without allowing the defences under general civil law to be raised.

(3) Most surprisingly, the rules on conformity have also been extended to cover services, within section 29 of the CRP Act.

The CRP Act may therefore be the starting point for a substantial change in the existing Latvian contract law as such. It is not known how the emergence of a new contract law will be handled by the Latvian legislator and Latvian courts.

III. Lithuania

All questions of contract law are dealt with in the sixth book of the Civil Code of 2000, which first deals with the law of obligations. The chapters following cover the law of contracts, followed by obligations arising on other grounds, and then provisions concerning particular contracts. Sales contracts are also regulated by the Law on Consumer Protection[79] (CPL), which is applicable only in the cases mentioned above.

The 23rd section of the fourth part of the sixth book of the Code contains provisions on sales contracts. Its paragraph (4) contains special norms on consumer sales contracts.

The rights of the consumer when he or she acquires goods that do not conform with the contract in Article 3 of the Sales Directive are set out in Article 6.363(4)

---

[78] Art. 16 of the CRP Act.

[79] The Law on Consumer Protection of the Republic of Lithuania, new wording of 2000.10.11, Official Gazette No. 85-2581, 2000.10.11, available at www3.lrs.lt/c-bin/eng/preps2?Condition 1=114309&Condition2.

of the Code. These are the right to have the goods brought into conformity by replacement (Article 6.363(4)(1)) or repair (Article 6.363(4)(3)) free of charge, the right to have an appropriate reduction in the price (Article 6.363(4)(2)), and the right to rescind the contract (Article 6.363(8)). The Code differs from the Directive in the manner of application of those rights. The Directive provides in Article 3(5) that the consumer is entitled to a reduction in the price or to have the contract rescinded, if the consumer is not entitled to other rights, mentioned above, or under other conditions as specified in the Sales Directive. The Code, however, provides in Article 6.363(4) that the consumer has a discretion to choose one of those rights—a problematic provision similar to the one under Latvian law (*supra* 4.B.II).

Article 4 of Directive 99/44 provides for a right of redress, and this right is indirectly enshrined in Article 6.280 of the Code. This part of the Code deals with questions of the law of torts, which is part of the chapter on obligations arising on grounds other than contract. According to Article 6.280(1), the person who has reimbursed the injury caused to another person has a right of redress equal to that reimbursement, if the law does not provide for a different amount. The Lithuanian rules on subrogation seem to be similar to those of Latvian law (*supra* 4.B.II) and make redress mandatory.

Article 6 of the Sales Directive lists some important requirements for the content of the guarantee. Special provisions of the Code on consumer sales contracts, namely Article 6.353(1), establish the seller's obligation to provide the necessary information about goods to the consumer, including terms of the guarantee. The Code regulates the term of the guarantee in Article 6.335—it states that the term of the guarantee begins to run from the moment of handover of the goods, unless the parties agree otherwise. It also covers other matters, none of which relate to the contents of the guarantee itself.

IV. Hungary

If we follow Vékás'[80] detailed account of the implementation of Directive 99/44 into Hungarian private law, there was agreement to amend the respective provisions of the Civil Code of 1959, and not to create a special law on consumer sales, as in Latvia and Poland. One of the reasons was the modern concept of liability of the seller based on the agreement; the concept used was 'defective performance', which is identical to 'lack of conformity' in the sense of Article 2 of the Directive. Some provisions of the implementing legislation became less 'consumer-friendly'. In the old Hungarian Civil Code, only positive knowledge of non-conformity excluded the seller's liability, while the Directive, in Article 2(3), extends it to the case where the 'consumer could not reasonably be unaware of the lack of conformity', which was adopted by section 305/A(2) of the Civil Code.

---

[80] See Vékás, *supra* note 13, at 41–68.

The remedies of Article 3 of the Directive were transposed into Hungarian law and extended by making use of the former case-law of the Hungarian Supreme Court, for example on giving the consumer a right to retain the purchase price in case of non-conformity. There is also a right to self-repair and to the reimbursement of such costs, if the seller does not complete the repair within an adequate time (section 306(3)).[81] As in the earlier law, the consumer must inform the seller of lack of conformity within two months, in accordance with Article 5(2) of Directive 99/44. This period may be extended. Lack of information leads not to a loss of remedies, but only to an obligation to pay the seller the additional costs caused by the delay (section 307, Civil Code). The general time limit for actions against a seller has been extended to two years, but only for consumer sales.

The seller has a right of redress against his or her prior seller for the costs of fulfilling the consumer's claims, provided that the latter has informed the seller about the lack of conformity. The time limit for redress is 60 days after fulfilling the consumer's claims, and not more than five years in all. This right of redress can be waived in part or completely[82]—a somewhat problematic solution with regard to Article 4 of Directive 99/44.

The Hungarian legislator also made clear that the contractual guarantee does not alter the consumer's rights in law (section 248, Civil Code). The guarantee is not a mandatory instrument. The rights under the guarantee have to be exercised similarly to the remedies for non-conformity. The transparency and form requirements of the guarantee have been transposed into law, but their lack does not avoid the claim.

Vékás[83] summarizes the Hungarian transposition of Directive 99/44 as follows:

> The transposition must be said to be a success. It is practically in full conformity with the directive, except for some minor errors. It must be particularly welcomed that the new rules have been organically integrated into the existing provisions of the Civil Code even where they go beyond the directive, and that the few special rules on consumer sales have been separated. In my opinion, the maintenance of non-mandatory rules including the right of redress must be clearly supported.

V. Poland

Poland has implemented Directive 99/44 not by amending its Civil Code of 1964, but by special Act of 27 July 2002, effective from 1 January 2003. At the same time it tried to create comprehensive consumer sales legislation, going further than Directive 99/44. The information requirements of the Act are dealt with *infra* at 5.B.V.

Section 1 defines its sphere of application similarly to the Directive. Sections 4–7 contain the transposition of Article 2 of the Directive. The provision in Article 2(4)

---

[81] See Vékás, *supra* note 13, at 65.

[82] Defended by Vékás, *ibid.*, at 67, referring to the freedom of contract principles which, however, are applicable here only to a limited extent.

[83] *Ibid.*, at 68.

on the cases where a seller is not bound by statements of the producer or his or her representative has been adopted by Polish law, with the exception of the alternative that 'at the time of conclusion of the contract the statement had been corrected'.

Section 8 of the Polish Act transposes Article 3 of Directive 99/44 on the rights of the consumer. The definition of 'free of charge' in Article 3(4) is extended to cover costs borne by the buyer, 'particularly costs of disassembly, delivery, labour, materials, as well as costs of another installation by other means'. The Act therefore confirmed the existence of a far-reaching right of the consumer to self-help, like Hungarian law. The limits of such self-help are not defined. The seller must react to a demand to repair or replace within 14 days. If the seller does not do so, the demand 'shall be deemed justified'.

Section 10 is concerned with time limits and prescription within the limits allowed by the Directive. Section 9 imposes a two-month notification period. Section 11 makes the rights of the consumer mandatory and tries to avoid their circumvention by a buyer's statement 'that he had the knowledge of the non-conformity of the consumer good with the agreement, or by opting to apply a foreign law'.

Section 13 contains detailed rules on warranties, as regards their contents, transparency, and the giving of the address of the warrantor 'or his representative in Poland'. It must be formulated in Polish. Violation of these requirements does not affect the validity of the warranty, as provided for in Article 6(5) of the Directive.

The Act does not contain any rules on the right of redress. This is left to the general provisions of the Polish Civil Code, which mean that they can be contracted out of in accordance with the general rules of civil law. It is not certain to what extent protection under standard-term legislation (*supra* 3.B.V) is available in this context.

5. INFORMATION

A. Generalities—EC Law as the Starting Point

Autonomy requires actors who are informed about their rights and duties. In traditional legal concepts, it is usually left to the actors themselves to acquire the necessary information that makes their freedom of action possible and effective. *Caveat emptor* as the general rule of autonomous transactions in contract law includes the responsibility to keep oneself informed. Autonomy is thus reduced to a formal concept based on the fiction that actors either have or can obtain the information needed to make decisions. Eventually they will have to 'buy' and pay for it if they do not want to rely on information conveyed through advertising.

Community law as a basically liberal order also started from this principle. However, it has increasingly recognized that autonomy in a substantive sense must be supplemented by the provision of adequate information. In the meantime, information requirements as regards citizens have become part of primary Community law itself, as seen especially in Article 153(1) EC. This contains the consumer's right to information, which of course also includes (pre-)contractual information, even though it has to be implemented by specific Directives. The objective of Community law, as a recent study by Rösler has stated, is the timely, specific, and complete disclosure of relevant information to the consumer as the structurally weaker party to a contract.[84] We will not go into details of the information paradigm in Community law, which can be found on three levels:

(1) the interdiction of deceptive and misleading information—a rule particularly applicable to marketing practices;

(2) the transparency principle in pre-contractual negotiations;[85] and

(3) specific information obligations in consumer Directives.[86]

B. Information Requirements in Contract Legislation of New Member States

I. Estonia

The Estonian Code of Obligations contains a general information rule concerning pre-contractual negotiations. Section 15(2) reads:

Persons who engage in pre-contractual negotiations or other preparations for entering into a contract shall inform the other party of all circumstances with regard to which the other party has, based on the purpose of the contract, an identifiable essential interest. There is no obligation to inform the other party of such circumstances of which the other party could not reasonably be expected to be informed.

Obviously, this broad obligation must be filled out by case-law which, at the time of writing, does not yet exist. It is worth mentioning that the information obligation is not limited to consumer contracts, even though it will have its main ambit there.

II. Latvia

The limited application of a general duty to act in good faith also underpins the legal regulation of pre-contractual duties on information in Latvian civil legislation. The Civil Code of 1937 regulates pre-contractual duties only in general terms. Thus, the scope of the *culpa in contrahendo* provision as a basis for pre-contractual information in the Latvian Civil Code is quite narrow, generally covering only intentional misconduct, and not negligence. In the light of this, it has been suggested in Latvian legal literature that amendments need to be made to the law, requiring the pre-contractual negotiations to be conducted in good faith, with the intention of entering into contractual relations.[87]

---

[84] See Rösler, *supra* note 15, at 148, 168.

[85] For its importance in the implementation of Community law see Case C-144/99, *Commission* v *Netherlands* [2001] ECR I-3541.

[86] For details see Reich, *supra* note 3, at 299–302.

[87] See Balodis, *supra* note 54.

The principle requiring transparency of pre-formulated terms on price or the subject matter of a contract (Article 4(2) of Directive 93/13) seems to be omitted and not transposed into the CRP Act at all. On the hand, the rules on the transparency of a guarantee in sales contracts have been introduced into the Latvian CRP Act (*supra* 4.B.II).

Latvia has specific legislation concerning the use of the Latvian language as the official State language (rather than Russian, which was the second or even first language in Soviet times). It is mostly concerned with State activities, but some effects spill-over into private law relations which are justified, according to section 2, by concerns of public security, public health, consumer protection, and the like. Thus, section 9 reads:

Contracts of natural and legal persons regarding provision of medical treatment, health care, public safety and other public services in the territory of Latvia shall be entered into the official language. If a contract is in a foreign language, a translation into the official language shall be attached thereto.

It is somewhat surprising that this strict rule is justified by concerns of consumer protection, because the consumer to be protected may not know Latvian at all. Latvian law also contains a general exception to rules on the use of language in private international law which normally would be either the language of the law applicable to the contract or the language in which the parties negotiated. It is also not clear what the consequences of disregarding this provision are: will the entire contract be avoided if it is drafted in a foreign language without a translation attached to it? This seems to be out of line with the principle of proportionality which the law itself mentions in section 2(2).

III. Lithuania

The Lithuanian Civil Code expressly obliges parties to reveal to each other information essential for the conclusion of a contract.[88] Furthermore, where confidential information is given by one party in the course of negotiations, the other party is under a duty not to disclose that information or to use it improperly for its own purposes, whether or not a contract is subsequently concluded.[89] A party which breaks this obligation is liable for the losses caused to the other party.[90] Article 6.164(2) provides that minimum losses in such situations are equal to the benefit received by the other party.

Under both the Law on Consumer Protection and the Civil Code, consumers are entitled to receive in the Lithuanian language (except when the use of the goods and services is known by custom) correct, complete, and transparent information concerning the terms under which goods and services are purchased, their quality,

[88] Art. 6.163(4) Civil Code.
[89] Art. 6.164(1) Civil Code.
[90] *Ibid.*

directions for use, a description of warranties and exchange period, procedures for termination of contracts for goods or services, and other relevant information which is significant to consumers.[91]

If the consumer was not provided with relevant information the consumer has the right to claim damages, or unilaterally to terminate the contract, reclaim sums paid by him or her, and claim other damages if the contract was concluded.[92] Moreover, if the seller fails to provide the necessary information, the seller is responsible for defects in the goods which occurred after the goods were delivered to the consumer, when the consumer proves that the defect occurred because of the lack of information.[93]

IV. Hungary

The Hungarian Civil Code contains a general information obligation in section 205(4) which reads:

The parties have to cooperate when concluding a contract and take care of the justified interests of the other side. Before concluding the contract they have to inform each other about the relevant essential circumstances concerning the contract to be concluded.

This rule has been extensively used by the Hungarian courts to impose information requirements, particularly in relations in which the parties are not equally informed. It is supplemented by specific information obligations which are derived from transposing EC Directives, namely on unfair contract terms and on consumer sales.

The Consumer Protection Act of 1997 gives the consumer two important rights to information:

- information with regard to the product or service purchased; and
- information about remedies—certainly an innovative provision.

V. Poland

Specific information requirements are included in the Act of 27 July 2002 on consumer sales (*supra* D.II.V). Section 2 contains a requirement for general information on price, unit price, and the conditions of a hire purchase or similar agreement. At the buyer's request the seller must 'issue a written[94] confirmation of the conclusion of the agreement, including the seller's mark bearing his address, date of sale and specification of the consumer good together with its amount and price'. Section 3 contains a requirement for sales in Poland 'to provide clear, understandable,

---

[91] Art. 6.353 Civil Code and Art. 5 Law on Consumer Protection.

[92] Art. 6.353(9) Civil Code.

[93] Art. 6.353(10) Civil Code.

[94] It is not clear whether this confirmation can also be in an electronic form, which seems to be required by Art. 9 of Directive 2000/31/EC of 8 June 2000 of the EP and the Council on Electronic Commerce, OJ 2000 L 178/1.

not misleading information in Polish, necessary for proper and full use of the consumer good'. There are detailed rules with regard to the placement of the information, instructions for use, maintenance manuals, all in Polish, and 'At the buyer's request the seller shall explain the meaning of each provision of the agreement'. The Polish language requirement, written into the Act on language which contains this requirement for 'legal transactions performed within the territory of Poland',[95] is, however, not without problems in the context of party autonomy and free movement of products and services.

6. CONTRACT LAW 'IN THE BOOKS' AND 'IN ACTION': 'NEW' RULES FOR 'OLD' MECHANISMS OF CIVIL JUSTICE?

A. A Summary of the 'New' Contract Law of 'New' Member States

The investigation made above has shown that the principles of autonomy, regulation, and information as basic requirements of a market-conforming contract law, integrating consumer protection requirements, have been adopted by all former socialist countries now members of the EU, but that the methods and instruments chosen for doing so differ widely. We have distinguished between a 'monist approach' (Estonia), a 'dualist approach' (Latvia), a 'parallel approach' (Lithuania), a 'modified uniform approach' (Hungary), and a 'mixed approach' (Poland). This shows the richness of European legal cultures after the enlargement process which will certainly give impetus to the emergence of a 'uniform' European contract law. European contract law is truly an experimental field and may even be used for trying out of a 'competition of better rules': for example, on how to implement general information requirements written into some modern contract legislation (Estonia, Lithuania, to some extent also Hungary and Poland); on redress of the final seller in consumer sales contracts (Latvia, Lithuania); on transparency of guarantees (Estonia, Latvia, Hungary, to some extent also Poland); in improving remedies under EU law (Lithuania, Hungary); and in prescribing spill-over effects to general contract law which has not yet been reformed (Latvia). At the same time, it warns against too much uniformity, and may discourage those who are optimistically promoting a 'European Civil Code'.

European law, in both its general principles and its specific Directives, has had an enormous impact on the contract law of the new Member States under scrutiny here. It is even more remarkable that this process has been accomplished before, and not after, membership. There may be certain deficiencies with regard to the implementation of Directives, for example on the hierarchy of consumer remedies in sales contracts (Latvia, Lithuania), but they cannot be said to be such as to endanger the European legal integration model—quite the contrary. They have strongly

---

[95] See Klapsa, 'Die Auswirkungen des Gesetzes über die polnische Sprache auf die Vertragpraxis' [2000] *WIRO* 233; Surdeck/Binieda, *supra* note 71, at 479.

reinforced general contract law principles like good faith and control over standard contract terms. They have allowed specific contract law, most notably on consumer protection, to 'spill-over' into general contract law. They have encouraged integrationist models of contract law which have clearly shown the deficits of a dualist model, as in Latvia. EU law has therefore been an instrument of transformation and modernization of contract law—similar to the situation in 'old' Member States like Germany.

This chapter is not concerned with the implementation of EC law as such and with possible violations of the obligations of the new Member States. Two seemingly contradictory trends should, however, be mentioned.

(1)   All the new Member States analysed here have made great efforts to bring their contract law in line with basic EC Directives before membership, even though they have done so via different methods, as they are entitled to do under Article 249(3) EC.

(2)   On the other hand, there is a certain tendency to extend consumer protection provisions into areas which are not covered by consumer law: for example, rules on the territorial application of consumer law (Estonia, Poland); the widening of the concept of consumer to certain B2B transactions (Latvia); applying the rules on pre-formulated contracts also to individually negotiated clauses (Hungary); and mandatory language rules beyond the accepted limits of party autonomy and free movement (Lithuania, Poland, and to some extent also Latvia).

(3)   Finally, ambiguities in EU Directives themselves create transposition problems particularly in new Member States: for example, the concept of unfair terms (Latvia, Hungary); redress of the seller (different solutions in Latvia/Lithuania on the one hand, Hungary on the other, and no solution in Poland, which creates problems with cross-border transactions); and consequences of individual failure to respect Directives.

At the time of writing, it was not known how these problems will be solved after membership.

B. 'Law in Action': Deficits in Civil Justice?

What much less is known about is the working of the 'reconstruction of contract law' in the countries under scrutiny. This is to some extent due to the relative 'youth' of the legislation under examination. Little case-law has emerged, and even less is known to the foreign observer. We simply do not know yet how the new 'law in the books' really works, and where the fault lines of new countries will arise.

This leads to a more fundamental problem: the weakness of the institutions of civil justice after the fall of socialism. Harmathy has said with regard to Hungary that 'the element of insecurity in contractual relationships may also be found in the form that the party crediting his contractual counterpart is unable to know whether the debtor will fulfil his obligations in accordance with the contract'.[96] The quality of judicial decisions in Hungary has been repeatedly criticized;[97] a theory of judicial precedent is only just emerging.[98] With regard to Poland, Letowska[99] criticized the lack of focus on the implementation of new laws; this is 'left to its own resources' (which are scarce). Torgans, the leading Latvian scholar of civil law, criticizes the 'excessive dogmatism or formalism' of Latvian court practice,[100] which makes a flexible adaptation to modern market conditions difficult. The Open Society Institute,[101] in a study done for the EC Commission, voiced concerns over judicial independence in some of the countries under scrutiny. Unfortunately, there is no up-to-date information on this.

A more general and highly critical discussion can be found in a substantial paper by Emmert.[102] Talking from his own experience, he sees problems in applying the law in the new Member States, not so much in the legislative framework but in the missing 'suitable structure . . . to ensure the application and enforcement of the new legal rules in practice'.[103] Emmert also identifies methodological weaknesses which are part of the Communist heritage. Judges are trained to apply written law only in a rather formal manner.

They have no training to overcome lacunae in the law, for example by recourse to general principles of law . . . The judges have no experience with the concept of justice in contrast to the concept of law.[104]

There is no professional legal argument, nor a thorough discussion of existing case-law. Citizens have no confidence in the working of civil justice.[105]

Legal education has to be reformed more rapidly to reflect not only the changes in legislation but also the (necessary) changes in legal culture.[106]

---

[96] See Harmathy, 'Hungarian Civil Law since 1990', 43 *Acta Juridica Hungarica* (2002) 1, at 17.

[97] See Küper, 'Zivilrechtsprechung in Ungarn: die Metro-Urteile und die ungarische Vertragsrechtsdogmatik' [1999] *WIRO* 366.

[98] See Pokol, 'Statutory Interpretation and Precedent in Hungary', 46 *Osteuroparecht* (2000) 262, at 274–88.

[99] See Letowska, 'Between Knowledge and Skill: Obstacles to Efficient Implementation of the Community Consumer Law in Poland', in M. Kepinski (ed.), *The Evaluation of the New Polish Legislation in the Matter of Consumer Protection from the European Perspective* (2001), Conference proceedings, Zakrzewo, 21–23 June 2001, at 19–32.

[100] See Torgans, 'Contract Law: Latvia and the EU', in University of Latvia, *supra* note 25, at 24, 31.

[101] See Open Society Institute (ed.), *Judicial Independence—Monitoring the EU Accession Process* (2001), at 16–69, with detailed recommendations for improvement which will not be taken up here.

[102] See Emmert, 'Administrative and Court Reform in Central and Eastern Europe', 9 *ELJ* (2003) 288.

[103] *Ibid.*, at 289.

[104] *Ibid.*, at 295.

[105] See Holmes, 'Citizen and Law after Communism', 7 *East European Con Rev* (1998) 1.

[106] See Emmert, *supra* note 102, at 302.

Critical academic discussion of case-law and regulatory action should be encouraged. The system of hierarchical court administration should be changed to allow for more self-administration.

Emmert points to structural problems of civil justice which are present to a greater or lesser extent in all countries studied here. On the other hand, with the improved quality of legislation, especially the adoption of new civil codes, as in Estonia and in Lithuania, the administration of justice will improve. Complicated problems of multi-level application of legislation from completely different traditions, as in Latvia and to some extent Poland, should be avoided in the interest of a more transparent and responsible administration of civil justice.

Some of the arguments of Emmert's study may seem anecdotal and exaggerated today. They need to be tested against the development of the countries studied here under the impact of full membership. To conclude, the enormous changes in substantive and procedural law, the role of the judiciary, training of legal personnel, and finally the adoption of the excessively complex *acquis* may necessitate a rethinking of these hypotheses. The Latvian judge at the ECJ, Egils Levits, is probably right in observing:

[Mastering interpretation methods regarding general clauses] has been a serious problem in Eastern European countries where these . . . methods were neither recognised nor used in the inherited socialist traditions of law. In the course of time the situation improved when the content of legal education slowly approached European (continental) education. In recent years, too, in Latvia it can be observed that civil servants' and judges' knowledge of interpretation methods is becoming better.[107]

---

[107] See Levits, 'General Clauses and Discretionary Power of Administrative Institutions and Courts' [2004] *Law and Justice* 2, at 9, para. 37.

Index